Joseph Foster

The Royal Lineage of our Noble and Gentle Families

Vol. 4

Joseph Foster

The Royal Lineage of our Noble and Gentle Families
Vol. 4

ISBN/EAN: 9783337779887

Printed in Europe, USA, Canada, Australia, Japan

Cover: Foto ©ninafisch / pixelio.de

More available books at **www.hansebooks.com**

The Royal Lineage

OF

OUR NOBLE AND GENTLE FAMILIES.

TOGETHER WITH

THEIR PATERNAL ANCESTRY.

COMPILED BY

JOSEPH FOSTER.

CORRESPONDING MEMBER OF THE "NEW ENGLAND HISTORIC GENEALOGICAL SOCIETY;"

Author of the "British Peerage and Baronetage,"
and
numerous other Genealogical Works.

PRINTED FOR THE AUTHOR,

21, BOUNDARY ROAD, FINCHLEY ROAD, LONDON, N.W.

1886.

CHART PEDIGREES, &c.

	PAGE
BLENNERHASSETT, Sir Rowland, Bart. (late M.P.)	562
CRAWLEY BOEVEY, Sir Thomas Hyde, Bart., of Flaxley Abbey, Gloucestershire	536
BOLITHO, Elizabeth, widow of John Borlase ...	637
BOULTON pedigree...	597
BOURCHIER, Philip Lennox Walter ...	607
FITZMAURICE pedigree ...	647
GUERIN, Col. Edmund Arthur ...	617
HILLIARD pedigree	600
HORNBY, Rev. James John, D.D., D.C.L., Provost of Eton College	623
HORTON, Joshua Thomas, Esq., of Howroyde, Yorks, J.P., D.L.	630
HORTON, Sydney George, Lieut., R.A. ...	635
JEBB, John Joshua, Esq., of Norton House, Lincolnshire	645
KEAYS, Frederick Edmund, Esq.	617
LLOYD, of Strancally Castle, pedigree ...	654
LYNES, Rev. John, M.A., of Sandesfort House, Dorset	580
M'GILLICUDDY pedigree ...	626
MAITLAND, Rev. Brownlow, M.A. ...	551
MARTIN, Henry Maclean, of Boston, U.S.A.	586
MELLISH, John Stafford, Esq.	547
De MOLEYNS, His Honour, Judge, Q.C.	659
PALMER, Rev. Abram Smythe, B.A.	569
PENNEFATHER, Alfred Richard, Esq.	663
PRESTON, Rev. John D'Arcy Warcop, M.A., of Askham Bryan Hall, Yorks, Rector of Freemantle	576
RAYMOND pedigree	639
ROBERTS, Major Bertie Mathew, D.L.	553
RUSSELL, Louisa C. E., wife of Capt. Theodosius	555
SHULDHAM, Edmund Anderson, Esq., of Dunmanway, co. Cork	610
STEWART, Misses Louisa and Grace	583
THORP, Charles William, F.R.C.S.I., M.D. ...	595
UNWIN, Charlotte Katherine, wife of Major-General Robert	615
WRIGHT, Charles Ichabod, of Stapleford Hall, Notts, and of Watcombe Park, near Torquay	650

MAITLAND, LIEUT.-GENERAL CHARLES LENNOX BROWNLOW, C.B., col. 1st Batt. Duke of Edinburgh's Regiment since May, 1884; Lieut. Tower of London 1876-84; J.P. Liberty of the Tower, military sec. to his father, General Sir Peregrine Maitland, in Kaffir War, 1846-7; a dep. assist. adjutant-general in Crimea; battles of Alma, Balaklava, Inkerman (dangerously wounded), and siege of Sebastopol (medal); knight Legion Honour, and Medjidie; lieut.-gov. Chelsea Hospital 1869-74; 20TH IN DESCENT FROM HENRY III.; born 27 Sept., 1823.

THE DESCENT OF LIEUT.-GEN. CHARLES LENNOX BROWNLOW MAITLAND, C.B., FROM THE BLOOD ROYAL OF ENGLAND.

ENRY III., born 1 Oct., 1206, succeeded when nine years of age; crowned at Gloucester by the Bishops of Winchester and Bath, 28 Oct., 1216, London being then held by Prince Louis of France (who was soon after defeated at Lincoln); was taken prisoner at the battle of Lewes, 1264, by Simon de Montfort, Earl of Leicester, together with Prince Edward, the Earl of Cornwall, his son Henry, and others; the Prince escaped from Hereford Castle, raised an army, and defeated the Earl of Leicester at the battle of Evesham, and released the King. In 1269 Prince Edward undertook the Holy War, and to obtain supplies sold Gascony to France for 30,000 marks; died at Westminster 16 Nov., 1272, having married, 14 Jan., 1236, Eleanor, 2nd daughter and coheir of Raymond Berengar, Count of Provence; she was crowned at Westminster 19th same month, took the veil, and died at Amesbury, Wilts, 25 June, 1291, having had, with other issue, 2 sons,

[1] **Edward** "Longshanks," King of England on the death of his father.

[2] Edmund, surnamed "Crouchback," Earl of Chester 1253, Earl of Lancaster 1267, Earl of Leicester and Steward of England 25 Oct., 1274, upon the forfeiture of Simon de Montfort, Earl of Leicester. The title of King of Sicily was bestowed upon him by Pope Alexander VI., but he never obtained possession; he went to the Crusade with his brother Edward, whence the name of Crouchback, afterwards misinterpreted; born 16 Jan., 1245; died during the wars in Gascony, 1296, buried in Westminster Abbey, having married 1st, April, 1269, Aveline, daughter and heir of William de Fortibus, Earl of Albemarle; she died without issue same year. He married 2nd, Blanche, Dowager Queen of Navarre and Countess Palatine of Champagne and Brye, daughter of Robert, Count of Artois (brother to St. Louis, King of France), and had, with other issue, a son,

HENRY, restored to the earldom of Leicester 1324, 3rd Earl of Lancaster and Leicester, and Steward of England on the reversal of his brother's attainder, 1 Edward III., 1327; he was one of the principal leaders in that confederacy which destroyed the power of the Spencers and deposed Edward II.; died 1345, having married Maud, daughter and heir of Sir Patrick Chaworth, and had, with an only son, 6 daughters, of whom

ELEANOR (5th daughter) died at Arundel, 11 Jan., 1372; married 1st, to John, Lord Beaumont, son and heir of Henry de Beaumont, Earl of Buchan, in Scotland, and had an only son, Henry, lineal ancestor of Beaumont of Cole Orton and Grace Dieu, co. Leic. (see Foster's *Baronetage*, and page 367 of this work)

She re-married in 1345, as 2nd wife to Richard FitzAlan, 9th earl of Arundel (ancestor of the Dukes of Norfolk, Earls of Berkeley, &c.); restored to the earldom (forfeited by his father's attainder) 4 Edward III., 1331; made his will 5 Dec., 1375; he died at Arundel, 24 Jan., 1375-6; buried at Lewes, and had, with 4 daughters, 3 sons, of whom the 2nd, viz.,

SIR JOHN DE ARUNDELL (adopted this surname instead of FitzAlan), Marshal of England upon the resignation of Percy, earl of Northumberland; had summons to parliament, 1, 2, and 3, Richard II.; made his will 26 Nov., 1379, in which he styles himself Sir John de Arundel, Knt., and desires to be buried in the Priory of Lewes; drowned off the coast of Ireland 15 Dec., 1379; *inquis. post-mortem*, 3 Rich. II.; married Alianor, daughter of John Maltravers, and granddaughter and (38 Ed. III.) co-heir of John Lord Maltravers; she died 10 Jan., 1405, having re-married as 2nd wife to Reginald, Lord Cobham, of Sterborough Castle, Surrey; he died 6 July, 4 Henry IV., 1403. Sir John de Arundell had 5 sons and 2 daughters.

[1] Sir John Arundell, Ch'r, Lord Maltravers in right of his mother, but never summoned, was in the Scottish wars of Ric. II., 1383; born 3 Nov., 1364; died 14 Aug., 1390; buried in Missenden Abbey. He married Elizabeth, daughter of Edward, Lord le Despencer, K.G.; she died 11 April, 1408, having (re-married as 2nd wife to Sir William la Zouche, of Harringworth, Knt., who died 13 May, 19 Richard II., 1396, leaving issue by a former wife) had 3 sons, of whom the eldest, John, became Earl of Arundell.
[2] Sir William Arundell, K.G., governor of Rochester Castle; made his will 1 Aug., 1400, to be buried in the priory at Rochester; names his "carnal brother, Sir Richard Arundell, Knt.," &c.
[3] Thomas, *alias* Edward, living 1375.
[4] Henry, living 1375.
[5] **Sir Richard,** of whom presently.
[6] Joan, wife of Echyngham.
[7] Margaret, married, before 1397, to William, Lord Roos, K.G., who died Sept., 1414.

SIR RICHARD ARUNDELL, Knt., lord of the manor of Wychampton, Dorset; governor of Bamborough Castle, Northumberland, and of the castle and city of Rochester; distinguished himself at the tournament at Smithfield, held in honour of the coronation of Isabel of France, after her marriage with Richard II., &c.; in the retinue of the King at the siege of Agincourt; mentioned in the will of Sir William Arundell, his brother, 1400, and in that of Agnes his widow 1401; made his first will 5 July, 8 Henry V., and the second 8 July, 1417, desires to be buried in the chapel of the Blessed Mary in the Abbey of Rochester; he died 3 June, 1419; married Alicia, relict of Roger Burley; she died 2 Aug., 1436, having had 3 daughters,

[1] Philippa Arundell, died s.p. before 5 Edward IV.
[2] Joan (2nd daughter and co-heir), married to Sir Thomas Willoughby, of Parham, Suffolk, "Bellator egregius," and had, with a daughter, 2 sons, of whom the elder.
Sir Robert Willoughby, of whom presently.
[3] Alianor (3rd daughter and co-heir) had the manor of Brandon; married to Sir William St. George, who died without issue, 11 Ed. IV., 1472.

SIR ROBERT WILLOUGHBY, was found to be next heir male to Robert, Lord Willoughby, who died 30 Henry VI.; married Cecily, 2nd daughter of Lionel, Lord Welles, K.G.; and died 30 May, 5 Edward IV., 1465, seized of the manors of Wychampton, &c., &c. He had at least 2 sons.

[1] Sir Robert Willoughby, Knt., died 24 or 27 March, 7 Edward IV., 1467, being in ward to the King.
[2] Sir Christopher Willoughby, K.B., aged 14 at his brother's death; had livery of his lands 14 Edward IV., Knight of the Bath at the coronation of Richard III.; made his will 1 Nov., 1498, proved 13 July following; married Margery, daughter of Sir William Jenney, of Knotteshall, Suffolk Knt., had 5 sons and 3 daughters.
(1) **William,** 8th Lord, of whom presently.
(2) Christopher, ancestor of Lord Willoughby, of Parham (see Foster's *Peerage*.) (3) George.
(4) Thomas, Chief Justice of Common Pleas, ancestor of Lord Middleton (see Foster's *Peerage*.)
(5) John (Willoughby).
(6) Dorothy, married to John Nevill, Lord Latimer.
(7) Catherine, married to Sir John Heydon, of Baconsthorp, Norfolk, Knt.
(8) Elizabeth, married to William, Lord Eure.

WILLIAM, 8TH LORD WILLOUGHBY, of Eresby, K.B.; had summons to parliament 17 Oct., 1 Henry VIII., 1509, to 15 April, 14 Henry VIII., 1523; had a special livery of his father's lands 19 Henry VII.; and in 24 Henry VII., upon the failure of issue male of Lord Welles, he was found to be one of his co-heirs; a Knight of the Bath at the coronation of Henry VIII.; served in the wars with France, 3 and 5 Henry VIII., at the taking of Therouenne, and at the siege of Tournay; made his will 4 May, 16 Henry VIII.; died at Hertford 19 or 27 Oct., 17 Henry VIII., 1525; buried at Mettingham, Suffolk; married 1st, Mary, daughtar of Sir William Hussey, of Sleaford, Knt.; she died s. p., and he married 2nd, Donna Maria de la Salinas, daughter of Don Diego Lopez, Sarmiento, Count

→ THE ❖ DESCENT ❖ OF ←

John Stafford Mellish, Esq.

FROM THE

Blood Royal  **of England.**

HENRY III., born 1 Oct. 1206, crowned 28 Oct. 1216, d. 16 Nov. 1272. = Eleanor, 2nd dau. and co-heir of Raymond Berengar, Count of Provence, d. 1291.

Edmund, Earl of Chester, of Lancaster, and of Leicester, b. 16 Jan. 1245, d. 1296. = Blanche (2nd wife), Queen Dowager of Navarre, dau. of Robert, Count of Artois.

Henry, 3rd Earl of Lancaster, &c. d. 1345. = Maud, dau. and heir of Sir Patrick Chaworth.

John de Beaumont (1st husband). = Eleanor, 5th daughter. = Richard FitzAlan, 9th Earl of Arundel (2nd husband), d. 24 Jan. 1375.

Sir John de Arundell (1st husband), Marshal of England, drowned 15 Dec. 1379. = Alianora, dau. of John, Lord Maltravers, d. 10 Jan. 1405.

Sir Richard Arundell, governor of Bamborough Castle, d. 3 June, 1419. = Alicia, relict of Roger Burley, she died 2 Aug. 1436.

Joan Arundell, 2nd dau. and co-heir. = Sir Thomas Willoughby, "Bellator egregius."

Sir Robert Willoughby, d. 30 May, 1465. = Cecily, 2nd dau. of Lionel, Lord Welles, K.G.

Sir Christopher Willoughby, K.B., d. 1498-9. = Margery, dau. of Sir William Jenney, of Knotteshall, Suffolk.

William, 8th Ld. Willoughby of Eresby, had summons to parl. 1509-23, K.B., d. 19 or 27 Oct. 1525. = Donna Maria de la Salinas (2nd wife), dau. of Don Diego Lopez, Sarmiento, Count de Salinas.

A, *continued above.*

A, *continued from below*

William, 8th Ld. Willoughby = Donna Maria de la Salinas.

Charles Brandon, Duke of Suffolk (1st husband), d. 21 Aug. 1545. = Catherine, Baroness Willoughby of Eresby, d. 22 Oct. 1580. = Richard Bertie, of Edenham (2nd husband), d. 9 April, 1582.

Peregrine Bertie, 10th Lord Willoughby of Eresby, sum. parl. 1581-97, d. 1599-1601. = Mary, dau. of John Vere, Earl of Oxford.

Robert, 11th Lord, sum. parl. 1605-25, K.B., Lord Great Chamberlain, cr. Earl of Lindsey 1626, K.G. 1631, sl. at Edge Hill 23 Oct. 1642. = Elizabeth, only child of Edward, 1st Lord Montagu, of Boughton, Northants, K.B., d. 30 Nov. 1654.

Montagu, 2nd Earl of Lindsey, K.G., Lord Great Chamberlain, d. 25 July, 1666. = Martha, widow of John Ramsay, Earl of Holderness, (1st wife).

Robert, 3rd Earl of Lindsey Lord Great Chamberlain, d. 8 May, 1701. = Elizabeth (2nd wife), dau. of Philip, Lord Wharton, bur. at Spilsby, 10 Oct. 1689.

Robert, 4th Earl, cr. Duke of Ancaster and Kesteven, 1715, L.G. Chamberlain, b. 20 Oct. 1660. d. 26 July, 1723. = Mary (1st wife), dau. of Sir Richard Wynne, of Gwydyr, Carnarvon, Bart., m. 30 July, 1678, d. 20 Sept. 1689.

Peregrine, 2nd Duke, Lord Great Chamberlain, b. 29 April, 1686, d. 1 Jan. 1742-3 = Jane, dau. and co-heir of Sir John Brownlow, of Belton, Bart., d. 25 Aug. 1736.

Lady Jane Bertie, m. 1760. = General Edward Mathew, governor of Grenada, 1784-9, d. 25 Dec. 1805.

Jane Matthew, m. 2 Sept. 1776 = Thomas Maitland, Esq., d. 2 Dec. 1797.

Gen. Sir Peregrine Maitland, G.C.B. col. 17th and 76th foot, lieut.-gov. of Upper Canada, 1818, of Nova Scotia, gov. and com.-in-chief Cape of Good Hope, 1843-6, b. 6 July, 1777, d. 30 May, 1854. = Lady Sarah Lennox, (2nd wife), dau. of Charles, 4th Duke of Richmond, m. 1 Oct. 1815, d. 1 Sept. 1873.

Charles David, Incumbt. of St. James, Brighton, m. Elizabeth Adye, dau. of J. Miller, Esq., and d. 12 Oct. 1865.

Jane, d. 18 May, 1816. = Richard Warren, lieut.-col. Scots Fusilier Guards, d. 1819.

Caroline, m. to Lt.-Col. Wm. Roberts, R.A.

Eliza, m. to Rev. G. Ranking, and d. s.p.

Browlow Charles Warren, m. 1841, Maria, dau of Sir S. B. Fludyer, R.N. and d. s.p. 17 Jan. 1874.

Mary Jane, m. 1st, 1825, to Rev. Cecil Smith, who died 1861, she m. 2ndly, 1867-8, to Rev. Jno. C. Pigot, and died 28 Aug. 1875.

Caroline Elizabeth Warren, m. 1835, to her cousin, Rev. John Warren, and d. s.p. 7 Jan. 1866.

Emily Aubrey Warren, m. 16 Feb. 1835, d. 2 Feb. 1881. = Sir Peter Stafford Carey, M.A. bailiff of Guernsey, 1845-83 recorder of Dartmouth, 1836-45.

Others died unmarried.

Charles Egerton Carey, B.A. b. 1841, m. 1874, Hannah, widow of J. Young, barrister-at-law.

Frances, m. 1851, to Col. Ernest W. Pelley, late 5th foot.

Amelia, m. 1858, to Cecil Smith, Esq. and died 18 Dec. 1880.

Caroline, m. 1860, to Lt.-Col. Julius A. Carey, and d. 1883.

Beatrice, m. 1867, to Thomas Brooksbank. Esq. barrister-at-law.

Emily.

Sophia Stafford Carey, m. 19 Aug. 1863, to Rev. Wm. John Mellish, M.A. rector of Winestead, Yorks. and d. 19 Aug. 1871.

Constance, d. 1877.

Ernest. Edward. Caroline. Fanny. Amelia.

Cecil. Janet. Caroline. Amy. Grace. Mabel. Susan.

Harold. Wilfred. Mervyn. Elaine.

Thomas.

John Stafford Mellish, b. 1864. Peter Bertie, b. 1866. Elizabeth. Dorothea.

de Salinas; she accompanied the Infanta, Katherine of Arragon, into England on her marriage with Arthur, Prince of Wales, and was one of her maids of honour after her marriage with Henry VIII., and had 2 sons and a daughter,

[1] Henry, and [2] Francis, both died young.
[3] Catherine, Baroness Willoughby of Eresby, daughter and co-heir; died 22 Oct., 1580; her wardship and marriage was granted to Charles Brandon, Duke of Suffolk, in 20 Henry VIII., whose fourth wife she became; he died 21 Aug. 1545, leaving by her 2 sons.
(1) Henry (Brandon), and
(2) Charles (Brandon), both died at Bugden, Hunts, 14 July, 1551.
CATHERINE, Duchess of Suffolk, re-married 1553, to Richard Bertie, of Edenham (son of Thomas Bertie, of Bersted, Kent, who had a grant of arms from Hawley, Clarencieux), fellow of Corpus Christi Coll., Oxon, M.A.; bred to the bar; sheriff of Lincoln 1564; made his will 23 Feb., 1581-2, died 9 April, 1582, aged 64, and had, with an only daughter, an only son.

PEREGRINE BERTIE, 10TH LORD WILLOUGHBY OF ERESBY, claimed and was allowed the barony; had summons to Parliament 16 Jan., 1581, to 24 Oct., 1597; admitted to Gray's Inn 1573; general of the forces in the Netherlands 30 Elizabeth; governor of Berwick at his death; born at Wesel, in the duchy of Cleve, Germany, 12 Oct., 1555; made his will at Berwick 7 Aug., 1599, proved 12 Sept., 1601; married Mary, daughter of John Vere, Earl of Oxford, and sister and heir of Edward, 17th Earl of Oxford; she died 1624, having had, with other issue, a son,

ROBERT BERTIE, 11TH LORD WILLOUGHBY; had summons to Parliament from 5 Nov., 3 James I., 1605, to 17 May, 1 Charles I., 1625, Knight of the Bath 5 Jan., 1604; admitted to Gray's Inn 1605; Lord Great Chamberlain of England; created Earl of Lindsey, co. Lincoln, 22 Nov., 1626; K.G. April, 1631; Lord High Admiral 11 Charles. I.; governor of Berwick, 1639; general of the King's forces 22 Aug., 1642; slain at Edge Hill fight 23 Oct., 1642, aged 60; buried at Edenham; married Elizabeth, only child of Edward, 1st Lord Montagu of Boughton, Northants, K.B.; she died 30 Nov., 1654, having had, with other issue, a son,

MONTAGU, 2ND EARL OF LINDSEY, K.G., Lord Great Chamberlain; had summons to Parliament by writ in his father's barony of Willoughby 31 Oct., 1640; Knight of the Bath at the coronation of Charles I., 1625, and gentleman of the bedchamber; capt. of the King's guards, 1639; was at both battles of Newbury and at the battle of Naseby, &c.; P.C. to Charles II.; lord lieut. of Lincolnshire 1660; K.G. 1 April, 1661; died 25 July, 1666, aged 58; buried at Edenham; he married 1st, Martha, widow of John Ramsay, Earl of Holderness, daughter of Sir William Cockayne, of Rushton Northants, Knt.; he married 2nd, Bridget, daughter and sole heir of Edward Wray, groom of the bedchamber to James I., and by her had a son, James, summoned to Parliament as Baron Norreys 1675, and created Earl of Abingdon, 1682 (see Foster's *Peerage*). By his 1st wife he had, with other issue, a son,

ROBERT, 3RD EARL OF LINDSEY, Lord Great Chamberlain; of the Privy Council, 12 Dec., 1666, lord lieutenant of Lincolnshire 1684, recorder of Lincoln; died 8 May, 1701; buried at Edenham; he married 1st, Mary, daughter and co-heir of John Massingberd, of London, merchant; he married 2nd, Elizabeth, daughter of Philip, Lord Wharton; she was buried at Spilsby, 10 Oct., 1689; he married 3rd, Elizabeth, widow of Sir Francis Henry Lee, of Ditchley, Oxon, Bart., daughter and heir of Thomas Pope, Earl of Downe; she died 1 July, 1719; buried at Edenham. By his 2nd wife he had, with other issue, a son.

ROBERT, 4TH EARL OF LINDSEY, Lord Great Chamberlain; M.P. Boston 1685-7, 1689, and Preston 1690; summoned to Parliament in the barony of Willoughby in his father's lifetime by writ 19 April, 1690; created Marquis of Lindsey 21 Dec., 1706, and Duke of Ancaster and Kesteven 26 July, 1715, with remainder to the heirs male of the body of his father by his wife Elizabeth Wharton; lord lieut. of Lincolnshire; P.C. to William III., Queen Anne, and George I.; born 20 Oct., 1660; died 26, July, 1723; married 1st, 30 July, 1678, Mary, daughter of Sir Richard Wynne, of Gwydyr, Carnarvon, Bart.; she died 20 Sept., 1689; he married 2nd, Albinia, daughter of Major-Gen. William Farrington, of Chislehurst, and had issue; (she re-married 6 April, 1726, to James Douglas, M.P., Clerk of the

Green Cloth to the Prince of Wales, and died 29 July, 1745, aged 46). By his 1st wife the Duke had a son and successor.

PEREGRINE, 2ND DUKE OF ANCASTER AND KESTEVEN, Lord Great Chamberlain; Vice-Admiral 1702; D.C.L., 1702; P.C. 1708; M.P., Lincolnshire, 1708-10, 1710-13, 1713-15; summoned to Parliament in his father's lifetime in the barony of Willoughby, by writ 16 March, 1714-15; lord lieutenant, Lincolnshire, 1733; lord warden of the forests north of Trent 1734; born 29 April, 1686; died 1 Jan., 1742-3; married Jane, daughter and co-heir of Sir John Brownlow, of Belton, Bart.; she died 25 Aug., 1736, having had, with other issue, a daughter,

LADY JANE BERTIE (3rd daughter) died ; married 1760, to General Edward Mathew, lieut. governor Island of Nevis ; governor of Grenada 1784-9; col. 62nd foot; general 1797; commander-in-chief West Indies; entered the Coldstream guards 1745; equerry to George III.; commanded a brigade of guards in America 1775 (son of General William Matthew); died 25 Dec., 1805, aged 78, having had a son and 3 daughters (*a*).

[1*a*] Brownlow (Bertie-Mathew), assumed the additional surname of Bertie in accordance with the testamentary injunction of the Duke of Ancaster; born ; died 29 April (? Sept.), 1826; married 2 April, 1807, Harriet Anne, daughter of North Naylor, Esq., H.E.I.C.S. (by his wife ——, sister of Admiral Sir Albemarle Bertie, Bart., K.C.B.); she died, having had 3 sons and 5 daughters,

(1) Brownlow (Mathew), died young.
(2) Bertie (Bertie-Matthew), lieut. 10th hussars; born 15 Dec., 1811; killed while hunting at Rome 19 Nov., 1844.
(3) Edward (Bertie-Mathew.)
(4) Jane (Bertie-Mathew), married to Field-Marshal the Marquis de la Marmora, s.p.
(5) Elizabeth. (6) Anne, died unmarried.
(7) Harriet Anne, died unmarried 23 Oct., 1881.
(8) Caroline, died unmarried.

[2*a*] **Jane (Mathew)**, twin with Anne; married 2 Sept., 1766, to Thomas Maitland, Esq., who died 2 Dec., 1797, having had 5 sons and 3 daughters (see next page).

[3*a*] Anne (Mathew), a twin with Jane; died married , 1798, as 1st wife to Rev. James Austen, rector of Steventon and Alton, Hants (eldest son of Rev. George Austen, rector of Dean and Steventon, by Cassandra, daughter of Rev. Thomas Leigh, rector of Harpenden, Oxon); he died , 1820, leaving by her an only daughter.

Jane Anna Elizabeth (Austen), died 1 Sept., 1872; married, 8 Nov., 1814, to Rev. Benjamin Lefroy, Rector of Ashe, Hants (3rd son of Rev. Isaac Peter George Lefroy, of Ashe); he died 27 Aug., 1829, having had a son and six daughters.

(1) George Benjamin Austen (Lefroy), civil service, born 18 May, 1818, married 17 Nov., 1853, Emma, daughter of Thomas Cracroft, Esq., of and has 2 sons and 4 daughters.
[1] Edward Cracroft (Lefroy), born 20 March, 1855.
[2] Franklin George, born 5 June, 1861.
[3] Florence Emma. [4] Jessie.
[5] Mary Isabella. [6] Louisa Langlois.

(2) Anna Jemima (Lefroy), died 17 Oct., 1855; married, 4 Sept., 1846, to Thomas Edward Preston Lefroy, Esq., judge of county courts (Circuit No. 55), 1868-80 (3rd son of Anthony Lefroy, Esq.), and had a son and 2 daughters.
[1] William Chambers (Lefroy), born 2 Feb., 1849.
[2] Jemima Anne. [3] Mary Georgina Langlois.

(3) Julia Cassandra (Lefroy). died 30 Jan., 1884, having married, Jan., 1861, as 2nd wife, to Sir George Kettilby Rickards, K.C.B. 1882, M.A. Trin. Coll., Oxon., 1835, fellow of Queen's Coll., prof. of political economy, 1851-6; a governor of Eton and Rugby Schools; barrister-at-law, Inner Temple, 1837, and a bencher; standing counsel to Speaker of House of Commons 1851-82.

(4) Georgiana Brydges (Lefroy), died , 1882; married, 28 Sept., 1847, to John Alured George Seymer Terry, Esq. (younger son of Stephen Terry, Esq., of Dummer House, Hants); he died Dec., 1874, having had 3 sons and 4 daughters.
[1] Edward Seymer (Terry), born 5 March, 1852; died on his voyage home from Melbourne, 2 Dec., 1872.
[2] Henry Alured, born July, 1855.
[3] Francis Austen, born Dec., 1864.
[4] Ethel Georgina.
[5] Caroline Louisa, married, 9 April, 1874, to George Charles Boutcher, Esq., now of Minnesota, Canada, and has a daughter.
Constance Caroline (Boutcher).
[6] Anna Jemima. [7] Beatrice Helen.

(5) Fanny Caroline (Lefroy), died 29 Jan., 1885.

(6) Louisa Langlois (Lefroy), married, 28 July, 1857, to Rev. Septimus Bellas, M.A., vicar of Monk Sherburne and Pamber, Hants (son of Richard Bellas, Esq.); he died 30 Nov., 1875, leaving an only daughter.
Margaret Bellas.

(7) Elizabeth Lucy (Lefroy), married, 10 May, 1859, to Rev. Arthur Loveday, M.A., Ball. Coll., Oxon, 1852; rector of Yattenden, Berks, since 1873, and has had 4 sons and a daughter.
Arthur Philip (Loveday), born 2 Jan., 1860; Charles Edward, born 21 March, 1864; Henry Thomas, born 21 Dec., 1867; Robert Bertie, born 17 July, 1869; Frances Charlotte, died 19 Feb., 1868.

[4*a*] Penelope Susan (Mathew), died 27 Aug., 1828, married 1st, to her cousin, David Dewar, Esq. (son of George Dewar, Esq., of Enham Place, Hants, and Lady Caroline Bertie, 4th daughter of Peregrine, 2nd Duke of Ancaster, see p. 175); he died 1794, leaving issue; she re-married 23 Oct., 1799, to Charles, 3rd son of Richard Cumberland, Esq., the dramatist; he died 12 May, 1835, having had 4 sons and 2 daughters (see page 382). By her 1st husband she had 2 sons and a daughter.

(1) George Edward Brownlow (Dewar); died at school, 1803.

(2) David Albemarle Bertie (Dewar), born 4 July, 1794; died 25 Nov., 1859; married, 1821, Annie Louisa, eldest daughter of Col. Richard Magenis, of Waringstown, co. Down (and his wife, Lady Elizabeth Anne Cole, daughter of William Willoughby, 1st Earl of Enniskillen—see Foster's *Peerage*); she died 19 Nov., 1855, having had 2 sons and a daughter.

[1] Albemarle (Dewar), of Doles, Hants, capt. 87th Royal Irish fusiliers; born 18th May, 1822; died 5 June, 1862; married 30 June, 1854, Jane, only daughter of late Felix O'Beirne, of Kilbride House, Drumsna, co. Leitrim, and had 2 sons and 3 daughters.

(1) Albemarle Willoughby O'Beirne (Dewar), born 15 June, 1855; married, 29 April, 1882, Florence Wilhelmina Rose, younger daughter of Col. Matthews.

(2) George Albemarle Bertie (Dewar), of Pembroke College, Oxford, born 3 Nov., 1862.

(3) Florence Jane Bertie.

(4) Adeliza, died in infancy.

(5) Adeliza Mary Bertie.

[2] George, born 1824; died unmarried 1850.

(3) Elizabeth Anne (Dewar), died 1 July, 1881; married, Sept., 1856, to Andrea Luigi, Marchese Taliacarne (son of Francesco, Marchese Taliacarne, by Donna Barbara, only daughter of Marchese Brignole, and grand-daughter of last Doge of Genoa), Minister Plenipotentiary of the King of Italy at the Court of Lisbon; he died Nov., 1867, having had a son and daughter.

(1) Arthur Bertie, Marchese Taliacarne, born 1859.

(2) Georgina Albinia (Marchesina).

(3) Jane Charlotte (Dewar), died unm. 8 June, 1837.

JANE (MATHEW), a twin with Anne, died 5 June, 1830; married, 2 Sept., 1776, to Thomas Maitland, Esq. (son of Richard Maitland); died 2 Dec., 1797, having had 5 sons and 3 daughters (*c*).

[1*c*] **Sir Peregrine** (Maitland), of whom, see page 552.

[2*c*] Thomas, died unmarried 12 Feb., 1800.

[3*c*] Edward (Maitland), died at sea, in an engagement, on board H.M.S. *Petrel*, Oct. 1805.

[4*c*] Charles David (Maitland); incumbent of St. James's, Brighton; formerly capt. R.A.; born 3 Sept., 1785; died 12 Oct, 1865; married, 15 April, 1814, Elizabeth Adye, daughter of John Miller, Esq. (and his wife Elizabeth, sister of Major-gen. P. Adye, R.A., and aunt to Lieut.-gen. Sir John Miller Adye, R.A., G.C.B., governor of Gibraltar); she died 13 Aug., 1874, having had 5 sons (*d*).

(1*d*-4*c*) Charles (Maitland), M.A., in holy orders, M.D.; author of "The Church in the Catacombs;" born 6 Jan., 1815; died 31 July, 1866; married, 5 Nov., 1842, Julia Charlotte, widow of James Thomas, Esq., daughter of Henry Barrett, Esq.; she died 29 Jan., 1864, having had a son and daughter.

[1] Peregrine Brownlow (Maitland), born 2nd May, died 28 Aug., 1845.

[2] Julia Caroline (Maitland), married, 18 July, 1861, to Rev. David Wauchope (see Don-Wauchope in Foster's *Baronetage*); M.A., Wadham Coll., Oxon., 1851; rector of Church Lawford, Warwick, since 1863; and has a son and 2 daughters.

(1) David Maitland (Wauchope), born 4 March, 1864.

(2) Anne Julia. (3) Caroline.

(4*d*-2*c*) Brownlow (Maitland), M.A., Trin. Coll., Camb., 1840; minister of Brunswick Chapel, Marylebone, 1849-70; sec. and chaplain to Gen. Sir Peregrine Maitland, G.C.B., governor of Cape of Good Hope (see p. 552), born 12 June, 1816; married, 1st, 19 July, 1848, Josephine, daughter of Alexander Erskine, Esq. (heir male of Erskine of Dun); she died 8 Dec., 1870, having had 3 sons and 2 daughters.

[1] Brownlow Erskine (Maitland), lieut. R.N.; born 26 June, 1850; died 23 Jan., 1881.

[2] Erskine Bertie (Maitland), of the Inner Temple; born 26 Oct., 1851; died 29 Oct., 1877.

[3] Alexander Charles (Maitland), b. 29 May, 1853.

[4] Josephine Fanny.

[5] Caroline Cecilia, died 2 Sept., 1878.

Rev. BROWNLOW MAITLAND married 2nd, 4 June, 1872, Emily, daughter of late Samuel Warren, Esq., Q.C., D.C.L., F.R.S., M.P., author of *Ten Thousand a Year*, and has a daughter.

[6] Mary Eleanor (Maitland).

(3*d*-4*c*) Edward (Maitland), novelist and essayist; born 27 Oct., 1824; married, 3 May, 1855, Esther Charlotte, daughter of William Bradley, Esq., of Sydney, N.S. Wales, and has a son,

Charles Bradley (Maitland), army surgeon; Indian medical service 1880; born 5 Jan., 1856.

(4*d*-4*c*) John Thomas (Maitland), R.N.; born 4 Aug., 1826; died 11 March, 1855; married, 1848, Mary Jane, daughter of Rev. Francis Pym, rector of Willian, Beds; (she re-married in Canada about 1856-7, to Wainwright), and had a son, Lionel; died Sept., 1873.

(5*d*-4*c*) Eardley (Maitland), col. R.A.; superintendent royal gun factory, Woolwich, 1 May, 1880 (asst. supt. 1872-7); military attaché, Turkey, 1877-8; served in Indian mutiny 1857-8; at relief of Lucknow mentioned in despatches; medal with 3 clasps; born 10 Nov., 1833; married, 29 May, 1855, Elizabeth Odell, daughter of Thomas Baillie, Esq.; she died 6 Aug., 1877, having had 2 sons and 3 daughters.

[1] Arthur Eardley (Maitland), lieut. 87th regiment; born 18 June, 1857; killed by a fall from the mess room window at Limerick, June, 1879.

[2] Edward William, born 31 Jan., died 20 March, 1860.

[3] Laura Frances Anne, died 24 March, 1861.

[4] Ella Laura Katherine. [5] Emily.

[5*c*] Brownlow James (Maitland), R.A.; born 2 Sept., 1788; mortally wounded at battle of Barossa, and died 31 Oct., 1811.

[6*c*] Jane (Maitland), died 18 May, 1816; married to Richard Warren, lieut.-col. Scots fusiliers; he died 1819, having had 5 sons and 5 daughters (*d*)

(1*d*-6*c*) Richard Brownlow (Warren), godson of Brownlow, Duke of Ancaster, born 15 July, 1805; died 16 Sept., 1808.

(2*d*-6*c*) Peregrine, born 3 Nov., 1806; died unmarried.

(3*d*-6*c*) Francis Samuel, born 8 Feb., died 4 Dec., 1808.

(4*d*-6*c*) Frederic Amelius, born 30 Aug., 1813; died

(5*d*-6*c*) Brownlow Charles (Warren), born 8 Nov., 1815; died s.p. 17 Jan., 1874; married, 1 Nov., 1841, Maria, eldest daughter of Sir Samuel Brudenell Fludyer, Bart. (see Foster's *Baronetage*); she died 25 March, 1884.

(6*d*-6*c*) Mary Jane (Warren), died 28 Aug., 1875; married 1st, 15 July, 1825, to Rev. Cecil Smith, of Lydeard House, Somerset; he died 12 May, 1861. She remarried 1867-8, to Rev. John Clare Pigot, of Thrumpton Lodge, Weston-super-Mare; he died 2 Dec., 1880. By her first husband she had a son,

Cecil (Smith), of Lydeard House, Somerset, J.P.; barrister-at-law, Inner Temple, 1852; born 31 May, 1826; married, 28 Sept., 1858, Amelia, daughter of Sir Peter Stafford Carey (see p. 552); she died 18 Dec., 1880, leaving a son and 6 daughters.

Cecil (Smith), born 5 Jan., 1860.

Janet Charlotte; Caroline Ellen; Amy; Grace; Mabel; Susan Constance.

THE DESCENT OF

Rev. Brownlow Maitland, M.A.,

FROM THE

Blood Royal  **of England.**

HENRY III., born 1 Oct. 1206, crowned 28 Oct. 1216, d. 16 Nov. 1272. = Eleanor, 2nd dau. and coheir of Raymond Berengar, Count of Provence, d. 1291.

Edmund, Earl of Chester, of Lancaster, and of Leicester, b. 16 Jan. 1245, d. 1296. = Blanche (2nd wife), Queen Dowager of Navarre, dau. of Robert, Count of Artois.

Henry, 3rd Earl of Lancaster, &c. d. 1345. = Maud, dau. and heir of Sir Patrick Chaworth.

John de Beaumont (1st husband). = Eleanor, 5th daughter. = Richard FitzAlan, 9th Earl of Arundel (2nd husband), d. 24 Jan. 1375.

Sir John de Arundell (1st husband), Marshal of England, drowned 15 Dec. 1379. = Alianora, dau. of John, Lord Maltravers, d. 10 Jan. 1405.

Sir Richard Arundell, governor of Bamborough Castle, d. 3 June, 1419. = Alicia, relict of Roger Burley, she died 2 Aug. 1436.

Joan Arundell, 2nd dau. and co-heir. = Sir Thomas Willoughby, "Bellator egregius."

Sir Robert Willoughby, d. 30 May, 1465. = Cecily, 2nd dau. of Lionel, Lord Welles, K.G.

Sir Christopher Willoughby, K.B., d. 1498-9. = Margery, dau. of Sir William Jenney, of Knottshall, Suffolk.

William, 8th Ld. Willoughby of Eresby, had summons to parl. 1509-23, K.B., d. 19 or 27 Oct. 1525. = Donna Maria de la Salinas (2nd wife), dau. of Don Diego Lopez, Sarmiento, Count de Salinas.

A,
continued above.

A,
continued from below.

William, 8th Ld. Willoughby = Donna Maria de la Salinas.

Charles Brandon, Duke of Suffolk (1st husband), d. 21 Aug. 1545. = Catherine, Baroness Willoughby of Eresby, d. 22 Oct. 1580. = Richard Bertie, of Edenham (2nd husband), d. 9 April, 1582.

Peregrine Bertie, 10th Lord Willoughby of Eresby, sum. parl. 1581-97, d. 1599-1601. = Mary, dau. of John Vere, Earl of Oxford.

Robert, 11th Lord, sum. parl. 1605-25, K.B., Lord Great Chamberlain, cr. Earl of Lindsey 1626, K.G. 1631, sl. at Edge Hill 23 Oct. 1642. = Elizabeth, only child of Edward, 1st Lord Montagu, of Boughton, Northants, K.B., d. 30 Nov. 1654.

Montagu, 2nd Earl of Lindsey, K.G., Lord Great Chamberlain, d. 25 July, 1666. = Martha, widow of John Ramsay, Earl of Holderness, (1st wife).

Robert, 3rd Earl of Lindsey, Lord Great Chamberlain, d. 8 May, 1701. = Elizabeth (2nd wife), dau. of Philip, Lord Wharton, bur. at Spilsby, 10 Oct. 1689.

Robert, 4th Earl, cr. Duke of Ancaster and Kesteven, 1715, L.G. Chamberlain, b. 20 Oct. 1660. d. 26 July, 1723. = Mary (1st wife), dau. of Sir Richard Wynne, of Gwydyr, Carnarvon, Bart., m. 30 July, 1678, d. 20 Sept. 1689.

Peregrine, 2nd Duke, Lord Great Chamberlain, b. 29 April, 1686, d. 1 Jan. 1742-3. = Jane, dau. and co-heir of Sir John Brownlow, of Belton, Bart., d. 25 Aug. 1736.

Lady Jane Bertie, m. 1760. = General Edward Mathew, governor of Grenada, 1784-9, d. 25 Dec. 1805.

Jane Matthew, m. 2 Sept. 1776 = Thomas Maitland, Esq., d. 2 Dec. 1797.

Gen. Sir Peregrine Maitland, G.C.B., col. 17th and 76th foot, lieut.-gov. of Upper Canada, 1818, of Nova Scotia, gov. and com.-in-chief Cape of Good Hope, 1843-6, b. 6 July, 1777, d. 30 May, 1854. = Lady Sarah Lennox, (2nd wife) dau. of Charles, 4th Duke of Richmond, m. 1 Oct. 1815, d. 8 Sept. 1873.

Charles David, Incumbt. of St. James, Brighton d. 12 Oct. 1865. = Elizabeth Ayde, dau. of J. Miller, Esq. m. 1814, d. 1874.

Jane, m. to Lieut.-Col. Warren.

Caroline, m. to Lt.Col. Wm. Roberts, R.A.

Eliza, m. to Rev. G. Ranking, and d. s.p.

Charles David Maitland, incum. of St. James, Brighton sometime capt. R.A. died 12 Oct. 1865.

Josephine (1st wife) dau. of Alex. Erskine, Esq. m. 1848, d. 1870. = Brownlow Maitland, M.A., Minister of Brunswick Chapel, Marylebone, 1849-70, b. 12 June, 1816. = Emily (2nd wife) dau. of late S. Warren, Esq. Q.C., m. 1872.

Edward Maitland, novelist and essayist, b. 1824, m. 1855, Edith, dau. of W. Bradley, Esq. of Sydney, N.S.W.

John Thomas R.N., m. 1848, Mary, dau. of Rev. F. Pym.

Eardley Maitland, col. R.A., suptdt. Royal gun factory, Woolwich, b. [illegible] m. [illegible], Elizabeth, dau. of T. Baillie, Esq. she d. 1877.

Alexander Charles, only surviving son, b. 29 May, 1853.

Josephine Fanny.

Mary Eleanor.

Charles Bradley, b. 5 Jan., 1856.

Ella Laura.

Emily.

(7*d*-6*c*) Caroline Elizabeth (Warren), died s.p. 7 Jan., 1866; married, 27 Aug., 1835, to her cousin, Rev. John Warren, rector of Graveley, Beds; he died 15 Aug., 1852.

(8*d*-6*c*) Charlotte, died 10 Sept., 1867

(9*d*-6*c*) Emily Aubrey (Warren), died 2 Feb., 1881; married, 16 Feb., 1835, to Sir Peter Stafford Carey, M.A., Oxon, barrister-at-law, Middle Temple, 1830; judge of court of record at Wells, 1838-45; professor of English law in Univ. Coll., London, 1838-45; recorder of Dartmouth, 1836-45; bailiff of Guernsey, 1845-83; and had a son and 7 daughters.

[1] Charles Egerton (Carey), of the Croft, Botley, Southampton; B.A., Exeter Coll., Oxon; born 19 July, 1841; married 23 Dec., 1874, Hannah, widow of J. Young, barr.-at-law, daughter of late Andrew Rogers, Esq., of Ryde, I.W.

[2] Frances (Carey), married 7 Aug., 1861, to Col. Ernest le Pelley, 5th foot (retired 1881), (son of Ernest le Pelley, Seigneur of Sark, and Amelia Carey his wife), and has 2 sons and 3 daughters,

(1) Ernest Brownlow (le Pelley), b. 1 June, 1862.

(2) Edward (Carey), born 2 Nov., 1870.

(3) Caroline Mary. (4) Fanny Ernestine.

(5) Amelia Maitland.

[3] Amelia (Carey), married 28 Sept., 1858, to Cecil Smith, Esq., and has a son and 6 daughters (see p. 550).

[4] Caroline (Carey), died 6 Feb., 1883; married 5 Dec., 1860, to Lieut.-Col. Julius Alphonso Carey (son of Sausmarez Carey, Esq.), formerly Belgian Consul at Alicante; A.D.C. to Lieut.-Gov. of Guernsey, and has had 4 sons and a daughter,

Harold Stafford (Carey), born 28 Sept.; 1861.
Wilfred Sausmarez, born 22 May, 1863.
Roland Warren, born 20 Jan., died 16 July, 1866.
Mervyn Dobree, born 8 Jan., 1877.
Elaine Biddulph.

[5] Beatrice (Carey), married 26 Dec., 1867, to Thomas Brooksbank, Esq., barr.-at-law, Inner Temple, 1849, and has a son,

Thomas Carey, born 12 July, 1878.

[6] Emily Jane.

[7] Sophia Stafford (Carey), died 19 Aug., 1871; married 19 Aug., 1863, to Rev. William John Mellish, M.A., Queen's Coll., Camb., 1855; rector of Winestead, Hull, since 1873; of Orston, Notts, 1855-72; and of Bardney, Linc., 1872-3 (son of William Mellish, Esq., of Guernsey, and Elizabeth Walter Lilly, his wife), having had 3 sons and 2 daughters,

John Stafford (Mellish), born 5 Aug., 1864.
Peter Bertie, born 25 Nov., 1866.
Charles Tillotson, b. 30 June, d. 19 Oct., 1871.
Elizabeth Aubrey. Dorothea Katherine.

[8] Constance Bertie (Carey), died 7 Jan., 1877.

(10*d*-6*c*] Eliza (Warren), died unmarried 14 Oct., 1868.

[7*c*] Caroline (Maitland), died 30 Nov. married, to Col. William Roberts, R.A.; he died 1851, having had 6 sons.

(1) William Maitland (Roberts), died unmarried.

(2) Brownlow Worsley, born 18 March, 1814.

(3 Henry Charles Roberts, major Bengal army; born 29 Nov., 1817; died married, 12 May, 1864, Jane, daughter of John Beckley, Esq., of Paignton, Devon, and has a son and 2 daughters.

Henry Maitland (Roberts), born 14 June, 1868.
Laura Maria; Edith Douglas.

(4) Peregrine (Roberts), born 1819; died unmarried 6 Aug., 1876.

(5) Edward Thomas, born 1820; died unmarried 1840.

(6) Bertie Mathew (Roberts), capt. 26th Cameronians and adjt. West Kent L.I. militia, retired with rank of Major D.L. Lancashire; born 11 Nov., 1822; married 1st, 1 July, 1852, Frances Jane Lennard, daughter of Gen. Sir William Cator, K.C.B. (see Lennard, Foster's *Baronetage*); she died 21 Sept., 1867; he married 2nd, 7 Nov. 1872, Laura Charlotte, widow of Alexander Forteath, Esq., of Newton, N.B., daughter of late Lieut.-gen. Henry Tufnell Roberts, C.B. By his 1st wife he had 2 sons.

[1] Harry Bertie (Roberts), B.A., Brasenose Coll. Oxon., 1876; curate of All Souls, Leeds, 1878 born 28 March, 1855.

[2] William Bertie (Roberts), lieut. R.W. fusiliers 1876; born 29 June, 1856; married 12 Oct., 1882, Camille, 2nd daughter of John Corbett, Esq., M.P., of Impney, Droitwich, and Ynys-y-Maengwyn, Towyn, Merioneth, and has a son,

Roger Harry Bertie, born 5 Oct., 1883.

(8*c*) Eliza (Maitland), died s.p. 1860; married to Rev. G. Ranking, who died

SIR PEREGRINE MAITLAND, G.C.B. (1852); Knight of Wilhelm and of St. Wladimir (1815); colonel 17th foot (1843); served in Flanders and in Spain, present at Corunna (silver war medal); in the expedition to the Scheldt, in 1809, commanded 1st brigade of guards at the battle of the Nive (gold medal); commanded 1st British brigade (2nd and 3rd battalions 1st foot guards) of 1st division at Waterloo; K.C.B. 1815; lieut.-governor of Upper Canada 1818; lieut.-governor Nova Scotia, and governor and commander-in-chief at Cape of Good Hope, 1843-6; general 1846; commander-in-chief at Madras, 1836-8; colonel 76th foot 1834-43; born 6 July, 1777; died 30 May, 1854; mar. 1st, 8 June, 1803, Hon. Louisa, daughter of Sir Edward Crofton, and his wife Anne, Baroness Crofton (see Foster's *Peerage*); she died 3 Nov., 1805, having had a son (*f*),

[1*f*] Peregrine (Maitland), lieut.-col. in the army, mil. sec. to Sir P. Maitland when com.-in-chief, Madras; born 1 May, 1804; died unmarried, 1837.

SIR PEREGRINE MAITLAND married 2nd, 9 Oct., 1815, Lady Sarah Lennox, 2nd daughter of Charles, 4th Duke of Richmond and Lennox (see Foster's *Peerage*); she died 8 Sept., 1873, having had 3 sons and 7 daughters (*f*).

[2*f*] **Lieut.-Gen. Charles Lennox Brownlow Maitland**, C.B., first-named (see p. 545).

[3*f*] George Bertie, born 6 April, 1830; died 8 April, 1831.

[4*f*] Horatio Arthur Lennox (Maitland), capt. R.N.; born 13 March, 1834.

[5*f*] Sarah (Maitland), married, 14 Jan., 1837, to Gen. Thomas Bowes Forster (son of Lieut.-Col. John Randall Forster); he died 21 March, 1870, having had 3 sons and 4 daughters.

THE DESCENT OF

Major Bertie Mathew Roberts, D.L.,

Late 26th Cameronians,

FROM THE

Blood Royal of England.

HENRY III., born 1 Oct. 1206, crowned 28 Oct. 1216, d. 16 Nov. 1272. = Eleanor, 2nd dau. and co-heir of Raymond Berengar, Count of Provence, d. 1291.

Edmund, Earl of Chester, of Lancaster, and of Leicester, b. 16 Jan. 1245, d. 1296. = Blanche (2nd wife), Queen Dowager of Navarre, dau. of Robert, Count of Artois.

Henry, 3rd Earl of Lancaster, &c. d. 1345. = Maud, dau. and heir of Sir Patrick Chaworth.

John de Beaumont (1st husband). = Eleanor, 5th daughter. = Richard FitzAlan, 9th Earl of Arundel (2nd husband), d. 24 Jan. 1375

Sir John de Arundell (1st husband), Marshal of England, drowned 15 Dec. 1379. = Alianora, dau. of John, Lord Maltravers, d. 10 Jan. 1405.

Sir Richard Arundell, governor of Bamborough Castle, d. 3 June, 1419. = Alicia, relict of Roger Burley, she died 2 Aug. 1436.

Joan Arundell, 2nd dau. and co-heir. = Sir Thomas Willoughby, "Bellator egregius."

Sir Robert Willoughby, d. 30 May, 1465. = Cecily, 2nd dau. of Lionel, Lord Welles, K.G.

Sir Christopher Willoughby, K.B., d. 1498-9. = Margery, dau. of Sir William Jenney, of Knotteshall, Suffolk.

William, 8th Ld. Willoughby of Eresby, had summons to parl. 1509-23, K.B., d. 19 or 27 Oct. 1525. = Donna Maria de la Salinas (2nd wife), dau. of Don Diego Lopez, Sarmiento, Count de Salinas.

A, continued above.

A, continued from below.

William, 8th Ld. Willoughby = Donna Maria de la Salinas.

Charles Brandon, Duke of Suffolk (1st husband), d. 21 Aug. 1545. = Catherine, Baroness Willoughby of Eresby, d. 22 Oct. 1580. = Richard Bertie, of Edenbam (2nd husband), d. 9 April, 1582.

Peregrine Bertie, 10th Lord Willoughby of Eresby, sum. parl. 1581-97, d. 1599-1601. = Mary, dau. of John Vere, Earl of Oxford.

Robert, 11th Lord, sum. parl. 1605-25, K.B., Lord Great Chamberlain, cr. Earl of Lindsey 1626, K.G. 1631, sl. at Edge Hill 23 Oct. 1642. = Elizabeth, only child of Edward, 1st Lord Montagu, of Boughton, Northants, K.B., d. 30 Nov. 1654.

Montagu, 2nd Earl of Lindsey, K.G., Lord Great Chamberlain, d. 25 July, 1666. = Martha, widow of John Ramsay, Earl of Holderness, (1st wife).

Robert, 3rd Earl of Lindsey, Lord Great Chamberlain, d. 8 May, 1701. = Elizabeth (2nd wife), dau. of Philip, Lord Wharton, bur. at Spilsby, 10 Oct. 1689.

Robert, 4th Earl, cr. Duke of Ancaster and Kesteven, 1715, L.G. Chamberlain, b. 20 Oct. 1660. d. 26 July, 1723. = Mary (1st wife), dau. of Sir Richard Wynne, of Gwydyr, Carnarvon, Bart., m. 30 July, 1678, d. 20 Sept. 1689.

Peregrine, 2nd Duke, Lord Great Chamberlain, b. 29 April, 1686, d. 1 Jan. 1742-3 = Jane, dau. and co-heir of Sir John Brownlow, of Belton, Bart., d. 25 Aug. 1736.

Lady Jane Bertie, m. 1760. = General Edward Mathew, governor of Grenada, 1784-9, d. 25 Dec. 1805.

Jane Matthew, m. 2 Sept. 1776 = Thomas Maitland, Esq., d. 2 Dec. 1797.

- Gen. Sir Peregrine Maitland, G.C.B., col. 17th and 76th foot, lieut.-gov. of Upper Canada, 1818, of Nova Scotia, gov. and com.-in-chief Cape of Good Hope, 1843-6, b. 6 July, 1777, d. 30 May, 1854. = Lady Sarah Lennox, (2nd wife), dau. of Charles, 4th Duke of Richmond, m. 1 Oct. 1815, d. Sept. 1873.
- Charles David, Incumbt. of St. James Brighton d. 12 Oct. 1865. = Elizabeth Adye, dau. of J. Miller, Esq.
- Jane, m. to Lieut.-Col. Warren.
- Caroline, m. to Lt.-Col. Wm. Roberts, R.A., who d. 1851.
- Eliza, m. to Rev. G. Ranking, and d. s.p.

Children of Caroline and Lt.-Col. Wm. Roberts:

- William M. Roberts d. unmarried.
- Brownlow Worsley Roberts, b. 18 Mar. 1814.
- Henry Charles Roberts, maj. Bengal army, b. 1817, m. 1864, Jane, dau. of John Beckley, Esq.
  - Henry Maitland Roberts, b. 1868.
  - Laura Edith.
- Peregrine d. 1876; Edward d. 1840.
- Frances (1st wife), dau. of Genl. Sir W. Cator, K.C.B. m. 1852, d. 1867. = Bertie Mathew Roberts, late capt. 26th Cameronians, maj. late West Kent L.I. militia, dept.-lieut. co. Lanc. b. 11 Nov. 1822. = Laura (2nd wife), widow of Alexander Forteath, Esq. of Newton, N.B. m. 1872.
  - Henry Bertie Roberts, B.A., Oxon. in holy orders, b. 28 March, 1855.
  - William Bertie Roberts, lieut. R. W. Fusiliers, 1876, b. 27 June, 1856. = Camille, 2nd dau. of John Corbett, Esq. M.P. m. 12 Oct. 1882.
    - Roger Harry Bertie, b. 5 Oct. 1883.

(1) Bowes Lennox (Forster), col. R.A.; asst.-adjutant and quarter-master-general, Dublin (1882); military secretary, Madras, 1867-71; brigade-major, Madras, 1871-74; served in New Zealand war 1860-1 (medal); born 9 Oct., 1837; married, 18 Jan., 1868, Jessie Kate, daughter of William Mackenzie, Esq., C.B., C.S.I., Inspector-Gen. of Hospitals, Indian Medical Dept. (retd.), Hon. Physician to the Queen, and has 4 sons and a daughter.

(1) William Anson Maitland Prendergast (Forster), born 21 April, 1869.

(2) Stuart Boscawen Erode Desbrisay, b. 5 Oct., 1870.

(3) George Norman Bowes, born 26 Oct., 1872.

(4) Lenox Weston Glendower, born 28 Sept., 1874.

(5) Isabella Gertrude.

(2) John Maitland (Forster), R.N.; born 10 Jan., 1839; died 18 Oct., 1854, on board H.M.S. *Bellerophon*, of wounds received in naval attack upon Sebastopol.

(3) Peregrine Henry (Forster), born 2 July, 1848.

(4) Susan Charlotte (Forster), married, 28 April, 1874, to Rev. Charles Garbett, M.A., Brasenose College, Oxford, 1864; vicar of Tongham since 1869, and has 4 sons and a daughter.

Cyril Forster (Garbett), born 6 Feb., 1875.
Basil Maitland, born 13 July, 1876.
Clement Steuart, born 21 July, 1877.
Leonard Gillilan, born 1 March, 1879.
Elsie Mary Katherine.

(5) Sarah Caroline (Forster), married 20 Oct., 1869, to Edward Howorth Greenly (eldest son of Charles Williams Greenly, Esq., of Titley Court, Herefordshire), and has a son and 3 daughters.

Walter Howorth (Greenly), born 2 Jan., 1875.
Alice Maud; Ethel Mary; Lucy Margaret.

(6) Emily Berlinga (Forster).

(7) Louisa Margaret Jane.

[6/] Caroline Charlotte (Maitland), married 17 July, 1837, to John George Turnbull, Esq., accountant-gen. at Madras; he died 2 Jan., 1872, having had 3 sons and 2 daughters,

(1) George Wilmot Maitland (Turnbull), major R.A., 1882; born 23 Nov., 1843; married 8 Nov., 1871, Annette, daughter of Comm. Featherston Acres, R.N.

(2) Henry John Lennox (Turnbull), lieut. R.H.A.; born 10 Aug., 1845; died May, 1881; married 7 Nov., 1871, Anna Carew, only daughter of Samuel Skurry Davenport, Esq., of Bognor, Sussex.

(3) Charles Frederick Alexander (Turnbull), capt. Duke of Cornwall's L.I. 1880; A.D.C. to Gen. the Hon. W. Feilding; extra A.D.C. to the Commander-in-Chief at Aldershot 1881-3; born 26 June, 1847.

(4) Caroline Maria (Turnbull), married 5 June, 1860, to Alexander William Adair, Esq., of Heatherton Park, Somerset (eldest son of Alexander Adair, Esq., of the same place); M.A. Oxon.; J.P. Somerset and Devon; Col. Comdt. 4th battalion (militia) Somerset L.I. 1870; at siege and fall of Sebastopol; formerly capt. 52nd foot (see Foster's *Peerage*, B. WAVENEY), and has had 2 sons and 3 daughters,

[1] Gerald (Adair), born 7 Nov., 1865.
[2] Nigel Adair, born 19 Jan., 1873; died same year.
[3] Evelyn Alice, married 29 April, 1883, to Joseph E , only son of Joseph Carter Wood, Esq., of Felcourt, Sussex.
[4] Mabel, died young.
[5] Kathleen, died young.

(5) Georgiana Sarah (Turnbull), married 5 Jan., 1864, to Allan Shafto Adair (4th son of above-named Alexander Adair, Esq., of Heatherton Park, Somerset), J.P. Middlesex and Herts, late capt. 13th light infantry; born 20 Dec., 1836, and has a son and daughter,

Desmond (Adair), born 20 Dec., 1865. Violet.

[7/] Georgina Louisa, died May, 1820.

[8/] Georgina Louisa (Maitland), died 5 Jan., 1852 married 2 Jan., 1844, as 1st wife to Rev. Sir Thomas Eardley Wilmot Blomefield, Bart. (see also page 584), vicar of All Saints, Pontefract, 1859-72; master of Archbishop Holgate's Hospital, Hemsworth, Yorks, 1872-8; he died 21 Nov., 1878, having had by her a son and 3 daughters,

(1) Sir Thomas Wilmot Peregrine (Blomefield), 4th Bart.; late lieut. 1st York rifle regiment of militia; born 31 Dec., 1848; married 5 Aug., 1874, Lilias, daughter of Major the Hon. Charles Napier, of Woodlands, Taunton (see B. Napier, Foster's *Peerage*), and has 3 sons and 2 daughters.

Thomas Charles Alfred (Blomefield), b. 27 June, 1875.
Nigel Napier, born 15 March, 1877.
Wilmot, born 26 Nov., 1878.
Lilias Marow; Nancy born 16 May, 1883.

(2) Caroline Sarah.

(3) Louisa Charlotte Emily, married 11 April, 1866, to Theodosius Stuart Russell (son of Rev. Edmund Russell, M.A., Cantab.), capt. late 1st West York militia; adjutant 24 Lanc. R.V.; chief constable W.R. York., and has 5 sons and 2 daughters.

Edmund Stuart Eardley Wilmot (Russell), born 15 June, 1869.
Charles Lennox Somerville, born 10 July, 1872.
Wilmot Peregrine Maitland, born 6 June, 1874.
Archibald George Blomefield, born 20 June, 1879.
Somerville Peregrine Brownlow, born 10 July, 1883.
Georgina Louisa Margaret.
Margaret Caroline Sarah.

(4) Georgina Salome, married 28 June, 1870, to Loftus Henry Martin, capt. 3rd battalion King's Own Light Infantry (S. York. regiment), late 69th regiment, and has 2 sons.

Loftus Wilmot (Martin), born 19 April, 1871.
Frank Henry Eardley, born 10 May, 1872.

[9/] Jane Bertie (Maitland), died 23 April, 1885.

[10/] Emily Sophia (Maitland), married 13 Jan., 1846, to Lord Frederic Herbert Kerr, admiral R.N. (retd.); groom in waiting to the Queen since 1868 (see Foster's *Peerage*, M. LOTHIAN), and has 3 sons and 6 daughters.

(1) Arthur Herbert (Kerr), born 10 Feb., 1862.

(2) Mark Edward Frederic, born 26 Sept., 1864.

(3) Frederic Walter, page of honour to the Queen 1879-83; born 20 May, 1867.

(4) Emily Georgina, married 6 Aug., 1866, as 2nd wife to Rev. and Hon. Francis Edmund Cecil Byng, M.A., Ch. Ch., Oxon.; chaplain in ordinary at St. James's Chapel since 1872; vicar of St. Peter's, S. Kensington from 1867; chaplain to Speaker of House of Commons since 1874; chaplain Hampton Court Palace 1865-7; hon. chaplain to the Queen 1867-72 (3rd son of George, Earl of Strafford, see Foster's *Peerage*), and has 2 sons and 3 daughters.

Ivo Francis (Byng), born 20 July, 1874.
Antony Schomberg, born 31 May, 1876.
Rachel Theodora. Irene Hilare.
Anne Dorothy Frederica, (sponsor H.R.H. Princess Frederica of Hanover).

(5) Sidney Katharine (Kerr). (6) Edith Harriet.

(7) Mary Frances (Kerr), married 3 April, 1880, to George Henry, 2nd son of late Thomas Longman, Esq., of Farnborough Hill, Hants, and of London.

(8) Constance Honoria. (9) Cecil Nona.

[11/] Eliza Mary (Maitland), married 14 July, 1857, to Major-gen. John Desborough, R.A., C.B. (retired 1877); Governor of Oxford Mil. Coll. 1876-83; served in China 1860 (medal), and has 3 sons and 4 daughters.

Charles Ernest Maitland (Desborough, b. 30 Nov., 1865.
Arthur Peregrine Henry, born 10 Sept., 1868.
John Bertie, born 19 March, 1874.
Leila Sarah Maitland. Emily Mary.
Henrietta Margaret. Madeline Annie.

THE DESCENT OF

Louisa Charlotte Emily,

Wife of Captain Theodosius Stuart Russell, Chief Constable of the West Riding of Yorkshire.

FROM THE

Blood Royal  **of England.**

HENRY III., born 1 Oct. 1206, crowned 28 Oct. 1216, d. 16 Nov. 1272. = Eleanor, 2nd dau. and co-heir of Raymond Berengar, Count of Provence, d. 1291.

Edmund, Earl of Chester, of Lancaster, and of Leicester, b. 16 Jan. 1245, d. 1296. = Blanche (2nd wife), Queen Dowager of Navarre, dau. of Robert, Count of Artois.

Henry, 3rd Earl of Lancaster, &c. d. 1345. = Maud, dau. and heir of Sir Patrick Chaworth.

John de Beaumont (1st husband). = Eleanor, 5th daughter. = Richard FitzAlan, 9th Earl of Arundel (2nd husband), d. 24 Jan. 1375.

Sir John de Arundell (1st husband), Marshal of England, drowned 15 Dec. 1379. = Alianora, dau. of John, Lord Maltravers, d. 10 Jan. 1405.

Sir Richard Arundell, governor of Bamborough Castle, d. 3 June, 1419. = Alicia, relict of Roger Burley, she died 2 Aug. 1436.

Joan Arundell, 2nd dau. and co-heir. = Sir Thomas Willoughby, "Bellator egregius."

Sir Robert Willoughby, d. 30 May, 1465. = Cecily, 2nd dau. of Lionel, Lord Welles, K.G.

Sir Christopher Willoughby, K.B., d. 1498-9. = Margery, dau. of Sir William Jenney, of Knotteshall, Suffolk.

William, 8th Ld. Willoughby of Eresby, had summons to parl. 1509-23, K.B., d. 19 or 27 Oct. 1525. = Donna Maria de la Salinas (2nd wife), dau. of Don Diego Lopez, Sarmiento, Count de Salinas.

A, *continued above.*

A, *continued from below.*

William, 8th Ld. Willoughby = Donna Maria de la Salinas.

Charles Brandon, Duke of Suffolk (1st husband), d. 21 Aug. 1545. = Catherine, Baroness Willoughby of Eresby, d. 22 Oct 1580. = Richard Bertie, of Edenham (2nd husband), d. 9 April, 1582.

Peregrine Bertie, 10th Lord Willoughby of Eresby, sum. parl. 1581-97, d. 1599-1601. = Mary, dau. of John Vere, Earl of Oxford.

Robert, 11th Lord, sum. parl. 1605-25, K.B., Lord Great Chamberlain, cr. Earl of Lindsey 1626, K.G. 1631, sl. at Edge Hill 23 Oct. 1642. = Elizabeth, only child of Edward, 1st Lord Montagu, of Boughton, Northants, K.B., d. 30 Nov. 1654.

Montagu, 2nd Earl of Lindsey, K.G., Lord Great Chamberlain, d. 25 July, 1666. = Martha, widow of John Ramsay, Earl of Holderness (1st wife).

Robert, 3rd Earl of Lindsey Lord Great Chamberlain, d. 8 May, 1701. = Elizabeth (2nd wife), dau. of Philip, Lord Wharton, bur. at Spilsby, 10 Oct. 1689.

Robert, 4th Earl, cr. Duke of Ancaster and Kesteven, 1715, L.G. Chamberlain, b. 20 Oct. 1660. d. 26 July, 1723. = Mary (1st wife), dau. of Sir Richard Wynne, of Gwydyr, Carnarvon, Bart., m. 30 July, 1678, d. 20 Sept. 1689.

Peregrine, 2nd Duke, Lord Great Chamberlain, b. 29 April, 1686, d. 1 Jan. 1742-3 = Jane, dau. and co-heir of Sir John Brownlow, of Belton, Bart., d. 25 Aug. 1736.

Lady Jane Bertie, m. 1760. = General Edward Mathew, governor of Grenada, 1784-9, d. 25 Dec. 1805.

Jane Matthew, m. 2 Sept. 1776 = Thomas Maitland, Esq., d. 2 Dec. 1797.

Gen. Sir Peregrine Maitland, G.C.B., col. 17th and 76th foot, lieut.-gov. of Upper Canada 1818, of Nova Scotia, gov. and com.-in-chief Cape of Good Hope, 1843-6, b. 6 July, 1777, d. 30 May, 1854. = Lady Sarah Lennox, (2nd wife), dau. of Charles, 4th Duke of Richmond, m. 1 Oct. 1815, d. 8 Sept. 1873.

Charles David, Incumbt. of St. James, Brighton d. 12 Oct. 1865. = Elizabeth Adye, dau. of J. Miller, Esq.

Jane, m. to Lieut.-Col. Warren.

Caroline, m. to Lt.-Col. Wm. Roberts, R.A.

Eliza, m. to Rev. G. Raoking, and d. s.p.

1 Lieut.-gen. Charles Lennox Brownlow Maitland, C.B., col. 1st batt. Duke of Edinburgh's regt., lieut. of the Tower of London, 1876-84, a dep. ass. adj.-gen. of division in America, lieut.-gov. of Chelsea Hospital, 1869-74, b. 27 Sept. 1833.

2 Horatio Arthur Lennox Maitland, cpt. R.N. b. 13 March, 1834.

3 Sarah Maitland, m. 14 Jan. 1837. = Gen. Thomas Bowes Forster, d. 21 March, 1870.

4 Caroline Charlotte Maitland, m. 17 July, 1837. = John George Turnbull, acct.-gen. Madras, d. 2 Jan. 1872.

5 Georgina Louisa Maitland (1st wife) m. 2 Jan. 1844 d. 5 Jan. 1852. = Rev Sir Thomas Eardley Wilmot Blomefield, Bart., d. 21 Nov. 1878.

6 Jane Bertie Maitland, d. 23 April, 1835.

7 Emily Sophia Maitland, m. 13 Jan. 1846. = Lord Frederic Herbert Kerr, adml. R.N. retd. groom-in-waiting to the Queen since 1868.

8 Eliza Mary Maitland, m. 14 July, 1857. = Major-Gen. John Desborough, R.A., C.B.

Sir Thomas Wilmot Peregrine Blomefield, 4th Bart. b. 31 Dec. 1848. = Lilias, dau. of the Hon. Charles Napier, m. 5 Aug. 1874.

Caroline Sarah Blomefield.

Louisa Charlotte Emily Blomefield. m. 11 April, 1866. = Captain Theodosius Stuart Russell, late 1st West York Militia, and Adjt. 24th Lanc. R.V., Chief Constable Yorkshire W.R.

Georgina Salome Blomefield, m. 23 June, 1870. = Loftus Henry Martin, Capt. (K.O.) Light Infantry.

Edmund Stuart Eardley Wilmot Russell, b. 15 June, 1863.

Charles Lennox Somerville Russell, b. 10 July, 1872.

Wilmot Peregrine Maitland Russell, b. 6 June, 1874.

Archibald George Blomefield Russell, b. 20 June, 1879.

Somerville Peregrine Brownlow Russell, b. 10 July, 1883.

Georgina Louisa Margaret Russell.

Margaret Caroline Sarah Russell.

THE DESCENT OF

Sir Thomas Hyde Crawley-Boevey,

Bart.,

Of Flaxley Abbey, Gloucestershire,

FROM THE

Blood Royal  **of England.**

EDWARD III., crowned 1 Feb. 1327, b. 13 Nov. 1312, d. 21 June, 1377. = Philippa, 3rd dau. of William, Count of Holland and Hainault, m. 24 Jan. 1328, d. 15 Aug. 1369.

Lionel of Antwerp, Duke of Clarence, Earl of Ulster, etc., K.G. = Elizabeth, dau. and heir of William de Burgh, Earl of Ulster (1st wife).

Philippa of Clarence, b. 16 Aug. 1355, m. 1368. = Edmund Mortimer, 3rd Earl of March and Lord of Wigmore, marshal of England, lieut. of Ireland, d. at Cork, 27 Dec. 1381.

Roger Mortimer, 4th Earl of March, etc., whom Richard II. nominated his successor to the throne, slain at Kenlis, Ireland, 20 July, 1398, aged 24. = Eleanor, dau. of Thomas Holland, Earl of Kent, descended from Edmund of Woodstock, Earl of Kent, son of Edward I.

Anne (1st wife), co-heir of her brother Edmund, Earl of March. = Richard, Earl of Cambridge (2nd son of Edmund of Langley, Duke of York, 4th son of Edward III.), beheaded 6 Aug., 1415.

Richard, 3rd Duke of York, Earl of Cambridge, etc., "the protector," fell at battle of Wakefield, 31 Dec. 1460. = Cicely, dau. of Ralph Nevill, Earl of Westmorland, d. 31 May, 1495.

Edward IV.

George, Duke of Clarence, attainted for high treason 1478, said to have been drowned in a butt of malmsey 18 Feb. 1478. = Isabel, dau. of Richard Nevill, Earl of Salisbury and Warwick, "the Kingmaker," d. 12 Dec. 1476.

Margaret, Countess of Salisbury, beheaded in the Tower 27 May, 1551, aged 72. = Sir Richard Pole, K.G., gent. of the bedchamber to Prince Arthur, d. 1505.

Henry Pole, Lord Montacute K.B., beheaded 9 Jan. 1539. = Jane, dau. of George Nevill, 2nd Lord Abergavenny,

A

continued above.

A

continued from below.

Henry Pole, Lord Montacute K.B. = Jane, dau. of George Nevill, 2nd Lord Abergavenny.

Catherine, eldest dau. and co-heir, d. 23 Sept. 1576. = Francis Hastings, 2nd Earl of Huntingdon, K.G., d. 23 June, 1561.

Sir George Hastings (2nd son), 4th Earl of Huntingdon. = Dorothy, 2nd dau. and co-heir of Sir John Port, of Etwall and Dale Abbey, co. Derby.

Henry Hastings, of Woodlands and Piddletown, Dorset. = Dorothy, dau. and co-heir of Sir Francis Willoughby, of Wollaton, Notts.

Henry Hastings, of Newington Butts, Surrey (3rd son), will dated 19, proved 21 Oct., 1668. = Susan (1st wife), dau. of Robert Offley, of London, merchant, bd. at St. Benet's, 29 Aug. 1661

Anne Hastings (eldest and only surviving dau. and co-heir), bapt. 2 Jan. 1624-5, m. 12 Oct. 1643, bd. 8 Jan. 1683-4. = John Ayleway, of London, citizen and merchant taylor, d. 7 Nov. 1677.

Susanna Ayleway (2nd wife) b. 15 March, 1647-8, m. 23 Feb. 1681-2, d. 6 June, 1732. = John White, of Paternoster, London, citizen and mercer, b. at Truro, 24 Jan. 1631, d. 1700.

Susanna White, m. before 1712, bd. at Flaxley, co. Glouc., 5 March, 1762. = John Lloyd, bd. at Christ Church, London, 6 Nov. 1744.

Susanna Lloyd, m. 31 Mar. 1743-4, bd. at Flaxley same day as her mother, 5 March, 1762. = Thomas Crawley-Boevey, of Flaxley Abbey, b. 11 Sept. 1709, d. 28 Nov. 1769.

Sir Thomas Crawley-Boevey, Bart., b. 14 Jan., 1744-5, d. 11 Aug. 1818. = Anne, 2nd dau. of Rev. Thos. Savage, M.A., of Broadway, m. 1769, d. 1816. | Charles Crawley, B.C.L., rector of Stowe Nine Churches, and of Broadway. | Susan Crawley, m. 1st to Edmund Bastard, 2nd to Sir Thomas Hyde Page, Knt. R E. | Katherine Crawley m. 1777, d. 9 Dec. 1842, = Rev. Duke Yonge, vicar of Cornwood, Devon.

Sir Thomas Crawley-Boevey, 3rd Bart., b. 28 Nov. 1769, d. 10 Jan. 1847. = Mary Albinia, dau. of Sir Thomas Hyde Page, Knt., m. 1807, d. 1835. | John Lloyd Crawley, rector of Heyford and Holdenby, m. Anne, dau. of Rev. Charles Crawley. | Charles Crawley, vicar of Hartpury, co Glouc., m. Catherine, dau. of Rev. Duke Yonge. | George Crawley, capt. R.N., m. Charlotte, dau. of Rev. Duke Yonge. | William Crawley, vicar of Flaxley, m Charlotte, dau. of Rev. Charles Crawley. | 6 daus.

Sir Martin Hyde Crawley-Boevey, Bart., verderer of the Forest of Dean, b. 1812, d 1862. = Elizabeth, eldest dau. of Rev. George William Daubeny, m. 9 June, 1836. | Albinia Anne, m. 14 Sept. 1843, d. 20 Jan., 1850. = Rev. George Barnston Daubeny. | Matilda Blanche, m. 1, Aug. 1839. = William Gibbs, of Tyntesfield, Somerset.

Sir Thomas Hyde Crawley-Boevey, Bart., b. 2 July, 1837. = Frances Elizabeth, only dau. of Rev. Thos. Peters, rector of Eastington, m. 25 July, 1865. | Walter Edward | Arthur, B.C.S., m. Annie, dau. of Major-Gen. Phayre, C.B. | Octavius, m. Dona Maria de Marga. | James, of Bombay, m. Frances, dau. of Dr. Newington. | Richard, in holy orders. Antony. | Martina Elizabeth, m. to Rev. W. C. Risley. | Sybella Mary.

Francis Hyde, b. 25 April, 1868.
Edward Martin, b. 2?th March, 1873.
Arthur Curtis, b. 10 July, 1874.
Thomas Russell, b. 22 March, 1880.
Albinia Frances.

CRAWLEY-BOEVEY, SIR THOMAS HYDE, BART., of Flaxley Abbey, Gloucestersire, high sheriff 1882, late lieut. 69th foot, elected a verderer of Her Majesty's Forest of Dean 1873, 20TH IN DESCENT FROM EDWARD III., born 2 July, 1837; married 25 July, 1865, Frances Elizabeth, only daughter of Rev. Thomas Peters, rector of Eastington, Gloucestershire, and has 4 sons and a daughter.

[1] Francis Hyde (Crawley-Boevey), born 25 April, 1868.
[2] Edward Martin, born 26 March, 1873.
[3] Arthur Curtis, born 10 July, 1874.
[4] Thomas Russell, born 22 March, 1880.
[5] Albinia Frances.

THE DESCENT OF SIR THOMAS CRAWLEY-BOEVEY, BART., FROM THE BLOOD ROYAL OF ENGLAND.

EDWARD III., KING OF ENGLAND, Earl of Chester, 1320, Duke of Aquitaine, Count of Ponthieu and Montreuil, 1325; crowned at Westminster in his father's lifetime, 1 Feb., 1327; defeated the Scots at Halidon Hill 1333. In 1339 he assumed the style of "King of France and England, and Lord of Ireland," and quartered the arms of France in the first quarter; gained a great naval victory over the French off Sluys, 1340, and won the celebrated battle of Cressy 26 Aug., 1346; 17 Oct. following the Scots were defeated at Neville Cross, and King David II. taken prisoner to London, where he remained nearly 11 years; his descendant,

SUSANNA (daughter of John Lloyd, see chart pedigree opposite), buried at Flaxley the same day as her mother, 5 March, 1762; married 31 March, 1743-4, to Thomas Crawley-Boevey, Esq., of Flaxley Abbey, Newenham, co. Gloucester, who died 28 Nov., 1769, having had 2 sons and 2 daughters.

[1] **Sir Thomas (Crawley-Boevey), Bart.**, whom see page 560.

[2] Charles (Crawley), B.C.L. Ball. Coll., Oxon., 1786; rector of Stowe Nine Churches, Northants, 1789-1849; and rector of Broadway, Worc.; born 25 April, 1750; died 4 Jan., 1849; married 12 April, 1784, Mary, daughter of George Abraham Gibbs, Esq., of Exeter (and sister of Rt. Hon. Sir Vicary Gibbs, chief justice of the Court of Common Pleas): she died 31 Oct., 1819, having had 2 sons and 7 daughters.

(1) Charles (Crawley), of Littlemore, Oxon., born 25 Sept., 1788; died 30 Sept., 1871; married 14 May, 1825, Eliza Katherine, daughter of Abraham Grimes, Esq., of Coton House, Warwickshire; she died 12 Oct., 1881, having had (with 2 sons who died young) a son,

CHARLES EDWARD (CRAWLEY), of Littlemore, born 17 Feb., 1827; married 1st, 16 April, 1850, Maria Walter Scott, daughter of William Wilson, Esq., of Wandsworth, Surrey; she died 16 Jan., 1862, having had a son and daughter.

[1] Charles William Scott (Crawley), born 4 Feb., 1858.

[2] Margaret Laura Scott.

CHARLES EDWARD CRAWLEY married 2nd, 23 April, 1867, Marion, daughter of George Charles Karop, Esq., of Copenhagen, and has 2 sons.

[3] Edward Robert John (Crawley), born 19 July, 1871.

[4] George Richard Eric, born 5 Dec., 1873.

(2) George Abraham (Crawley), of Whitehall Place, and Fitzroy Farm, Highgate, Middx, solicitor; born 26 Sept., 1795; died 24 July, 1862; married 20 Sept., 1826, Caroline, daughter of David Powell, Esq., of Loughton, Essex; she died 18 Dec., 1875, having had 3 sons and 8 daughters.

[1] Robert Townsend, M.A. Ch. Ch., Oxon., 1858; rector of North Ockendon, Essex, since 1869; vicar of Cressing, 1866-9; born 13 Feb., 1832; married 20 Jan., 1857, Louisa Marianne, daughter of Rev. James Charles Clutterbuck, rector of Long Wittenham, Bucks, and has 4 sons and 4 daughters,

Robert Francis, born 3 Sept., 1858; Charles Henry, born 7 July, 1859; George Herbert, born 16 Nov., 1863; James Henry, born 18 July, 1865; Mary; Elizabeth Margaret; Caroline Bertha; Louisa.

[2] George Baden, born 4 Sept., 1833; died 23 Nov., 1879, having married 6 Aug., 1863, Eliza Inez, eldest daughter of Henry G. Hollier, Esq., of East Farleigh, Kent, and had 6 sons and 2 daughters,

George Abraham, born 1864; Henry Ernest, born 1865; Leonard Russell, born 1866; Eustace, born 1868; John Kenneth, born 1872; Arthur Stafford, born 1876; Caroline Inez; Georgina Beatrice, a posthumous daughter, born 27 May, 1880.

[3] Charles David, M.A. Ch. Ch., Oxon., 1865; vicar of East Harnham, Wilts, since 1875; born 13 July, 1835; unmarried.

[4] Mary, married 31 Aug., 1859, to Rev. Henry Manning Ingram, M.A. Trin. Coll., Camb., 1853; B.A., 38th wrangler, 1847; rector of Aldrington since 1879; 2nd Master of Westminster School, 1861-80, and has 5 sons and 2 daughters,

Henry Hugh (Ingram), born 17 May, 1861; Charles Frederick, born 20 Aug., 1862; Francis Manning, born 6 Nov., 1864; Robert Antony, born 11 Feb., 1866; Arthur David, born 3 March, 1869; Anne Caroline, twin with Robert Antony; Edith Mary.

[5] Caroline, unmarried. [6] Anne, died 1850.

[7] Edith, unmarried.

[8] Fanny, died 12 April, 1865, having married 1 May, 1861, to Rev. George Edward Jelf, M.A. Ch. Ch., Oxon., 1859; canon resid. of Rochester cathedral since 1880; vicar of St. Matthew, Blackmoor, Hants, 1868-74; vicar of Saffron Walden, 1874-82; hon. canon St. Albans, 1878-80; and had a son and 3 daughters.

(1) Edward (Jelf), born 13 March 1865.

(2) Edith Louise. (3) Mary Agnes.

(4) Fanny, died 1871.

[9] Agnes, married 28 Dec., 1869, to Rev. Thomas Robinson, B.A., and has 2 sons and a daughter.

George Villiers (Robinson), born 14 Jan., 1872; Clement Crawley, born 25 Aug., 1874; Agnes Irene.

[10] Willielmina, unmarried.

[11] Bertha, died 26 Dec., 1870, having married 5 June, 1866, to Col. Thomas Lowndes, Burmese police service, and had a son and daughter.

Maurice (Lowndes), born 4 Nov., 1869; Bertha Caroline.

(3) Ann (Crawley), died 2 May, 1863; married 21 April, 1806, to her cousin, Rev. John Lloyd Crawley (2nd son of Sir Thomas Crawley-Boevey, Bart.; see Foster's *Baronetage*); he died 18 Oct., 1850, having had 8 sons and 2 daughters (see p. 560).

(4) Mary, died unmarried 16 April, 1865.

(5) Susan, died unmarried 1881.

(6) Elizabeth, married 1811, to Rev. George William Daubeny, of Seend House, Wilts (son of Ven. Archdeacon Daubeny); he died 5 June, 1860, leaving issue (see p. 776).

(7) Isabella, died young.

(8) Caroline, died 13 Feb., 1850; married 9 July, 1817, to her cousin George Henry Gibbs, Esq., of Bedford Square, Midd., and afterwards of Clifton Hampden, Oxfordshire, and Aldenham, Herts; he died 21 Aug., 1842. having had issue (see p. 750).

(9) Charlotte, married 8 Oct., 1822, to her cousin Rev. William Crawley (youngest son of Sir Thomas Crawley-Boevey, Bart.; see Foster's *Baronetage*); he died 17 Dec., 1858, leaving issue (see p. 561).

[3] Susanna (Crawley), died ; married 1st, to Edmund Bastard, Esq., of South Warnford, Devon; 2nd, in 1777, to Sir Thomas Hyde Page, Knt., R.E.; he died 20 June, 1821.

[4] Catherina (Crawley), died 9 Dec., 1842; married, 12 March, 1777, to Rev. Duke Yonge, vicar of Cornwood, Devon (son of Rev. John Yonge, of Puslinch, Devon); he died 3 Dec., 1823, having had 5 sons and 4 daughters.

(1) Duke (Yonge), vicar of Antony, Cornwall; born 13 Oct., 1779; died 29 July, 1836; married 14 May, 1806, Cordelia Anne, daughter of Samuel Colborne, of Lyndhurst, Hants (sister of F.M. Lord Seaton, G.C.B., G.C.M.G., G.C.H., &c.); she died 20 July, 1856, aged 82, having had 3 sons and 2 daughters.

[1] Duke John (Yonge), in holy orders; born 9 May, 1809; died 10 January, 1846; married ; Elizabeth, daughter of Roberts, of (she re-married to Capt. Scott), and had 3 sons.

(1) Duke Dowton (Yonge), R.N., died 1878.

(2) Kenneth Arthur Duke (Yonge).

(3) Walter Francis Duke (Yonge).

[2] John Francis Duke (Yonge), of Plymouth, M.D.; born 30 January, 1814; died 25 Dec., 1879; married 1st, Elizabeth Alice, daughter of Holmes, Esq., of ; he married 2ndly, 19 July, 1869, Mary, daughter of David Jones, Esq.; by his 1st wife he had 3 sons.

(1) Francis Arthur Holmes (Yonge), died .

(2) James Frederic Moore.

(3) Stephen Duke.

[3] Frederick Duke (Yonge) in New Zealand; formerly R.N.; born 24 March, 1816; married

[4] Arthur Duke (Yonge), born 11 June, 1825; married , 1870, Lucy, daughter of John Williams, Esq., of Bruges, and has a daughter,

Alethea Duke (Yonge), born at Florence, 8 Nov., 1872.

[5] Cordelia Anne Duke, died August, 1864 married , to Major-Gen. Oldfield, R.A., A.D.C. to the Queen; died .

[6] Alethea Duke, died s.p. 18 Feb., 1847; married 8 Oct., 1842, as 1st wife, to Lt.-Col. Edward Bond, 53rd regt., who died 4 July, 1880.

(2) Charles (Yonge), in holy orders, a master at Eton born 14 May, 1781; died 29 May, 1830; married Dec., 1811, Elizabeth, daughter of Joseph Lord, Esq., of Pembroke; she died 11 Jan., 1868, having had 4 sons and 2 daughters.

[1] Charles Duke (Yonge), regius professor of modern history, Queen's Coll., Belfast, and fellow of the Royal University; born 30 Nov., 1812; married 15 Aug., 1837, Anne, daughter of James Vincent Bethell, Esq., of Hereford.

[2] John Eyre (Yonge), M.A. King's Coll., Camb., 1843, some time fellow; rector of Hempstead with Lessingham since 1876; rural dean, 1881; assist.-master Eton, 1840-75; born 10 April, 1818; married 19 Dec., 1844, Hon. Catherine Charlotte Lysaght, daughter of George, 4th Baron Lisle, and has had 3 sons and 5 daughters.

(1) George (Yonge), M.A., Trin. Hall, Camb., 1877; wrangler; curate of Sparham, Norfolk, since 1882; born 10 Oct., 1850; married 17 July, 1883, Ann, daughter of Rev. T. S. Norgate.

(2) John Harry, born 30 March, 1852; married 4 April, 1883, Emma, daughter of late Dr. Sherlock.

(3) Charles Francis Lysaght, born 11 Oct., 1858.

(4) Elizabeth Catherine.

(5) Mary Isabel, married 20 Aug., 1872, to Rev. Denys Nelson Yonge, vicar of Broxted, Suffolk (see page 817).

(6) Lucy Sarah, married 28 Dec., 1881, to Rev. John Paget Davies, rector of Street, Surrey.

(7) Charlotte Fortescue.

(8) Gertrude Augusta Jane, died, 1858.

(9) Margaret Alice.

[3] James Arthur, born 9 March, 1822; died s.p. Sept., 1864; married 28 Aug., 1860, Hannah, daughter of R. Rogers, of Kilkee, Ireland; she remarried to Charles Egerton Carey, Esq.

[4] George Edward (Yonge), treasurer of the County of Southampton, born 4 July, 1824; married 6 Oct., 1859, Lucy, daughter of Gideon Acland, and had a son,

George Acland, born 23 Sept., 1861; died 6 Oct., 1870.

[5] Elizabeth Catherine, died unmarried 1836.

[6] Charlotte Frances, died 28 Sept. 1860; married 9 Nov., 1841, to Rev. John Finch Mason, rector of Brignall, Yorkshire, and of Aldenham Lodge, Herts; who died 16 Dec., 1874, and had 6 sons and 7 daughters.

(1) John (Mason), born 24 June, ; died .

(2) William Bryant Finch, born 8 Sept., ; died .

(3) George Finch, born 3 Jan., .

(4) Arthur Finch, born 24 Feb., ; died .

(5) Henry Charles Finch, born 1 July, .

(6) John Henage Finch, born 13 July, ; died .

(7) Mary Elizabeth, died youn.

(8) Mary Alethea Jane.

(9) Ada Charlotte Frances, married to Charles Duncan Royds, Esq., of the Grange, Roestock, St. Albans.

(10) Elizabeth Catherine.

(11) Helen Maria, died young.

(12) Georgina Emily, died young.

(13) Gertrude Beatrice, died young.

(3) John George (Yonge), born 1786; died , 1806.

(4) James (Yonge), B.A. Exeter Coll., Oxon., M.D. Edin., born 11 March, 1793; died s.p. 3 Jan., 1870; married 1st, 20 Feb. 1820, Margaret, daughter of Sir Thomas Crawley-Boevey, Bart., (see page 561); she died 22 April, 1867, having had 2 sons and 2 daughters, who all died young; he married 2ndly, 25 Aug., 1868, Anna Susanna, daughter of George Couch, Esq., of Ford, Devonport.

(5) William Crawley (Yonge), of Otterbourne, Hants, J.P., served at Waterloo with 52nd light infantry; born 2 June, 1795; died 26 Feb., 1854; married 25 Oct., 1822, Frances Mary, daughter of Rev. Thomas Bargus, vicar of Barkway, Herts; she died 30 Sept., 1868, having had a son and daughter.

[1] Julian Bargus (Yonge), of Otterbourne, Hants, M.A. Balliol Coll., Oxon., formerly in Rifle Brigade, born 31 Jan., 1830; married 9 Sept., 1858, Emma Frances, daughter of Col. Edward Walter, 3rd Bombay light cavalry, and has 3 sons and 3 daughters.

(1) Francis Arthur (Yonge), born 23 Nov., 1861.

(2) Maurice Edward, born 26 March, 1867.

(3) George Alan David, born 1 March, 1871.

(4) Helen Emma.

(5) Louisa Alethea, m. 7 Aug., 1884, to Rev. Thos. Henry Arlington Bowles, of Arlington, Devon.

(6) Joanna Angela.

[2] Charlotte Mary (Yonge) author of "The Heir of Redclyffe," "Heartsease," &c.; born 11 Aug. 1823.

(6) Susannah (Yonge), died s.p. 29 Sept., 1832; married 1825 to Jerome Roach, Esq.

(7) Catharina, died 2 Jan., 1858; married 30 Aug., 1811, to Rev. Charles Crawley, vicar of Hartpury, son of Sir Thomas Crawley-Boevey, Bart., he died 17 Jan., 1856, having had 2 sons and 5 daughters (see next page).

(8) Charlotte, died 8 April, 1836; married 1st, Aug. 1806, to George Crawley, Capt. R.N., who died 5 March, 1810 (see next page); she re-married 6 Jan., 1825, to Rev. Thomas Jones, D.D., rector of Exeter Coll., Oxon.; he died 7 Aug. 1838; by her first husband she had a daughter.

Georgiana, married 1 Jan., 1831, to Rev. Hugh Polson, of Bourton-on-the-Water, and had 3 sons and 2 daughters.

[1] Charles Henry (Polson), born 30 Oct., died 5 Nov., 1831.

[2] Arthur Crawley (Polson), born 20 Jan., 1833; died , 1864.

[3] George Henry (Polson), born 28 Jan., 1834.

[4] Catherine Rosalie, born 25 May, 1835; married 11 Dec., 1860, to Arthur Proctor Pickering, of London, solicitor, and has a son and daughter.

Umfraville (Pickering), born 28 April, 1863; Alethe Mary.

[5] Georgiana Alethe, born 28 Feb., 1838; died 1881; married 15 Oct., 1861, as 1st wife to Charles Warren Adams, Esq., and had a daughter.

Charlotte Alethe Rosalie (Adams), born 1862.

(9) Anne Duke (Yonge), died 22 June, 1845; married 15 Dec., 1830, as 1st wife, to Thomas Julian Pode, Esq., of Plympton Erle, Devon; he died 9 Feb., 1857; having had 5 sons and 3 daughters.

[1] John Duke (Pode), of Slade, Devon, J.P., M.A. New Coll., Oxon. (some time fellow), barrister-at-law, Inner Temple; born 6 Nov. 1832; married 30 Aug. 1860, his cousin Augusta Boevey, youngest daughter of Rev. Charles Crawley, Vicar of Hartpury, &c., (see next page) and has 3 sons and a daughter.

Ernest Duke Yonge (Pode), born 2 Aug. 1862; Cyril Augustin, born 29 April, 1866; Arthur Crawley, born 4 July, 1870; Beatrice Catharina.

[2] James Yonge (Pode), born 23 Dec. 1833, died 17 Nov. 1834.

[3] William Yonge (Pode), of Plympton Erle, born 16 June, 1835.

[4] Charles Coleridge (Pode), scholar of Exeter Coll., Oxon., B.A., M.B., &c., born 3 April, 1841, died 25 May, 1873.

[5] Edward (Pode), educated at Exeter Coll., Oxon., born 26 Sept. 1842; married 6 Oct. 1866, Elizabeth Davey, daughter of Richard Clifton, of Ashwater, Devon, she died 13 May, 1883.

[6] Anne Catharina, married 30 July, 1861, to William John Woollcombe, Esq., of Plympton Erle (3rd son of late Vice-Admiral George Woollcombe), and has had 8 sons and 2 daughters.

(1) William, born 1 July, 1862; died 7 Aug., 1873.

(2) James Yonge, born 5 Sept., 1863.

(3) Walter Ley, born 23 Feb., 1865.

(4) Maurice, midshipman, R.N., born 18 April, 1868.

(5) Reginald, born 11 April, 1870.

(6) Charles Kenneth, born 8 Nov., 1871.

(7) Alfred, born 11 April, 1873.

(8) John, born 19 Jan., 1875.

(9) Mary Catharina.

(10) Frances Jane.

[7] Charlotte Cordelia, married 26 Aug. 1862, to Rev. Duke Yonge, of Puslinch and Combe, Devon, and of Burrell, Cornwall, M.A. Exeter Coll., Oxon., 1849; patron and rector of Newton Ferrers, 1877 to 1881; he died 7 Oct. 1881, and had 6 sons and 4 daughters.

(1) John (Yonge), of Puslinch, &c.; born 18 Dec. 1864.

(2) Charles Burell, born 6 April, 1866.

(3) Geoffrey, born 20 Sept., 1867.

(4) Duke Mohun, born 18 April, 1869.

(5) James Upton, born 17 April, 1872.

(6) Ambrose Pode, born 19 Dec. 1878.

(7) Katharine. (8) Dorothea.

(9) Cordelia Elizabeth. (10) Alethea.

(8) Frances Alethea (Pode), married 6 Feb., 1873, to Rev. Thomas Harold Frederick Hickes, M.A. Pem. Coll., Oxon., 1870, chaplain of St. Michael's House, Cheddar, &c., since 1878, and has 2 sons and a daughter.

George (Hickes), born 8 March, 1874.
Thomas Duke, born 27 Nov., 1876.
Mary Yonge.

SIR THOMAS CRAWLEY-BOEVEY, of Flaxley Abbey, aforesaid, s. as 2nd baronet on the death of his kinsman Sir Charles Barrow 10 Jan., 1789, s.p., by virtue of the limitation of the patent; born 14 Feb., 1744-5; died 11 Aug., 1818, having married 20 Feb., 1769, Anne, 2nd daughter of Rev. Thomas Savage, M.A., of Broadway, Worcester, &c., rector of Standish, by Eleanor, his wife, only daughter and heir of Thomas Barrow, of Field Court, parish of Hardwicke (uncle of Sir Charles Barrow, Bart.); she died 10 Sept., 1816, having had 5 sons and 6 daughters.

[1] **Sir Thomas**, 3rd Baronet, of whom presently.
[2] John Lloyd Crawley, rector of Heyford and Holdenby, Northants, 1809-50, B.A. St. Mary Hall, Oxon., 1798; born 21 Feb., 1775; died 18 Oct., 1850, having married 21 April, 1806, his cousin Anne, daughter of Rev. Charles Crawley, LL.B., rector of Stowe (see page 558); she died 2 May, 1863, having had 6 sons and a daughter.
(1) John Lloyd, vicar of Arlingham, Glouc., 1837-48, M.A. Trinity Coll., Oxon., 1834; born 10 June, 1808; drowned in the Severn, 30 Aug., 1848, having married 25 June, 1839, Mary Elizabeth, daughter of Rev. John Sayer, vicar of Arlingham; she died 11 May, 1880, having had a son and 3 daughters.
John Lloyd, in New Zealand, late lieut. R.N., born 1 Nov., 1845, unmarried; Mary Elizabeth Sayer; Ellen Sayer; Selina Charlotte Sayer.
(2) George, born 8 Nov., 1810; died s.p 2 Sept., 1854, having married 8 Aug., 1850, Emily Anne Frances, 2nd daughter and coheir of Right Rev. William Grant Broughton, D.D., bishop of Sydney.
(3) Charles Gibbs, commr. R.N., retd., born 17 April, 1812.
(4) Henry, rector of Stowe Nine Churches 1849, M.A. Balliol Coll., Oxon., 1842; born 7 July, 1813; married 1st, 15 Jan., 1857, Emma, daughter of Mr. John Tollington, of Leicester; she died 6 May, 1858. He married 2ndly, 4 Oct., 1870, his cousin Mary, daughter of Rev. Charles Crawley, and had by 1st wife a daughter
Emma Anne, born 28 April, 1858.
(5) Thomas William, rector of Heyford, Northants. 1851, M.A. Pembroke Coll., Oxon., 1834; born 21 Aug., 1815; married 5 May, 1853, Hannah Elizabeth, daughter of Jeffery Carter, of Heyford, and has had with other issue 7 sons and 3 daughters.
[1] Thomas William, late clerk in the foreign office, born 12 Feb., 1854; died 4 Jan., 1885; married 23 Sept., 1875, Emily, eldest daughter of Walter Mingay and Emily Rochfort, of Acton, Middlesex, and had a daughter.
Cecilia Emily Augusta Elizabeth.
[2] Antony Frazer Hughes Riddell, born 1 Aug., 1855,
[3] Henry Hughes, born 7 Aug. 1856.
[4] George Burridge, lieut. Bengal S.C., served in Afghanistan; born 10 March, 1858; married, and has a son.
[5] Charles Purrier, born 20 Aug., 1859; married, and has a son, born 10 Dec., 1880
[6] John Sayer, born 8 March, 1867.
[7] Vicary Gibbs, born 9 May, 1868.
[8] Albinia Hawksley.
[9] Emily Gibbs.
[10] Ellen Daubeny.
(6) Alfred, born 4 Aug., 1824; unmarried.
(7) Eleanora, married 26 September, 1833, to Henry Norris, Esq., of Swalcliffe, Oxon., and has 2 sons and 4 daughters.
[1] Henry Crawley (Norris), of Chacombe House, Banbury, Oxon., J.P., major Oxfords. hussars, late capt. 8th hussars, A.D.C. to the Duke of Marlborough, K.G., when Lord Lieutenant of Ireland, 1876-7; born 9 Feb., 1841; married 17 Jan., 1867, Mary, daughter of Rt. Hon. Sir William Bovill, and has 2 sons and a daughter.
Henry Everard du Cane (Norris), born 27 April, 1869; John, born 17 April, 1870; Dorothy.
[2] George Hugh, lieut. Oxfords. hussar yeo. cavly. barrister-at-law Inner Temple 1870, M.A. Exeter Coll., Oxon.; born 26 June, 1843.
[3] Ellen Hamilton (Norris). [4] Anne Henrietta.
[5] Albinia Georgiana, married July, 1863, to Rev. Henry Clark Powell, rector of Wylye, Wilts, since 1882, vicar of Stanton St. Bernard, 1877-82, provost of Inverness cathedral.
[6] Mary Elizabeth.
[3] Charles Crawley, vicar of Hartpury, Glou., and hon. canon of Gloucester cathedral; born 28 Nov. 1780; died 17 Jan., 1856, having married 30 Aug., 1811, his cousin Catharina, daughter of Rev. Duke Yonge, of Cornwood, Devon (see preceding page), she died 2 Jan., 1857, having had 2 sons and 5 daughters.
(1) Charles Yonge, B.A., minor canon of Gloucester cathedral, rector of Taynton, Glouc., 1864, M.A. Oriel Coll., Oxon., 1848; born 2 Mar. 1813; died 5 June, 1876, having married 3 June. 1845, Harriet, only daughter of James Wintle, of Saintbridge, co. Gloucester, and has a son and daughter.
[1] Charles James, born 2 Mar. 1850, married 1880, Maude, daughter of Buck, Esq.
[2] Harriet Maria, died 26 July, 1881; married 6 April, 1875, to Oliver Henry Atkins Nicolls, lieut.-col. R.A., and has a son and daughter.
Oliver Charles Crawley (Nicolls), born 3 June, 1878; Georgina Harriet, died 26 July, 1881.
(2) George John Lloyd, curate of Bartley Green, Northfield, Worcestershire, B.A. Ch. Ch., Oxon., 1844; born 20 Feb., 1820; died unmarried 8 Nov., 1874.
(3) Catherina Duke, married 28 July, 1864, to Rev. Henry Low, M.A. 1845, fell. Exeter Coll., Oxon.; he died 18 Nov. following.
(4) Charlotte Elizabeth, died unmarried 25 Nov. 1864.
(5) Mary, married 4 Oct. 1870, as second wife, to her cousin, Rev. Henry Crawley, rector of Stowe Nine Churches.
(6) Anna Cordelia.
(7) Augusta Boevey, married 30 Aug. 1860, to John Duke Pode, Esq., of Slade, Devon, J.P., barrister-at-law Inner Temple, late fellow New Coll., Oxon. (see preceding page), and has three sons and a daughter.
Ernest Duke Yonge (Pode), born 2 Aug. 1862; Cyril Augustin, born 29 April 1866; Arthur Crawley, born 4 July, 1870; Beatrice Catharina.
[4] George Crawley, capt. R.N., born 23 Dec. 1781; died 5 March, 1810, having married Aug. 1806, his cousin Charlotte, daughter of Rev. Duke Yonge, of Cornwood, Devon; she died 8 April, 1836, having (re-married 6 Jan., 1825, to Rev. Thomas Collier Jones, D.D., rector of Exeter Coll., Oxon., who died 7 Aug., 1838), had an only daughter,
Georgiana, married 1 Jan., 1831, to late Rev. Hugh Polson, of Bourton-on-the-Water, and had 3 sons and 2 daughters (see preceding page).
[5] William Crawley, vicar of Flaxley, M.A. Bras.

Coll., Oxon, 1816; born 24 Dec. 1790; died 17 Dec. 1858, having married 8 Oct. 182*, his cousin Charlotte, youngest daughter of Rev. Charles Crawley, LL.B. (see page 558); she died 14 Dec. 1878, having had with other issue a son and three daughters.

(1) William Savage, born 27 July, 1823; married 30 April, 1857, Clara Mary Ann, daughter and coheir of John Dennil Maddock, of Lescard Manor, Cheshire, and has had with other issue 5 sons and a daughter,

William Evelyn Maddock, of Le Mars, Iowa, U.S.A., born 20 Jan. 1859; John Dennil Maddock, born 20 Jan., 1861; Alured Geoffrey Maddock, of Iquique, Peru, born 4 Dec., 1863; Francis Herbert Maddock, born 20 March 1865; Arthur Alain Maddock, born 3 Aug. 1868; Clara Cecelia Maddock.

(2) Charlotte Sybella, married 13 Sept. 1849, to John Sayer, of Pett place, Charing, Kent, barrister-at-law L.I., and has 4 sons and 2 daughters.

[1] John (Sayer), barrister-at-law L.I. 1875, born 3 July, 1850.

[2] George, born 7 Sept., 1853.

[3] William, born 7 Nov., 1854.

[4] Arthur, born 15 Aug. 1856.

[5] Mary, married 1882, to Rev. John Robert Lawrence, M.A. Ch. Church, Oxon, 1877, curate in charge of Moorlynch since 1882.

[6] Sibella Fanny.

(3) Joanna Gibbs. (4) Margaret Susanna.

[6] Susannah (Crawley-Boevey), died unmarried 16 Sept., 1851.

[7] Katherine, died s.p. ; married as 2nd wife 2 Dec., 1822, to Rear-admiral Ballard, of Bath.

[8] Eleanor, died Sept., 1802; married 11 June, 1801, to Rev. Richard Iremonger (son of Joshua Iremonger, Esq., of Wherwell, Hants); he died 31 May, 1819, having had an only son,

Richard (Iremonger), born Sept, 1802.

[9] Mary, died unmarried Sept., 1835.

[10] Elizabeth, died unmarried 9 March, 1870.

[11] Margaret, married 12 Jan., 1820, as 1st wife to her cousin James Yonge, M.D., of Plymouth, who died 3 Jan., 1870 (see p. 559).

SIR THOMAS CRAWLEY-BOEVEY, 3rd baronet, born 28 Nov., 1769; died 10 Jan., 1847, having married 28 Oct., 1807, Mary Albinia, daughter of Sir Thomas Hyde Page, Knt.; she died 18 Feb., 1835, leaving a son and 2 daughters.

[1] **Sir Martin Hyde Crawley-Boevey,** succeeded as 4th baronet.

[2] Albinia Anne, died 20 Jan., 1850, having married 14 Sept., 1843, to her cousin Rev. George Barnston Daubeny, and had issue (see p. 776).

[3] Matilda Blanche, married 1 Aug., 1839, to William Gibbs, of Tyntesfield, Somerset, who died (see p. 749).

SIR MARTIN HYDE CRAWLEY-BOEVEY, 4th baronet, verderer of the Forest of Dean 1847; capt. Glouc. yeomanry cavalry, and capt. 12th Glouc. R.V.; born 25 May, 1812; died 14 Oct., 1862, having married 9 June, 1836, Elizabeth, eldest daughter of Rev. George William Daubeny (see p. 776), and had 10 sons and 2 daughters.

[1] **Sir Thomas Hyde Crawley-Boevey,** 5th and present baronet, first-named (see p. 557).

[2] John, born 1, died 29 July, 1838.

[3] Francis Gibbs, born 15th Jan., 1839; died, 6 Dec., 1866.

[4] Walter Daubeny Crawley-Boevey, born 13 April, 1841.

[5] Edward Barnston Crawley-Boevey, lieut. R.A., born 20 March, 1844; married 11 June, 1884, Katherine, 2nd daughter of late Rev. Henry Bolton Power, vicar of Bramley, Surrey.

[6] Arthur William Crawley-Boevey, M.A. Balliol Coll., Oxon., 1880; barrister-at-law L.I. 1868; Bo.C.S. 1868; born 12 Aug., 1845; married 16 Sept., 1873, Annie Maria, 2nd daughter of Gen. Sir Robert Phayre, K.C.B., A.D.C. to the Queen, and has a son,

Martin, born 17 Sept., 1883.

[7] Octavius Charles Crawley-Boevey, born 24 Nov., 1846; married 2 Sept., 1871, Dona Maria de Marga, of Arequypa, Argentine Republic, and has had 3 sons and 3 daughters.

Santiago Charles, born , 1872.
Edward Maximo, born , 1875.
Alfred Martin, born 26 April, 1879; died 3 March following.
Maria Margarita Elisa. Mary Isabel. Rose Agnes. Lilian Maud Antonia.

[8] James Henry Crawley-Boevey, of Bombay, solicitor, born 2 July, 1848; married at Bombay 7 Dec., 1878, Frances Georgina Hayes, youngest daughter of late Dr, Charles Hayes Newington, of Ticehurst, Sussex, and has 2 sons and daughter,

Charles Arthur, born 9 Dec., 1879; son, born 17 Sept., 1884.
May Frances, born 22 Sept., 1881.

[9] Richard Lloyd Crawley-Boevey, M.A. University Coll., Oxon., 1878; vicar of Flaxley 1883; curate of Haslingden, Manchester, 1881-3; curate of Kirkby, Liverpool, 1876-81; born 22 March, 1852.

[10] Antony P Crawley-Boevey, born 1854.

[11] Martina Elizabeth, married 3 Sept., 1868, to Rev. William Cotton Risley, M.A. Exeter Coll., Oxon., 1858; rector of Shalstone, Bucks, since 1878; vicar of Titley, Herefordshire, 1876 7, and has a son and 3 daughters,

Martin William Cotton (Risley), born 1 June, 1869.
Ethel Blanche. Mabel Alice. Evelyn Martina.

[12] Sybella Mary.

THE DESCENT OF

Sir Rowland Blennerhassett,

Bart., M.P.

FROM THE

Blood Royal  **of England.**

EDWARD III., crowned 1 Feb., 1327, b. 13 Nov., 1312, d. 21 June, 1377. = Philippa, 3rd dau. of William, Count of Holland and Hainault, m. 24 Jan. 1328, d. 15 Aug. 1369.

Edmund, Duke of York, K.G., 5th son, d. at Langley, 1 Aug. 1402. = Isabel (1st wife), youngest dau. and co-heir of Peter, King of Castile, m. 1372.

Constance of Langley. = Thomas, 6th Baron le Despencer, cr. Earl of Gloucester, 1397, beheaded at Bristol, 16 Jan. 1400.

Isabel le Despencer, b. 26 July, 1400, m. 27 July 1411, d. 26 Dec. 1440. = Richard Beauchamp, Lord Bergavenny (1st husband), cr. Earl of Worcester 1420, d. 1422.

Elizabeth Beauchamp, Baroness Bergavenny, b. at Hanley Castle, 16 Dec. 1415, d. 18 June, 1447 (1st wife). = Sir Edward Nevill, sum. to parl. as Baron Bergavenny, 1450-72, d. 18 Oct. 1476.

Sir George Nevill, Lord Bergavenny, sum. to parl. 1482-92, d. 20 Sept. 1492. = Margaret (1st wife), dau. and heir of Sir Hugh Fenne, of Sculton, d. 28 Sept. 1485.

Sir Edward Nevill, of Addington Park, Kent, beheaded on Tower Hill, 9 Jan. 1538-9. = Eleanor, widow of Ralph, 8th Lord Scrope, of Masham, dau. of Andrew, Lord Windsor.

——— Royden (1st husband). = Catherine Nevill = Clement Throckmorton, of Hanley, Warwickshire, d. 19 Oct. 1594.

A, continued above.

A, continued from below.

Catherine Nevill = Clement Throckmorton.

Martha Throckmorton, bur. at Southwick, 30 Dec. 1600, aged 49. = George Lynne, of Southwick Hall, Northants, bur. there 29 Nov. 1617.

George Lynne, of Southwick Hall, d. 5 Nov. 1606. = Isabel, sister of Sir Anthony Forrest, of Morborn, Hunts, Knt.

Martha Lynne = John Blennerhassett, of Ballyseedy, co. Kerry, M.P. Tralee, 1661.

Robert Blennerhassett = Avice, dau. and co-heir of Jenkin Conway, d. April, 1663.

Henry Blennerhassett = Dorcas, dau. of Francis Crumpe, Esq., Killarney.

Robert Blennerhassett = Frances, dau. of Richard Yeilding, Esq., of Tralee.

Sir Rowland Blennerhassett, cr. a baronet, 22 Sept. 1809, d. 14 March, 1821, aged 81. = Melicent Agnes, dau. of Richard Yeilding, Esq., of Rathkeale, co. Limerick.

Sir Robert Blennerhassett, 2nd baronet, b. 26 Jan. 1769, d. 21 Sept. 1831. = Rosanna, only dau. of Arthur Blennerhassett, Esq., of Fortfield, m. 1790, d. 4 Feb. 1828.

- Rowland d. unmarried.
- Sir Arthur Blennerhassett, 3rd bart. b. 30 July, 1794, d. Feb. 1849. = Sarah, dau. of John Mahony, m. 26 July, 1826, d. 11 July, 1866. = Frederick Randall, of Highbury, (2nd husband), m. 16 May, 1850.
- Henry, of royal navy, d. 1811.
- William, d. un. 1837.
- Robert, of Mount Rivers co. Kerry, b. 1797, d. 1862. = Sarah, dau. of Alexander Eagar, M.D., m. 1838, d. 1856.
- Catherine, m. 22 May, 1822, to Rev. Edw. Fitz Gerald Conyers, of Castle-town Conyers. =

Sir Rowland Blennerhassett, 4th baronet, b. 5 Sept., 1839. = Countess Charlotte, only dau. of Count Charles de Leyden, m. 9 June, 1870.

Rosanna.

- Arthur Charles Bernard, b. 1871.
- Rowland William b. 1882.
- Lewis Paul,
- Marie Carola Franciska Roselyne.

BLENNERHASSETT, Sir Rowland, of Churchtown, and Blennerville, co. Kerry, 4th Baronet, M.P. co. Galway 1865-74, co. Kerry 1880 to Nov. 1885, J.P., D.L.; 17th in descent from Edward III; born 5th September, 1839; married, 9th June, 1870, the Countess Charlotte, only daughter of late Charles, Count de Leyden, and has had 3 sons and a daughter.

[1] Arthur Charles Bernard, born 14 April, 1871.
[2] Paul Charles William Roland Marmaduke, born 4 Dec 1877; died 25 Aug. following.
[3] Rowland Lewis William Paul, born 6 Oct. 1882.
[4] Marie Carola Franciska Roselyne.

Arms—Gu., a chevron erm. between three dolphins, embowed arg.
Crest—a wolf sejant ppr.
Motto—Fortes fortuna juvat.
Seats—Churchtown, near Killarney, and Blennerville, Tralee.

The Descent of
Sir Rowland Blennerhassett, Bart., M.P.,
from the Blood Royal of England.

EDWARD III., King of England, Earl of Chester 1320, Duke of Aquitaine, Count of Ponthieu and Montreuil, 1325; crowned at Westminster in his father's lifetime, 1 Feb., 1327; defeated the Scots at Halidon Hill, 1333. In 1339 he assumed the style of "King of France and England, and Lord of Ireland," and quartered the arms of France in the first quarter; gained a great naval victory over the French off Sluys, 1340, and won the celebrated battle of Cressy 26 Aug., 1346; 17 Oct. following the Scots were defeated at Neville Cross, and King David II. taken prisoner to London, where he remained nearly 11 years. Instituted the order of the Garter 1349. His son, the Black Prince, defeated the French at the battle of Poictiers, 19 Sept., 1356, and brought King John prisoner to London, where he remained nearly five years (for further particulars, see *Royal Lineage*, Foster's *Peerage*). The King died at Sheen, Surrey, 21 June, 1377, having had, with other issue,

EDMUND of Langley, 5th son, born at King's Langley, Herts, 5 June, 1341; Lord of Tindale, K.G., Earl of Cambridge by charter 13 Nov. 1362; constable of Dover Castle; warden of the Cinque Ports, 12 July, 1376; a commissioner during the tutelage of his nephew Richard II.; commanded an army in Portugal in support of the claim of John of Gaunt to the throne of Castile, 1381; created Duke of York 6 Aug. 1385; Warden of the kingdom during the King's absence in Ireland, 1394-5; died at Langley, 1 Aug. 1402, married 1st, 1372, Isabel, younger daughter and co heir of Peter (the Cruel), King of Castile and Leon; her will dated 6 Dec. (6 Rich. II.), 1382. The Duke married 2ndly, Joane, daughter of Thomas Holland, Earl of Kent; she re-married 1st, to William, Lord Willoughby of Eresby; 2ndly, to Henry, Lord Scrope; and lastly, to Henry Bromflete, Lord Vescy, for which marriage they had a pardon 14 Aug. 4 Hen. V.; she died s. p. By his 1st wife the Duke of York had with 2 sons an only daughter.

CONSTANCE, married to the ill-fated Thomas, 6th Baron Le Despencer, two years old at his father's death, had summons to parliament 30 Nov. (20 Richard II.), 1396; and 18 July

(21 Richard II.), 1397; in the latter year he obtained the reversal of the Act of Parliament, declaring his ancestors, Hugh 3rd and Hugh 4th Barons, traitors. Created Earl of Gloucester, 29 Sept. 1397 (by virtue of his descent from Hugh le Despencer by his wife Eleanor, daughter and co-heir of Gilbert de Clare, Earl of Gloucester, by his wife, Joan of Acre, daughter of Edward I.); Richard II. granted him several manors, and he shared the misfortunes of that monarch, for he was degraded in the 1st Parliament of Henry IV.; was captured at Bristol when attempting to escape from the kingdom, and beheaded by the rabble in the market-place 16 Jan., 1400, had with other issue a daughter.

ISABEL LE DESPENCER, sister and eventually (1414) sole heir of Richard Le Despencer; born (posthumous) at Cardiff, 26 July, 1400; died 26 Dec., 1440; made her will 1 Dec., 1439, proved 4 Feb., 1439-40; to be buried at Tewkesbury; she married 1st, "on he day of the Seven Sleepers," 27 July, 1411, to Richard Beauchamp, Lord Bergavenny, though his name does not appear among the barons of Parliament in 1417 and 1419; created Earl of Worcester 1420 (son of William, Lord Beau champ de Bergavenny by his wife Joane daughter of Richard, and co-heir of her brother Thomas, Earls of Arundel); he died 1422, being mortally wounded at Meaux, in France; buried at Tewkesbury; she re-married to her husband's cousin, Richard Beauchamp, 5th Earl of Warwick, K.G., by whom she also had issue; he died 30 April, 1438; by her 1st husband, the Earl of Worcester, she had an only daughter,

ELIZABETH BEAUCHAMP, Baroness Bergavenny, or Baroness Beauchamp of Bergavenny; born at Hanley Castle, co. Worcester, 16 Dec. 1415; died 18 June, 1447; buried at the Carmelites, Coventry; married before 1426, as 1st wife, to Sir Edward Neville (6th son of Ralph, 1st Earl of Westmorland, though 4th son by his 2nd wife, Joan Beaufort, daughter of John of Gaunt); had livery with his wife of the lands, but *not* of the castle of Bergavenny, 14 Henry VI.; knighted by John, Duke of Bedford, at Leicester, Whitsuntide, 4 Henry VI, with his brothers, William and George Nevill (Lord Latimer), and the king himself; had summons to parliament as a baron from 5 Sept. (29 Henry VI.), 1450, to 19 Aug. (12 Edward IV.), 1472; in 10 Edward IV. he was a commissioner of array for Kent to oppose the Duke of Clarence and the Earl of Warwick; he married 2ndly (dispensation 15 Oct., 1448), Catherine Howard, sister of John, first Duke of Norfolk (see vol. i. page 5); and died 18 Oct., 1476, leaving by his first wife, with other issue, a son.

SIR GEORGE NEVILL, Lord Bergavenny; had livery of the lands of his father and mother, 12 Jan. (16 Edward IV.), 1476-7; one of the barons at the coronation of Richard III.; served in the wars in France; knighted for his services at the battle of Tewkesbury by Edward IV. at Barton, 9 May, 1471; had summons to parliament 15 Nov., 1482, to 12 Aug., 1492; born at Raby Castle, co. Durham, 1440; died 20 Sept., 1492; buried at Lewes Priory, Sussex; will dated 1 July, 1491; proved 1492 (see *Testamenta Vetusta*, page 406); he married 1st, Margaret, daughter and heir of Sir Hugh Fenne, of Sculton Burdeleys, Norfolk, and of Braintree, Essex, treasurer of the household to Henry VI.; she died 28 Sept., 1485. His widow, Elizabeth, made her will 14 April (proved 19 June), 1500 describing herself as of Berghdenne, parish of Chartham, Kent, widow, and naming her 4 husbands; her 2nd was Richard Naylor, citizen of London, her 3rd Robert Bassett, and her last husband John Stokker, Lord Bergavenny had by his 1st wife with 3 daughters 5 sons.

[1] GEORGE, succeeded as 3rd Lord Bergavenny.
[2] William, died s. p.
[3] **Sir Edward Nevill**, of Addington Park, of whom presently.
[4] Sir Thomas, of Mereworth, Kent, speaker of the House of Commons, 1514-23; died 29 May, 1542, leaving a daughter.
[5] Sir John, a knight of Rhodes.

SIR EDWARD NEVILL, of Addington Park, Kent, knight banneret for his bravery at the siege of Therouenne, 5 Hen. VIII.; one of the commanders of the forces under the Duke of Suffolk in the expedition to France, 15 Hen. VIII.; a gentleman of the bedchamber at the christening of Prince Edward, 15 Oct., 1537; but on 3 Nov. in the following year he was imprisoned

in the Tower, and 3 Jan. indicted for "devising to maintain, promote and advance one Reginald Pole, late dean of Exeter, enemy to the king beyond the sea, and to deprive the king," was attainted and beheaded on Tower Hill 9th of same month, 1538-9; married Eleanor, widow of Ralph, 8th Lord Scrope, of Masham, daughter of Andrew, Lord Windsor, and had with 3 sons 4 daughters, of whom the eldest, viz.:—

CATHERINE, married 1stly to ——— Royden, and, 2ndly, to Clement Throckmorton, of Haseley, Warwick, sewer to the Queen temp. Henry VIII.; a commander at the siege of Boulogne, 1544 (son of Sir George Throckmorton, co. Warwick, by Katherine Vaux, also of royal descent); he died 19 Oct., 1594 (? 18 Oct., 1599), having had 6 sons and 7 daughters.

[1] Job (Throckmorton), of Haseley, supposed author of "Sir Martin Mar Prelate"; born 28 Jan., 1545; by his wife Dorothea, daughter of Thomas Vernon, of Houndhill, Salop, he had, with other issue, a son, Sir Clement, knight of the shire for the county of Warwick temp. Eliz., Jas. I. and Chas. I., grandfather of Sir Clement, M.P. Warwick, 1661, &c.
[2] Edward, born 31 May, 1542.
[3] Henry, born 9 Feb., 1552.
[4] Kenelm, born 25 May, 1557.
[5] Josiah, born 10 June, 1558.
[6] Clement, of Ansley, co. Warwick, born 20 Dec., 1561; married Elizabeth Ludford, widow, daughter of — Harcourt, of Staffordshire, and had a son and 3 daughters.
[7] Frances, married to Henry Medley, of Titley, Isle of Wight.
[8] Katherine, married 1st to Thomas Harby, of Adston, Northants; she re-married to George Dryden; and lastly, to John Wilmer, of Throwley.
[9] Amphelice, born 22 June, 1544.
[10] **Martha**, married to George Lynne, of Southwick, Northants; of whom presently.
[11] Ursula, born 19 Nov., 1555; married to Thomas Bigges, of Lenchwike, co. Worc.
[12] Susanna (Throckmorton).
[13] Mary, born 21 Sept., 1563; married to Giles Foster, of Bois, co. Glouc.

MARTHA THROCKMORTON (4th daughter of Clement, above named), buried at Southwick 30 Dec., 1600, aged 49; married to George Lynne, of Southwick Hall, Northants (son and heir of George Lynne, of Southwick, by his wife Amicia, daughter of Sir Edward Montagu, lord chief justice of England, ancestor of the Duke of Manchester; see Foster's *Peerage*); he was buried at Southwick 29 Nov., 1617, having had at least 4 sons and 9 daughters.

[1] **George Lynne**, of whom presently.
[2] Fitzwilliam, vicar of Southwick, 1599.
[3] Guy.
[4] Walter, vicar of Moulton, co. Linc., where he was buried s.p. 15 March, 1638-9; made his will 3 Oct., 1638, proved by Lydia his wife 11 May, 1639.
[5] Alice, married to George Sandford, of Bassetts in Willinghall, Essex, and had 6 sons and 2 daughters, viz.: George, Robert, Edmond, Arthur, Thomas, William, Alice, and another daughter named Matthew.
[6] Anne, married to Nicholas Bestow, of Holton-le-Moor, co. Linc., who was buried in the chapel there 18 Sept., 1653, leaving issue.
[7] (daughter), married to Holland, of Lancashire.
[8] Margaret, married to John Fosbrook, of Cranford, Northants, and had issue.
[9] Mary, married to Edward Lisle, of Yarwell, Northants (son of Reginald Lisle, of Moxhull Hall, Warwickshire).
[10] Jane, baptised at Southwick 5 Dec., 1592; married there 11 Feb., 1617-18, to Martin Johnson, of Spalding, Lincolnshire, gent., and had issue.
[11] (daughter), married Stemrode.
[12] (daughter), married to Rev. John Cranford, vicar in 1609 of Cranford, Northants.
[13] Elizabeth, married to Edward Pickering, of Aulkmondbury, Hunts, and had a son, Edward, who was dead in 1613.

GEORGE LYNNE, of Southwick Hall, died 5, buried in Southwick church 6 Nov., 1606; inquisition post mortem 26 August, 5 James I.; he married Isabella, daughter of Myles and sister of Sir Anthony Forrest, of Morborn, Hunts, Knt., where she was baptised 26 July, 1575; had 4 sons and 6 daughters.

[1] GEORGE (**Lynne**), of whom see p. 667.
[2] William died before 4 March, 1669-70; married at St. Bartholomew the Great, London, 24 May, 1631, Elizabeth, daughter of Anthony Whetenhall, of Tenterden, Kent, and had at least 5 sons.
[3] Clement, a soldier in the Low Countries, where he died.
[4] Miles, died young.
[5] Frances, died unmarried. [6] Anne, died unmarried.
[7] Isabella, died unmarried.
[8] **Martha**, married to John Blennerhassett, of Ballyseedy, co. Kerry, named below.
[9] Cordelia, married to Rev. William Hardwick, vicar in 1619 of Swineshead, and in 1631 of Bicker, both in Lincolnshire.
[10] Anne, married to Rev. George Kirkham, vicar in 1631 of Bicker aforesaid; he died 1636.

MARTHA (daughter of George Lynne aforesaid), married to John Blennerhassett, Esq, of Ballyseedy, co. Kerry; M.P. Tralee, 1661; (eldest son of Robert Blennerhassett, Esq., of Ballycarty, and his wife Elizabeth Conway); he made his will 18 Oct., 1673, proved 14 Sept., 1676, and had 3 sons and 3 daughters.

[1] John (Blennerhassett), of Ballyseedy, M.P. Tralee, Dingle, and co. Kerry; high sheriff, 1658; his will

proved 1667; married Elizabeth, daughter of Sir Edward Denny, Knt., of Tralee; she was born 25 Feb., 1635, and had 2 sons and a daughter (see p.691).
[2] **Robert,** of whom presently.
[3] Thomas, of Littur, co. Kerry, made his will 8 June 1695, married Ellen, daughter of Anthony Stoughton, of Ratto, co. Kerry, clerk of the court of Castle Chamber (by his wife Honora, daughter of Dermot O'Brien, Lord Inchiquin), and had 6 daughters (see Raymond *Pedigree*, p.639).
[4] Mary (Blennerhassett), married to Capt Thomas Wren, of Littur, co. Kerry, and had a son (ancestor of the family still seated there); and a daughter Martha, married to William Fitz Gerald.
[5] Alice, married to Edmond Conway, of Cloghane (son of Capt. James Conway, of Castle Conway, co. Kerry, by Elizabeth, daughter and sole heir of Edmond Roe, by his wife, Alice, daughter of Jenkin Conway), and had a son.
James Conway, of Cloghane, married, 1st, Catherine, daughter of Patrick Fitzgerald, of Gallerus, son of the Knight of Kerry (see p. 213); he married, 2nd, Honora, daughter of Rev. Vere Hunt, by his wife, Constance, daughter of Sir William Piers, of Tristernagh, co. Westmeath, 2nd Bart.); by his 1st wife he had an only daughter,
Alice Conway, married, as 1st wife, to Col. John Colthurst, of Ballynally, and had 3 sons and 2 daughters (see page 715).
6] Lucy, married to John Walker, a lieut. in the English army, 1641, and had a daughter,
Martha Walker, married, about 1680, to Thomas Shiercliffe, of Castle Gregory, and died 1683, leaving 2 daughters.
(1) Alice (Shiercliffe), married to Edward Rice, and had 4 daughters.
[1] Christian (Rice), married to Edward Conway, and had an only surviving child,
Mary Rice, died 15 July, 1825; married 18 May, 1784, to John Hurly, Esq., clerk of the crown and peace for Kerry; he died 26 Nov., 1829, leaving issue.
[2] Alice.
[3] Mary, married to Richard, youngest son of Henry Blennerhassett, and had issue (see next page).
[4] Martha (Rice)
(2) Martha (Shiercliffe), of Moyalla, co. Cork.

ROBERT BLENNERHASSETT (son of John Blennerhassett and Martha Lynne), married Avice, daughter and co-heir of Jenkin or Edward Conway, of Killorglin or Castle Conway, co. Kerry, with whom he acquired the greater part of the estates granted to John Conway; she died April, 1663, having had 3 sons and 5 daughters.

[1] John Blennerhassett, of Castle Conway, co. Kerry, (Captain) known as "Black Jack," married Elizabeth, 3rd daughter of Rev. Benjamin Cross, D.D., Blackhall, Oxford, rector of Christ Church, Cork, and of Spettisbury, Dorset; she died 22 March, 1732, aged 63, having had 6 sons and 4 daughters (see page 593A
2] Thomas (Blennerhassett), married Jane Darby, of Wales, and had 3 sons and 4 daughters (see page589).
[3] **Henry,** of whom presently.
[4] Catherine, married 1st, to Richard, son of Capt. Richard McLough in, of Bally Downey, and had 2 daughters (see page600); she re-married to John Conway, and had a daughter.
Mildred (Conway), married , to Thomas Jeffcott, of Tonarigh, and had issue.
[5] Avice, married to Thomas, son of Captain Thomas Spring, of Ballycr spin, co, Kerry, and had 4 sons and 4 daughters (see page592).
[6] Alice, married to Walter, brother of Capt. Thomas Spring aforesaid, and had a son and 4 daughters.
(1) Thomas (Spring), married Anne Fitz-Maurice, Duaghnafealy, and had William and Thomas, 1732.
(2) Avice, married to Thomas, 3rd son of John Blennerhassett, of Ballyseedy, and had 3 sons (see p 692).
(3) Anne, married to Rev. Thomas Frankland, prebendary of Cloyne.
(4) Martha, married to Capt. John Thwaite, of Cumberland.
(5) Jane (Spring), married 1st, 6 Nov., 1729, to Thomas Eagar, of Ballyhar, and had 3 sons and 4 daughters (see p. 592); 2nd, to Brewster, and 3rd, to William Dunscombe, of Cork
[7] Lucy (Blennerhasset), married to John Plaguavan, a Frenchman, and had 2 sons and 2 daughters.
(1) John Plaguavan, of Cork, married Elizabeth Laird, or Lane, of Cork; she made her will 18 Dec., 1760, proved 27 April, 1771, and had at least 2 sons and 2 daughters.
John. Henry, born 20th June, 1736, Mary and Lucy.
(2) George.
(3) Jane (Plaguavan), made her will 11 Jan., 1781, proved 23 January following, buried in St. Peter's, Dublin; she married , to John Poujade, a Frenchman, and had a son and 2 daughters.
[1] John Poujade.
[2] Mary, made her will 1 Jan., 1802, proved 25 May, 1803; married (deed 21 Dec., 1758) to Henry, 2nd son of Samuel Blennerhassett, named below.
[3] Avice (Poujade.
(4) Avice (Plaguavan).
[8] Anne, married to Dennis Hurly, of Knocklong, co. Limerick, and had 5 sons and 3 daughters.

HENRY BLENNERHASSETT, married Dorcas, daughter of Francis Crumpe, Esq. of Killarney (by his wife Dorcas, 2nd daughter of Robert Orpen, Esq.), and had 7 sons and 4 daughters.

[1*a*] Arthur (Blennerhassett), a doctor of the Sorbonne in France.
[2] John. [3*a*] William.
[4*a*] **Robert,** of whom see page 572.
[5*a*] Samuel (Blennerhassett), married Catherine, daughter of Ven. Maurice Connor, Archdeacon of Ardfert, (see page 722), and had 4 sons and 3 daughters (*b*).
(1*b*-5*a*) Thomas, died s.p.
(2*b*-5*a*) Henry (Blennerhassett), of Dublin, solicitor, married (deed 21 Dec., 1758), Mary, daughter of John Poujade, Esq., named above, made her will 1 Jan., 1802, proved 25 May, 1803, she had 2 sons and 3 daughters (*c*).
[1*c*-2*b*] John Henry Blennerhassett, of Tralee; died 15 Aug., 1841; married 1st. Elizabeth, daughter of John O'Connell, of Kiltannon, near Rathkeale, and had 1 son and 3 daughters (*d*).
(1*d*-1*c*) Henry, died unmarried.
(2*d*-1*c*) Catherine, died unmarried.
(3*d*-1*c*) Mary, died unmarried.
(4*d*-1*c*) Anne, married 1822, as 1st wife, to Rowland Tallis Eagar, Esq. (see p.573).

JOHN HENRY BLENNERHASSETT, married 2nd, 1818, Veronica, daughter of Robert Montgomery, Esq., of co. Down; she died in Tralee, , 1828, having had 5 daughters *(d)*.

(5*d*-1*c*) Veronica Montgomerie, married 15 Sept., 1840, to John Grey Porter Atthill, LL.D., late Chief Justice St. Lucia, and of Kingstown, barrister-at-law, and had 2 sons and 6 daughters.

[1] William Eyre Blennerhassett (Atthill), M.D., born 14 April, 1848; married 9 July, 1872, Augusta Jane Vine, daughter of late E. Edmonds, J.P., D.L., Wilts, and has

[2] Robert Maunsell Eyre (Atthill), born 15 Nov., 1853; married 6 Feb., 1878, Agnes Sarah, 3rd daughter of late Alfred Parker, Esq., and has a son and daughter,

Robert Blennerhassett (Atthill), born 2 Dec., 1880.

Agnes Isabel Blennerhassett.

[3] Veronica Montgomerie, married , to Capt. William Alexander Russwurm.

[4] Henrietta Margaret Eyre, married , to Frederick Arthur Selwyn.

[5] Emilie Gertrude, married to C. de Giraudy.

[6] Isabel Blennerhassett, married , to C. Birch, Esq.

[7] Laura Adela Herbert (Atthill), youngest daughter, married 1st, to Ernest Francis Hercules Rickard; she re-married 14 Jan., 1880, to Richard Copeland, of Croydon.

[8] Helena Grace, died 3 Feb., 1883.

(6*d*-1*c*) Henrietta, died Dec., 1883; married July, 1844, to George Newenham Woolley, Esq., of Buckden, Hunts, and had a son, George, of Leicester, and a daughter, deceased.

(7*d*-1*c*) Elizabeth, married 6 Sept., 1842, to Hon. John Thicknesse-Touchet (brother of George, 23rd Lord Audley, see Foster's *Peerage*); he died 21 July, 1861, having had one son and 4 daughters.

[1] George John (Thicknesse-Touchet), born 27 April, 1847; died 11 Nov., 1866.

[2] Elizabeth.

[3] Maria Jane, died 15 Feb., 1867.

[4] Charlotte Anna, married 16 June, 1875, to Thomas Jesson, Esq., of Great Houghton House, near Northampton, and has 2 sons and 2 daughters,

Thomas Touchet (Jesson), born 17 July, 1879; George Arthur Touchet, born 31 May, 1885; Gertrude Anne, Dorothy Charlotte.

[5] Dorothea Susan, married 24 Jan., 1878, as 2nd wife, to Rev. and Hon. Charles Samuel Twisleton (see Foster's *Peerage*, B. SAYE AND SELE), p.

(8*d*-1*c*) Anna Sarah, married 30 Oct., 1843, to Francis Green Tincler, of Dublin, solicitor; he died 17 June, 1877, having had 4 sons and a daughter.

[1] George Samuel Boxwell (Tincler), of Dublin, solicitor, born 16 Aug., 1846; married 1873, Eva, daughter of late Capt. Chas. Kirkwood, R.N., of Barra, co. Mayo, and has 2 sons and 2 daughters.

George Blennerhassett (Tincler), born 11 March, 1875; Charles Knox Kirkwood, born 5 Oct., 1880; Ida Emyly; Eva Mabel.

[2] Blennerhassett Montgomery (Blennerhassett), assumed that surname in lieu of his patronymic, 1829, surgeon-major Army Medical Department; born 18 Nov., 1849; married April, 1875, Gertrude Harcourt, daughter of Capt. R. Wilcox, R.N., of Kingstown, co. Dublin; she died April, 1878, leaving a daughter,

Venice Maud (Blennerhassett), born 6 April, 1876.

[3] Charles Lewis (Blennerhassett), also assumed that surname in lieu of his patronymic, 1883; born 5 Oct., 1852; married 3 Feb., 1883, Katherine Elizabeth, daughter of William Paxton, Esq., of Palmeira-square, Brighton.

[4] Ernest Blennerhassett (Tincler), also assumed that surname in lieu of his patronymic, 1885, lieut. R. Enniskillen (27th) Fusiliers, born 29 June, 1863.

[5] Louise Agnes (Tincler), born 7 Aug., 1844; married, 1st, Nov. 1866, to Gordon Archdall, M.D.; she re-married to John Adolphe Poirey, Esq.

(9*d*-1*c*) Jemima, died unmarried.

[2*c*-2*b*] Edward Francis, died unmarried.

[3*c*-2*b*] Mary, died 28 Dec., 1859, aged 95; married (lic. 30 April, 1791) to Capt. Thomas Blennerhassett, who died in Brussels 1825, leaving issue, see p. 593*a*.

[4*c*-2*b*] Jane (Mrs. Armstrong) had a daughter, Mary.

[5*c*-2*b*] Charlotte, died 6 Feb., 1847; married 1793, to Rowland Eagar, J.P., collector of Excise; he died, s.p., 5 Dec., 1830 (see page 573).

(3*b*-5*a*) John; (4*b*-5*a*) William.

(5*b*-5*a*) Frances, married to Daniel McCarthy, Esq.

(6*b*-5*a*) Mary.

(7*b*-5*a*) Annie, died s.p.; married, 1st, as 2nd wife to John Hoare, Esq., of Coolfada, co. Cork, and of Dromeare, co. Kerry (she re-married, 1st, to John Blennerhassett, of Rosbeigh (see page 742), and, lastly, to John Moore Eagar) (see page 592).

[6*a*] Edward (Blennerhassett).

[7*a*] Richard (Blennerhassett), of Ballymacprior, co. Kerry, married June, 1780, Hon. Elizabeth de Moleyns, daughter of Thomas, 1st Lord Ventry (see page 664); she died 29 Oct., 1844, having had 3 sons and 5 daughters *(e)*.

(1*e*-7*a*) Henry (Blennerhassett), M.D., born 1783; died 1861; married Anne Bell, a Scotch lady; she died 1852, having had 11 sons and 4 daughters.

[1] William, died unmarried.

[2] Richard, M.D., died unmarried.

[3] Henry, and [4] Thomas, both died young.

[5] Thomas (Blennerhassett), of Laune Mount, Killorglin; born 10 Sept., 1821; married Feb., 1866, his cousin Eliza, daughter of Thomas Barry; she died s.p. 1872 (see next page).

[6] Rowland, M.D., born ; died , 1877; married Maria, sister of Capt. Henry Haire, of the Fermanagh militia (she re-married), and had three sons and 2 daughters.

(1) Hamilton. (2) Thomas, died at school, 1881.

(3) Townsend. (4) Rhoda Charlotte, died 1863, aged 15. (5) Harriet.

[7] Aremberg (Blennerhassett), now in America, married Elizabeth, sister of Capt. Henry Haire, and has issue. [8] Henry, died young.

[9] Townsend (Blennerhassett), of Ballymacprior, Killorglin, capt. Kerry mil., born 11 Feb., 1829; drowned in Castlemain Bay, 20 June, 1867, in attempting to save the life of a boatman; married Sept., 1854, Catherine, daughter of Alexander Eager, M.D. (see page 574); she died June, 1873, leaving a daughter,

Annabella Charlotte (Blennerhassett), died 1 July, 1882; married 14 April, 1880, to Edward Abram McGillycuddy, Esq., (see p. 628), and had a son,

Townsend Blennerhassett (McGillycuddy), born 27 July, 1882.

[10] Edward (Blennerhassett), M.D., born 24 June, 1838; died at Valentia Island, 24 March, 1874; married 13 Feb., 1862, Cherry Greene, daughter of Samuel Alleyne Rothwell, Esq., of Newtown, and has 2 sons,

Irvine, born 9 Dec., 1864.

Edward Townsend, born 14 Feb., 1872.

[11] Frederick, [12] Elizabeth, and [13] Elizabeth, all died young.

[14] Charlotte, died 20 June, 1872, aged 41.

[15] Maria, died young.

(2e-7a) Arthur Thomas (Blennerhassett), of Ballymacprior, co. Kerry; married Nov., 1829, Sarah daughter of Hon. Richard de Moleyns (BARON VENTRY, see page 661), and had 3 sons and 4 daughters.

[1] Richard (Blennerhassett), M.D.; ; died 1868; married Elizabeth, daughter of Capt. Wilberforce Bird, R.N., uncle of the Archbishop of Canterbury, and had, with a son, died young, a daughter, Lucy.

[2] Henry, died young. [3] William, in the army.

[4] Madeline, died unmarried.

[5] Eliza Jane, married April, 1862, to Capt. Robert Rowland Conyers (2nd son of Rev. Edward Fitzgerald Conyers, see page 575), and had 4 sons.

(1) Edward. (2) Robert.

(3) Alured. (4) Frederick William.

[6] Charlotte, married 1st to Capt. Henry Haire, of the Fermanagh militia, he died s.p.; she re-married to Francis, eldest son of Francis Spring Walker, of Limerick, both dead s.p. (see below).

[7] Evelyn Florence, married 16 July, 1872, to William de Moleyns, eldest son of Rev. William de Moleyns (see page 662), and has 3 sons and a daughter.

(3e-7a) Townsend, died unmarried.

(4e-7a) Elizabeth, died 21 Dec., 1857; married , to William, son of Sir Rowland Blennerhassett, 1st Bart.; he died 1842, having had 2 sons and 2 daughters (see page 575).

(5e-7a) Theodora, married 1824, to Edward Supple Eagar, Esq., and had 6 daughters (of whom (5) Louisa married as 3rd wife to Richard Ellis, of Glenascrone, see page 601).

(6e-7a) Charlotte, married , to Thomas Barry, Esq., and had 4 sons and 3 daughters.

[1] Thomas (Barry) died unmarried, 1841.

[2] James, died unmarried 1873.

[3] Henry, died young. [4] Richard, went abroad.

[5] Eliza, died s.p., 1872; married Feb., 1860, to her cousin, Thomas Blennerhassett (see preceding page).

[6] Jane, married to Christopher, 2nd son of James Royse Yeilding, Esq., and died in America (see page 572).

[7] Charlotte, married, 1st, to her cousin, John Walker, Esq. (see below); and 2ndly, to William, son of Francis Spring of Castlemaine, who had no issue.

(7e-7a) Mary, died 6 April, 1872, aged 83; married , to Francis Walker, of Lahern; he died 22 Dec., 1848; having had a son and 4 daughters.

[1] John Walker, born 1811; married his cousin Charlotte, daughter of Thomas Barry aforesaid (she remarried to William, son of Francis Spring), and had 3 sons and a daughter.

(1) Francis (Walker), married Kate, daughter of Edward Spring, and has 3 sons; Francis, Walter, and Barry.

(2) Thomas, in India. (3) John. (4) Charlotte.

[2] Eliza, died 30 Nov., 1877; married 21 July, 1827, to Francis Spring Walker, of Belville, co. Limerick, he died 5 June, 1865, having had 2 sons and a daughter.

(1) Francis Walker, married his cousin, Charlotte Haire, née Blennerhassett, both died s.p. (see above).

(2) Anster FitzGerald Walker, M.D., born 7 June, 1842; married 29 Jan., 1873; Margaret, daughter of Dr. John Peppard (see page 573), and has a son

Francis Spring (Walker), born 6 Jan. 1876.

(3) Helen Mary, married 1859, to James Grady FitzGerald Conyers, Esq., Liskennet, near Croome, co. Limerick (see page 575).

[3] Arabella, unmarried.

[4] Charlotte, married 1st, to John Upton, of Ashgrove, co. Limerick, and 2ndly, to Stephen Brazil, by whom 2 children.

[5] Maria (Walker) unmarried.

(8e-7a) Arabella (Blennerhassett), born 1797; died July 1875; married 1st, 3 April, 1825, to Lieut.-col. Frederic Jones, he died May, 1832; she re-married 1841, to Major Hartley; by her 1st husband she had a son and daughter.

[1] Edward Kent (Jones) major in the army, born 1 March, 1829, died July 1877; married

[2] Elizabeth, born 3 Jan., 1826.

[8a] Dorcas (Blennerhassett), mar. to John Godfrey, of Ballingamboon, co. Kerry, and had a son and 3 daughters *(f)*.

(1f-8a) William (Godfrey), married Henrietta Brabazon Eccleston, of Drogheda, and had 3 sons and 2 daughters; his 3rd son, Henry, was father of John Blennerhassett Godfrey, M.D.

(2f-8a) Dorcas (Godfrey), married to Robert Twiss, Esq., of Killintierna, co. Kerry, who died 29 Jan., 1771, having had a son and 2 daughters.

[1] George (Twiss), married Honoria Meredith (see page 512).

[2] Catherine (Twiss), married to William Hilliard, Esq., son of Christopher Hilliard, of Knockeanish, or "the Barn," and died s p.

[3] Avice, married to Thomas Marshall, of Riverville.

(3f-8a) Mary (Godfrey), 3rd daughter, married to A. Spring, Esq.

(4f-8a) Avicia (Godfrey), 2nd daughter, married to William Twiss, of Ballybeg, brother of Robert Twiss, Esq., of Killintierna, and had, with other issue, a son and 4 daughters *(g)*.

[1g-4f] William (Twiss), married his first cousin Henrietta, daughter of William Godfrey, above-named, and had at least 3 sons and 2 daughters.

[2g-4f] Catherine (Twiss), married to David FitzGerald, of Ardrival, co. Kerry, Esq., and had a son, William, of Ardrival, barrister-at-law.

[3g-4f] Dorcas (Twiss), married 22 Jan. 1782, to Caleb Palmer, of Kenmare, co. Kerry, who died 25 March, 1794, having had 5 sons and 3 daughters *(h)*.

(1h-3g) Abraham (Palmer), of Dublin and of Ash grove, co. Kerry; born 10 Dec., 1782; died 1860; married 1805, Margaret, eldest daughter of Major Edward Orpen, of Killowen, co. Kerry; she died having had 6 sons and 3 daughters *(i)*.

[1i-1h] Edward Orpen (Palmer), of Ashgrove, and of Killowen, co. Kerry; born 1 May, 1807; died 13 May, 1883; married at Killintierna 5 Oct., 1841, Elizabeth Agnes, 3rd daughter of Capt. Robert Hutchinson Herbert, R.N., of Lakeview, Killarney (see page 770), and had 2 sons and 3 daughters.

(1) Abraham Henry Herbert (Palmer), vicar of St. Peter's, Cheltenham, B.A. Trin. Coll., Dublin, 1865; born 29 Jan., 1843; married 28 Oct., 1872, Eveline Cecilia, 3rd daughter of Every Carmichael, Esq., of Monktown, co. Durham, and has 4 sons,

Edward Orpen Herbert (Palmer), born 8 Nov., 1873; Harold Bland Herbert, born 8 Sept., 1876; Reginald Arthur Herbert, born 26 Dec., 1877; Geoffrey de Montmorency Herbert, born 1 Mar., 1883.

(2) Robert, died young. (3) Elizabeth Agnes.

(4) Margaret Dorcas. (5) Agnes Laura.

[2i-1h] Caleb Richard (Palmer), of Ashbrook, Raheny, co. Dublin, and of Fusthane, co.

✣ THE ✣ DESCENT ✣ OF ✣

Rev. Abram Smythe Palmer, B.A.

FROM THE

Blood Royal  **of England.**

EDWARD III., crowned 1 Feb., 1327, b. 13 Nov., 1312, d. 21 June, 1377. = Philippa, 3rd dau. of William, Count of Holland and Hainault, m. 24 Jan. 1328, d. 15 Aug. 1369.

Edmund, Duke of York, K.G., 5th son, d. at Langley, 1 Aug. 1402. = Isabel (1st wife), youngest dau. and co-heir of Peter, King of Castile, m. 1372.

Constance of Langley. = Thomas, 6th Baron le Despencer, cr. Earl of Gloucester, 1397, beheaded at Bristol, 16 Jan. 1400.

Isabel le Despencer, b. 26 July, 1400, m. 27 July 1411, d. 26 Dec. 1440. = Richard Beauchamp, Lord Bergavenny (1st husband), cr. Earl of Worcester 1420, d. 1422.

Elizabeth Beauchamp, Baroness Bergavenny, b. at Hanley Castle, 16 Dec. 1415, d. 18 June, 1447 (1st wife). = Sir Edward Nevill, sum. to parl. as Baron Bergavenny, 1450-72, d. 18 Oct. 1476.

Sir George Nevill, Lord Bergavenny, sum. to parl. 1482-92, d. 20 Sept. 1492. = Margaret (1st wife), dau. and heir of Sir Hugh Fenne, of Sculton, d. 28 Sept. 1485.

Sir Edward Nevill, of Addington Park, Kent, beheaded on Tower Hill, 9 Jan. 1538-9. = Eleanor, widow of Ralph, 8th Lord Scrope, of Masham, dau. of Andrew, Lord Windsor.

A, *continued above.*

A, *continued from below.*

Sir Edward Nevill = Eleanor Scrope.

Royden (1st husband). = Catherine Nevill. = Clement Throckmorton, of Hanley, Warwickshire, d. 19 Oct. 1594.

Martha Throckmorton, bur. at Southwick, 30 Dec. 1600, aged 49. = George Lynne, of Southwick Hall, Northants, bur. there 29 Nov. 1617.

George Lynne, of Southwick Hall, d. 5 Nov. 1606. = Isabel, sister of Sir Anthony Forrest, of Morborn, Hunts, Knt.

Martha Lynne = John Blennerhassett, of Ballyseedy, co. Kerry, M.P. Tralee, 1661.

Robert Blennerhassett = Avice, dau. and co-heir of Jenkin Conway, d. April, 1663.

Henry Blennerhassett = Dorcas, dau. of Francis Crumpe, Esq., Killarney.

Dorcas Blennerhassett = John Godfrey, of Ballingamboon, co. Kerry.

Avicia Godfrey = William Twiss, of Ballybeg.

Dorcas Twiss, married 22 Jun. 1782. = Caleb Palmer, of Kenmare, co. Kerry, d. 25 March, 1794.

Abraham Palmer, of Dublin and Ashgrove, co. Kerry, m. 1805, Margaret, dau. of Major Orpen, of Killowen, and d. 1860.

William Twiss Palmer, B.A., in holy orders, m. his cousin, Catherine, dau. of William Twiss, of Tullaree.

George Palmer, m. 1818, Margaret, dau. of John Giles, of Castledrum, and d. 1844.

Thomas, d. young.
Caleb, d. unmarried, 1875.

Avice, m. to Rev. W. Peacock.
Isabella, m. to James Eagar.
Catherine, m. to Rev. John Carey.

Edward Orpen Palmer, of Ashgrove and of Killowen, co Kerry, b. 1 May, 1807, d. 13 May, 1883. = Elizabeth Agnes, 3rd dau. of Capt. Herbert, R.N., m. 5 Oct., 1841.

Anne (1st wife), dau. of Capt. Ralph Smythe, 7th Dragoon Guards, m. 23 Oct., 1839, d. 20 Dec., 1852. = Caleb Richard Palmer, of Ashbrook, co. Dublin, and of Fusthane, co. Kerry. = Harriet Sophia (2nd wife), dau. of Richard Archer, Esq., m. 28 April, 1855.

Other issue see page 568.

Abraham Henry Herbert Palmer, B.A., Vicar of St. Peter's, Cheltenham, b. 29 Jan., 1843. = Eveline Cecilia, 3rd dau. of Evory Carmichael, Esq., m. 28 Oct., 1872.

Elizabeth.
Margaret.
Agnes.

Abram Smythe Palmer, B.A., in holy orders, b. 23 July, 1844. = Frances, dau. of Echlin Molyneux Q.C., Chairman of co. Meath.

Other issue see page 570.

Edward Orpen Herbert, b. 8 Nov., 1873.
Harold Bland Herbert, b. 8 Sept., 1876.
Reginald Arthur Herbert, b. 26 Dec. 1877.
Geoffrey de Montmorency Herbert, b. 1 March, 1883.

Geoffrey Molyneux, b. 8 Oct., 1882.

Gladys Mary.

Kerry; born 3 Feb., 1809; married 1st, 23 Oct., 1839, Anne, daughter of Capt. Ralph Smythe, 7th dragoon guards; she died 20 Dec., 1852, having had a son and 5 daughters *(k)*.

(1*k*-2*i*) Abram Smythe (Palmer), B.A. Trin. Coll., Dublin, clerk in holy orders, author of *Folk Etymology*, &c.; born 23 July, 1844; married 9 July, 1875, Frances, daughter of Echlin Molyneux, Q.C., chairman co. Meath, and has a son and daughter.

Geoffrey Molyneux (Palmer), born 8 Oct., 1882; Gladys Mary.

(2*k*-2*i*) Henrietta Adelaide.

(3*k*-2*i*) Sarah Maria, married 26 Jan., 1866, to Robert Freeman, Esq., of the Bank of Ireland, s.p.

(4*k*-2*i*) Margaret Anna, married 1st, 13 Sept., 1869, to Rev. Luke King, LL.D., who died s.p. 22 July, 1873; she re-married, 30 March, 1875, to William Harrison Peard, Esq., of Riverstown, co. Cork, and has 3 sons and 3 daughters.

William Harrison (Peard), born 30 March, 1877; John Richard, born 25 Dec., 1882; Henry Harrison, born 19 Dec., 1884; Ethel Woodley; Mabel Anna; Josephine Maud.

(5*k*-2*i*) Anna Victoria, married 30 Nov., 1872, to George Hamilton King, M.A. Trin. Coll., Dublin, headmaster Bective College, Dublin, and has had 4 sons and 3 daughters.

George Lucas Stephen (King), born 26 Dec., 1873; died

William Ashe, born 29 Aug., 1880.

Edward Eccleston, born 22 May, 1882; died

Richard Burnet Palmer, born 6 Dec., 1883.

Magdalen Annie; Nora Aileen; Violet Hamilton

(6*k*-2*i*) Emily Theodora, married 23 April, 1878, to Rev. James Torrens, incumbent of Charlemont, co. Armagh, since 1882, and has 2 sons and 2 daughters.

Theodore Wilson (Torrens), born 16 June. 1879; Louis Palmer, born 4 Dec., 1880.

Emily Theodora; Elizabeth May.

Mr. CALEB R. PALMER married, 2ndly, 28 April, 1855, Harriet Sophia, daughter of Richard Archer, Esq., and had a son and 2 daughters *(k)*.

(7*k*-2*i*) Herbert Albert Orpen (Palmer), born 14 April, 1861; died 28 Dec., 1863.

(8*k*-2*i*) Kathleen Augusta, married 16 Aug., 1882, to Arthur William Panton, fellow Trin. Coll., Dublin, and has a daughter,

Harriette Sarah (Panton).

(9*k*-2*i*) Edith Harriette Orpen.

(3*i*-1*h*) Henry Orpen (Palmer), barrister-at-law, died unmarried.

[4*i*-1*h*] Abraham, and [5*i*-1*h*] Charles, died young.

[6*i*-1*h*] William Palmer, of Roxborough, co Armagh, J.P.; born 20 Nov., 1820; died 19 Dec., 1882; married 17 June, 1844, Emma Margaret, daughter of William Armstrong, C.E., and had 3 sons and 7 daughters.

(1) Abraham William (Palmer), born 21 Dec., 1849; married 15 Aug., 1881, Jane, only child and sole heir of late Alexander Stitt, of Freedruff Lodge, Drogheda, and has 2 sons.

Abraham Richard Alexander, born 6 April, 1883; William Benjamin Armstrong, born 29 June, 1884.

(2) Benjamin Armstrong (Palmer), M.B. Glasgow, L.R.C.S. Edin.; born 30 March, 1852; married 1 June, 1882, Susan Georgina, daughter of James Browne, Esq., of Kilmalogue House, and had a son.

Orpen William Armstrong (Palmer), born 4 March, 1883, died 1 Feb. 1884.

(3) Richard Armstrong, born 12 Aug., 1855.

(4) Elizabeth, died 27 Dec., 1856, aged 11.

(5) Margaret Isabel, married 7 March, 1871, to Archibald John Turretin, Esq., of Newtown, co. Down.

(6) Isabella, died 13 Aug., 1874, aged 21.

(7) Emma Dorcas, married to John Cosgrove, Esq., of Belfast, and has a son, William Thomas (Cosgrove), born 4 June, 1883.

(8) Elizabeth Violet Lily.

(9) Ida Mary Ethel.

(10) Florence Christian Evelyn.

[7*i*-1*h*] Lucinda, died in infancy.

[8*i*-1*h*] Dorcas Maria, born 12 Nov., 1817.

[9*i*-1*h*] Margaret Lucy, born 26 Aug., 1826; died unmarried.

(2*h*-3*g*) William Twiss (Palmer); in holy orders, B.A. Trin. Coll., Dublin, born 12 Dec., 1784; married his cousin, Catherine, daughter of William Twiss, of Tullaree, and had 2 sons and 2 daughters.

[1] William Twiss (Palmer), of Vancouver Island.

[2] Caleb, of Albany, N.Y.

[3] Harriet Ann, of Albany.

[4] Jane, married, 1st, to John Williams, of Callinafercy House, co. Kerry; and 2ndly to John William Taylor, of Hamilton, Upper Canada; by her first husband she had 2 daughters.

(1) Anne Mary (Williams), married to James Hewat, Esq., of Saxe Coburg Place, Edinburgh.

(2) Elizabeth Georgina (Williams), married to Mr. Ralph Caldwell Crafton, of Bramley Hill, Croydon.

(3*h*-3*g*) George (Palmer), born 7 Oct., 1786; died 14 Oct., 1844; married 28 July, 1818, Margaret, daughter of John Giles, of Castledrum (by his wife Jane Sullivan); she died Jan., 1860, having had 3 sons.

[1] Caleb, born 6 Oct., 1819; died unmarried, 23 Dec., 1882.

[2] John, born 2 July, 1821; died unmarried, 14 June, 1860.

[3] Abram Giles, of Clounagillon, co. Kerry; born 2 Aug., 1823; married 10 Oct., 1854, Mary, daughter of Patrick Hanaffin, of Miltown Market.

(4*h*-3*g*) Thomas, born 10 July, 1791; died young.

(5*h*-3*g*) Caleb, born 10 April, 1793; died unmarried, 24 Sept., 1875.

(6*h*-3*g*) Avice, born 28 Dec., 1783; died 30 Jan., 1858; married 3 Dec., 1808, to Rev. William Peacock, who died at Longford 9 Aug., 1813, having had 2 sons and a daughter.

[1] John (Peacock), born 3 June, 1811; living unmarried Sept., 1849.

[2] William (Peacock), F.R.C.S.E., surgeon-major, born 4 Dec., 1813; died 9 Sept., 1849; married 18 Dec., 1845, Sarah, daughter of Samuel Parker, of Kingstown, co. Dublin, and had a son and 2 daughters,

William (Peacock), capt. R.E., born 20 April, 1848; Letitia; Sarah.

[3] Dorcas, born 4 Sept., 1809; died 24 Aug., 1810.

(*7h-3g*) Isabella (Palmer), born 24 Dec., 1787; died 23 May, 1858; married 25 April, 1820, to James Eagar, collector of customs, Scarborough; and also at New Ross (son of Thomas Eagar, of Rathpogue); he died 24 March, 1844, having had, with 4 daughters, who all died unmarried, 4 sons.

[1] Thomas (Eagar), of the Bank of Ireland, Dublin; born 23 Sept., 1823; died 4 Sept., 1863; married 14 July, 1855, Lydia, daughter of John Langley, Esq., of Brittas Castle, co. Tipperary; she died 1869, having had, (with other issue, died young) 2 sons and a daughter,

James, born 1 Sept., 1856; Thomas, born 17 Jan., 1860; Isabella.

[2] Caleb, born 14 Nov., 1827; died 22 Aug., 1834.

[3] Francis, born June 1828; died Feb., 1829.

[4] Alexander (Eagar), of Dublin, born 13 March, 1830; married 13 Sept., 1862, Elvira Ellen, daughter of William Deverell, Esq., of Ballycarroll House, Queen's co., and has had 7 sons and 5 daughters.

George William Deverell (Eagar), born 16 Sept., 1864; died 15 May, 1884. Edward Alexander, born 27 April, 1868. Boyce Deverell, born 15 Nov., 1869. Eusebius Francis, born 23 July, 1874; died 4 Jan., 1881. Caleb Palmer, born 23 July, 1876. Alexander, born 27 Nov., 1877. Robert William Deverell, born 22 June, 1879; died 6 Jan., 1881. Alexandra, Isabella Mary Lavinia Barbara, Elvira Eleanor, Ursula Georgina.

(*8a-3g*) Catherine (Palmer), born 23 July, 1789; died 4 Jan., 1876; married 30 Nov., 1822, to Rev. John Carey, who died at Drogheda 2 March, 1874, having had 3 sons and 3 daughters.

[1] Malcolm (Carey), of Linden Cottage, Jamaica, Long Island, New York, born 6 Oct., 1823; married, and has issue.

[2] Robert James (Carey), born 23 Oct., 1826; died 15 Dec., 1844.

[3] John, born 28 Feb., 1828; died 23 May, 1848.

[4] Anne Jane. [5] Isabella.

[6] Dorcas (Mrs. O'Neill).

[*4g-4f*] Jane (Twiss), died in 1841.

[*5g-4f*] Avice (Twiss), married to Richard Purcell, of Gurtnaconroe, co. Cork, and had a son and a daughter.

(1) Richard (Purcell), born ; married Barbara, daughter of Robert Crofts, Esq., and had issue.

(2) Avice (Purcell), married to Bartholomew Purdon, Esq.

[*9a*] Avicia (Blennerhassett), married to John Yeilding, Esq., of Tralee (son of Richard Yeilding, Esq., and Miss Haines), and had a son and 2 daughters (*l*).

(*1l-9a*) James (Yeilding), born 26 Nov., 1717; married 1st, Dorcas, daughter of Samuel Crumpe, Esq. (by Lucy, daughter of Thomas McLoughlin and Ann, 2nd daughter of Sir Francis Brewster), and had a daughter (*m*).

[*1m-1l*] Lucinda, married to Henry Eagar, of Faha, 2nd son of Alexander Eagar, of Castle Ballymalis and Droumavally, co. Kerry, and had 6 sons and 4 daughters (*n*).

(*1n-1m*) James (Eagar), died unmarried.

(*2n-1m*) Alexander, "an officer 3rd garrison battalion, drowned returning from America."

(*3n-1m*) John, died unmarried.

(*4n-1m*) Henry Yeilding (Eagar), capt. and paymaster 90th foot; died 12 June, 1858, aged 75; married Emily, eldest daughter of John Lynch, Esq., of Dromin; she died having had 2 daughters.

[1] Bessy Charlotte, died young.

[2] Elizabeth, married to Cotton Way, 28th Bombay native infantry, and has, with other issue,

(1) Henry Edward Cotton (Way), Bo. S.C., lieut. the East Yorkshire (15th) regt.; born 6 Feb., 1858.

(2) Alfred Cotton (Way), lieut. the South Wales Borderers; probationer Indian Staff Corps; born 16 Dec., 1860.

(*5n-1m*) Charles (Eagar), died unmarried.

(*6n-1m*) Geoffrey (Eagar), of Ballyard, lieutenant in the Royal York Rangers; deputy registrar of Ardfert and Aghadoe; born ; died ; married Blanche, daughter of Bryan McMahon, Esq., registrar of the diocese of Limerick, Ardfert, and Aghadoe, and had 5 sons and 4 daughters.

[1] Henry McMahon (Eagar), lieut. 90th and 62nd regts.; born 1825; died 18 Sept., 1855, aged 30; married 1847, Catherine Avice Spring, daughter of James Day Eagar, Esq., of Coolgarriff (see page 593), and had 3 sons and a daughter.

(1) Geoffrey Edward MacMahon (Eagar), born 28 Jan., 1848; married 9 April, 1877, Elizabeth Helen Kate, only surviving daughter of Joseph Jaques, of London, and has 2 sons and a daughter.

Henry Llewellyn Spring (Eagar), born 23 Feb., 1878; Geoffrey Edward Clarence, born 18 April, 1882; Maude Helen Louise,

(2) Henry, born 31 Dec., 1854.

(3) James, died young.

(4) Avice, died young.

[2] Bryan, of United States army; fell at battle of Chattanooga.

[3] Geoffrey, died unmarried.

[4] James McMahon, late capt. Kerry militia, born 26 June, 1833.

[5] John Yeilding, late lieut. Kerry militia.

[6] Susan, died unmarried.

[7] Dorcas, died 1870; married 1859, to George Raymond, of Kerry, who died s.p. 1869 (see p. 573).

[8] Blanche, married 1855, to John William Weekes, Esq. (see next page).

[9] Lucinda Yeilding (Eagar), died unmarried 8 Sept., 1856, aged 21.

(*7n-1m*) Dorcas, married , 1791, as 2nd wife to John Eagar, Esq., of Ballyhar (2nd son of Thomas Eagar, Esq., of Cottage and Ballyhar, co. Kerry), and had 3 sons and 2 daughters (see page 593).

(*8n-1m*) Rose Anne, died unmarried.

(*9n-1m*) Lucinda, married 1st, , to Dr. O'Sullivan; 2ndly, to William Seymour, of Cork.

(*10n-1m*) Arabella (Eagar), died unmarried 10 June, 1860, aged 78.

JAMES YEILDING married 2ndly, daughter of William Carrick, or Carrique (by his wife Rose Ponsonby, of Crotto), and had a son and daughter (*m*).

[*2m-1l*] John (Yeilding), barrister-at-law, married Elizabeth, daughter of Thomas Henry Royse, Esq., of Nantenan, co. Limerick, and had a son.

(1) JAMES ROYSE (YEILDING) sold his landed property; married Harriet, daughter of Christopher Hilliard (see page 601), and had issue (now settled in America), of whom,

Christopher, 2nd son, married Jane, daughter of Thomas Barry, whom see page 568.

(2o-2m) Martha Ford Royse (Yeilding, married to Christopher Delmege, of Castle Park, co. Limerick; he died 1859, having had a son and 4 daughters.

[1] John Christopher (Delmege), of Castle Park aforesaid, J.P. cos. Limerick, Clare, and Cork; high sheriff co. Limerick, 1880; barrister-at-law, King's Inns, 1841; born married 1845, Katherine, 2nd daughter of James O'Grady, Esq., of Raheen, co. Limerick (see Foster's *Peerage*, V. GUILLAMORE); she died 1869, having had 2 sons and 4 daughters.

(1) Christopher John (Delmege), late 48th regiment, born 1847.

(2) James O'Grady. (3) Maria Julia.

(4) Matilda. (5) Kathleen. (6) Annabella.

[2] Isabella, died ; married to Robert Atkins Lidwill, Esq., of Clonmore and Cormackstown, co. Tipperary, J.P.; he died 1850, having had 2 sons and 3 daughters.

(1) Robert Atkins (Lidwill), of Clonmore and Tomslake, Riverine, Australia; born 24 April, 1840; married 27 Jan., 1866, Mary Jane Cowen, daughter of Wm. Florence, Esq., of Richmond, M.D., and has a son and daughter.

Mark Cowley, born 7 April, 1878.

Matilda Florance.

(2) Thomas Lidwill, died unmarried.

(3) Matilda, married to her cousin, Thomas Brown, Esq.; he died Jan., 1877.

(4) Mary, married 1875, to Henry Loftus Hogen, Esq.

(5) Isabella.

[3] Martha (Delmege), married to Saml. Caswell, Esq., of Blackwater, co. Clare, J.P.

[4] Eliza, married 21 June, 1858, to Daniel Meares Maunsell, Esq., of Ballywilliam, co. Limerick, J.P.; s.p.

[5] Annabella.

[3m-1l] Avis (Yeilding) married to John Weekes, and had a son.

JOHN YEILDING WEEKES, lieut. in the Limerick Militia, died Oct., 1842; married Agnes, daughter of Samuel Sealy, Esq., of Maglass, co Kerry; high sheriff, 1810 (by his wife, Elizabeth Raymond, see p. 641), she died Jan. 1872, having had, with other issue, 2 sons and 4 daughters.

[1] John William (Weekes), died 1872; married 1855, Blanche, daughter of Geoffrey Eagar, Esq., aforesaid (see preceding page).

[2] Sealy (Weekes), of 30 Randall street, Baltimore, born 23 Sept., 1828; married 15 June, 1859, Matilda, daughter of Samuel Phillips, of Phillipsborough, Queen's co., and has had 4 sons and 4 daughters.

John Yeilding (Weekes), born 5 March, 1864; Charles Clement, born 14 Nov., 1868; Clement Peat, born 27 Sept., 1875; William Albert Edward, born 26 August, 1880, died 27 Oct., 1881; Maude Selina, Agnes Isabella, Ida Florence, Blanch Ethel.

[3] Elizabeth (Weekes), married 9 Sept., 1847, to Jerome Quill, Esq., J.P. co. Kerry (son of Thomas Quill and his wife Ellen King), and had 4 sons and 3 daughters.

(1) Richard Henry (Quill), M.B., surgeon-major, served in Afghanistan and Central Asia; born 8 June, 1848.

(2) John Jerome, capt. R.M., served in the Ashantee war; born 18 Dec., 1849, married Maud Agnetta Simpson.

(3) Berkeley Crosbie, capt. 2nd batt. York and Lancashire regt., served in Egypt, at battle of Tel-el-Kebir; born 4 May, 1852.

(4) Arthur Sealy, born 26 Sept., 1862.

(5) Agnes Sophia.

(6) Isabel, married 25 Jan. 1881, to Charles E. Leahy, Esq., of Tralee, and has 3 sons.

Richard (Leahy), born 16 Oct., 1881.

Percy Edward, born 5 Nov., 1882.

Charles Farquharson Nash, b. 10 June, 1884.

(7) Elizabeth Helen, died young

[4] Isabella, died 12 Aug., 1863, having married Jan., 1863, to Col. Frank Fitzpatrick, of Indian army.

[5] Agnes Jane (Weekes), married 19 June, 1858, to William James Eagar, of Blennerville (son of late John Frederick Eagar, Esq.), and has 2 sons and 3 daughters.

William John Alton (Eagar), born 24 Dec., 1859.

Henry Arthur, born 13 Jan., 1861.

Agnes Elizabeth. Kathleen Alice.

Isabella Blanche Lucy

[6] Margaret Clementina, married 19 Dec., 1872, to William England Young, Esq., of Limerick, who died 30 Oct., 1879, leaving a daughter.

Agnes Isabella Williamina, born Jan., 1874.

(2l-9o) Dorcas (Yeilding).

(3l-9o) Lucy (Yeilding), married to Rev. E Lombard, and had, with other issue, a son,

Rev. John Lombard, died 3 Jan., 1847, having married Dora Purefoy, who died 13 March, 1815, leaving a son,

Rev. John Newman Lombard, rector of Carrigaline; died 18 July, 1855, having married Elizabeth Catherine Swan, who died July, 1880, leaving a son,

Rev. John Lombard, M.A., rural dean, rector of Booterstown; chaplain to Lord-Lieut. of Ireland; married 1857, Maria J. Hart, and has 3 sons.

(1) John Newman. (2) Edmond.

(3) Thomas G F

[10o] Alice (Blennerhassett), married to Daniel Ferris, of Muckinagh, and had, with other issue,

Edward (Ferris), R.C. priest.

[11o] Lucy, married to John, son of Daniel Heafy, Esq., and had Blennerhassett and other issue.

ROBERT BLENNERHASSETT, of Mount Rivers (son of Henry Blennerhassett, see page 566); married Frances, daughter of Richard Yeilding, Esq., of Tralee (by his wife, Belinda Bateman), and had 2 sons and 4 daughters (*r*).

[1r] **Sir Rowland**, created a baronet, of whom see page 574.

[2r] Arthur, of Fortfield, co. Kerry, married Catherine, daughter of James Hickson, Esq., of Fermoyle, and had an only son and daughter.

(1) Robert (Blennerhassett), married his cousin, Catherine, daughter of Robert Hickson, of Fermoyle, and died s.p.

(2) Rosanna, died ,1828; married 27 May, 1790, to her cousin, Sir Robert Blennerhassett, 2nd Bart., who died 21 Sept., 1831, leaving issue (see page 575).

[3r] Belinda, married to her cousin Charles Hurly, and had issue.

[4r] Alice, married 9 June, 1758, to James Eagar, Esq., of Castle Ballymalis; he died , 1806, aged 76, having had a son and 6 daughters (*s*).

(1s-4r) Rowland Eagar, Esq., J.P., collector of excise, 1808-26; died s.p 5 Dec., 1830; married , 1793, Charlotte, daughter of Henry Blennerhassett, Esq., of Dublin; (see page 567) she died 1850, aged 77.
(2s-4r) Frances, married 1781, to Richard Eagar, of Gortdromakeiry; he died , 1850, aged 96, having had 7 sons and 3 daughters *(t)*.

[1t-1st] Geoffrey (Eagar), died unmarried.

[2t-1st] Edward (Eagar), married 1st Jemima, daughter of Rev. James M'Dowall, and had 2 sons and a daughter,

(1) Richard Edward (Eagar), of Wellington, N.Z.; married Eleanor, daughter of Rev. John Eamblen, and has issue.

(2) Geoffrey (Hon.), Under Secretary Finance and Trade, 1879, Minister of Public Works, 1859-63, M.L.C., New South Wales; representative for West Sydney, 1863, 1865; married Mary Anne, daughter of William Bucknell, Esq., of Yeovil, Somerset.

(3) Frances, wife of H. Waldegrave, Esq., of New Zealand.

Edward Eagar married 2ndly Ellen, daughter of Nicholas Mooney, commander R.N., and had at least 3 sons and a daughter.

(4) Nicholas Henry (Eagar), of Sidney, New South Wales; married Louisa, daughter of John Morris, Esq., and has issue.

(5) William, of London, solicitor; died married Anne, daughter of John Wilkins, of London, solicitor.

(6) Francis. (7) Ellen.

[3-1ts] James, and [4t-1s] Henry; both died unmarried.

[5-1ts] Rowland, married Anne, daughter of Edward Hickson, Esq., and has 2 sons and 3 daughters.

Edward. Richard. Frances. Maria Anne. Alice.

[6t-1s] Richard, died unmarried 17 March, 1831.

[7t-1s] Sidney, married , daughter of John Martin, of Killarney, and had 3 sons and 2 daughters.

David. Martin, died s.p. Richard. Philippa. Frances.

[8t-1s] Alice. [9t-1s] Marvel. [10t-1s] Charlotte.

(3s-4r) Belinda, married as 2nd wife to Francis, son of James Eagar and Avice Hurley.

(4s-4r) Barbara, married to Joseph Webb.

(5s-4r) Agnes, married to Wm. Mason, and had 5 sons and a daughter.

[1] Alexander (Mason), married, 1st Cherry, daughter of John Sealy, Esq., J.P., of Rockfield, and had 2 sons and 2 daughters.

(1) William, died young. (2) John.
(3) Anne, died young. (4) Susan.

Alexander Mason, married, 2ndly, Cherry, daughter of Thomas Ledman, Esq., of Billcrough, and grand daughter of Anthony Raymond, Esq., of Ballyloughran (see page 641), and had 2 sons and 5 daughters.

(4) William Ledman (Mason), M.D., of St. Austell.
(5) Alexander Raymond. (6) Frances.
(7) Jane Maria. (8) Agnes Eagar.
(9) Cherry Anne. (10) Thomasina Elizabeth.
(11) Anne.

[2] Oliver. [3] William. [4] Rowland.

[5] Thomas (Mason), married Jane Fuller, of Dingle, and had issue.

[6] Mary (Mason), married to John Mason, Esq., of Gorthbrack, and had 3 sons—Oliver, William, and Rowland, who died unmarried.

(6s-4r) Mary (5th daughter), married to Rev. Thomas Nash, B.A Trin. Coll., Dublin, curate of Ballynacourty, co. Kerry, and had a son and 2 daughters.

[1] Webb (Nash), baptized at Ballynacourty, 27 Nov., 1797; died s.p.

[2] Mildred (Nash), baptized at Ballynacourty, 10 Feb., 1793; died 1872; married to George Raymond, lieut. 57th regt., served in the Peninsula, and had 3 sons and a daughter.

(1) George (Raymond); died s.p. 1869; married Dorcas, 2nd daughter of Geoffrey Eagar (see page 571), she died s.p.

(2) Thomas, died young.

(3) William Webb (Raymond), B.A. Trin. Coll., Dublin, 1854; incumbent of Ballyheigue, 1881; vicar of Ballyseedy, 1857-69; of Kilflyn, 1869-81; born 1 Jan., 1827; married 15 April, 1856, Annie, daughter of Joseph Coneys, Esq., of Galway, and has a son and 6 daughters.

George (Raymond), B.A. Trin. Coll., Dublin, 1881; born 8 April, 1859; Mildred Maude Mary, Kathleen Alice Cyrilla, Anna Coneys, Mary Sybil, Blanche Geraldine, Yolande Laura Gabriella.

(4) Mary, died young.

[3] Alice (Nash), baptized at Ballynacourty, 22 July, 1795; married to Alexander, son of William Hilliard.

(7s-4r) Harriet, married John Bride; line extinct.

[5r] Mildred, married to Tallis Eagar, Esq., of Culleenymore (son of James Eagar, by his wife Margaret, daughter of Thomas Day, Esq., of the Manor), and had a son and 5 daughters.

(1) Rowland (Eagar), of Lahard, and Culleenymore, married Jane, 2nd daughter of James Eagar, of Cottage, J.P. (see page 593), and had a son and daughter.

[1] Rowland Tallis (Eagar), of Cottage and Ballymalis, born 1800; married 1st 1822, Anne, daughter of John Henry Blennerhassett, Esq., of Tralee (see page 566); she died , having had 2 sons and 3 daughters.

(1) John Henry, born , 1823; died s.p.
(2) Morgan O Connell Busteed, died young.
(3) Jane. (4) Anne, died unmarried.
(5) Frances, died young.

Mr. Rowland Tallis Eagar married 2nd, 1841, Lucinda, youngest daughter of Oliver Stokes, of Tralee, J.P. (by his wife Elizabeth Day see page 440), she died, having had a son and 2 daughters.

(6) Oliver Stokes Eagar, M.D., surgeon-major; served in Ashantee war; retired 1881; born 8 Oct., 1843; married 7 Nov., 1885, Wilhelmina, widow of Major H. M. Sandes (see page 824), daughter of Hugh Eldon Yeilding, Esq. (see next page).

(7) Margaret. (8) Honoria.

[2] Catherine, married to Rev. John Boate.

(2) Lucy. (3) Sarah. (4) Alice.
(5) Frances, died unmarried. (6) Melicent.

[6r] Sarah (Blennerhassett), died Sept., 1826; married 10 Sept., 1776, to John Eagar, Esq., of Ardrinane, J.P.; he died 1814, aged 63, having had 5 sons and a daughter *(u)*.

(1u-6r) Alexander Eagar, M.D., born Nov. 1779; died 16 July, 1817; married 24 Sept., 1811, Annabella, 3rd daughter of Richard Yeilding, Esq., of Cloghers (by his wife, Anne Massy), she was born 14 March, 1781; died 2 May, 1872, having had 4 daughters.

[1] Annabella, married 17 July, to John Peppard, M.D., who died 15 April, 1881, having had a son and 7 daughters.

(1) Richard (Peppard), born 17 April, 1845; murdered in New Zealand by the Maoris, 1868.

(2) Isabella Alexina.

(3) Margaret Whitaker, married 29 Jan. 1873, to Anster FitzGerald Walker, M.D. (see page 568), and has a son,

Francis Spring (Walker), born 6 Jan., 1876.

(4) Sarah Robertina, married 8 Oct., 1872, to Robt. Gillispie, brigade surgeon, and has 2 daughters
Annabella (Gillispie); Jane Agnes.
(5) Kate Mary. **(6)** Frances. **(7)** Alexina.
(8) Mary, married 30 Dec., 1879, to Rev. Francis Morgan Dean, rector of Kilrush, co. Wexford, and has 3 sons and a daughter.
Francis Peppard Sneyd (Dean), born 3 Feb., 1881; William Frederick Morgan (Dean), born 8 Oct., 1883; Edward George Dean, born 1 April, 1885; Mary Alice Dean.
[2] Sarah, died 25 Feb., 1856; married 4 Sept., 1838, to Robert 3rd son of Sir Robert Blennerhassett, Bart.; he died s.p. 2 July, 1862 (see next page).
[3] Catherine (Eagar), died June, 1873; married Oct., 1854, to Townsend Blennerhassett, capt. Kerry militia (9th son of Henry Blennerhassett, M.D., see page 567), born 11 Feb., 1829; drowned 20 June, 1867, leaving an only daughter.
Annabella Charlotte (Blennerhassett), died 1 May, 1882; married 14 April, 1880, to Edward Abram McGillycuddy, Esq. (see page 628), and had a son,
Townsend Blennerhassett (McGillycuddy), born 27 April 1882.
[4] Alexina Frances (posthumous daughter), married 12 May, 1846, to her cousin John Eagar, Esq. (see below).
(2*u*-6*r*) Robert (Eagar), of Dingle, born 4 June, 1784; died 18 July, 1843; married 5 Aug., 1810, Margaret, daughter of John Eagar, Esq., sovereign of Dingle; she died 2 April, 1846, having had 3 sons.
[1] John (Eagar), of Ardrinane, born 15 July, 1811; died s.p. 14 Dec., 1848; married 12 May, 1846, his cousin, Alexina Frances, youngest daughter of Dr. Alexander Eagar, named above.
[2] Alexander, died young.
[3] Thomas, of Ardrinane, M.A., hon. canon of Manchester, 1884; rector of Ashton-under-Lyne since 1870, and rural dean; vicar of Audenshaw, Manchester 1844-70; born 18 June, 1814; married 1st, 12 Aug., 1846, Mary, daughter of Stephen Taylor, Esq., of Ashton, co. Lanc.; he married 2nd, 13 Feb., 1873, Sarah Anne, widow of Rev. J. H. C. Wright, rector of Wolverlow; by his 1st wife he had (with 3 sons who died in infancy) a son and 2 daughters.
(1) Robert Taylor Sumner (Eagar), of Stourbridge, M.D., born 10 May, 1849; married 1878, Caroline, daughter of Joseph Webb, Esq., of Coalbourne House, co. Staff s.p.
(2) Mary Elizabeth, married 27 Sept., 1882, to William E. Garforth, Esq., J.P. of Halesfield, Normanton.
(3) Margaret Eliza, died 18 July, 1878.
(3*u*-6*r*) Rowland Blennerhassett (Eagar), born 1786; died 20 April, 1843; married , 1813, Marianne, daughter of Oliver Mason, J.P., and had 2 sons and 2 daughters.
[1] John (Eagar), settled in America, born 14 May, 1816; married 28 Aug., 1855, Alicia, widow of William Brereton, daughter of John Frederick Eagar, Esq., and has a son,
Rowland Henry, born 5 April, 1856.
[2] Rowland, born 4 March, 1822; died in America, leaving 2 daughters.
[3] Theodora, married to William Hickson, Esq.
[4] Sarah (Eagar), died young.
(4*u*-6*r*) Frederick, died s.p.
(5*u*-6*r*) Tallis, died s.p.
(6*u*-6*r*) Frances, born July, 1781; died , 1854; married , 1796, to Richard Massy Yeilding, of Belview, co. Limerick (son of Richard Yeilding, of Belview, co. Limerick by his wife, Agnes Massy), and had 7 sons and 6 daughters *(v)*.

[1*v*-6*u*] William Richard (Yeilding), born Jan., 1800; died April, 1854, having married 7 March, 1818, Mary, daughter of Hugh Massy, of Stagdale, co. Limerick; she died 21 June, 1881, having had 2 sons and a daughter.
(1) Richard Massy (Yeilding), born 1819; married, Charlotte, daughter of Rev. Charles Townley, and had a son,
Charles William, died 1884, aged 38.
(2) Hugh Eldon (Yeilding), of New Park, co. Limerick; born 6 May, 1829; married 11 Jan., 1849, Margaret, daughter of Augustus Richard Yeilding, Esq. (son of Richard Yeilding, of Cloghers), and has 3 sons and 3 daughters.
[1] William Richard (Yeilding), lieut. Bengal staff (late 54th regt.), in march to Candahar; born 13 Jan., 1856; married 9 Dec., 1881 Teresa, daughter of Richard Wyndham Magrath Fitzgerald, of Limerick.
[2] Godfrey Massy, born 20 Jan., 1857; lost at sea 23 May, 1874.
[3] Hugh Blennerhassett, born 11 Oct., 1866.
[4] Frances Augusta, married, 1st, to Dawson Massy, surgeon Bengal staff; she re-married 2 Aug., 1859, as 2nd wife to Vere Hunt, of High Park, co. Tipperary, and had a son and two daughters.
Vere Robert (Hunt), born 26 Nov., 1875.
Mary, born 15 April, 1871, and Frances, born 3 Sept., 1872.
[5] Mary Wilhelmina married, 1st, 10 April, 1876, to Major Henry Moore Sandes, of Kerry militia (see page 822); he died s.p., 13 Dec. 1883; she re-married, 7 Nov., 1885, to Major Oliver Stokes Eagar (see pages 410 and 573).
[6] Margaret Constance Evelyn Venetia.
(3) Frances Mary, married, 1st to John Lloyd Fitzgerald, of Ballydonoghue House, co Kerry, barrister at-law, she re-married the Rev. E. Pepper, rector of Castle Derwent and Prebendary of St. Patrick's Cathedral, Dublin, died 5 April 1872.
[2*v*-6*u*] Richard, and **[3*v*-6*u*]** Eagar (Yeilding), emigrated to America; the latter became M.P. for Ottawa City, and died about 1873, both s.p.l.
[4*v*-6*u*] Alexander and **[5*v*-6*u*]** Alexander, both died young.
[6*v*-6*u*] Alexander, born 1817; married Bessie Cussen, of Rockfield, co. Limerick.
[7*v*-6*u*] Rowland Frederick, civil engineer; died about 1850.
[8*v*-6*u*] Agnes, died young.
[9*v*-6*u*] Sarah, o.s.p., married to Benjamin Cox, of Mount Pleasant, co. Clare.
[10*v*-6*u*] Belinda, died unmarried.
[11*v*-6*u*] Frances, married to Henry Prittie Bayley, and has issue.
[12*v*-6*u*] Annabella, died 1849; married July, 1844, to John, grandson of Sir Rowland Blennerhassett, Bart., he died 14 Dec., 1847, having had a daughter,
Letitia Melicent (see next page).
[13*v*-6*u*] Mary, died young.

SIR ROWLAND BLENNERHASSETT, of Blennerville, was created a baronet 22 Sept., 1809; died 14 March, 1821, aged 81, having married Melicent Agnes, daughter of Richard Yeilding, Esq., of Bellevue, Croom, co. Limerick, and had 5 sons *(w)*.

[1*w*] Sir Robert, succeeded as 2nd Baronet.

[2w] Richard Francis, born 23 May, 1772; died s.p. Nov., 1827, having married Agnes Anne, daughter of Sir Barry Denny, Bart. (see page 724); she died 19 Dec., 1842.

[3w] Arthur, of Blennerville, born 27 Oct., 1776; died 31 May, 1839, having married Sept., 1799, Hon. Ellen Jane Mullins, daughter of Thomas, Lord Ventry (see page 664); she died 24 Dec., 1846, having had a son and 2 daughters.

(1) Rowland, s.p.

(2) Melicent Agnes, married as 1st wife to Rev. Edward Maynard Denny, rector of Listowel, &c. (see page 724), and had 2 daughters,

[1] Theodora Denny, died s.p.

[2] Penelope Jane, married 18 April, 1860; to Alexander O'Donnell, Esq., (see Foster's *Baronetage*); he died 1867, leaving an only daughter.

Melicent Agnes O'Donnell), married 27 June, 1883, to Edwin Thomas, Esq., of Raheir, co. Mayo

(3) Theodora, died 25 July, 1845, having married 18 Oct., 1836, as 1st wife, to Richard Chute, Esq., of Chute Hall, co. Kerry; he died 13 Sept., 1862, leaving issue.

[4w] Rowland, of Tralee and Kells, &c.; born 26 Dec., 1780; died 12 April, 1854, having married Letitia, eldest daughter of John Hurly, Esq., of Tralee, clerk of the crown (by his wife Mary Conway); she died , having had 3 sons and 5 daughters.

(1x-4w) John, born 1812; died 14 Dec., 1847, having married July, 1844, Annabella, youngest daughter of Richard Yeilding, of Belview, co. Limerick (see preceding page); she died 1849, and had a daughter,

Letitia Melicent.

(2x-4w) Richard Francis, of Kells, co. Kerry; born 1819; died 16 Feb., 1854, having married 13 Oct., 1849 Honoria, youngest daughter of Major William Carrique-Ponsonby, of Crotto, co. Kerry she (re-married to James Barry, M.D., of Villa Nova, near Valentia), died 3 Dec., 1883, leaving an only son.

Rowland Ponsonby, of Kells, M.P. co. Kerry 1872-4, 1874-80, and since 1880; born 22 July, 1850; married 21 Sept., 1876, Mary Beatrice, 3rd daughter of Walter Armstrong, Esq., and has a son born 29 June, 1879.

(3x-4w) Rowland, born 3 Dec., 1822; died unmarried Sept., 1840.

(4x 4w) Melicent Agnes, died 1843; married to John Collis, Esq., of Barrow, and had, with other issue, a son,

Thomas, settled in Australia married Arabella, daughter of William Collis, of Lismore, and has issue.

(5x-4w) Mary, died 7 Nov., 1883; married April 1836, to Rev. George Purdon, who died 21 June, 1842, having had 2 sons and 2 daughters.

[1] Rowan (Purdon), born 8 January, 1838.

[2] Rowland (Purdon), major in the army, capt. 85th regt., born 26 Nov., 1838; died unmarried 25 May 1883.

[3] Letitia Mary Anne, married to Rev. John Collins, rector of Ballyheigue, co. Kerry; he died leaving a son and 2 daughters.

Barry George (Collins), Mary, Letitia.

[4] Sophia, died unmarried. [5] Lucy died in infancy.

[6x-4w] Letitia Mary Anne, died unmarried.

[7x-4w] Lucy, died unmarried.

[8x-4w] Alice, married 1 July, 1869, to Charles Chute, Esq., of Tralee (son of Pierce Chute, of Brennan); he died 24 May, 1884 (see page 640).

[5w] William, twin with Rowland, born 26 Dec., 1780; died 1842, having married Elizabeth, daughter of Richard Blennerhassett, of Ballymacprior (see page 568); she died 21 Dec., 1857, having had 2 sons and 2 daughters.

(1) Frederick, born 1808; died s.p. 16 July, 1860.

(2) Rowland, died s.p. April, 1838.

(3) Melicent Agnes, died unmarried.

(4) Charlotte, died unmarried 1842, aged 25.

SIR ROBERT, 2nd baronet, born 26 Jan., 1769; died 21 Sept., 1831, having married 27 May, 1790, his cousin Rosanna, only daughter of Arthur Blennerhassett, of Fortfield, co. Kerry (see page 572); she died 4 Feb., 1828, having had with other issue 5 sons and a daughter.

[1] Rowland, died s.p.

[2] **Sir Arthur**, succeeded as 3rd baronet.

[3] Henry, midshipman R.N., died 26 July, 1811.

[4] Robert, of Mount Rivers, co. Kerry; born 27 July, 1797; died s.p. 2 July, 1862, having married 4 Sept., 1838, Sarah, daughter of Alexander Eagar, M.D., of Tralee and Ardrinane, co. Kerry (see preceding page); she died 25 Feb., 1856.

[5] William, born 1800; died unmarried 1837.

[6] Catherine, died Nov., 1869, having married 22 May, 1822, to Rev. Edward Fitzgerald Conyers, of Castletown Conyers, co. Limerick, rector of Knockane, Killarney he died 25 June, 1856, having had 4 sons.

(1) Charles (Conyers), of Castletown Conyers; born 4 Apl., 1823; married 1st, Agnes, daughter of Col. Graham, of Meiklewood, Stirling (see page 440); he married 2ndly, Margaret, daughter of Francis Drew, Esq., of Drews Court, co. Limerick.

(2) Robert Rowland (Conyers), capt. in the army; born May, 1826; married April, 1862, his cousin Eliza, daughter of Arthur Thomas Blennerhassett, Esq., of Ballymacprior (see page 568), and has 4 sons.

Edward, Robert, Alured, Frederick William.

(3) James Grady FitzGerald (Conyers), of Liskennet, near Croome, co. Limerick; born Sept., 1831; married 1859 his cousin Helen Mary, daughter of Francis Spring Walker, of Bellville aforesaid (see page 568).

(4) Edward, unmarried.

SIR ARTHUR, 3rd baronet, born 30 July, 1794; died Feb, 1849, having married 26 July, 1826, Sarah, daughter of John Mahony, she died 11 July, 1866, having (re-married 16 May, 1850, to Frederick Randall, of Highbury) had a son and daughter.

[1] **Sir Rowland**, 4th and present baronet (see page 563).

[2] Rosanna.

THE DESCENT OF

Rev. John D'Arcy Warcop Preston,

Of Askham Bryan Hall, Yorks., M.A., Rector of Freemantle,

FROM THE

Blood Royal  **of England.**

Edward I., crowned 19 Aug. 1274, b. 17 June, 1239, d. 7 July, 1307. = Eleanor (1st wife) dau. of Ferdinand III., King of Castile, d. 27 Nov. 1290.

John, Count of Holland, etc. (1st husband), d. s.p. = Elizabeth, d. 5 May, 1316, aged 32. = Humphrey de Bohun, Earl of Hereford, etc. (2nd husband), fell at Boroughbridge, 16 March 1321.

James Butler, Earl of Carrick and Earl of Ormonde (1st husband), d. 6 June, 1337. = Eleanor de Bohun. = Sir Thomas de Dagworth (2nd husband), had summons to parlt. 13 Nov. 1347.

Petronilla Butler (1st wife) = Gilbert, Lord Talbot, sum. to parlt., d. 24 Aug. 1387.

Elizabeth Talbot = Sir Henry de Grey, Lord Grey de Wilton, d. 1395.

John Darcy, 6th Baron Darcy = Margaret de Grey = Sir Thomas Swinford (2nd husband).

Sir John Darcy, of Torksey, co. Linc. = Joan, dau. of John, Lord Greystoke.

Richard Darcy o.v.p. (1st husband). = Eleanor, dau. of John, 4th Lord Scrope, of Masham. = William Claxton, of East Bridgeford, d. 1496.

Sir William Darcy, of Torksey. = Euphemia, dau. of Sir John Langton, of Farnley, Yorks.

Sir Thomas Darcy, K.G., sum. to parlt., beheaded 20 June, 1538. = Dowsabel (1st wife) dau. and heir of Sir Richard Tempest, knt., of Ridlesdale, Northumberland.

A, *continued above.*

A, *continued from below.*

Sir Thomas Darcy = Dowsabel Tempest.

Sir George Darcy, knighted at Tournay, restored in blood, etc. Baron Darcy d. 24 Aug. 1557. = Dorothy, dau. and heir of Sir John Melton, of Aston, Yorks.

John, 2nd Baron Darcy = Agnes, dau. of Thomas Babington, of Dethick, co. Derby.

Michael Darcy, o.v.p. 15 Dec. 1588. = Margaret, dau. of Thos. Wentworth, Esq., buried 13 Nov. 1614. = Jasper Blytheman (2nd husband).

Anne Darcy = Henry Savile, of Copley, Yorks.

Mary (1st wife) dau. of William West, of Firbeck. = William Savile, of Copley. = Rosamond (2nd wife) widow of John Booth, of Glossop, m. 1639.

William Savile, of Cridling Park, Yorks. = Katharine, dau. of Arthur Ingram, of Knottingley, Yorks, d. 16 Jan. 1692-3.

Mary Savile = William Maude, of York, proctor and notary, buried there 14 Jan., 1714-15.

Mary Maude, bap. 27 Aug. 1698, m. 7 Feb. 1722-3, d. 24 April, 1758. = Darcy Preston, of Askham Bryan, Yorks, d. 16 Nov. 1749.

John Preston, rector of Marston, and prebendary of York, m. 10 March, 1763 = Jane (2nd wife) sister of Peter Consett, of Brawith Hall, Yorks.

Darcy Preston, of Askham Bryan, Yorks, admiral R.N., d. 21 Jan., 1847. = Sophia, 4th dau. of Hon. Sir George Nares, a judge of Common Pleas, d. Jan., 1833.

Louisa, m. 16 April, 1793, d. 1839, = Rev. John Fletcher Muckleston, D.D., prebendary of Lichfield and Wolverhampton, d. 1844.

Elizabeth, (1st wife), dau. of Peter Spence, M.D. m. 1821, d. 1833. = John D'Arcy Jervis Preston, of Askham Bryan, M.A., in holy orders. = Hannah (2nd wife) dau. of Sir John St. Leger Gillman, Bart., m. 1835.

Wm. Preston, J.P. Sussex, capt. R.N. d. Dec. 1851. = Hamilton Mary, dau. of John Mangles, Esq. M.P. of Woodbridge, Surrey.

4 daughters.

John D'Arcy Warcop Preston, of Askham Bryan Hall, Yorks. M.A. Oxon., rector of Freemantle since 1871, b. 27 Jan., 1824. = Emily Anne Augusta 3rd dau. of Rev John Bligh Brownlow, m. 11 May, 1858.

Charles Edward Preston, major, m 1875, Emmeline, dau. of P. S. F. Martin, Esq.

D'Arcy Spence Preston, rear-adml., R.N., b. 1827.

William Warcop Peter Consett, of Brawith Hall, Yorks. =

5 daughters.

Hannah Elizth., m 1870, to Rev. Edward Barher, B.A., vicar of Carleton. =

D'Arcy Brownlow, b. 19 July, 1860. Walter Charles, d. 2 May, 1885. Roland D'Arcy, b. 1 July, 1867. Arthur John, b. 4 Nov., 1871. Alice Elizabeth. Edith, d. 1882.

Charles. Thomas. Winifred. Constance.

PRESTON, JOHN D'ARCY WARCOP, of Askham Bryan Hall, Yorks., M.A., Worcester College, Oxford, 1847; rector of Freemantle since 1871; vicar of Sandgate, Kent, 1859-69; of Stonegate, Sussex, 1869-71; 21ST IN DESCENT FROM EDWARD I.; born 27 Jan., 1824; married 11 May, 1858, Emily Anne Augusta, 3rd daughter of late Rev. John Bligh Brownlow, incumbent of Sandgate (see Foster's *Peerage*, B. LURGAN), and has had 4 sons and 2 daughters.

[1] D'Arcy Brownlow, born 19 July, 1860.
[2] Walter Charles, R.N., born 18 Feb., 1864; died 2 May, 1885.
[3] Roland D'Arcy, born 1 July, 1867.
[4] Arthur John, born 4 Nov., 1871.
[5] Alice Elizabeth.
[6] Edith, died 31 Jan., 1882.

THE DESCENT OF
REV. JOHN D'ARCY WARCOP PRESTON.
FROM THE BLOOD ROYAL OF ENGLAND.

EDWARD I., so named after Edward the Confessor; born at Westminster, 17 June 1239, knighted at Burgos, 1254, created Earl of Chester; crowned at Westminster, 19 Aug., 1274, king of England, lord of Ireland, duke of Aquitaine; he subdued the principality of Wales 1283, claimed and exercised feudal superiority over Scotland; died at Burgh-on the-Sands, Cumberland, 7 July, 1307, buried in Westminster Abbey; by his 1st wife, Eleanor, daughter of Ferdinand III., king of Castile, who died 27 Nov., 1290, he had, with other issue, a daughter,

ELIZABETH, died 5 May, 1316, aged 32; she married 1st to John, Count of Holland and Zealand, and Lord of Friesland, who died s.p.; she re-married to Humphrey de Bohun, Earl of Hereford and Essex, Lord of Brecknock, and constable of England; served in the wars against Scotland, taken prisoner at the battle of Stryvelin 7 Edward II., was exchanged for the wife of Robert Bruce; he fell at the battle of Boroughbridge, Yorks, 16 March, 1321, leaving, with other issue, a daughter,

ELEANOR DE BOHUN, married 1st, 1327, to James Butler, Earl of Carrick (eldest son of Edmund Butler, created Earl of Carrick 1 Sept., 1315), created Earl of Ormond 2 Nov., 1328; founded the friary of Carrickbeg-on-the-Suir, 1336; he died 6 Jan., 1337, buried at Waterford; she re-married before 1344 to Sir Thomas de Dagworth, the celebrated warrior who brought Charles de Blois, Duke of Britany, a prisoner to the Tower, 21 Edward III., had summons to parliament 13 Nov., 1347, had a son, Nicholas; by her 1st husband she had, with a son James, 2nd Earl of Ormond, a daughter.

PETRONILLA BUTLER, married as 1st wife to Gilbert, Lord Talbot, who had summons to parliament, 36 Edward III. until 10 Richard II; served in the wars with France, 33, 43, and 46 Edward III.; in 1 Richard II. was in the King's fleet at sea, of which Michael de la Pole was admiral for the north; 7 years after he was summoned to be at Newcastle upon Tyne with horse and arms, &c., to march against the Scots; he died 24 Aug., 1387, leaving, with a son, Sir Richard, ancestor of the Earls of Shrewsbury, a daughter,

ELIZABETH TALBOT, married to Sir Henry De Grey, 6th baron; had summons to parliament 1 Dec., 50 Edward III., 1376, as "Henr' Grey de Shirland," and from 4 Aug., 1 Richard II., 1377, to 20 Nov., 18 Richard II., 1394, as "Henr' Grey De Wilton;" was in the retinue of John of Gaunt in his expedition to Gascony; he died 1395; he had, with an only son, Richard, a daughter,

MARGARET DE GREY, married 1st to John Darcy, 5th Baron Darcy; had summons to parliament 19 Aug., 23 Richard II., 1399, to 21 Sept., 12 Henry IV, 1411, in which year he died. She re-married to Sir Thomas Swinford. By Lord Darcy she had, with other issue, a son,

SIR JOHN DARCY, of Torksey, co. Lincoln, Knt.; died 32 Henry VI.; escheat 35 Henry VI.; he married Joan, daughter of John, Lord Greystoke; she died 34 Hen. VI.; escheat 32 Hen. VI No. 15; and had, with other issue, a son,

RICHARD DARCY; died in the lifetime of his father; married Eleanor, daughter of John, 4th Lord Scrope, of Masham. She re-married about 29 April, 38 Hen. VI., 1460, to William Claxton, of East Bridgeford, Notts, who died 18 May, 1496. Richard Darcy left a son,

SIR WILLIAM DARCY, of Torksey, 4 years old at his grandfather's death; married Euphemia, daughter of Sir John Langton, of Farnley, Yorkshire, Knt., and had a son,

SIR THOMAS DARCY, K.G., had summons to parliament as "Thomas Darcy de Darcy, Chl'r.," from 17 Oct., 1 Hen. VIII., 1509, to 3 Nov., 21 Hen. VIII., 1529, and with the designation of "de Temple Hirst," 5 Jan., 25 Hen. VIII., 1534, and as "Thomas Darciæ, Chl'r.," 8 June, 28 Henry VIII., 1536; one of the Lords who marched with Thomas, Earl of Surrey, to the relief of Norham Castle, 12 Hen. VII., and the year following made a knight of the King's body; constable of Bamborough Castle, Northumberland; captain of the town and castle of Berwick-upon-Tweed; warden of the east and middle marches towards Scotland; constable and steward of the lordship of Sheriff Hutton, Yorkshire; a privy councillor; joined in Ask's rebellion ("The pilgrimage of grace"); convicted of high treason, and beheaded on Tower Hill, 20 June, 1538; married 1st, Dowsabel, daughter and heiress of Sir Richard Tempest, Knt., of Ridlesdale, Northumberland; he married 2nd, Elizabeth, widow of Ralph Nevill, sister of William Sandys, first Lord Sandys, of the Vine; by his 1st wife he had, with other issue, a son,

SIR GORGE DARCY, knighted at Tournay by Hen. VIII., and restored in blood, with the dignity of Baron Darcy to him and his heirs male, by act of parliament, 2 Ed. VI., 1548; died 24 August, 4 and 5 Philip and Mary, 1557; he married Dorothy, daughter of Sir John Melton, of Aston, Yorks, and had, with other issue, a son,

JOHN, 2nd Baron Darcy, married Agnes, daughter of Thomas Babington, of Dethick, co. Derby, and had an only son,

MICHAEL DARCY; died 15 Dec., 1588, in his father's lifetime; married Margaret, daughter of Thomas Wentworth, of Wentworth Woodhouse; she re-married to Jasper Blytheman, of New Lathes, Yorks, and was buried at Wentworth, 13 Nov., 1614; by her 1st husband she had a son and 2 daughters.

[1] John, 3rd Lord Darcy, married 4 times, but died without surviving issue, in 1635.
[2] Margaret (Darcy), died unmarried.
[3] Anne, married to Henry Savile, of Copley, Yorks; aged 7 in 1585, and had 8 sons and 4 daughters.
(1) Thomas (Savile), of Copley; married twice, and had 2 sons and a daughter (see Foster's *Yorkshire Collection*).
(2) Henry, died s.p. (3) Michael, died s.p.
(4) John, of Copley; died 1644, leaving a son and daughter.
(5) **William Savile**, of whom presently.
(6) Darcy, attorney-at-law, died unmarried.
(7) Anthony, died unmarried.
(8) Henry, died unmarried.
(9) Margaret, married to Rowland Dand, of Mansfield Woodhouse, Notts.
(10) Annie, married to Thomas Squire, of Thornhill.
(11) Elizabeth, married 1st, to George Pulleyn, M.D. and 2ndly, to — Fox.
(12) Jane (Savile), living 1666.

WILLIAM SAVILE, of Copley aforesaid, married 1st, Mary, daughter of William West, of Firbeck, Yorks, and had a daughter, Elizabeth, married to her cousin John, son and heir of Rowland Dand aforesaid. He married 2ndly, at Arksey, 30 May, 1639, Rosamond, widow of John Booth, of Glossop, co. Derby, youngest daughter of John Frank, of Pontefract, and had a son,

WILLIAM SAVILE, of Cridling Park, Yorkshire; married Katharine, daughter of Arthur Ingram, of Knottingley, Yorkshire, she died 16 Jan., 1692-3; buried in York Minster, having had 3 daughters.

[1] Ann (Savile), married to John Smithson.
[2] Mary (Savile), married to William Maude, of Belfreys, York, proctor and notary; he was buried 14 Jan., 1714-15, having had 6 sons and 4 daughters.
(1) William (Maude), born 12 April, 1694.
(2) Savile, baptized 22 May, 1702; died 2 Nov. following.
(3) Savile, buried 30 May, 1704.
(4) Arthur, born 1704. (5) Thomas, died young.
(6) Major, baptized 2 Jan., 1709-10.
(7) Catherine, baptized 26 Sept., 1695; married to William Dawson.
(8) **Mary**, married to Darcy Preston (see below).
(9) Ann, died young.
(10) Rosamond (Maude); baptized at Belfreys, York, 5 April, 1708; married to William Herdsman.
[3] Dorothy (Savile); married to John Keane.

MARY MAUDE (2nd daughter of William Maude and Mary Savile, aforesaid), baptized 29 Aug., 1698; died 24, buried at Belfreys 27 April, 1758; married in York Minster, 7 Feb., 1722-3, as 2nd wife to Darcy Preston, of Askham Bryan by purchase in 1745, town clerk of York 1719, (son of Thomas Preston, organist of York Minster, by his wife Elizabeth, widow of Henry Harrison, of Allerthorpe, daughter and heir of Darcy Conyers, of Holtby, Yorks); he died 16, buried at Belfreys 19 Nov., 1749, having had 3 sons and 8 daughters *(a)*.

[1a] D'Arcy (Preston), baptized 1726.
[2a] William (Preston), born 1730.
[3a] **John (Preston)** of Askham Bryan, rector of Marston (see page 584).
[4a] Mary, born 1724 [5a] Margaret, born 1727.
[6a] Elizabeth, born 1729.
[7a] Rosamond (Preston), baptized at Belfreys, York, 10 Feb., 1731-2; married to Rev. George Haggitt.
[8a] Anne, baptized 3 Aug., 1733; married at Belfreys 21 Oct., 1751, to Rev. Richard Barnard.
[9a] **Mary**, married to HENRY BOULTON, of whom immediately.
[10a] Cordelia, born, 1736.
[11a] Elizabeth Preston, born 1741; married to Rea.

MARY PRESTON (5th daughter of Darcy Preston aforesaid), baptized at Belfreys, York, 29 Dec., 1734; died Feb., 1779; buried at Uppingham, Rutland; married 9 Feb., 1756, as 3rd wife to Henry Boulton, of Moulton, Lincolnshire, J.P., member of the Board of Green Cloth (son of Henry Boulton, of Stixwold, who was son of Henry Boulton, of Stixwold, by his wife, Elizabeth, only child of Norton Bryan, Esq., of Bolingbroke, co. Linc.); he died 10 Dec., 1788, having had 4 sons *(e)*,

[1e] **Henry (Boulton)**, of Moulton, and of the Middle Temple, barrister-at-law, died 11 March, 1828, aged 71, of whom presently (see p. 582).
[2e] James, died s.p.
[3e] **D'Arcy (Boulton)**, of whom hereafter (see p. 597).
[4e] George (Boulton), M.A. of Pembroke Hall, Cambridge, vicar of Westbury-cum-Sutton, Camb., rector of Oxendon, Northants, 56 years; born 12 Aug., 1761; died 16 Aug., 1843; married 8 Dec., 1791, Catherine, daughter of Rev. Christopher Hatton Walker, M.A., rector of Harrington, Northants, and of Kibworth, Leicestershire; she died 8 May, 1850, having had 3 sons and 7 daughters *(f)*.
(1f-4e) Henry Towers (Boulton), born about 1792, died about 1836-7.
(2f-4e) D'Arcy (Boulton), born 13 Oct., 1801; died 4 Oct., 1856; married 29 May, 1834, Ann Eliza, daughter of Thomas Hartley, Esq., having had, with other issue, 2 daughters,
Ann Hartley (Boulton). Eliza Catherine.
(3f-4e) James, born ; died an infant.
(4f-4e) Catherine, died 26 Nov., 1867; married 17 Sept., 1816, to Rev. Thomas Warren Mercer, M.A., vicar of Northallerton, Yorks; he died 21 Aug., 1827, having had a son and 2 daughters.
[1] Thomas (Mercer), solicitor, born 28 Oct., 1818; died unmarried, 29 Oct., 1879.
[2] Elizabeth Catherine (Mercer), married 20 Dec., 1838, to Philip William Newsam, of Warwick, solicitor; he died 6 June, 1873, having had 2 sons and 7 daughters.
(1) Clement (Newsam), born 29 Sept., 1848.
(2) Walter, born 1 Aug., 1852.
(3) Mary, died in infancy.
(4) Catherine, died in infancy.
(5) Henrietta.
(6) Anne, married 14 June, 1866, to Rev. Hewett Linton, vicar of Abram, co. Lanc., since 1878, &c., and has 7 sons and a daughter,
Philip (Linton), born 4 June, 1869; Hewett, born 20 Sept., 1870; Walter, born 7 May, 1872; Frederick, born 31 Oct., 1876; Francis Alfred, born 2 May, 1878; Clement, born 10 Nov., 1879; Christopher George, born 29 July, 1883; Annie.
(7) Frances, died ; married 2 July, 1868, to Joseph Paddison, Esq., of Melton Mowbray, solicitor, who died s.p.
(8) Georgiana, died unmarried 30 July, 1879.
(9) Laura (Newsam).
[3] Mary (Mercer), died unmarried, 17 Dec., 1877, aged 57.
(5f-4e) Anna (Boulton), died 23 Aug., 1864.
(6f-4e) Mary, died .
(7f-4e) Georgiana, married to John Marriott, Esq., and had 4 sons and 2 daughters.

THE DESCENT OF

Rev. John Lynes, M.A.,

Of Sandesfort House, Dorset.

FROM THE

Blood Royal  **of England.**

EDWARD I., crowned 19 Aug. 1274, b. 17 June, 1239, d. 7 July, 1307. = Eleanor (1st wife) dau. of Ferdinand III., King of Castile, d. 27 Nov. 1290.

John, Count of Holland, etc. (1st husband), d. s.p. = Elizabeth, d. 5 May, 1316, aged 32. = Humphrey de Bohun, Earl of Hereford, etc. (2nd husband), fell at Boroughbridge, 16 March 1321.

James Butler, Earl of Carrick and Earl of Ormonde (1st husband), d. 6 June, 1337. = Eleanor de Bohun. = Sir Thomas de Dagworth (2nd husband), had summons to parlt. 13 Nov. 1347.

Petronilla Butler (1st wife) = Gilbert, Lord Talbot, sum. to parlt., d. 24 Aug. 1387.

Elizabeth Talbot = Sir Henry de Grey, Lord Grey de Wilton, d. 1395.

John Darcy, 6th Baron Darcy = Margaret de Grey = Sir Thomas Swinford (2nd husband).

Sir John Darcy, of Torksey, co. Linc. = Joan, dau. of John, Lord Greystoke.

Richard Darcy o.v.p. (1st husband). = Eleanor, dau. of John, 4th Lord Scrope, of Masham. = William Claxton, of East Bridgeford, d. 1496.

Sir William Darcy, of Torksey. = Euphemia, dau. of Sir John Langton, of Farnley, Yorks.

Sir Thomas Darcy, K.G., sum. to parlt., beheaded 20 June, 1538. = Dowsabel (1st wife) dau. and heir of Sir Richard Tempest, knt., of Ridlesdale, Northumberland.

A, continued above.

A, continued from below.

Sir Thomas Darcy = Dowsabel Tempest.

Sir George Darcy, knighted at Tournay, restored in blood, etc. Baron Darcy d. 24 Aug. 1557. = Dorothy, dau and heir of Sir John Melton, of Aston, Yorks.

John, 2nd Baron Darcy = Agnes, dau. of Thomas Babington, of Dethick, co. Derby.

Michael Darcy, o.v.p. 15 Dec. 1588. = Margaret, dau. of Thos. Wentworth, Esq., buried 13 Nov. 1614. = Jasper Blytheman (2nd husband).

Anne Darcy = Henry Savile, of Copley, Yorks.

Mary (1st wife) dau. of William West, of Firbeck. = William Savile, of Copley. = Rosamond (2nd wife) widow of John Booth, of Glossop, m. 1639.

William Savile, of Cridling Park, Yorks. = Katharine, dau. of Arthur Ingram, of Knottingley, Yorks, d. 16 Jan. 1692-3.

Mary Savile = William Maude, of York, proctor and notary, buried there 14 Jan., 1714-15.

Mary Maude, bap. 27 Aug. 1698, m. 7 Feb. 1722-3, d. 24 April, 1758. = Darcy Preston, of Askham Bryan, Yorks., d. 16 Nov. 1749.

Mary Preston (3rd wife), m. 9 Feb. 1756, d. Feb. 1779. = Henry Boulton, of Moulton, co. Linc., d. 10 Dec. 1788.

Henry Boulton, of Moulton, barrister-at-law, d. 11 March, 1828. | James d. s.p. | D'Arcy Boulton, a judge in Upper Canada, d. 1834, aged 72. | George Boulton, M.A., Camb., vicar of Westbury, co. Camb., rector of Oxendon, Northants, b. 12 Aug., 1761, d. 16 Aug., 1841. = Catherine, dau. of Rev. C. H. Walker, M.A., rector of Harrington, Northants, m. 8 Dec., 1791, d. 8 May, 1850.

Henry. Darcy. James. | Catherine, d. 1867, m. 1816, to Rev. Thomas Warren Mercer, M.A., who d. 1827. | Anna. Mary. | Georgiana m. to John Marriott. | Frances, m. 28 Oct., 1817, d. 25 March, 1866. = Thomas Lynes, of Great Oxendon, Northants, m. 28 March, 1817, d. 10 Nov., 1875. | Elizabeth Caroline, d. 1832, 1st wife of Rev. H. R. Rokeby, who d. 1870.

Rev. John Lynes, M.A., b. 1821, m. 1853, Mary, dau. of B. Hodgetts, Esq. | George Boulton Lynes, of Ivy Depôt, Albemarle, co. Virginia, b. 1833, m. 1856, Harriet, dau. of T. Spencer. | William Lynes, of Toronto, Clerk Common Pleas, &c., d. 1880, m. 1856, Elizabeth, dau. of D. Horsell, Esq. | Rev. Robt. Francis Lynes, M.A., of Wyke Lodge, b. 1835, m. 1861, Louisa, dau. of R. H. Swaffield, Esq. | Elizabeth, d unm. Frances, m. 1847, to Peter S. Dixon, who d. 1857. | Caroline, m. 1847, to Henry Hall Dixon, who d. 1870. | Laura Lynes, m. 1851, to Philip Grove, of Eastcote, Northants.

(Children of Rev. John Lynes:) John. Thomas. | Booth. Frances.

(Children of George Boulton Lynes:) Thomas. John. Spencer. | George. Robert. | Agnes, m. 1867, to George P. Gilbert, Esq. | Frances. Ethel.

(Child of William Lynes:) Ada, m. 1877, to George B. Gordon, barrister-at-law.

[1] John (Marriott), of Braybrooke, Market Harborough born
[2] Richard Walker, vicar of Aldborough, Yorks, since 1854; B.A., Lincoln College, Oxford, 1851; M.A., 1854; b. 21 Jan., 1829; m. 3 Feb., 1857, Anna Maria, daughter of late Rev. Robert Philip, s.p.
[3] William Henry, vicar of Thrussington, co. Leic., since 1867; M.A., Lincoln College, Oxford, 1857.
[4] Charles Hayes (Marriott), of Leicester, M.D. London, 1863; M.B., 1859; F.R.C.S. Eng. (exam.), 1859; M.A, 1858; L.S.A., 1857 (Univ. Coll.); surgeon, Leicester Infirmary; consulting surgeon, Leic. and Rutland County Lunatic Asylum; born 19 Oct., 1834; married 25 Oct, 1864, Lucy, daughter of late Rev. John Gibson, vicar of Furneux-with-Brent Pelham, Herts, and has had 6 sons and 2 daughters.

Charles Bertram (Marriott), born 1 Oct., 1868
Cecil Edward, born 1 June, 1870.
John Reginald, born 20 Oct., 1871.
Ernest Jenner, born 18 March, 1873.
Harold Henry, born 20 Jan., 1875.
George Eustace Arthur, born 5 Nov., 1877, and died 27 Feb., 1879.
Lucy Evelyn. Ella Kathleen.

[5] Katherine (Marriott), married 5 June, 1861, to Rev. Montagu Francis Finch Osborn, M.A., Merton College Oxford, 1848; rector of Kibworth-Beauchamp, Leic., since 1851; rural dean of Gartree, 1866 (see Foster's *Baronetage*), and has 2 sons and 3 daughters.

Francis Wilfrid (Osborn), born 22 April, 1862.
Montagu John, born 19 Feb., 1869.
Margaret. Catharine Louisa. Hilda.

[6] Georgina (Marriott).

(8*h-4*) Frances (Boulton), died 25 March, 1866; married 28 Oct., 1817, to Thomas Lynes, of Great Oxendon, Northants, sometime chairman of the Union Board, Market Harborough (2nd son of John Lynes, Esq., of Kirkby Mallory, Warwickshire); he died 10 Nov., 1875, having had 4 sons and 4 daughters (*g*).

[1*g-8*] John (Lynes), of Sandesfort House, Wyke Regis, Weymouth, M.A., Christ Church College, Cambridge, 1847; formerly vicar of Buckland Monachorum, Devon; born 6 March 1821; married 17 Nov., 1853, Mary Campion, daughter of Booth Hodgetts, Esq., and has 3 sons and a daughter.

John (Lynes), born 21 Jan., 1863.
Thomas, born 4 June, 1865.
Booth Hodgetts, born 23 April, 1867.
Frances Mary.

[2*g-8*] George Boulton (Lynes), of Ivy Depôt, Albemarle co., Virginia, born 8 March, 1833; married 5 July, 1856, Harriet, daughter of Thomas Spencer, Esq., of Earl's Shinton, Hinckley, Leic., and has 5 sons and 3 daughters.

(1) Thomas (Lynes), born 6 July, 1860.
(2) John, born 11 March, 1862.
(3) Spencer, born 2 May, 1863.
(4) George, born 9 Aug., 1868.
(5) Robert, born 24 Jan., 1870.
(6) Agnes (Lynes), married 26 Oct., 1876, to George Percy Gilbert, Esq., of Ivy House, Albemarle co., Virginia, U.S.
(7) Frances. (8) Ethel.

[3*g-8*] William (Lynes), clerk in Common Pleas, and clerk in Queen's Bench office, Osgoode Hall, Toronto, 1864-71; born 3 June, 1834; died 8 July, 1880; married 24 April, 1856, Elizabeth, daughter of Bartholomew Horsell, Esq., of Wootton Bassett, Wilts (she re-married 18 April, 1881, to Francis William Bell, Esq., of St. Louis, U.S.A.), and had one daughter.

Ada Elizabeth (Lynes), married 18 March, 1877, to George Burrows Gordon, Esq., barrister-at-law, Winnipeg.

[4*g-8*] Robert Francis (Lynes), of Wyke Lodge, Weymouth, M.A., St. John's College, Oxford, 1864; formerly curate of Fleet, Dorset; born 10 Oct., 1835; married 7 Feb., 1861, Louisa Eliza Josephine, daughter of Robert Hassall Swaffield, Esq., of West Down Lodge, Weymouth.

[5*g-8*] Elizabeth, died unmarried, 21 Nov., 1842.

[6*g-8*] Frances (Lynes), married 9 Feb., 1847, to Peter Sydenham Dixon, cotton spinner (eldest son of Peter Dixon Esq., of Holme Eden, Cumberland); he died 14 March, 1857, having had 2 sons and 2 daughters.

(1) Francis Peter (Dixon), born 17 March, 1849.
(2) Sydenham Lynes, born 27 Dec., 1852.
(3) Caroline. 4 Gertrude Catherine.

[7*g-8*] Caroline (Lynes), married 12 May, 1847, to Henry Hall Dixon, Esq. (2nd son of aforesaid Peter Dixon, Esq., of Holme Eden, Cumberland); he died 16 March, 1870, having had 7 sons and 4 daughters.

(1) Henry Sydenham (Dixon), born 4 May, 1848, married 17 Aug., 1868, Louisa Anne, daughter of Robert Ashfield Cooper, Esq., of London; she died 27 Feb., 1875, having had 3 sons and 2 daughters.

Hamilton (Dixon), born 3 Sept., 1872.
Percival, born 10 Sept., 1873.
Rawdon, born 5 Oct., 1875; died 18 March, 1876.
Morna. Paulina.

(2) Charles Walter (Dixon), born 21 Aug., 1850.
(3) Arnold Edward (Dixon), in South America, born 23 Sept., 1852; married 25 Feb., 1875, Rachell Palmer Stewart, daughter of late Capt. A. Steward Wardell, 5th dragoon guards
(4) Alfred Lynes, born 2 April; died 30 Dec., 1854.
(5) Alfred Herbert, born 22 Feb., 1857.
(6) Wilfred Lynes, born 12, died 27 Aug., 1859.
(7) Archibald Ernest, born 30 June, 1863.
(8) Fanny Finlay.
(9) Sydney Caroline, died 18 July, 1862.
(10) Caroline Lynes. (11) Edith Katharine.

[8*g-8*] Laura (Lynes), married 12 Nov., 1851, to Philip Grove, Esq., of Eastcote Northants (son of Rev. John Worrall Grove, D.D.), and has had 7 sons and 2 daughters.

(1) Benjamin (Grove), born and died 6 Oct., 1852.
(2) Philip Sydney, born 25 Sept., 1857.
(3) Reginald Parker, born 23 Aug, 1859.
(4) Charles Edward, born 10 Aug, 1861.
(5) Darcy Boulton, born 4 Aug., 1864; died 28 Jan., 1865.
(6) John Worrall, born 9 Oct., 1866.
(7) Percy Lynes, born 16 Sept., 1871.
(8) Anna Laura, died young, 12 Aug., 1855.
(9) Laura Sybil.

(9*f-4*) Elizabeth (Boulton) died young.
(10) Caroline (Boulton), died 20 April, 1832; married 26 July, 1827, as 1st wife to Rev. Henry Ralph Rokeby, of Arthingworth Manor House, Northants, formerly Com. R.N., subsequently rector of Arthingworth, and lord of the manor; he died 20 May, 1870, having had a son and 2 daughters.

[1] Henry Ralph Rokeby, B.A., Trinity College, Cambridge, 1854; rector of Arthingworth, and lord of the manor, since 1870; vicar of Preston Deanery 1855-9; born 2 June, 1831; married 7 Feb, 1861, Mary Jane, daughter of Rev. Thomas Barbot Beale, of Brettenham Park, Suffolk, and has 3 sons and a daughter.

Henry Langham (Rokeby), born 26 Nov., 1861.
Ralph Thomas, born 28 June, 1863.
Arthur Willoughby, born 7 June, 1866.
Caroline Mary.
[2] Isabella Caroline (Rokeby), married 2 May, 1855, to Rev. George Frederick Pearson, M.A., Worcester College, Oxford, 1858; vicar of Funtington, Chichester, since 1874; vicar choral of York Minster 1857-62; vicar Felpham, near Bognor, 1871-4.
(3) Anna Maria (Rokeby).

HENRY BOULTON, of Moulton, co. Linc., and of the Middle Temple, barrister-at-law, born died 11 March, 1828, *æt.* 71; married 1st, 17 April, 1781, Susannah, eldest daughter and co-heir of Mr. Serjeant James Forster (by Susannah, his wife, daughter and co-heir of Sir John Strange, Master of the Rolls), she died 5 Sept., 1788, having had 3 sons and 2 daughters (*h*).

[1*h*] Henry (Boulton), born 21 Sept., 1785; died 22 March, 1786.
[2*h*] Henry (Boulton), vicar of Sibsey, co. Linc., born 19 May, 1787; died unmarried, 13 July, 1825.
[3*h*] Anthony (Boulton), D.D., of Moulton, rector of Preston Capes, and subsequently of Sampford Peverell, Devon, born 5 June, 1788; died 23 May, 1854; married 29 June, 1819, Harriet, 3rd daughter of Thomas Lane, Esq., of Selsden, Surrey (elder sister to her father-in-law's 5th wife), she died 26 Aug., 1853, having had 6 daughters (*i*).
(1*i*-3*h*) Maria Antonia Eliza (Boulton), died 1821.
(2*i*-3*h*) Antonia Maria, married 2 March, 1848, to lieut.-general Alfred Augustus Chapman (reserve), formerly in 48th regiment, and commanded the 18th R.I. regiment 7 years, and has had 5 sons and a daughter.
[1] Frederick William Boulton (Chapman), born 10 Sept., 1850; died 13 Oct., 1862.
[2] Alfred Stephen, capt. Royal Welsh fusiliers, 1883; born 4 July, 1852; married 12 Dec., 1882, Fanny Georgina, daughter of Lieut-Col. Tritton, 10th Hussars, and has a daughter.
Audrey Frances Maxwell.
[3] Edward Poore (Chapman), lieut. R.N., born 12 June, 1854; married 20 Dec., 1881, Alice Gertrude, daughter of Frederick Boulton, Esq, and has a daughter,
Sylvia Alice, born 15 Dec., 1883.
[4] D'Arcy Richard, 29th regt., born 25 Sept., 1856.
[5] Harry Remnant, born 25 July, 1858; died 14 Feb., 1871. [6] Alfreda Emily.
(3*i*-3*h*) Harriet Elizabeth (Boulton), died in infancy.
(4*i*-3*h*) Elizabeth Harriet, died in infancy.
(5*i*-3*h*) Emma Anne, died in infancy.
(6*i*-3*h*) Mary, married 23 Aug., 1849, to Samuel John Maclurcan, major 1st Devon militia, capt 48th and 19th regiments; he died 2 March, 1868, having 4 sons and 5 daughters.
[1] Thomas Alfred Boulton (Maclurcan), officer in Bombay port trust, born 9 July, 1850; married 9 May, 1883, Fanny Sophia, youngest daughter of Capt. Bingham, of Bombay Ordnance dept.
[2] Donald Samuel Boulton, chief officer British India Steam Service; born 14 April, 1853.
[3] John Lewis Rooke, lieut. R.M.L.I. born 12 Feb., 1858; married 12 Dec., 1882, Claire Russell, 2nd daughter of Alfred Mortimer, Esq.
[4] Charles Hare, born 5 Jan., 1862.
[5] Mary Harriet (Maclurcan) married 12 Dec., 1871, to John Edward Simeon, 97th regiment. (See Foster's *Baronetage*.)
[6] Alice Emily (Maclurcan), married 16 Sept., 1873, to Richard Richards Breffney Ternan, of the Army Pay dept.; late lieut. Buffs, East Kent regt.; and has a son and daughter,
Alexander Gore Breffney (Ternan), born 17 Dec., 1876.
Alice Mary Breffney.
[7] Frances Antonia, married 5 July, 1881, to D Solomon, Esq., of the Stock Exchange, and has 2 daughters.
Helen Christine (Solomon).
Phyllis Lorna.
[8] Edith Blanche.
[9] Evelyn Florence.
[4] Susannah (Boulton), died 27 Sept, 1786.
[5] Mary, died unmarried, 1-16 Dec., 1856.

HENRY BOULTON married, 2nd, 4 Oct., 1790, Mary, daughter of John Francklin, Esq., of Great Barford, Beds.; she died 4 Sept., 1795, having had 3 children, the 2nd named John; all died in infancy. He married 3rd, 27 Dec., 1796, Harriet, youngest daughter of Rev. Baptist Isaac, of Whitwell, Rutland; she died 3 March, 1806, having had 2 daughters.

[6*h*] Harriet (Boulton), died 26 March, 1865, married Sept., 1828, to Rev. Henry de Foe Baker, M.A., St. Catherine's Hall, Cambridge, vicar of Greetham, Rutland, warden of Browne's Hospital, Stamford; he died 3 July, 1845, having had a son and daughter.
(1) Henry de Foe (Baker), M.A., Jesus College, Cambridge, 1858, rector of Thruxton, Andover, 1873; rural dean, Andover, 1878; born ; married 1st, 13 Aug., 1861, Eleanor Isabella, only daughter of William Charleton, Esq., of Brixton, Surrey; she died 21 June, 1869, having had 3 sons.
[1] D'Arcy (Baker), born 12 July, 1862; died 26 April, 1885.
[2] Henry Charleton, born 17 Nov., 1864.
[3] Donald, born 18 Feb., 1865.
Rev. H. DE FOE BAKER married 2nd, 2 July, 1872, Frances Arabella Dyke, eldest daughter of late Edward Dyke Poore, of Syrencott, Wilts, and has a son and 3 daughters.
[4] Ryce Dyke Poore, born
[5] Frances Mary (Baker).
(2) Harriet Elizabeth, married , to Lieut.-col. Jeremie Peyton Jones, (reserve, late 8th foot), son of Jeremy Jones, Esq., of the War Department, s.p.
[7*h*] Elizabeth (Boulton), married 29 Jan, 1824, to her cousin, George Strange Boulton, Esq., of Coburg, Upper Canada (see page 598).

HENRY BOULTON married, 4th, 9 May, 1807, Mary Winifreda, daughter of Lieut.-col. Durell; she died 9 April, 1808, leaving a daughter,

[8*h*] Anna Maria, married 27 July, 1830, to Donald Christopher Baynes, 3rd son of Sir Christopher Baynes, Bart., of Harefield Place, Middlesex (see Foster's *Baronetage*), LL.B., Sidney Sussex College, Cambridge, 1844, sometime an officer in the 62nd regiment; curate of Thruxton, 1847-64; Andover, 1873-5; he died, s.p., 18 Jan., 1884.

THE DESCENT OF

Misses Louisa and Grace Stewart,

Of Calcutta,

FROM THE

Blood Royal of England.

EDWARD I., crowned 19 Aug. 1274, b. 17 June, 1239, d. 7 July, 1307. = Eleanor (1st wife) dau. of Ferdinand III., King of Castile, d. 27 Nov. 1290.

John, Count of Holland, etc. (1st husband), d. s.p. = Elizabeth, d. 5 May, 1316 aged 32. = Humphrey de Bohun, Earl of Hereford, etc. (2nd husband), fell at Boroughbridge, 16 March 1321.

James Butler, Earl of Carrick and Earl of Ormonde (1st husband), d. 6 June, 1337. = Eleanor de Bohun. = Sir Thomas de Dagworth (2nd husband), had summons to parlt. 13 Nov. 1347.

Petronilla Butler (1st wife) = Gilbert, Lord Talbot, sum. to parlt., d. 24 Aug. 1387.

Elizabeth Talbot = Sir Henry de Grey, Lord Grey de Wilton, d. 1395.

John Darcy, 6th Baron Darcy = Margaret de Grey = Sir Thomas Swinford (2nd husband).

Sir John Darcy, of Torksey, co. Linc. = Joan, dau. of John, Lord Greystoke.

Richard Darcy, o.v.p. (1st husband). = Eleanor, dau. of John, 4th Lord Scrope, of Masham. = William Claxton, of East Bridgeford, d. 1496.

Sir William Darcy, of Torksey. = Euphemia, dau. of Sir John Langton, of Farnley, Yorks.

Sir Thomas Darcy, K.G., sum. to parlt., beheaded 20 June, 1538. = Dowsabel (1st wife) dau. and heir of Sir Richard Tempest, knt., of Ridlesdale, Northumberland.

A, *continued above.*

A, *continued from below.*

Sir Thomas Darcy = Dowsabel Tempest.

Sir George Darcy, knighted at Tournay, restored in blood, etc. Baron Darcy d. 24 Aug. 1557. = Dorothy, dau and heir of Sir John Melton, of Aston, Yorks.

John, 2nd Baron Darcy = Agnes, dau. of Thomas Babington, of Dethick, co. Derby.

Michael Darcy, o.v.p. 15 Dec. 1588. = Margaret, dau. of Thos. Wentworth, Esq., buried 13 Nov. 1614. = Jasper Blytheman (2nd husband).

Anne Darcy = Henry Savile, of Copley, Yorks.

Mary (1st wife) dau. of William West, of Firbeck. = William Savile, of Copley. = Rosamond (2nd wife) widow of John Booth, of Glossop, m. 1639.

William Savile, of Cridling Park, Yorks. = Katharine, dau. of Arthur Ingram, of Knottingley, Yorks, d. 16 Jan. 1692-3.

Mary Savile = William Maude, of York, proctor and notary, buried there 14 Jan., 1714-15.

Mary Maude, bap. 27 Aug. 1698, m. 7 Feb. 1722-3, d. 24 April, 1758. = Darcy Preston, of Askham Bryan, Yorks, d. 10 Nov. 1749.

John Preston, rector of Marston, and prebendary of York, m. 10 March, 1763. = Jane (2nd wife) sister of Peter Consett, of Brawith Hall, Yorks.

Darcy Preston, of Askham Bryan, Yorks, admiral R.N., d. 21 Jan., 1847. = Sophia, 4th dau. of Hon. Sir George Nares, a judge of Common Pleas, d. Jan., 1833.

Louisa, m. 16 April, 1793, d. 1839, = Rev. John Fletcher Muckleston, D.D., prebendary of Lichfield and Wolverhampton d. 1844.

John Muckleston, B.A., incumbent of Wychnor, 1842-72; m. Mary, dau. of T. Levett, Esq., of Wychnor Park, and died s.p., July, 1877.

Rowland Muckleston, fellow 1836-55, tutor, and vice-provost Worcester Coll., Oxford, M.A., 1836, rector of Dinedor, Herefordshire, 1855, rural dean, etc., b. 29 Aug., 1811, d. 1884.

Louisa, d. 11 May, 1871, m. 12 Aug., 1842, to Robert Stewart, Esq., of Torquay, he died 26 Sept., 1865.

Ann, m. 1st to Arthur Battersby, who died s.p. = Frederick Cuerton Travers Smyth, Esq. (2nd husband) m. 13 July, 1840, d. 19 July, 1870.

Mary, m. to Capt. Puckford, R.N., both dead, s.p.s

Robert Stewart, b. 28 Jan., 1844, d. 10 Oct., 1876. = Millicent Banerjea, m. Jan., 1875.

Amy, m. 2 Aug., 1883, to James Grange, Esq. of Dover.

Henry Travers Smyth, only issue, b. 10 Feb., 1846. = Lucy Maria Emily, dau. of late Rev. Samuel Henry Duntze, m. 6 Jan., 1870.

Louisa Mary. Grace Muckleston.

Frederick Duntze Travers-Smyth, b. 25 Sept., 1870. George Muckleston, b. 23 Jan., 1873.

Florence Anne Travers-Smyth. Constance Mary, d. 25 Dec., 1878.

HENRY BOULTON married, 5th, 4 May, 1815, Emma, 4th daughter of Thomas Lane, Esq., of Selsden, Surrey, and youngest sister of his eldest son's wife; she died 15 Aug., 1864, having had an only son,

[9*h*] James (Boulton), M.R.C.S. Eng. 1838, L.S.A. 1837 (Middlesex), surgeon to county Prison; 21ST IN DESCENT FROM EDWARD I; born 6 May, 1816; married 1st, 12 Feb., 1839, Ann Kentish Cordelia, daughter of William Mathews, solicitor, Pontypool; she died 24 July, 1840, having had a daughter.

(1) Emma Agnes Anne (Boulton) died young, 24 April, 1841.

MR. JAMES BOULTON married 2ndly, 4 May, 1841, Catherine, youngest daughter, and one of the ten children of Rev. Thomas Addams Williams, vicar of Usk (by his second wife, Annabel, youngest daughter of Samuel Marsh, Esq., of Clapham, M.P. for Chippenham); she died 31 March, 1872; he married 3rd, 15 July, 1875, Emma, daughter of Robert Boatfield, of Barnstaple, Devon. By his second wife he had 3 sons.

(2) James Bowyer D'Arcy (Boulton), C.E., of Usk, born 5 March, 1842.

(3) Donald Fludyer (Boulton), of Usk, Mon., M.R.C.S. Eng. 1866, L.S.A. 1867 (St. Barth.), born 20 July, 1843, married 15 Aug., 1868, Clara, daughter of William Gething, of Newport, Mon., and has 2 daughters.

[1] Catherine Annabella Mary (Boulton).

[2] Edith Augusta.

(4) Charles Anthony (Boulton), of Usk, Mon., born 3rd Jan., 1847.

JOHN (Preston) of Askham Bryan, rector of Marston, and prebendary of York (see page 579); born 18 May, 1738; married 1st, Dorcas Jackson; 2ndly, at Holy Trinity, King's-square, York, 10 March, 1763, Jane, sister of Peter Consett, of Brawith Hall, Yorks, and had with 5 daughters (of whom Louisa, married to Rev. John Fletcher Muckleston, D.D., see chart pedigree, page 583), an only son.

D'ARCY PRESTON, of Askham Bryan, D.L., Yorkshire, N. and W. Ridings, admiral R.N. 1841; served at the storming of Fort Royal, Martinique, 1794, and at the reduction of the island of St. Lucia; baptized at St. Michael's, Ousebridge, York, 23 Feb, 1762; died 21 Jan., 1847; married 29 June, 1792, Sophia, 4th daughter of Hon. Sir George Nares, a judge of Common Pleas, and sister of Dr. Nares, regius professor of modern history, Oxford; she died Jan., 1833, having had 5 sons and 2 daughters (*b*)

[1*b*] **John D'Arcy Jervis Preston** (of whom presently).

[2*b*] Edward (Preston), royal navy, died unmarried.

[3*b*] William (Preston), capt. R.N., of Borde Hill House, Sussex, J.P.; born ; died Dec., 1851; married 23 Oct., 1833, Hamilla Mary, daughter of John Mangles, Esq., M.P., of Woodbridge, Surrey, and had a son and 3 daughters (*d*).

(1*d* 3*b*) Darcy Harrington (Preston), B.A., Trin. Coll., Camb., 1866; in holy orders 1868 71; born 19 Nov., 1844; married 22 Nov., 1866, Harriet, daughter of Thomas Vipan, Esq., of Sutton, Isle of Ely; she died 30 Jan., 1873. leaving 2 sons and 3 daughters.

William Darcy (Preston), born 7 November, 1869.

Bertram Harrington, born 23 Oct., 1870.

Emily Mary; Edith; Harriett.

(2*d*-3*b*) Frances.

(3*d*-3*b*) Ellen Jane, married 15 Sept., 1858, as 2nd wife to Lieut.-Col. Thomas Stannard MacAdam, of Blackwater, co. Clare, and has 2 sons and 2 daughters.

Frank Robert Preston (MacAdam), lieut. 1st batt. P.W.O. West Yorkshire regt., born 26 Aug., 1859; Walter, lieut. R.E., born ;

Charlotte Honor; Grace.

[4*b*] Charles (Preston), in the army; died s.p. 1 Jan., 1861; married, 1847, Mary Sullivan, daughter of John Dalton, Esq., of Slenningford, Yorks (see Foster's *Yorkshire Collection*); she re-married, 1862, as 2nd wife to Rev. William Fisher, M.A. canon of Salisbury.

[5*b*] D'Arcy (Preston), H.E.I.C.S., married Jessie, daughter of Col. Forest, and died s.p.

[6*b*] Sophia.

[7*b*] Anne (Preston), married to Edward Probyn Nares, and had, with other issue, a son,

Edward Nares, capt. R.N.; married July, 1863, Augusta Frances, daughter of late William John Law, Esq., of Horsted, Sussex (see page 264); she died 28 Jan., 1865, leaving a daughter,

Agnes Sophia (Nares), born 19 Jan., 1865.

JOHN D'ARCY JERVIS PRESTON, of Askham Bryan, M.A., Merton College, Oxford, 1823, in holy orders; born 28 March, 1794; died 5 Aug., 1867; married 1st, 3 April, 1821, Elizabeth, daughter of Peter Spence, of Kensington, M.D.; she died Jan., 1833, having had 4 sons and 5 daughters (*c*).

[1*c*-1*b*] **John D'Arcy Warcop (Preston)**, first-named (see page 577).

[2*c*-1*b*] Charles Edward (Preston), major, born 16 April, 1826; married, 14 July, 1875, Emmeline, 2nd daughter of Philip S. Feake Martin, Esq., of Alvediston, Wilts, s.p.

[3*c*-1*b*] D'Arcy Spence, rear-admiral R.N., born 26 May, 1827, unmarried.

[4*c*-1*b*] William Worcup Peter Consett, of Brawith Hall, Yorks., J.P., D.L. *N.R.*, assumed the name and arms of Consett in compliance with the testamentary injunction of Peter Consett, Esq., of Brawith Hall, Yorks.; born 6 Jan., 1833; married 10 Nov., 1864, Harriet Georgiana Edith, eldest daughter of Lord Charles Lennox Kerr (see Foster's *Peerage*, MARQUIS OF LOTHIAN), and has 2 sons and 6 daughters.

D'Arcy Preston (Consett), born 28 March, 1870

Montagu William, born 15 April, 1871; Violet Elizabeth, Victoria Florence, Winifred Edith, Mildred Sophia, Vera Margaret, Cordelia Mary.

[5c-1b] Fanny (Preston), married 19 October, 1853, as 2nd wife to Rev. Sir Thomas Eardley Wilmot Blomefield, Bart. (see also page 554); he died 21 Nov., 1878, leaving by her 2 sons and 2 daughters.

(1) Malcolm (Blomefield), born 1 June, 1858.

(2) Arthur Hugh, born 1 Dec., 1862.

(3) Laura Elizabeth, married 2 Aug., 1882, to Rev. Alfred Ernest Jalland, of Wakefield, and has a son and daughter.

Ernest Henry (Jalland), born 23 June, 1883.

Ethel Mary, born 27 May, 1884.

(4) Margaret Edith.

[6c-1b] Sophia Elizabeth (Preston), married 3 April, 1850, to Rev. John Blomefield, M.A., vicar of All Saints, Knightsbridge, since 1873; of St. George, Leeds, 1857-73 (brother of late Rev. Sir T. E. W. Blomefield, Bart., aforesaid), and has had with other issue 2 sons and 4 daughters.

Eardley Wilmot (Blomefield), born 7 Jan., 1855.

Laurence Woodyeare, born 8 Oct., 1870.

Sophia Mary, Emily Louisa, Margaret Ellen, Annie Hamilla.

[7c-1b] Jane (Preston).

[8c-1b] Margaret Laura, married April, 1858, to Rev. Constantine Barnard Yeoman, M.A., Trin. Coll. Cambridge, 1848; vicar of Manfield, Yorks, since 1860; of Yeddingham, 1848-54; vicar of Marholm, Northants, 1854-60; J.P. Yorks, North Riding, and has 7 daughters,

Margaret Constance (Yeoman); Harriot Emily; Sophia Bruce; Laura Cecilia; Eva Dorothy; Charlotte; Mary.

[9c-1b] Emily Anne, married 30 Sept., 1868, as 2nd wife to Rev. John Fountain Woodyeare-Woodyeare, of Crookhill, Yorks, who died s.p.s. 25 July, 1880.

REV. JOHN D'ARCY JERVIS PRESTON married 2ndly, 1835, Hannah Elizabeth, 2nd daughter of late Sir John St. Ledger Gilman, Bart., she died , leaving an only daughter.

[10c-1b] Hannah Elizabeth Preston, married 12 October, 1870, to Rev. Edward Barber, B.A., vicar of Carleton, Yorks, since 1870, and has a son and 3 daughters.

Charles Edward Gillman (Barber), born 12 Oct., 1871; Frances Mary; Winnifred Hough; Constance Elizabeth.

THE DESCENT OF

Henry Maclean Martin,

Of Boston, U.S.A.,

FROM THE

Blood Royal  of England.

EDWARD III., crowned 1 Feb., 1327, b. 13 Nov., 1312, d. 21 June, 1377. = Philippa, 3rd dau. of William, Count of Holland and Hainault, m. 24 Jan. 1328, d. 15 Aug. 1369.

Edmund, Duke of York, K.G., 5th son, d. at Langley, 1 Aug. 1402. = Isabel (1st wife), youngest dau. and co-heir of Peter, King of Castile, m. 1372.

Constance of Langley. = Thomas, 6th Baron le Despencer, cr. Earl of Gloucester, 1397, beheaded at Bristol, 16 Jan. 1400.

Isabel le Despencer, b. 26 July, 1400, m. 27 July 1411, d. 26 Dec. 1440. = Richard Beauchamp, Lord Bergavenny (1st husband), cr. Earl of Worcester 1420, d. 1422.

Elizabeth Beauchamp, Baroness Bergavenny, b. at Hanley Castle, 16 Dec. 1415, d. 18 June, 1447 (1st wife). = Sir Edward Nevill, sum. to parl. as Baron Bergavenny, 1450-72, d. 18 Oct. 1476.

Sir George Nevill, Lord Bergavenny, sum. to parl. 1482-92, d. 20 Sept. 1492. = Margaret (1st wife), dau. and heir of Sir Hugh Fenne, of Sculton, d. 28 Sept. 1485.

Sir Edward Nevill, of Addington Park, Kent, beheaded on Tower Hill, 9 Jan. 1538-9. = Eleanor, widow of Ralph, 8th Lord Scrope, of Masham, dau. of Andrew, Lord Windsor.

——— Royden (1st husband). = Catherine Nevill. = Clement Throckmorton, of Hanley, Warwickshire, d. 19 Oct. 1594.

A, continued above.

A, continued from below.

Catherine Nevill = Clement Throckmorton.

Martha Throckmorton, bur. at Southwick, 30 Dec. 1600, aged 49. = George Lynne, of Southwick Hall, Northants, bur. there 29 Nov. 1617.

George Lynne, of Southwick Hall, d. 5 Nov. 1606. = Isabel, sister of Sir Anthony Forrest, of Morborn, Hunts, Knt.

Martha Lynne = John Blennerhassett, of Ballyseedy, co. Kerry, M.P. Tralee, 1661.

Robert Blennerhassett = Avice, dau. and co-heir of Jenkin Conway, d. April, 1663.

John Blennerhassett, "Black Jack" of Castle Conway, co. Kerry. = Elizabeth, 3rd dau. of Rev. Benjamin Cross, D.D., she d. 22 March, 1732.

Conway Blennerhassett, of Castle Conway, M.P. Tralee, 1723-4, b. 3 Oct. 1693, d. 7 June, 1724. = Elizabeth, dau. of Col. Harman, of Bawne, co. Longford.

Conway Blennerhassett, of Castle Conway, and of Killorglin, co. Kerry, b. 3 June, 1720. = Elizabeth, dau. of Major Thomas Lacy.

Catherine Blennerhassett = Capt. Robert Agnew, of Howlish, co. Durham.

Elizabeth Agnew, youngest dau. m. 20 May, 1792, d. 27 Feb. 1830. = Rev. Austin Martin, incumbent of Tarbert, co. Kerry, d. 15 May, 1831.

1 Austin Robert, b. 1793, d. 1795.
3 Edward, b. 1797, d. 1798.
2 Henry James Martin, M.R.C.S.E., b. 17 Feb. 1795, d. 8 Oct. 1870. = Mary, dau. of Cap. Alex. Maclean, m. 20 Oct., 1823, d. Jan. 1842.
4 Montgomery Agnew Martin, d. 1869, m. 1827, Catherine, dau. of Fr. M'Gillicuddy.
5 William Wynne b. 1802, d. 1820.
6 Charles, b. and d. 1805.
7 Rev. Robert Agnew Martin, d. 1875 m. Frideswide, da. of R. Sandys, Esq. she d. 1880.
6 daughters.

Henry Austin Martin, of Boston, U.S.A., M.D., A.M., b. 23 July, 1824, d. 7 Dec., 1884. = Frances Coffin, dau. of (Hon.) Nathan Crosby, LL.D., of Lowell, Mass., U.S.A., m. 9 Aug., 1848.
Alexander Donald William, b. 12 Jan., 1829.
Austin Maclean, died young.

Henry Maclean Martin, of Boston, b. 15 May, 1849. = Caroline, dau. of David D. Colton, of San Francisco, m. 10 Nov. 1894.
Stephen Crosby, M.D., b. 13 Sept. 1850.
Austin Agnew, A.B., LL.D., b. 3 Nov., 1851.
Francis Coffin, A.B., M.D., b. 22 March, 1858.
Frances Moody, b. 3 April, 1855, d. 17 Mar., 1857.

MARTIN, HENRY MACLEAN, of Boston, U.S.A., 19TH IN DESCENT FROM EDWARD III., born 15 May, 1849; married 10 Nov., 1884, Caroline, daughter of David D. Colton, of San Francisco.

THE DESCENT OF
HENRY MACLEAN MARTIN, OF BOSTON, U.S.A.,
FROM THE BLOOD ROYAL OF ENGLAND.

EDWARD III., KING OF ENGLAND, Earl of Chester 1320, Duke of Aquitaine, Count of Ponthieu and Montreuil, 1325; crowned at Westminster in his father's lifetime, 1 Feb., 1327; defeated the Scots at Halidon Hill, 1333. In 1339 he assumed the style of "King of France and England, and Lord of Ireland," and quartered the arms of France in the first quarter; gained a great naval victory over the French off Sluys, 1340, and won the celebrated battle of Cressy 26 Aug., 1346; 17 Oct. following the Scots were defeated at Neville Cross, and King David II. taken prisoner to London, where he remained nearly 11 years. Instituted the order of the Garter 1349. His son, the BLACK PRINCE, defeated the French at the battle of Poictiers, 19 Sept., 1356, and brought King John prisoner to London, where he remained nearly five years (for further particulars, see *Royal Lineage*, Foster's *Peerage*). The King died at Sheen, Surrey, 21 June, 1377, having had, with other issue,

EDMUND OF LANGLEY, 5th son, born at King's Langley, Herts, 5 June, 1341; Lord of Tindale, K.G., Earl of Cambridge by charter 13 Nov. 1362; constable of Dover Castle; warden of the Cinque Ports, 12 July, 1376; a commissioner during the tutelage of his nephew Richard II.; commanded an army in Portugal in support of the claim of John of Gaunt to the throne of Castile, 1381; created DUKE OF YORK 6 Aug. 1385; Warden of the kingdom during the King's absence in Ireland, 1394-5; died at Langley, 1 Aug. 1402, married 1st, 1372, Isabel, younger daughter and co heir of Peter (the Cruel), King of Castile and Leon; her will dated 6 Dec. (6 Rich. II.), 1382. The Duke married 2ndly, Joane, daughter of Thomas Holland, Earl of Kent; she re-married 1st, to William, Lord Willoughby of Eresby; 2ndly, to Henry, Lord Scrope; and lastly, to Henry Bromflete, Lord Vescy, for which marriage they had a pardon 14 Aug. 4 Hen. V.; she died s. p. By his 1st wife the Duke of York had with 2 sons an only daughter.

CONSTANCE, married to the ill-fated Thomas, 6th Baron Le Despencer, two years old at his father's death, had summons to parliament 30 Nov. (20 Richard II.), 1396; and 18 July 21 Richard II.), 1397; in the latter year he obtained the reversal of the Act of Parliament, declaring his ancestors, Hugh 3rd and Hugh 4th Barons, traitors. Created Earl of Gloucester, 29 Sept. 1397 (by virtue of his descent from Hugh le Despencer by his wife Eleanor, daughter and co-heir of Gilbert de Clare, Earl of Gloucester, by his wife, Joan of Acre, daughter of Edward I.); Richard II. granted him several manors, and he shared the misfortunes of that monarch, for he was degraded in the 1st Parliament of Henry IV.; was captured at Bristol when attempting to escape from the kingdom, and beheaded by the rabble in the market-place 16 Jan., 1400, had with other issue a daughter.

ISABEL LE DESPENCER, sister and eventually (1414) sole heir of Richard Le De Spencer; born (posthumous) at Cardiff, 26 July, 1400; died 26 Dec., 1440; made her will 1 Dec., 1439, proved 4 Feb., 1439-40; to be buried at Tewkesbury; she married 1st, "on the day of the Seven Sleepers," 27 July, 1411, to Richard Beauchamp, Lord Bergavenny, though his name does not appear among the barons of Parliament in 1417 and 1419; created Earl of Worcester 1420 (son of William, Lord Beau champ de Bergavenny by his wife Joane daughter of Richard, and co-heir of her brother Thomas, Earls of Arundel); he died 1422, being mortally wounded at Meaux, in France; buried at Tewkesbury; she re-married to her husband's cousin, Richard Beauchamp, 5th Earl of Warwick, K.G., by whom she also had issue; he died 30 April, 1438; by her 1st husband, the Earl of Worcester, she had an only daughter,

ELIZABETH BEAUCHAMP, Baroness Bergavenny, or Baroness Beauchamp of Bergavenny; born at Hanley Castle, co. Worcester, 16 Dec. 1415; died 18 June, 1447; buried at the Carmelites, Coventry; married before 1426, as 1st wife, to Sir Edward Neville (6th son of Ralph, 1st Earl of Westmorland, though 4th son by his 2nd wife, Joan Beaufort, daughter of John of Gaunt); had livery with his wife of the lands, but *not* of the castle of Bergavenny, 14 Henry VI.; knighted by John, Duke of Bedford, at Leicester, Whitsuntide, 4 Henry VI., with his brothers, William and George Nevill (Lord Latimer), and the king himself; had summons to parliament as a baron from 5 Sept. (29 Henry VI.), 1450, to 19 Aug. (12 Edward IV.), 1472; in 10 Edward IV. he was a commissioner of array for Kent to oppose the Duke of Clarence and the Earl of Warwick; he married 2ndly (dispensation 15 Oct., 1448), Catherine Howard, sister of John, first Duke of Norfolk (see page 5); and died 18 Oct., 1476, leaving by his first wife, with other issue, a son.

SIR GEORGE NEVILL, Lord Bergavenny; had livery of the lands of his father and mother, 12 Jan. (16 Edward IV.), 1476-7; one of the barons at the coronation of Richard III.; served in the wars in France; knighted for his services at the battle of Tewkesbury by Edward IV. at Barton, 9 May, 1471; had summons to parliament 15 Nov., 1482, to 12 Aug., 1492; born at Raby Castle, co. Durham, 1440; died 20 Sept., 1492; buried at Lewes Priory, Sussex; will dated 1 July, 1491; proved 1492 (see *Testamenta Vetusla*, page 406); he married 1st, Margaret, daughter and heir of Sir Hugh Fenne, of Sculton Burdeleys, Norfolk, and of Braintree, Essex, treasurer of the household to Henry VI.; she died 28 Sept., 1485. His widow, Elizabeth, made her will 14 April (proved 19 June), 1500 describing herself as of Berghdenne, parish of Chartham, Kent, widow, and naming her 4 husbands; her 2nd was Richard Naylor, citizen of London, her 3rd Robert Bassett, and her last husband John Stokker, Lord Bergavenny had by his 1st wife with 3 daughters 5 sons.

[1] GEORGE, succeeded as 3rd Lord Bergavenny.
[2] William, died s. p.
[3] **Sir Edward Nevill**, of Addington Park, of whom presently.
[4] Sir Thomas, of Mereworth, Kent, speaker of the House of Commons, 1514-23; died 29 May, 1542, leaving a daughter.
[5] Sir John, a knight of Rhodes.

SIR EDWARD NEVILL, of Addington Park, Kent, knight banneret for his bravery at the siege of Therouenne, 5 Hen. VIII.; one of the commanders of the forces under the Duke of Suffolk in the expedition to France, 15 Hen. VIII.; a gentleman of the bedchamber at the christening of Prince Edward, 15 Oct., 1537; but on 3 Nov. in the following year he was imprisoned in the Tower, and 3 Jan. indicted for "devising to maintain, promote and advance one Reginald Pole, late dean of Exeter, enemy to the king beyond the sea, and to deprive the king," was attainted and beheaded on Tower Hill 9th of same month, 1538-9; married Eleanor, widow of Ralph, 8th Lord Scrope, of Masham, daughter of Andrew, Lord Windsor, and had with 3 sons 4 daughters, of whom the eldest,

CATHERINE, married 1stly to ——— Royden, and, 2ndly, to Clement Throckmorton, of Haseley, Warwick, sewer to the Queen temp. Henry VIII.; a commander at the siege of Boulogne, 1544 (son of Sir George Throckmorton, co. Warwick, by Katherine Vaux, also of royal descent); he died 19 Oct., 1594 (? 18 Oct., 1599), having had 6 sons and 7 daughters (see page 565), of whom

MARTHA THROCKMORTON (4th daughter), buried at Southwick 30 Dec., 1600, aged 49; married to George Lynne, of Southwick Hall, Northants (son and heir of George Lynne, of Southwick, by his wife Amicia, daughter of Sir Edward Montagu, lord chief justice of England, ancestor of the Duke of Manchester; see Foster's *Peerage*); he was buried at Southwick 29 Nov, 1617, having had with 9 daughters, 4 sons (see page 565), of whom the eldest

GEORGE LYNNE, of Southwick Hall, died 5, buried in Southwick church 6 Nov., 1606; inquisition post mortem 26 August, 5 James I.; he married Isabella, daughter of Myles and sister of Sir Anthony Forrest, of Morborn, Hunts, Knt., where she was baptised 26 July, 1575; had with 4 sons (see page 565) 6 daughters, of whom,

MARTHA, married to John Blennerhassett, Esq., of Ballyseedy, co. Kerry; M.P. Tralee, 1661; (eldest son of Robert Blennerhassett, Esq., of Ballycarty, and his wife Elizabeth Conway); he made his will 18 Oct., 1673, proved 14 Sept., 1676, and had 3 sons and 3 daughters.

[1] John (Blennerhassett), of Ballyseedy, M.P. Tralee, Dingle, and co. Kerry; high sheriff, 1658; his will proved 1667; married Elizabeth, daughter of Sir Edward Denny, Knt., of Tralee; she was born 25 Feb., 1635, and had 2 sons and a daughter (see page 691).
[2] **Robert,** of whom presently.
[3] Thomas, of Littur, co. Kerry, made his will 8 June 1695, married Ellen, daughter of Anthony Stoughton, of Rattoo, co. Kerry, clerk of the court of Castle Chamber (by his wife Honora, daughter of Dermot O'Brien, Lord Inchiquin), and had 6 daughters (see Raymond *Pedigree*, page 639).
[4] Mary (Blennerhassett), married to Capt. Thomas Wren, of Littur, co. Kerry, and had a son (ancestor of the family still seated there); and a daughter Martha, married to William Fitz Gerald.
[5] Alice, married to Edmond Conway, of Cloghane (son of Capt. James Conway, of Castle Conway, co. Kerry, by Elizabeth, daughter and sole heir of Edmond Roe, by his wife, Alice, daughter of Jenkin Conway), and had a son.

James Conway, of Cloghane, married, 1st, Catherine, daughter of Patrick Fitzgerald, of Gallerus, son of the Knight of Kerry (see p. 213); he married, 2nd, Honora, daughter of Rev. Vere Hunt, by his wife, Constance, daughter of Sir William Piers, of Tristernagh, co. Westmeath, 2nd Bart.); by his 1st wife he had an only daughter,

Alice Conway, married, as 1st wife, to Col. John Colthurst, of Ballyhally, and had 3 sons and 2 daughters (see page 715).

[6] Lucy, married to John Walker, a lieut. in the English army, 1641, and had a daughter,

Martha Walker, married, about 1680, to Thomas Shierc!iffe, of Castle Gregory, and died 1683, leaving 2 daughters.

(1) Alice (Shiercliffe), married to Edward Rice, and had 4 daughters.

[1] Christian (Rice), married to Edward Conway, and had an only surviving child,

Mary Rice (Conway), died 15 July, 1825; married 18 May, 1784, to John Hurly, Esq., clerk of the crown and peace for Kerry; he died 26 Nov., 1820, leaving issue.

[2] Alice.
[3] Mary, marr'ed to Richard, youngest son of Henry Blennerhassett, and had issue (see page 567).
[4] Martha (Rice).

(2) Martha (Shiercliffe), of Moyalla, co. Cork.

ROBERT BLENNERHASSETT (son of John Blennerhassett and Martha Lynne), married Avice, daughter and co-heir of Jenkin or Edward Conway, of Killorglin or Castle Conway, co. Kerry, with whom he acquired the greater part of the estates granted to John Conway; she died April, 1663, having had 3 sons and 5 daughters (*a*).

[1*a*] **John,** of whom see page 593*a*.
[2*a*] Thomas (Blennerhassett), married Jane Darby, of Wales, and had 3 sons and 4 daughters (*b*).

(1*b*-2*a*) John; (2*b*-2*a*) Chiswell; and (3*b*-2*a*) Arthur; one of whom had a son,

Thomas Blennerhassett, of Annadale, co. Kerry, many years treasurer of Kerry; married Alicia Brunton, widow, daughter of John Philip O'Brien, of Kilowa, co. Clare, and had with 5 sons a daughter.

ANNE BLENNERHASSETT, died 13 Aug., 1856; married Oct., 1800, to Peter Thompson, of Tralee, treasurer of Kerry (on the death of his father-in-law); he died 3 Jan., 1850, having had 5 sons and 2 daughters (*c*).

[1*c*] David Peter (Thompson) of Stonestown and Park, King's co., J.P., born 1803; died 7 Jan. 1845; married 2 Dec., 1838, his cousin Anna Maria, eldest daughter of George Thompson, Esq., of Clonskeagh Castle, and had 3 sons and 2 daughters.

(1 Peter Hamlet (Thompson), of Stonestown and Park, King's co., J.P., High Sheriff 1875; born 1839; died, 1883; married, 28 Aug., 1873, Mary Anne, daughter of John W. Tarleton, Esq., of Killeigh, King's co.
2 George Irwin (Thompson), an officer 96th regt., died Jan, 1867.
3 Blennerhassett David, of Claremont, co. Westmeath.
4 Ellen Wade, married Jan., 1866, to

lieut.-col., Henry A. Little, Bengal Staff Corps, late of Royal Fusiliers.

(5) Hannah Gerrard, died July, 1868; married, June, 1866, to H. W. Cuppage, 49th Light Infantry.

[2c] Thomas Blennerhassett (Thompson), born 1804; died, 1853; married, 1828, Meliora, daughter of John Young, Esq., of Philpot'stown, and had ason and daughter.

(1) Peter Henry, lieut., 88th regt.; died unmarried 1854.

(2) Mary Anne, married 5 Feb., 1856, to William Rynd, Esq., of Messina.

[3c] William.

[4c] Henry, capt., 74th Highlanders, died unmarried.

[5c] Robert Acheson (Thompson) of Sandville, co. Kerry, born ; married 30 Oct., 1841, Christina Frances, daughter of Francis Christopher Bland, Esq., of Derriquin, co. Kerry (see page 771)), and has had 4 sons and 2 daughters.

(1) Peter (Thompson), born 9 Aug., 1845; died unmarried.

(2) Robert Acheson, born 5 Sept., 1848; died unmarried

(3) Edward Herbert, born 21 Nov., 1851; died unmarried.

(4) William, M.D.R.N., born 18 Jan., 1854.

(5) Lucy Ann

(6) Clara Dalinda, died 8 Oct., 1873, having married 21 Sept., 1871, to George Anthony Denny, M.D. (see page 726); he died March, 1873, leaving an only daughter

Ethel (Denny).

(6c) Annie died young.

[7c] Alicia (Thompson) married 1820, to Ven. Arthur Blennerhassett Rowan, archdeacon of Ardfert, rector of Kilgobbin, who died 14 Aug., 1861, having had 2 sons and 3 daughters.

(1) Major William Rowan, of Belmont, Tralee, born 25 March, 1830; married first, 1859, his cousin Katherine, daughter of Thomas Higginbotham Thompson, of Clonskeagh Castle, co. Dublin; she died having had 3 sons and 2 daughters.

[1] Thomas Thompson (Rowan), lieut. R.A., born 22 Nov., 1861.

[2] Arthur Blennerhassett. [3] Arthur.

[4] Martha Alice. [5] Annie.

MAJOR ROWAN married secondly 16 Oct., 1877, Katharine Wilhelmina, daughter of Richard Huggard, of Tralee, solicitor (see page 640), and has a daughter.

[6] Marion Annie (Rowan).

(2) Arthur E D . (3) Annie.

(4) Meliora died. (5) Arabella (Rowan) died.

(4b-2a) Elizabeth, married to William Conron, and had a daughter, Mary, 1733.

(5b-2a) Avice, married to Rev. Thomas Collis, vicar of Dingle, and had 3 daughters.

[1] Jane, married 1st, to Rev. Frederick Mullins, eldest brother of Thomas, 1st Lord Ventry; he died s.p.; she re-married, as 2nd wife, to Rev. Arthur Herbert, of Cahirnane and Currens, rector of Tralee, and had a daughter (see pages 380 and 660).

[2] Mary, 1733. [3] Isabella, 1733.

(6b-2a) Jane, married 9 Aug., 1731, to Maurice O'Connell, Esq., of Imlaghmore, co. Kerry (eldest son of Geoffrey O'Connell, of Kilkeevera, co. Kerry, by Elizabeth, daughter of Edmond Conway of Glanbeigh), and had a son and daughter.

(1) Geoffrey O'Connell, married Elizabeth Conway, of Glanbeigh, and had a son,

Thomas O'Connell, M.D., of Tralee, who married Ellen, daughter of David Tuohy, of Tralee, and had a son and a daughter,

(2) Mary (O'Connell), died Oct., 1836; married 3 June, 1802, to her cousin, Daniel O'Connell, of Darrynane, co. Kerry, "the liberator;" M.P. Clare 1828-30, co. Waterford 1830, co. Kerry, 1831, Dublin 1832-6, Kilkenny 1836-7, Dublin 1837-41, co. Cork 1841-7; admitted to Gray's Inn 26 April, 1796; barrister-at-law King's Inns, Q.C. (son of Morgan O'Connell, of Carhen and Iveragh, co. Kerry (see Foster's *Baronetage*); born 6 Aug., 1775; died 15 May, 1847, having had 4 sons and 3 daughters (*d*).

[1-*d*] Maurice Daniel (O'Connell), M.P. Clare 1831-2, Tralee 1832-7, 1838-53; admitted to Gray's Inn 27 Jan., 1824; died 18 June, 1853, having married , 1832, Frances Mary, only daughter of John Binden Scott, Esq., of Cahircon, co. Clare, and had 2 sons and 2 daughters (*e*).

(1*e*-1*d*) Daniel, of Darrinane Abbey, co. Kerry, J.P., D.L. and high sheriff; born 20 Nov., 1836; married 25 April, 1861, Isabella Mary, daughter of Denis Shine Lawlor, Esq., of Castlelough and Grenagh House, co. Kerry, and has 5 daughters.

Isabella Mary; Kathleen; Margaret Gertrude; Eileen; Frances.

(2*e*-1*d*) John Maurice, born 12 April, 1839; married 9 Aug., 1873, Mary Kathleen, only daughter of Daniel McCartie, Esq., of Ardnageeha, co. Cork, and has a son and 6 daughters.

Daniel Maurice, born 18 Sept., 1878.

Anna Mary; Mary Helena; Kate Mary Monica; Frances Mary Laura; Aileen Mary; Jane Mary.

(3) Fanny, died 1878.

(4) Mary, married 25 Nov., 1858, to Daniel McCartie, Esq., of Headfort, co. Kerry, and has 5 sons and 4 daughters.

Denis (McCartie), born 28 Oct., 1862.

Maurice, born 29 May, 1864.

Daniel Joseph, born 9 Aug., 1865.

Charles John, born 27 Dec., 1866.

Jeremiah Joseph, born 7 Dec., 1877.

Jane; Frances Mary; Mary; Elizabeth Catherine Mary.

[2*d*] Morgan, M.P. co. Meath, 1832-41; registrar of deeds, Ireland, 1848-68; born 31 Oct., 1804; died s.p., 20 Jan., 1885; married 23 July, 1840, Kate Mary, daughter of Michael Balfe, Esq., of South Park, co. Roscommon.

[3*d*] John, M.P. Youghal 1832-7, Athlone 1837, Kilkenny 1841, Limerick 1847-51, Clonmel 1853-7; clerk of the hanaper, Ireland; barrister-at-law, admitted to King's Inns, Hilary, 1831; called Michaelmas, 1837; born 24 Dec., 1810; died 24 May, 1858, having married 28 March, 1838, Elizabeth, daughter of James Ryan, LL.D., of Jubilee Hall, co. Dublin; she died 9 April, 1877, having had 3 sons and 5 daughters (*f*).

(1*f*-3*d*) Daniel, admitted to King's Inns, Hilary, 1859; called 1864; born 23 March, 1839; drowned 1 June, 1872.

(2*f*-3*d*) John, C.E. of Bombay, a capt. of Volunteers; born 26 Feb., 1843; married 27 March, 1873, Mary, daugeter of Henry Baldwin, Esq., of Dublin, and has 3 sons and a daughter.

John Henry, born 24 April, 1875; Daniel John Joseph Patrick, born 27 Nov., 1879; Henry John Joseph Patrick, born 25 June, 1881; Mary Margaret.

(3*f*-3*d*) Morgan John Joseph Patrick, 1st Hampshire, capt. 37th regt., A.D.C. to lieut.-gen. com.-in-chief Cape 1880; born 27 Oct., 1845; died unmarried 22 Sept., 1881.

(4*f*-3*d*) Elizabeth, married 9 Aug., 1869, to

James Sullivan, of Kilkenny, J.P., and has 3 sons and 6 daughters.

Richard (Sullivan), born 29 Aug., 1872; John, born 16 Dec., 1874; James Joseph, born 19 March, 1885; Elizabeth; Frances; Mary; Eleanor; Kathleen; Alice.

(5*f*-3*d*) Mary, married 26 Nov., 1867, to Andrew Nugent Comyn, Esq., of Ballinderry, co. Galway, J.P., and of Ryefield, co. Roscommon, and has had 4 sons and 4 daughters.

Nicholas O'Connell (Comyn), born 19 June, 1869; John, born 21 May, 1871, died 1881; Andrew David, born, 23 Sept., 1872; Lewis, J. J .P. Ward, born March, 1878; Elizabeth Mary; Mary Sabina, died , 1883; Geraldine Mary; Eily Mary.

(6*f*-3*d*) Eily (O'Connell), a nun.

(7*f*-3*d*) Kathleen, married 29 July, 1885, to Capt. Michael Joseph Balfe, of South Park, co. Roscommon.

(8*f*-3*d*) Alice.

[4*d*] Daniel, M.P. Dundalk 1846-7, Waterford 1847-8, Tralee 1853-63; commissioner of income tax 1863; capt. Kerry militia; admitted to King's Inns, Easter 1838; born 22 Aug., 1816; married 23 Oct., 1866, Ellen Mary, daughter of Ebenezer Foster, Esq., of Cambridge, and has 4 sons and 3 daughters.

Daniel John Foster William, born 19 Jan., 1873; Maurice Francis Joseph Benedict, born 21 March, 1874; Geoffrey Owen Morgan Leo, born 18 Feb., 1876; Morgan Macfarlane, born 1 Dec., 1879; Eily Mary Foster; Mary Elizabeth Kathleen; Dorothy.

[5*d*] Ellen (O'Connell), died 27 January, 1883; married 1825, to Christopher FitzSimon, of Glancullen, co. Dublin and Ballinamona, co. Wicklow; J.P., D.L., clerk of the crown and hanaper; M.P. co. Dublin 1832,5, 1835-7; he died 25 July, 1856, having had with other issue, 4 sons and 3 daughters (*g*).

(1*g*-5*d*) Christopher O'Connell (FitzSimon), of Glancullen, co. Dublin, J.P., D.L., and of Ballinamona, co. Wicklow; high sheriff 1861; born 12 Aug., 1830; died 16 Nov. 1884, having married 1 Aug., 1866, Agnes Teresa, daughter of late Capt. Richard Leyne, of Annagh, co. Kerry (see page 629), and had 4 sons and a daughter.

Christopher James O'Connell, born 30 June, 1867. Richard O'Connell, Daniel O'Connell, Edward O'Connell, Ellen O'Connell.

(2*g*-5*d*) Thomas O'Connell, married and died.

[3*g*-5*d*] Henry O'Connell (FitzSimon), of Ballinamona, co. Wicklow; J.P. co. Dublin, married and has issue.

(4*g*-5*d*) Maurice O'Connell, died unmarried.

(5*g*-5*d*) Mary O'Connell, (FitzSimon), died 26 May, 1877; married 19 Nov. 1849, to Henry Edward Redmond, Esq. of Dungarvan, resident magistrate since 1860; served in 2nd Queen's and (lieut.) 54th regts.; and has had 8 sons and a daughter.

(1) Gabriel O'Connell FitzSimon (Redmond), of Copppoquin, co. Waterford, M.D., born 15 Oct., 1850; married 1st, 30 Oct., 1873, Catalina Netterville, daughter of late Edwar Netterville Barron, Esq., of Ballynacourty House, co. Waterford; she died 10 Feb., 1877, leaving a daughter.

[1] Mary Catalina Gabriella.

Dr. Redmond married 2ndly, 1 Sept., 1881, Helen, eldest daughter of John Quinlan, of Clonkerdin House, co. Waterford, deputy clerk of Lieutenancy, and has 2 sons and a daughter.

[2] Henry Edward, born 28 June, 1882.

[3] John Raymond, born 4 June, 1883.

[4] Clarissa Ellen.

(2) Christopher Douglas (Redmond) died 30 Sept., 1855.

(3) Henry Douglas Johnstone (Redmond), of 104th or Royal Munster Fusileers, late 2nd West India regt., born 10 Aug., 1853.

(4) Daniel O'Connell, died 10 Oct., 1855.

[5] Raymond O'Connell, born 6 Aug., 1856, died 11 May, 1880.

(6) Thomas O'Connell, born 21 Dec., 1858; married July, 1881, Nellie Butler, and has Henry Edward, and John.

(7) Christopher FitzSimon, died 15 Aug., 1863.

(8) John Johnstone, born 19 Feb., 1864.

(9) Ellen Philadelphia, born 21 July, 1865.

[6*g*-5*d*] Ellen O'Connell (FitzSimon), married 1st, 26 April, 1859, to Charles Bianconi, D.L., co. Tipperary (son of Charles Bianconi and Eliza Hayes), he died 2 March, 1864, having had 4 daughters.

(1) Ellen O'Connell (Bianconi), married 19 Aug., 1880, to Victor E. Collins, Esq.

(2) Elizabeth O'Connell (Bianconi), married 30 May, 1882, to Clement Ryan, Esq., of Scarteen, co. Limerick.

(3) Charlotte Mary, died March, 1864, a twin with

(4) Katharine Mary.

Mrs. Charles Bianconi re-married 28 March, 1867, to Patrick Charles Hayes, Esq., and has had 4 sons and 5 daughters.

(5) Christopher O'Connell (Hayes), born 27 Dec., 1867; (6) Henry O'Connell, born 10 Jan., 1868; (7) Charles O'Connell, born 20 Jan., 1872; (8) Daniel O'Connell, born 12 April, 1883, died 22 Nov., 1884; (9) Mary O'Connell; (10) Henrietta O'Connell; (11) Emily O'Connell; (12) Gertrude O'Connell; (13) Alice O'Connell.

[7*g*-5*d*] Catherine O'Connell (FitzSimon) married, to Col. George Ludlow Kennedy Hewett, of the Indian Army, and has 4 sons and 8 daughters.

James, Christopher, George, Henry, Eliza, Ellen, Mary, Christina, Georgina, Kathleen, Maud, Rosalie.

(6*d*) Catherine (O'Connell), married 1832, to Charles O'Connell, Esq. (son of Daniel O'Connell, of Iveragh); M.P. co. Kerry, 1832; he died 23 Jan., 1845, having had, with daughters, an only son,

[1] Daniel O'Connell, of Ballynabloun, co. Kerry, J.P.; born 6 Jan., 1842; married, 1st, 1867, Milly, only daughter of late Joseph Lindsay Curtis, Esq., of Cork; she died , 1870; he married 2ndly, 31 Jan., 1877, Helen Josephine, 2nd daughter of Sir Joseph Neale McKenna, of Ardogena, co. Waterford, M.P. Youghal, and has a son,

Charles, born , 1878.

(7*d*) Elizabeth, married 7 April, 1831, to Nicholas Joseph ffrench, of ffrench Lawn, co. Roscommon, J.P. and resident magistrate (only son of Christopher ffrench, deputy constable of the castle of Athlone); he died 11 Aug., 1842, having had 3 sons and 3 daughters (*k*).

[1*k*-7*d*] Daniel O'Connell ffrench, of Dublin, barrister-at-law, assistant-registrar of deeds, Ireland; born 26 Oct., 1832; married 16 Oct., 1856, Nora Mary, daughter of Maurice O'Connor, M. D. of Tralee, and had 7 sons and 6 daughters, of whom survive,

Nicholas O'Connell (ffrench), born 30 Nov., 1858. Morgan O'Connell, born 28 Nov., 1868. Christopher O'Connell, born 10 Nov., 1871. Jane Mary O'Connell, Elizabeth Ellen O'Connell, Leonora O'Connell, Mary O'Connell, Cecilia O'Connell, Alice O'Connell.
[2k-7d] Christoper O'Connell, born 28 March, 1837; married 21 July, 1883, Eleanor, 2nd daughter of late Wm. Deane Butler, Esq., F.R.S.A., of Dublin
[3k-7d] Nicholas O'Connell, born 13 June, 1842; died 23 Oct., 1882.
[4k-7d] Harriett O'Connell, married 1866, to Thomas Anthony Wright, Esq., who died s.p. 26 Sept., 1884.
[5k-7d] Mary O'Connell, married 21 July, 1859, to J. F. FitzGerald, Esq., of Kinneigh House, co. Kerry, J.P.
[6k-7d] Alice O'Connell.
(7b-2a) Alice, married to Thomas, son of Dennis Hurly, of Knocklong, co. Limerick.
[3a] **Henry**, of whom (see page 566).
[4a] Catherine, married 1st, to Richard, son of Capt. Richard McLoughlin, of Bally Downey, and had 2 daughters (see page 600); she re-married to John Conway, and had a daughter.
Mildred (Conway), married to Thomas Jeffcott, of Tonarigh, and had issue.
[5a] Avice, married to Thomas, son of Captain Thomas Spring, of Ballycrispin, co. Kerry, and had 4 sons and 4 daughters.
(1) Thomas Spring, of Ballycrispin, barrister-at-law, King's Inns; married 3 Dec., 1730 (? 15 Dec., 1733), Hannah, youngest daughter of Francis Annesley, Esq., of Ballyshannon, co. Kildare (see Foster's *Peerage*, E. ANNESLEY), and had a son,
THOMAS SPRING, of Ballycrispin, born 3 June, 1735; married Catherine, daughter of Ven. Edward Wight, rector of Rathronan and archdeacon of Limerick; she made her will 28 July, 1785, proved 7 Sept. following (? married also Jane, youngest daughter of Lieut.-Col. Thomas Maunsell, of Thorpe Malsor, Northants), and had an only child,
CATHERINE, married 10 Aug., 1785, to Stephen Edward Rice, of Mount Trenchard, co. Limerick (see page 532), father of Lord Monteagle.
(2) Edward, in the Prussian service, 1733.
(3) Francis (Spring), of Bally Crispin, married his cousin Catherine, eldest daughter of John Mason, Esq., of Bally MacEligot and Ballydowney (by Ann MacLoughlin, see page 600), and had a son and 2 daughters.
[1] John (Spring), born 23 June, 1730; married Mary, daughter of Rev. Thomas Collis, of , and had 3 sons.
(1) Francis, died unmarried.
(2) Thomas, J.P., married Catherine, elder daughter of Capt. James Eagar, of Cottage, who died s.p. 1850, aged 83 (see next page).
(3) William Collis (Spring), lieut.-col. 57th regt., born 1770, died 14 August 1825, having married Sept. 1807, Anne, daughter of Col. Carter, 16th regt.; she died 19 Feb., 1853, having had 5 sons.
[1] William (Spring), lieut.-col. 44th regt.; born 30 Sept., 1808; died 10 March, 1860; married May, 1834, Mary Isabella, daughter of Col. Tidy, C.B. (and great granddaughter of Rev. John Skelly, by his wife, Lady Elizabeth Gordon, daughter of Alexander, 2nd Duke of Gordon), and had 2 sons and 2 daughters.
(1) Charles William Gordon (Spring), of Castlemayne, co. Kerry; lieut. R.N.; born 9 April, 1850.
(2) Herbert George Charles, born 8 Oct., 1854.
(3) Mary Gordon.
(4) Frances Caroline Gordon.
[2] John, lieut. 9th regt.; died unmarried.
[3] Robert, major in the army, born 24 May, 1814; married 7 Feb., 1850, Caroline Emily, daughter of Lt.-Gen. Henry Raleigh Knight, s.p.
[4] Thomas, major in the army, married, and had 2 daughters.
[5] Francis (Spring), capt. 57th regt., born 15 Sept., 1821. killed in the Indian mutiny, 8 July, 1857; married 2 April 1853, Sara, daughter of Lt.-Col. Edward Day; she re-married 4 Aug., 1859 to Thomas M. Hamilton Jones, Esq. (see page 438), and had a son and daughter.
William Edward Day (Spring), capt. 24th regt., born 6 June, 1855; Anne Eleanor Frances.
[2] Avice, born 23 Dec., 1734.
[3] Catherine, married 16 Feb., 1760, to Capt. James Eagar, of Cottage, co. Kerry, J.P., who died 1818, aged 87, having had 4 sons and 3 daughters (see below, &c.).
(4) John. (5) Alice. (6) Anne.
(6) Mary (Spring). (7) Annabella.
[6a] Alice, married to Walter, brother of Capt. Thomas Spring aforesaid, and had a son and 4 daughters.
(1) Thomas (Spring), married Anne FitzMaurice, of Duaghnafealy, and had William and Thomas, 1732.
(2) Avice, married to Thomas, 3rd son of John Blennerhassett, of Ballyseedy, and had 3 sons (see page 692).
(3) Anne, married to Rev. Thomas Frankland, prebendary of Cloyne.
(4) Martha, married to Capt. John Thwaite, of Cumberland.
(5) **Jane** (Spring), of whom (see below).
[7a] Lucy (Blennerhassett), married to John Plaguavan, a Frenchman, and had 2 sons and 2 daughters (see p. 556).
[8a] Anne, married to Dennis Hurly, of Knocklong, co. Limerick, and had 5 sons and 3 daughters.

JANE SPRING (4th and youngest daughter of Walter Spring, by his wife Alice Blennerhassett), died 1776; married 1st, 6 Nov., 1729, as 2nd wife, to Thomas Eagar, of Cottage and Ballyhar, co. Kerry; she re-married to — Brewster, and lastly to William Dunscombe, of Cork; by her 1st husband she had 3 sons and 4 daughters.

[1] James Eagar, of Cottage, J.P. co. Kerry; capt. of the Laune Rangers Yeomanry corps; died 1817, aged 86; married 16 Feb., 1760, Catherine, daughter of Francis Spring, of Ballycrispin (see above); she died , having had 4 sons and 3 daughters.
[1] Thomas Spring (Eagar), of Cottage, J.P. co. Kerry; died 1808, married 25 Nov., 1801, Mary, daughter of Samuel Raymond, Esq., of Ballyloughran, co. Kerry; J.P.; high sheriff 1773; (see p. 641); she died , 1808, leaving a son and 2 daughters.
(1) James Raymond (Eagar), sold "Cottage" to his cousin Rowland Tallis Eagar; born 1815, died unmarried.
(2) Frances, died unmarried.
(3) Catherine, married 1824, to William FitzMaurice Sealy, Esq., and settled in America.
[2] Francis Spring (Eagar), B.A., Trin. Coll., Dublin, in holy orders, died unmarried, 1807.
[3] John Moore (Eagar), of Ashill, died ; married 1st, Elizabeth, daughter of Ephraim Peet, of Cork; he married 2nd, Ann, widow

of John Blennerhassett, of Rossbeigh, daughter of Samuel Blennerhassett, Esq. (see page 567); by his 1st wife he had a son and daughter.

(1) James Peet (Eagar), died unmarried.

(2) Elizabeth, married to George Beale, of Cork.

[4] James Day (Eagar), of Coolgariff, a Peninsula veteran, served at the siege of Badajoz, and at the battles of Salamanca, Fuentes d'Onore, and Ciudad Rodrigo; died 28 March, 1854, aged 82; married, 1815, Avice, daughter of Robert Eagar, Esq., of Listry (by his wife Anne, daughter of Denis Hurley, see preceeding page); she died 21 April, 1838, aged 53, having had 3 sons and 2 daughters.

(1) James Heaviside (Eagar), died unmarried.

(2) Robert, rector of Killorglin, and rural dean, B.A., Trin. Coll., Dublin, born married 5 Nov., 1868, Dorothea Anne Chute, 2nd daughter of Wm. John Neligan, Esq., of Tralee, by his wife Dorothea, daughter of Richard Chute, Esq., Chute Hall, and has an only surviving son.

James Robert Conway Blennerhassett (Eagar), born 1 May, 1873.

(3) Thomas Spring, B.A. Trin. Coll., Dublin, in holy orders; died unmarried, July 1862.

(4) Anna Maria.

(5) Kate Avice, married to Lieut. Henry McMahon Eagar, who died 18 Sept., 1855, leaving issue (see p. 571).

[5] Catherine Eagar, died s.p. , 1850, aged 83; married to Thomas Spring, Esq., J.P. (see p. 592).

[6] Jane, married to Rowland Eagar, Esq., of Culleenymore, and had a son and daughter (see p. 573).

[7] Avice, married to George Kennedy, surgeon R.N., had a son and 2 daughters.

(1) Frank Kennedy, married Aphra, daughter of James Fisher, Esq., and had a daughter, Eva Fisher, married Nov. 1882, to William Graham, Fleet surgeon, R.N.

(2) Jane (Kennedy).

(3) Catherine, married , to Robert Hickson, Esq., and had a daughter, married to George Garrow Green, Esq., of Ahinrone, King's co., inspector Royal Irish Constabulary.

[2] John (Eagar), of Ballyhar; died 1813, aged 80; married 1st, sister of Capt. Carey, of co. Cork; 2nd, 1791, Dorcas, daughter of Henry Eagar, of Faha (by his wife Lucy, daughter of James Yeilding (see page 571); and had 3 sons and 2 daughters.

(1) Thomas (Eagar), died young.

(2) John Henry (Agar), sold Ballyhar, 1834; born ; died , 1837; married Elizabeth, daughter of John Lynch, of Dromin (by his wife Elizabeth, daughter of Geoffrey Eagar, Esq., of Glenfleck), and had 5 sons and 5 daughters

[1] John Henry (Agar), M.D.; a member of legislative assembly, Antigua; died at Parham, 3 Nov., 1853, aged 39.

[2] Henry (Agar), lieut. Ceylon rifles; born ; married , Frances, daughter of James Chamberlain, Esq., of Chamherst Nor- and had a daughter, Elizabeth, unmarried.

[3] Rowland, assist.-surgeon on staff, Ceylon, died there unmarried, 22 Oct., 1852.

[4] Thomas, and [5] James, died young.

[6] Eliza. Charlotte, living 1885.

[7] Emily, died 21 April, 1854; married 29 Nov., 1843, as 1st wife, to William Paston Purnell, of Stancombe Park, co. Gloucester, J.P., C.B., col. 90th regt., served in the Crimea and India, ensign of the yeomen of the guard; died 14 May, 1869, leaving a daughter, Emily Anne.

[8] Dorcas, died unmarried.

[9] Lucinda, died unmarried 1862-3.

[10] Jane, died unmarried 1881.

(3) Thomas (Agar), in holy orders, B.A. Trin. Coll., Dublin, died unmarried, June, 1836.

(4) Lucinda, died unmarried 1881.

(5) Jane, married 1826 to Michael MacSheehy, Esq., of Killarney, and had 2 sons and a daughter.

[1] Brian (MacSheehy), LL.D., Head Inspector, National Board of Education.

[2] John, solicitor to the Corporation and City of Dublin. [3] Dorcas Jane.

[3] Walter (Eagar), of Killarney; married Alice, daughter of Richard Mason (see p. 600), and had an only surviving son and 3 daughters.

(1) James Walter (Agar), of Woodmount; born 23 June, 1783, died 1 Sept., 1859, aged 76; married 1st, of April, 1808, Rachel, daughter of Abel Benjamin Orpen, Esq., of Ballintemple; and had 3 sons living and 4 daughters.

[1] John Orpen (Agar), born ; died Feb., 1836; married July, 1834, Anne, daughter of John Dowman, of Cork (by Mary Jane, sister of Lieut.-General Sir John Rolt); and had a son, Walter Agar, M.D., born 10 Nov., 1835, died in 1866.

[2] Thomas, died unmarried.

[3] Richard Walter (Agar), born died married Catherine, daughter of Patrick Galwey, Esq., of Cork (she re-married to Thomas Walters, J.P., high sheriff city of Cork), and left a son and daughter.

(1) Walter, died young.

(2) Kate, married, March 18 , to William Henry Lyons, Esq., J.P. Cork, High Sheriff co. Cork, (son of late Sir Wm. Lyons); he died

[4] Susan; [5] Alice; [6] Anne; [7] Mary Jane, all died unmarried.

James Walter Agar, married 2ndly, 1835, Susan, daughter of John Shelton, Esq., J.P., of Rossmore House, co. Limerick; she died 29 April, 1879, having had 3 sons and a daughter.

[8] Walter James (Agar), of Laurence estate, Dikoya, Ceylon, born 6 July, 1838, married 22 Feb., 1873, Barbara Maria Roper, daughter of Washington Finlay, Esq., of Sainte Adresse, France (see p. 103), and has 3 sons and 2 daughters.

Walter James (Agar), born 13 July, 1876; Roper Shelton, born 8 Sept., 1878; Robert Charles, born 28 Jan., 1883; Annie Susan Eliza, Maria Willington Roper.

[9] Charles Shelton (Agar), of Forres estate, Maskelyia, Ceylon, born 16 Oct., 1840, married 13 April, 1871, Mary Elizabeth, daughter of Frederick George Rumley, Esq., of Middleton, co. Cork, she died 30 Nov. 1878, having had 2 sons and 2 daughters.

Charles Walter, born 2 Jan., 1872; James Walter, born 14 Dec., 1875; Jane Elizabeth, Mary.

[10] John Shelton (Agar), of Kandy, Ceylon, born 23 Oct., 1842, married 1872, Emily, only daughter of Gotlieb Cruwell, Esq., of Ceylon, and has 4 sons a and 5 daughters.

Shelton Gotlieb, born 12 Dec., 1873; Oliver Cruwell, born 28 March, 1876; Walter Richmond Reckham, born 3 Jan., 1879; John Shelton, born 18 Nov., 1881; Susan Eliza; Avice Sophia Wellington; Eliza Maria; Dorcas Mary; Dorothy Sophie.

[11] Eliza Willington (Agar), married 20 Aug., 1862, to George Sydney Bird, Esq., he died in Australia, in 1866, having had 3 sons.

George Frederick (Bird), born 26 June, 1863; Walter James, born 17 July, 1865; Charles Henry George, born 4 Dec., 1867.

(2) Alice, married to Capt. Chidley Coote, who died

(3) Jane, married to Thomas Mason, who died.
(4) Avice, died 1859, aged 84; married 1 Aug., 1809, to William, eldest son of Frederick Eagar, Esq., of Groinmore, and had 5 sons.
[1] Frederick (Eagar), of police force, London and Windsor, born 14 June, 1811; married, and had issue.
[2] Thomas, born 28 Feb., 1812; married, but s.p. 1881.
[3] Walter, born Oct., 1814; married, and has issue.
[4] Robert, born Nov., 1816.
[5] John, born Oct., 1818; died 1847.
[4] Avice, married to Lowther Godfrey, Esq.
[5] Martha, died unmarried.
[6] Margaret, married to John O'Sullivan, Esq., of Carhirdion, co. Kerry.
[7] Jane, married 1805, to Thomas Giles, of Wood Lodge, Esq., and had 2 daughters.
(1) married to Rev. Kerrin, rector of Ardfert.
(2) married to Giles Shelton, Esq., of co. Limerick.

JOHN BLENNERHASSETT, of Castle Conway, co. Kerry, (Captain) known as "Black Jack," married Elizabeth, 3rd daughter of Rev. Benjamin Cross, D.D., Blackhall, Oxford, rector of Christ Church, Cork, and of Spettisbury, Dorset; she died 22 March, 1732, aged 63, having had 6 sons and 4 daughters.

[1] **Conway**, of whom (see next page).
[2] John (Blennerhassett), born 6 April, 1696; married Anne, daughter of Col. James Dawson, of Ballynacourty (otherwise New Forest), co. Tipperary, and had at least 2 sons and a daughter.
(1) Dawson, born 23 Oct., 1725; died unmarried.
(2) John, born 12 Oct., 1726; died young.
(3) Elizabeth, married 13 July, 1754, to Robert Bolton, of Brazeel, co. Dublin, who died 1798, leaving 2 sons.
[3] Benjamin (Blennerhassett), born 13 Sept., 1698; married Susanna, daughter of Very Rev. John Richards, dean of Ardfert, and had a daughter, Susanna, died unmarried.
[4] Thomas, born 13 Aug., 1700; married 9 March, 1735, Mary Frankland, and had a daughter born the following year.
[5] Edward, of Rosbeigh, Kerry, born 31 Mar., 1705; made his will 6 Nov., 1774; married Mary, daughter of Capt Edward Fitzgerald (by his wife Jane Leader), and had 3 sons and 5 daughters.
(1 John, rector of Tralee; born Jan., 1733; died , 1803; married 2 Feb., 1765, Louisa, daughter of Capt. Thomas Goddard (see Mullins, page 661); had 4 sons and 4 daughters.
[1] Thomas, capt. Kerry militia; died in Brussels, 1825; married (lic 30 April, 1791) Mary, daughter of Henry Blennerhassett and Mary Poujade (see page 567); she died 28 Dec., 1859, having had 5 sons and 5 daughters.
(1) John, baptized 10 June, 1792.
(2) Henry, living 1802.
(3) Goddard, (4) Conway, and (5) Arthur, all died s.p.
(6) Louisa, baptized 4 July, 1794; wife of Wade.
(7) Eliza, died 18 Feb., 1868; married 2 Nov., 1840, to William Henry Garvey, Esq., who died 28 March, 1872, having had 2 sons.
[1] Thomas Blennerhassett Garvey, M.A., M.B.
[2] Charles Henry, died unm., 28 Jan., 1868.
(8) Charlotte, bapt. 7, and buried 18 Oct., 1801.
(9 Charlotte, bap. 30 June, 1803; died unmarried.
(10) Letitia, wife of Dr. William Bruce.
[2] John Blennerhassett, of Dublin, solicitor; married 1st, 10 Jan., 1794, Mary Anne, daughter of Robert Phaire, of Temple Shannon, co Wexford (by his wife, Lady Ricardia Annesley), and had 2 sons.
(1) Goddard (Blennerhassett), died 1833; married Sarah, daughter of Sir Abraham Bradley King, Bart. (see Foster's *Baronetage*); she died 23 Dec., 1870, leaving 2 daughters only.
(2) Aldworth (Blennerhassett), capt. 73rd regt., served at Waterloo.
JOHN BLENNERHASSETT, married 2ndly, daughter of Very Rev. Robert Gorges, D.D, dean of Kilmacduagh, vicar of Dunboyne and Kilbrew, co. Meath; he married 3dly, 1841, Frances Louisa, daughter of Richard Digby, Esq. (by his wife, Frances Herbert; see page 380); by his 2nd wife he had 2 daughters.
(3) Rachel (Blennerhassett), married to General Thomas Gordon Higgins, R.A.
(4) Frances, died 21 Nov., 1845; married 18 March, 1837, to Rev. Francis Plimley Voules, B.A., Wadham Coll. Ox., 1831; rector of Middle Chinnock, Wilts, since 1841; conduct of Eton Coll., 1837-41, and had 3 sons and 2 daughters.
[1] Gordon Blennerhassett (Voules), private secretary to the parliamentary secretary of the Admiralty, since 1879, born on 8 Sept., 1839; married, 12 July, 1866, Frances Cotton, daughter of James Minchin, Esq., and has 2 sons and 3 daughters.
Francis Minchin, born 9 May, 1867; Arthur Blennerhassett, born 15 Sept., 1870; Cherry Marion, Margaret Rose Frances, Evelyn Dorothy Felicia.
[2] Frank Herbert (Voules), of the royal naval reserve, born 1841.
[3] Stirling Cookesley (Voules), B A., (late scholar) Linc. Coll. Ox., 1866. M.A, 1870; rector of Ashley, Staff. principal Sydney Coll. Bath, 1874-9; sometime assistant master at Marlbro Coll.; born 4 Jan., 1843; married 1st, 6 August, 1874, Isabella Sophia, daughter of Frederick Hookey Bond, of Weston-super-Mare, she died May, 1881; he married 2ndly, 16 Dec., 1885, Emily Mary, youngest daughter of late Rev. C. S. Royds, rector of Haughton. By his 1st wife he had a daughter,
Ethel Victoria.
[4] Eliza Maria. [5] Fanny Elizabeth.
[3] Conway, and [4] Goddard, both died s.p.
[5] Elizabeth, baptized 17 May, 1772; married to Edward Fuller, capt. in the old Kerry regt. he died , having had 3 sons and 3 daughters.
(1) Thomas Harnett Fuller, of Glashnacree, co. Kerry, born Sept., 1806; married 1st, Dec., 1832, Frances Diana, daughter of Francis Christopher Bland, Esq., of Derriquin Castle, co. Kerry, J.P., D.L. (by Lucinda, daughter of Arthur Bastable Herbert (see page 771); she died 23 April, 1872; he married 2ndly, 8 May, 1873, Eliza, daughter of Richard Harris Purell, Esq., of Annabella Park, Mallow (by his wife Louisa, daughter of William Leader, of Mount Leader); by his 1st wife he had a son and 2 daughters.
[1] James Franklin Fuller, of Glashnacree, co. Kerry, F.S.A.; Fellow of Royal Institute of British Architects, 1872, and of the Architects of Ireland; of Founder's kin to Oriel, Queen's, and New Colleges, Oxford, to King's and Sidney Sussex, Cambridge, and to Winchester College; 23RD IN DESCENT FROM EDWARD I., through his father, and 19TH through his mother (see Chart Pedigree, page 207); born 16 Aug.,

1835; married 28 Aug., 1860, Helen, daughter of John Prospère Guivier (and grand-daughter of General Guivier, who fell in the retreat from Moscow), and has had 2 sons and 3 daughters.
(1) Franklin Bland (Fuller), lieut. R.A., born Jan., 1863; died 13 June, 1882.
(2) Harnett John, born 14 Dec., 1866.
(3) May Florence.
(4) Adela Bessie. (5) Evelyn Melicent.
[2] Louisa (Fuller), married 3 July, 1862, to her cousin, Arthur Hyde, Esq. (eldest son of Frederick Hyde, Esq., J.P., of Hollywood, co. Kerry (see page 771), and has had 2 sons and 2 daughters.
Arthur Herbert (Hyde), born 11 April, 1863; Thomas Bland, born 15 Nov., 1867; Frances Lucy; Emma Louisa, died 26 Oct., 1873.
[3] Bessie (Fuller).
(2) Edward Goddard (Fuller), died s.p.
(3) John Blennerhassett (Fuller), died s.p.
(4) Louisa (Fuller), died unmarried.
(5) Ann (Fuller) married 16 Aug., 1836, to Ven. Nathaniel Bland, B.A., Trin. Coll., Dublin, 1831, archdeacon of Aghadoe, 1862, late rector of Knockane and of Aghadoe, both in Kerry, he died s.p. 25 Feb., 1885.
(6) Elizabeth (Fuller) married 28 Oct, 1836, to Sir Arthur Helps, K.C.B., D.C.L., clerk of the Privy Council 1859-75, the personal friend and literary adviser of the Queen, author of "Friends in Council" and numerous works, B.A., Trin. Coll., Cambridge, 1838 (son of Thomas Helps and Ann Frisquett, Plucknett); he died 7 March, 1875, aged 62, having had 2 sons and 4 daughters.
[1] Charles Leonard (Helps), rector of Clowne since 1870, born 10 July, 1841; married 2 July, 1868, Emily, daughter of late James Theobald, Esq, J.P., of Grays and Thurrock Nunney, Somerset, and Hyde Abbey, Hants., and has a son.
Arthur Leonard, born 30 March, 1872.
[2] Edmund Arthur (Helps), H.M. Inpector of Schools, born, 10 May, 1843; married 24 July, 1884, Mary Alice, daughter of A. J. Tapson, Esq., M.B., of Gloucester Gardens, Hyde Park.
[3] Alice Plucknett (Helps).
[4] Melicent (Helps), married 3 Nov., 1864, to William Henry Stone, Esq., of Lea Park, Surrey, J.P., D.L., J.P. Hants, M.P. Portsmouth 1865-73, and has a son and daughter.
Arthur William (Stone), born 5 Feb 1866; Melicent, born 5 Sept., 1868.
[5] Rose Elizabeth. [6] Lucy Hester (Helps).
[6] Louisa, married to Rev. Thomas Cole, died s.p.
[7] Catherine, twin with Letitia, married to Finn, and had a son and 2 daughters.
(1) Patrick Finn, of Cork.
(2) Katherine, married to John Saunders, o.s.p.
(3) Christina, married to W H Cotter, and had Barry, Catherine, Joseph, and Louisa, all in America.
[8] Letitia, twin with Catherine, married, 1st, to Major Ponsonby, and had 2 daughters (Louisa and Mary); she remarried to William Lindsay, Esq., of Tarbert, and had 3 sons and a daughter.
(3) Joseph (Lindsay), in Australia.
(4) Blennerhassett.
(5) William. (6) Letitia.
(2) Robert.
(3) Conway, rector of Ardfert, born May, 1736; died s.p. 1805. (4) Avis. (5) Anne.
(6) Jane, wife of Hilliard Giles.

(7) Elizabeth Connell, wife of Samuel K. Williams, of Miltown, and had with other issue a daughter.
HELENA SUSAN (WILLIAMS), married to John Bourke, son of Robert Leech, of Runroe, co. Sligo, and had 6 sons and 2 daughters.
[1] Robert (Leech), died s.p.
[2] William (Leech) born 1798; married Elizabeth Clarke MacDougall and had a son. Rev. John William; died s.p.
[3] George Williams (Leech) of Rathkeale Abbey, co. Limerick, J.P., barrister-at-law, born 30 Aug., 1810; died 6 Oct., 1878; married, first, 12 Nov, 1834, Anna Maria, daughter of General George Bellasis; she died leaving a son.
(1) Robert S B (Leech) late barrack-master, Mauritius; formerly capt. 94th regiment, born 21 May, 1836.
GEORGE W. LEECH married secondly 28 Sept., 1846, Catherine, daughter of Hunt Walsh Chambré, Esq., of Hawthorn Hill, co. Armagh, she died having had 2 sons and 4 daughters.
(2) Hunt Walsh Chambré (Leech), B.A., L.L.D. Trin. Coll., Dublin, and of King's Inns, barrister-at-law, 1883; collector magistrate, Krian-Perah; born 20 Dec., 1847; married 1884, Kathleen Elizabeth, 3rd daughter of Rev, John Leech, D.D., of Mitchelstown.
(3) John Bourke Massy (Leech) born 21 July, 1854.
(4) Helen Susanna (Eiline), married to Lorimore Corbett, Esq.
(5) Catherine Rebecca married
(6) Eliza Georgina.
(7) Mary, married to Francis Buckworth, Esq.
GEORGE W. LEECH, married thirdly, 1869, Elizabeth Winefred, eldest daughter of Henry E. Hemphill, Esq., of co. Dublin, and had with other issue a daughter.
(8) Ethel (youngest daughter), died at Brunswick, Germany, 15 Dec., 1883.
[4] James (Leech) of the Civil Service.
[5] John Bourke, died unmarried, 1859.
[6] Arthur Blennerhassett (Leech), J.P., Sligo, late major rifle volunteers.
[7] Eliza, died unmarried. [8] Julia (Leech).
[6] Arthur (Blennerhassett), born 19 Feb., 1708; married 1st, Mildred, daughter of Capt. Joshua Markham (by Mildred, daughter of Sir Francis Brewster, of Brewsterfield, co. Kerry, Knt.); he married 2nd, 18 Feb., 1734, Sarah, daughter of George Gun, Esq., of Rattoo (by his wife Sarah, daughter of Ven. Thomas Connor, Archdeacon of Ardfert) (see page 722); by his 1st wife he had a son, Joshua.
[7] Anne, born 24 Jan., 1694; married 1st to Dennis M'Gillycuddy, of The Reeks, and had 4 sons and 3 daughters (see page 627); and 2nd, Jan., 1731, to Thomas, son of Arthur Herbert, of Currens, and had a son and daughter, Arthur and Charity, in 1733.
[8] Elizabeth, born 20 Nov., 1702; married to Townsend Gun, of Rattoo, Esq.; he died 1730, having had at least 2 daughters,
(1) Katherine, born 4 July, 1725.
(2) Elizabeth Margaret, born 14 Sept., 1736; married 5 Oct., 1755, to Thomas, 1st Lord Ventry (see p. 661).
[9] Tryphena, born 21 Jan., 1703; married to Ulick FitzMaurice, of Duaghnafealy (see page 647).
[10] Mary, born 23 April, 1707; married ("herself") to Raymond FitzMaurice, brother of Ulick (see note page 647).

CONWAY (Blennerhassett), of Castle Conway, M.P. Tralee 1723-4; admitted to the Middle Temple, 30 Nov., 1710; king's counsel; born 3 Oct., 1693; died 7 June,

1724; married Elizabeth, daughter of Col. Wentworth Harman, of Bawne, co., Longford, a captain of the battle axe guards, and had a son and 2 daughters.

1] Conway (Blennerhassett), of Castle Conway, and of Killorglin, co. Kerry; born 3 June, 1720; married, Elizabeth, daughter of Major Thomas Lacy, and had 3 sons and 6 daughters.

(1) John, and (2) Thomas died young.

(3) Harman (Blennerhassett), a "United Irishman," deeply implicated in the rebellion, sold his estates to Lord Ventry, fled to America, and settled in Canada; married his niece, Margaret, daughter of Robert Agnew, of Howlish, named below, and had issue.

(4) Susanna, died 13 Dec., 1819; married 31 Oct., 1763, to John, 26th Lord Kingsale, who died 24 May, 1822, leaving issue (see page 783).

(5) Elizabeth, married, as 1st wife, to Daniel McGillycuddy, and died s.p. (see page 627).

(6) Catherine, married to Capt. Robert Agnew, of Howlish, co. Durham (son of Brigadier-gen. James Agnew, who was son of James Agnew, of Bishop Aukland, co. Durham, Major 7th Dragons, by his wife Margaret Wilkinson, of Kirkbrigg, and grandson of Sir James Agnew, 4th Bart.), and had a son and 5 daughters.

[1] Major Andrew (Agnew), married 1792, Martha, daughter of John, Lord Kingsale, and died s.p.

[2] Catherine, Mrs. Whiteside, died s.p.

[3] Margaret, married to Harman Blennerhassett (see above).

[4] Mary, died 16 March, 1846; married, as 2nd wife, to Col. Edward Stafford, of Maine, co. Louth, High Sheriff 1795, he died 1802, having had 2 sons and 4 daughters.

[1] Edward Norton (Stafford), born and died 1793.

[2] Berkeley Buckingham (Stafford), of Maine, co. Louth, high sheriff 1828; born 25 March, 1797; died Aug., 1847; married 3 July, 1818, Anne, 3rd daughter of Lieut.-colonel Patrick Duff Tytler (by Isabella, daughter of James Erskine, a lord of session; see Foster's *Peerage*, E. ROSSLYN); she died , having had 4 sons and 2 daughters.

[1] Sir Edward William Stafford, K.C.M.G. 1879, of Maine, co. Louth, and Lansdowne, Christchurch. New Zealand; prime minister N.Z. 1856-61, 1865-9, 1872, M.L.C, 1855-78; born 23 April, 1820; married, 1st, 24 Sept., 1846, Emily Charlotte only child of Col. William Wakefield (see page 844), and granddaughter of Sir John Shelley-Sidney, Bart; she died s.p 18 April, 1857; he married 2ndly, 5 Dec., 1859, Mary, 3rd daughter of Thomas Houghton Bartley, barrister-at-law, I.T. speaker L.C. New Zealand and has 3 sons and 3 daughters.

[1] Edward Tytler Stafford Howard, born 24 May, 1862.

[2] Humphrey de Bohun Howard, born 31 March, 1864.

[3] Berkeley Howard, born 24 Oct., 1869.

[4] Anne Isabella.

[5] Mary Montgomerie.

[6] Edith Margaret.

(2 Berkeley Buckingham de Bohun Howard (Stafford), curate of Tillington 1866-74, &c.; born 23 Aug., 1822.

(3) Hugh Henry Tytler de Toeni (Stafford), of Nelson, New Zealand; born 19 April, 1824; died 29 Nov., 1880; married Jan., 1860, Caroline, daughter of William Wood, Esq., and has 3 sons and 2 daughters.

[1] William, born Oct., 1860.

[2] Berkeley Buckingham.

[3] Hugh Henry Archibald.

[4] Isabella Erskine.

[5] Emily Margaret.

(4) Patrick Plunkett Leslie, late col. Indian army, born 13 July, 1826.

(5) Isabella Erskine.

(6) Mary Montgomerie.

[3] Augusta Buckingham, died 1807.

[4] Clementina Louisa, died 18 July, 1873.

[5] Thomasine Palmer, died 1834; married to Rev. John Herman Stafford incumbent of St. Paul's, Liverpool, and had, with other issue, 2 sons,

(1) John Herman (Stafford), managing director, Yorkshire and Lancashire Railway.

(2) Brabazon.

[6] Frances Anne, died 7 June, 1831; married 19 Jan., 1820, to Rev. Patrick Brewster, who died 26 March, 1859; having had, with other issue, a daughter,

Frances, only surviving child.

[5] Susan, Mrs., Kilburne.

[6] **Elizabeth (Agnew)**, died at Tarbert, 27 Feb., 1830; married 20 May, 1792, to Rev. Austin Martin, incumbent of Tarbert, co. Kerry; he died at Drogheda, 15 May, 1831, having had 7 sons and 6 daughters of whom see below.

(7) Margaret, married to Capt. Coxon; and had a daughter.

(8) Anne, died 21 March, 1828; married 24 Oct., 1786, to Hon. Michael de Courcy, admiral of the blue (brother of John, Lord Kingsale), who died 22 Feb., 1824, leaving issue (see page 782).

(9) Avice, died unmarried

[2] Avice, born 10 June, 1718.

[3] Margaret, born 27 Oct., 1721; married to Capt. William Gun (son of Francis Gun and Roche), and had at least a daughter.

Elizabeth Gun, married to John Henry Fitzgerald, of Fortfield and Garrihees, and had an only son.

Francis Fitzgerald, of Garrihees; married Anne, daughter of Pierce Chute, of Tralee, J.P., and had issue.

ELIZABETH AGNEW (youngest daughter of Capt. Robert Agnew, of Howlish, co. Durham, named above), died at Tarbert, 27 Feb., 1830; married 20 May, 1792, to Rev. Austin Martin, incumbent of Tarbert, co. Kerry, he died at Drogheda, 15 May, 1831, having had 7 sons and 6 daughters.

(1) Austin Robert (Martin), born 4 Oct., 1793; died 20 Feb., 1795.

(2) Henry James (Martin), M.R.C.S.E., born 17 Feb., 1795; died 8 Oct., 1870; married 20 Oct. 1823, Mary, daughter of Capt. Alexander Maclean, of Hudson's Bay Company's service; she died Jan., 1842, having had 3 sons.

[1] Henry Austin (Martin), of Boston, U.S.A.; M.D., A.M.; born 23 July, 1824; died 7 Dec., 1884; married 9 August, 1848, Frances Coffin, daughter of (Hon.) Nathan Crosby, LL.D., of Lowell, Mass., U.S.A., and has had 4 sons and a daughter.

(1) **Henry Maclean (Martin)**, first named, see page 587.

THE DESCENT OF

Charles William Thorp,

F.R.C.S.I., M.D.

FROM THE

Blood Royal  **of England.**

EDWARD III., crowned 1 Feb., 1327, b. 13 Nov., 1312, d. 21 June, 1377. = Philippa, 3rd dau. of William, Count of Holland and Hainault, m. 24 Jan. 1328, d. 15 Aug. 1369.

Edmund, Duke of York, K.G., 5th son, d. at Langley, 1 Aug. 1402. = Isabel (1st wife), youngest dau. and co-heir of Peter, King of Castile, m. 1372.

Constance of Langley. = Thomas, 6th Baron le Despencer, cr. Earl of Gloucester, 1397, beheaded at Bristol, 16 Jan. 1400.

Isabel le Despencer, b. 26 July, 1400, m. 27 July 1411, d. 26 Dec. 1440. = Richard Beauchamp, Lord Bergavenny (1st husband), cr. Earl of Worcester 1420, d. 1422.

Elizabeth Beauchamp, Baroness Bergavenny, b. at Hanley Castle, 16 Dec. 1415, d. 18 June, 1447 (1st wife). = Sir Edward Nevill, sum. to parl. as Baron Bergavenny, 1450-72, d. 18 Oct. 1476.

Sir George Nevill, Lord Bergavenny, sum. to parl. 1482-92, d. 20 Sept. 1492. = Margaret (1st wife), dau. and heir of Sir Hugh Fenne, of Sculton, d. 28 Sept. 1485.

Sir Edward Nevill, of Addington Park, Kent, beheaded on Tower Hill, 9 Jan. 1538-9. = Eleanor, widow of Ralph, 8th Lord Scrope, of Masham, dau. of Andrew, Lord Windsor.

——— Royden (1st husband). = Catherine Nevill. = Clement Throckmorton, of Hanley, Warwickshire, d. 19 Oct. 1594.

A, *continued above.*

A, *continued from below.*

Catherine Nevill = Clement Throckmorton.

Martha Throckmorton, bur. at Southwick, 30 Dec. 1600, aged 49. = George Lynne, of Southwick Hall, Northan's, bur. there 29 Nov. 1617.

George Lynne, of Southwick Hall, d. 5 Nov. 1606. = Isabel, sister of Sir Anthony Forrest, of Morborn, Hunts, Knt.

Martha Lynne = John Blennerhassett, of Ballyseedy, co. Kerry, M.P. Tralee, 1661.

Robert Blennerhassett = Avice, dau. and co-heir of Jenkin Conway, d. April, 1663.

John Blennerhassett, "Black Jack" of Castle Conway, co. Kerry. = Elizabeth, 3rd dau. of Rev. Benjamin Cross, D.D., she d. 22 March, 1732.

Conway Blennerhassett, of Castle Conway, M.P. Tralee, 1723-4, b. 3 Oct. 1693, d. 7 June, 1724. = Elizabeth, dau. of Col. Harman, of Bawne, co. Longford.

Conway Blennerhassett, of Castle Conway, and of Killorglin, co. Kerry, b. 3 June, 1720. = Elizabeth, dau. of Major Thomas Lacy.

Catherine Blennerhassett = Capt. Robert Agnew, of Howlish, co. Durham.

Elizabeth Agnew, youngest dau. m. 20 May, 1792, d. 27 Feb. 1830. = Rev. Austin Martin, incumbent of Tarbert, co. Kerry, d. 15 May, 1831.

7 sons, as pages 594 and 596. | Elizabeth, m. Feb., 1820, to Richard Standish, lieut. R.N. | Anne and Jane both d. young. | Mary, m. to Pierce Leslie, of Tarbert, co. Kerry. | Charlotte Hester d. young. | Susan, b. 31 Oct., 1812, m. 1 Jan., 184[illegible] = Gabriel Thorp, M.B., d. 23 Jan., 1877.

Charles William Thorp, F.R.C.S.I., M.D., b. 9 April, 1842. = Edith, dau. of Francis Spencer, of Worksop, Notts., m. 4 Aug., 1869. | Austin Robert, born 1844, died 1860. John Gabriel, d. 1851. | Gabriel Browne, b. 5 Nov. 1855. | 1 Elizabeth Mary. 3 Alice Susan. | 2 Mary Gabriella, m. 187[illegible] to Henry W. Smyth, who d. 18[illegible]

Spencer, b. 1872. Austin, b. 1873. | Harold, b. 1875. Norman, b. 1879. | Gerald, b. 1881. Ethel. | Norah. Kathleen.

(2) Stephen Crosby, M.D., born 13 Sept., 1850.
(3) Austin Agnew, A.B., LL.B., born 3 Nov., 1851.
(4) Francis Coffin, A.B., M.D., born 22 March, 1858.
(5) Frances Moody, born 3 April, 1855; died 17 March, 1857.
[2] Alexander Donald William, born 12 Jan., 1829.
[3] Austin Maclean; died young.
(3) Edward, born 9 July, 1797; died 17 Oct., 1798.
(4) Montgomery Agnew (Martin), born 4 Sept., 1800; died at Flimby, Tralee, co Kerry, 23 Dec., 1869; married 17 Jan., 1827, Catherine, daughter of Francis M'Gillicuddy (see page 625); she died 9 Oct., 1872, having had 3 sons and 5 daughters.
[1] Austin, born 5 April, 1830; died at Shanghai, 13 Feb. ——
[2] Francis M'Gillicuddy, born 7 Jan., 1833.
[3] Montgomery Agnew (Martin), born 14 March, 1834; married 1 July, 1868, Matilda, daughter of James Crosbie Leslie, Esq., of Tarbert, co. Kerry, and has 4 sons and 3 daughters.
Montgomery Agnew (Martin), born 2 Nov., 1870.
Austin Henry, born 2 April, 1875.
Frank M'Gillicuddy, born 5 Aug., 1877.
James Crosbie, born 19 May, 1880.
Kathleen Mary M'Gillicuddy.
Annie Sarah. Matilda Leslie.
[4] Catherine Maria, born 31 Dec., 1827; died 6 Jan., 1828.
[5] Eliza Anne, born 20 Dec., 1828.
[6] Mary, born 14 May, 1831; died March, 1832.
[7] Sarah Maria, born 27 Nov. 1835; died 10 May, 1871, having married, 8 June, 1853; to Robert Ralph Smyth, of Fort Lion Castle, and left an only daughter,
Frideswide Catherine Emily.
[8] Eliza Anne, married 18 Oct., 1852, as 3rd wife, to Gorges Graham, 2nd son of William Graham, of Kingstown, co. Meath; he died 18 Aug., 1879, having had 5 sons and 4 daughters.
Gorges (Graham) born 10 Oct., 1859; William Montgomery, born 17 July, 1862; Oliver MacGillycuddy, born 19 Feb., 1865; Francis Agnew, born 21 May, 1867; died 6 June following; Francis Anthony, born 20 March, 1870; Mary Jane; Catherine Sarah Delia; Elizabeth Ida, Margaret Maria.
(5) William Wynne, born 19 May, 1802; died 3 Oct., 1820.
(6) Charles, born 19 Feb., died 1 March, 1805.
(7) Robert Agnew (Martin), rector of Moyliscar. co. West meath, born 16 Sept., 1806; died s.p. 15 July, 1875; married Frideswide Catherine Harriette, eldest daughter of Robert Sandys, Esq., of Crevaghmore, co. Longford, she died 4 April, 1880.
(8) Elizabeth, died April, 1878; married Feb., 1820, to Richard Standish, lieut. R.M., who died May, 1861, having had 7 sons and 4 daughters.
[1] Richard Nash (Standish), B.A. Trinity Coll., Dublin, incumbent of Manor Hamilton, 1868-77; born 2 Nov., 1820; married 13 Dec., 1849, Elizabeth, daughter of Lieut.-col. Charles Cox, s.p.
[2] Austin Martin (Standish), col. and adj.-gen. in Confederate Army; killed near Montery, Mexico, by Cortine's guerillas, in 1864; married 1857, Mildred, daughter of Gov. Parsons, and sister to Lieut.-gen. Parsons, and had 3 sons.
(1) Richard Adolphus, born 6 Dec., 1857; died unmarried, 3 Oct., 1884.
(2) Austin D'Arcy, of Jefferson City, Missouri, physician, born 31 Oct., 1859
(3) Monroe Parsons, of St. Louis, Missouri, born 14 Jan., 1861.
[3] John Langford (Standish) of N.S. Wales.
[4] William Henry (Standish), of Rockhampton, Queensland, married Jane
[5] Thomas, of Lexington, Missouri, major in Confederate States Army, born 25 Dec., 1829; married 29 Dec., 1868, Adelia, daughter of Joseph Shewalton, and has had 3 sons and 2 daughters.
(1) Austin Gustavus, born 13 Oct., 1869; died Sept., 1870.
(2) Glin Limerick, born 15 May, 1871.
(3) Richard Shewalton, born 8 Feb., 1877.
(4) Ellen Elizabeth.
(5) Adelia Drite.
[6] Valentine, died unmarried , 1872.
[7] Montgomery Agnew, died unmarried, 1867.
[8] Elizabeth Jane, married 17 Dec., 1862, to Rev. Charles Holte Ensell, B.A. Trin. Coll., Dublin, 1858; vicar of Lucan, 1862-71; of Arnside, Westmoreland, 1872-6; of St. Paul, Truro, &c., 1876-9; chaplain at Havre, 1879-81, &c., &c.; and has had a son and daughter,
(1) Charles Standish (Ensell); born 1 Jan., 1868.
(2) Elizabeth, died 5 Feb., 1864.
[9] Millicent Anne, married 1855, to (Hon.) Edward King Cox, member S. Australian Legislative Council; he died 25 July, 1884, having had 4 sons and 2 daughters,
(1) Richard Standish (Cox), born 1856.
(2) Elizabeth, died unmarried.
(3) Mary Constance, married to John Anderson.
[10] Jane, married 15 Sept., 1877, to John Minchin Harnett, Esq., of Glin Lodge, co. Limerick, J.P., of River View, Queenstown, co. Cork, and has a daughter,
Elizabeth Catherine (Harriett).
[11] Mary Frideswide, married 14 Oct., 1868, to Rev. Edward Augustus Lester, M.A. Trin. Coll., Dublin, 1868; vicar of Bishop's Nympton, Devon, since 1882, &c., and has 6 sons and 3 daughters.
Augustine Standish (Lester), born 12 March, 1875; Cecil, born 11 April, 1876; Charles Valentine, born 2 April, 1877; Richard Standish, born 23 May, 1878; William Alexander, born 12 May, 1879; Arthur Cyril, born 13 Dec., 1883; Elizabeth Matilda, Kathleen Maud, Millicent Mary.
(9) Anne, born 8 May, 1796; died 31 Dec. following.
(10) Jane, born 8 Sept., 1803; died 3 June, 1804.
(11) Mary, born 20 Jan., 1808; married
to Pierce Leslie, of Tarbert, co. Kerry, and had (some say 22 children) 2 sons and a daughter.
Austin Martin (Leslie).
(12) Charlotte Hester, born 20 Oct., 1809; died 5 March, 1810.
(13) Susanna, born 31 Oct., 1812; married 1 Jan., 1840, to Gabriel Thorp, M.B. Trin. Coll., Dublin; he died 28 Jan., 1877, having had 4 sons and 3 daughters
[1] Charles William (Thorp), F.R.C.S.I., M.D., born 9 April, 1842; married 4 Aug., 1869, Edith, daughter of Francis Spencer, of Worksop, Notts., and has had 6 sons and 3 daughters,
Spencer (Thorpe) born 15 Feb., 1872; Austin, born 23 Oct., 1873; Harold, born 4 April, 1875; Norman, 24 March, 1879; Gerald, born 21 January, 1881; Martin, born 3 Jan., 1883, died 25 Nov., 1884; Ethel, Norah, Kathleen.
[2] Austin Robert, born 8 Jan., 1844; died 15 March, 1860.
[3] John Gabriel, born 31 August, 1851; died 1 Nov. 1851.
[4] Gabriel Browne, born 5 Nov., 1855.
[5] Elizabeth Mary.
[6] Mary Gabriella, married 1879, to Henry W. Smyth, Esq., who died 1883.
[7] Alice Susan

BOULTON D'ARCY EDWARD, of Shell River, Manitoba, barrister-at-law, lieut.-col. 3rd regiment cavalry, active militia of Canada; 21ST IN DESCENT FROM EDWARD I.; born 2 Feb., 1814; married 29 Aug., 1838, Emily, daughter of Charles Heath, late lieut.-col. H.E.I.C.S., and has had 3 sons and 7 daughters,

[1] Charles Arckoll (Boulton), of Shell River, Manitoba, major 46th regiment Canada militia, formerly capt. H.M. 100th or Royal Canadian regiment of infantry; born 17 April, 1841; married 4 Feb., 1874, Augusta, daughter of Richard Latter, Esq., and has a daughter,
Ellen Mary (Boulton).
[2] George D'Arcy (Boulton), of Highland Park, Lake County, Illinois, U.S.A., and of Chicago, banker; born 13 June, 1844; married 16 Sept., 1868, Emily Ada, daughter of Richard J. Street, Esq., of Hamilton City, Ontario, and has had 3 sons and 5 daughters.
George Allan Heath, born 6 Jan., died 20 Sept., 1871; Reginald Arthur, born 15 Nov., died 29 Nov., 1872.
Kenneth Percival, born 7 Aug., 1876.
Ethel D'Arcy. Alice Marjorie. Elsie Beatrice.
Helen Wray. Muriel Heath.
[3] D'Arcy Edward, of St. Louis, Missouri, U.S.A., born 9 Jan. 1852.
[4] Agnes Mary.
[5] Emily (Boulton), married 30 June, 1868, to John Robinson Cartwright, of Toronto, Canada, barrister-at-law (son of John Cartwright, of Kingston, barrister), and has 2 sons and a daughter,
John Macaulay (Cartwright), born Nov., 1872.
Stephen, born Oct., 1874. Mabel.
[6] Mary Jane (Boulton), died 4 July, 1874; married 26 Jan., 1858, to Roland Clement Strickland, Esq., of Lakefield, Ontario, Canada.
[7] Marjorie Wallace.
[8] Elizabeth Frances, married to Thomas Grimshawe, jun., of Whiteside Cove, Walhalla, North Carolina, U.S.A.
[9] Alice Sayer, married to Charles Nield, of Dunedin, Florida.
[10] Sarah Maude.

THE DESCENT OF
D'ARCY EDWARD BOULTON, ESQ.,
OF SHELL RIVER, MANITOBA,
FROM THE BLOOD ROYAL OF ENGLAND.

EDWARD I., so named after Edward the Confessor; born at Westminster, 17 June, 1232, knighted at Burgos, 1254, created Earl of Chester; crowned at Westminster, 19 Aug, 1274, king of England, lord of Ireland, duke of Aquitaine; he subdued the principality of Wales, 1283, claimed and exercised feudal superiority over Scotland; died at Burgh-on-the-Sands, Cumberland, 7 July, 1307, buried in Westminster Abbey; by his 1st wife, Eleanor, daughter of Ferdinand III., king of Castile, who died 27 Nov., 1290, he had issue; their descendant

D'ARCY BOULTON, one of H.M. Judges in Upper Canada, (3rd son of Henry Boulton, by his wife, Mary Preston, see page 579,) born 1762; died 1834; married 18 Dec., 1782, Elizabeth, 3rd and youngest daughter and co-heir of Mr. Serjeant James Forster (by Susannah his wife, daughter and co-heir of Sir John Strange, Master of the Rolls); she died , having had 6 sons and 2 daughters (*a*),

[1*a*] **D'Arcy** (Boulton), of Toronto, auditor-general of Canada, of whom (see page 599).

[2a] Henry John (Boulton), attorney-general of Canada, and chief justice of Newfoundland, afterwards of Toronto; born in London 22 June, 1790; died at Toronto 18 June, 1870; married 29 April, 1818, Eliza, daughter of Ephraim Jones, Esq., of Brockville, Ontario; she died 21 May, 1868, having had (with others, who died in infancy, 4 sons and 5 daughters (*b*).

(1*b*-2*a*) William Henry Forster (Boulton), born 16 Jan., 1819; died in infancy.

(2*b*-2*a*) Henry John (Boulton), of Toronto, born 26 April, 1824; died June, 1876; married 23 Sept., 1852, Charlotte, only child of Henry Rudyerd, of Whitby, Yorks, lieut. 15th regiment, and has had 4 sons and 4 daughters,

[1] Henry Rudyerd (Boulton), born 18 Nov., 1856.

[2] Reginald Rudyerd, born 20 Oct., 1859.

[3] Charles Rudyerd, born 27 June, 1861; died 28 Dec., 1863.

[4] Wolfrid Rudyerd (a twin with his sister Marion), born 19 Oct., 1870.

[5] Madeleine, died 11 Sept., 1865.

[6] Charlotte Constance Rudyerd.

[7] Elizabeth Rudyerd.

[8] Marion Rudyerd (a twin with her brother Wolfrid).

(3*b*-2*a*) Charles Knightley, born 27 Sept., 1827; thrown from his horse and killed 21 Dec., 1846.

(4*b*-2*a*) George D'Arcy (Boulton), alderman and president of the City Council of Toronto, born 7 May, 1834; married 6 Oct., 1860, Juliana Mary, eldest daughter of Thomas Gibbs Ridout, Esq., of Toronto, and has 2 sons and 4 daughters,

Gerald D'Arcy (Boulton), born 5 Oct., 1867.
Arthur Henry, born 29 Nov., 1868.
Florence Mary. Laura Milicent.
Helen Madeline. Adeline Marion.

(5*b*-2*a*) Harriet Eliza, married 22 May, 1843, as 2nd wife to Clarke Gamble, of Pinehurst, Toronto, Esq., barrister-at-law, and has 6 sons and 2 daughters,

[1] John Henry (Gamble), capt. 17th regiment, born 12 July, 1844; died 14 July, 1879.

[2] Francis Clarke (Gamble), born 23 Oct., 1848; married Sarah Elleanor, daughter of Clarke, Esq., and has had a daughter, who died young.

[3] Alleyne Woodbridge, born 26 Dec., 1850.

[4] Raynald D'Arcy, born 12 May, 1853.

[5] Harry Dudley, born 12 April, 1855.

[6] Arthur Gordon, born 16 May, 1858.

[7] Elizabeth Sophia (Gamble), married , to Charles Edward Bowker, Esq., of Whittlesea, Cambridge, and has a son and daughter,

Edward Clarke (Bowker). Catherine Louisa.

[8] Harriet Emily (Gamble), married 27 April, 1880, to Isidore Frederick Hellmuth, barrister-at-law, of the Inner Temple.

(6*b*-2*a*) Sophia, died 3 Nov., 1871; married 15 June, 1842, to James Forlong, col. 43rd light infantry, and had 4 sons and 3 daughters.

[1] Herbert James (Forlong), of Toronto, born 15 Dec., 1846.

[2] Arthur Henry, born .

[3] Charles Albert, lieut. R.N.

[4] George Frederick. [5] Sophia Eliza.

[6] Alice, married to Rev. Charles, of , G Bethune, M.A., son of late bishop of Toronto, and has a son,

Herbert (Bethune).

[7] Agnes Georgina.

(7*b*-2*a*) Elizabeth, died 20 April, 1844; married, , to (Hon.) John Hillyard Cameron, of the Meadows, Toronto, and had an only son.

Hillyard Henry Angus (Cameron), major the Bedford regiment since 1881; adjutant to auxiliary forces, 1875-81; born, 29 March, 1844; married , Mary, daughter of Ferguson, Esq., and has 2 daughters.

(8) Clara Louisa, married 5 Oct., 1847, as 2nd wife to John Cayley, Esq., formerly of Toronto (6th son of John Cayley, of St. Petersburgh, see Foster's *Baronetage*), and has 2 sons and 2 daughters.

[1] Claud Thornton (Cayley), of Bickley, Kent, born 9 June, 1854; married , and has a son and daughter; a son, born 2 July, 1882; a daughter, born 16 July, 1883.

[2] Francis Osmund, of Toronto, born 30 Sept., 1856.

[3] Adela Sidney (Cayley), married 8 May, 1873, to Christopher Wolston, M.D., of Croydon, Surrey, and has a daughter,

Adela Maud (Wolston).

[4] Clara Louisa.

(9*b*-2*a*) Charlotte Augusta, married 1 May, 1873, to William Henry Crawford, Esq., of Quebec, and has 2 daughters,

Charlotte Augusta (Crawford). Clara Mildred.

[3a] Charles (Boulton), born 15 June, 1797; died 27 Feb., 1809.

[4a] George Strange (Boulton), of Coburg, Upper Canada, barrister-at-law; for 26 years member of the Legislative Council; lieut.-col. of militia; born 11 Sept., 1797; died 13 Feb., 1869; married 1st, 29 Jan., 1824, Elizabeth, daughter of Henry Boulton, Esq., of Moulton, by his 3rd wife (see p. 582), she died 4 Oct., 1838; he married 2nd, 23 April, 1840, Anne Maria, widow of adj.-gen. Nicholas Fairley Beck, daughter of Jonathan Walton, Esq., she died, s.p., 12 Dec., 1862; by his 1st wife he had a son and 2 daughters.

(1) Edward Trevor (Boulton), born 11 Feb., 1830; died unmarried.

(2) Harriet.

(3) Georgiana (Boulton), died 8 May, 1864; married 10 July, 1848, to Rev. John Walton Romeyn Beck, rector of Peterborough, Canada (son of Nicholas Fairly Beck, adj.-gen.), and had 7 sons and a daughter.

[1] George Fairley (Beck), born 10 Jan., 1851.

[2] Harry Thatcher, born 21 Aug., 1853.

[3] Arthur Romeyn, lieut. R.N., born 11 Feb. 1855; lost in H.M.S. *Atalanta*.

[4] Nicholas du Bois, born 4 May, 1857.

[5] Geoffrey Strange, born 6 June, 1859.

[6] Charles Beauclerc, born 18 Sept., 1863.

[7] Anna Maria.

[5a] James (Boulton), of Toronto, barrister-at-law, born 27 July, 1801; died Aug., 1878; married 1st, 20 May, 1823, Susannah, daughter of Elisha Beaman, Esq., she died July, 1827, having had a son and daughter,

(1) D'Arcy (Boulton), born 29 March, 1825; died s.p. 14 Feb., 1875; married Louisa, daughter of Thomas Corbett, Esq., of Perth.

(2) Esther.

JAMES BOULTON married 2nd, 16 Feb., 1830, Harriet, daughter of Dr. Thorn; she died Jan., 1839, having had 2 sons and 2 daughters.

(3) Alexander Gregg, born 26 Nov., 1830, died April, 1869.

(4) Forster James, born 21 Sept., 1832, died married , Jane, daughter of Col. Graham, and had a son,

Claude Forster (Boulton).

(5) Susannah Margaret, married , 1855, to John Small, Esq., of Toronto, s.p.

(6) Harriet Eliza.

JAMES BOULTON married 3rd, 18 May, 1843, Margaret Nielina, daughter of Major Thomas Fortye, 8th regiment, (by his wife Jane Athol Gordon, daughter of John Campbell, Esq.), and had 3 sons, and 2 daughters.

(7) James Lorn Fitzroy, born 29 April, 1848; died 21 Oct., 1863.

(8) Eustace Colin Campbell, born 5 July, 1853; died 28 July, 1854.
(9) Frederick Campbell Melfort, born 25 Nov., 1850; married 1 June, 1881, Amy or Emma Augusta, daughter of William Dickson, Esq., of Woodlawn, Niagara, and grand-daughter of W. H. Draper, C.B., chief justice of Canada, and has a daughter,
Florence Athol Gordon, born 17 May, 1882.
(10) Adeline Georgina Mary, died 13 Feb., 1883; married 13 April, 1868, to George Lee le Mesurier Taylor, lieut. Bedford regt., and had a son.
George Arthur Campbell (Taylor), born 22 Jan., 1869.
(11) Edith Louisa, married 15 Nov., 1871, to Samuel Nordheimer, Esq., of Genedyth, Toronto, and has 2 sons and 7 daughters.
Stuart Fitzroy Boulton (Nordheimer), born 16 Dec. 1872.
Samuel May (Nordheimer), born 20 May, 1876.
Julie Niellina Boulton. Athol Gordon Boulton.
Matilda Adeline Boulton.
Errol Louise Boulton (twin with) Edith Vera Boulton.
Cecil Evelyn Boulton. Estelle Mary Boulton.
[6] William (Boulton) in holy orders; born 1 Dec., 1805; died 31 May, 1834; married 14 Oct., 1829, Frances, daughter of Capt. Carew, R.N., and had 2 sons and 2 daughters.
(1) William Somerville (Boulton), of Toronto, C.E., born 21 July, 1830; drowned in s.s. *Hungarian*, off Cape Sable, Newfoundland, 19 Feb., 1860-3; married 30 May, 1854, Caroline Howorth, daughter of Col. Graham, of Devonshire Terrace, Hyde Park, having had a son and 2 daughters.
John Graham (Boulton), born 12 Oct., 1856.
Dora Caroline. Anna Frances.
(2) Henry Carew, born 23 Sept. 1833; married 1864, Martha Jane Cowin, daughter of Hill, Esq., and has had 2 daughters.
Frances Charlotte (Boulton).
Anne Hill, died young.
(3) Caroline, died 18 March, 1874; married 21 Jan., 1857, to G. Wilgress, Esq. (son of Col. Wilgress, of Montreal), and had 2 sons and 2 daughters.
(4) Anne (a twin with Henry Carew), died young.
[7b] Elizabeth (Boulton), died 11 April, 1789.
[8b] Harriet Elizabeth, born 29 Oct., 1803.

D'ARCY BOULTON, of Toronto, auditor-general of Canada, born 3 June, 1785; died 20 April, 1846; married, 1809, Sarah Anne, daughter of Christopher Robinson, Esq., of Kingston, Canada; she died 20 Aug., 1863, having had 5 sons and 3 daughters (*c*).

[1c] John Andrew (Boulton), of Toronto, born July, 1810; died unmarried 1829.
[2c] William Henry (Boulton), of the Grange, Toronto, barrister-at-law, many years mayor of Toronto, and representative of that city during several parliaments; born 19 April, 1812; died s.p. 1 Feb., 1874; married
Harriette Elizabeth, daughter of Thos. Dixon, Esq., of Amsterdam, who resided as consul of the Netherlands in Boston, Mass.; she re-married 30 Sept., 1875, to Professor Goldwin Smith.
[3c] **D'Arcy Edward** (Boulton), first-named (see page 597).
[4c] Beverley Robert, died unmarried, 1840.
[5c] John Boulton (Boulton), of Toronto, born 12 Oct., 1829; married, 1 Oct. 1857, Martha Rowan, daughter of William Gamble, Esq., and has 4 sons and 5 daughters.
(1) Christopher Robinson (Boulton), born 10 Sept., 1859.
(2) Arthur St. George, born 25 Oct., 1862.
(3) Herman Eugene, born 21 Dec., 1864.
(4) John D'Arcy, born 3 Oct., 1873.
(5) Mary Augusta.
(6) Laura Louisa Brenchley.
(7) Emily Grace.
(8) Amy Madeleine.
(9) Edith Adelaide
[6c] Mary Sayer (Boulton), died 23 Aug., 1837; married 10 Dec., 1833, as 1st wife to Clarke Gamble, Esq., of Toronto, barrister-at-law, and had a son and daughter.
(1) John Clarke (Gamble), born 31 July; died 4 Aug., 1837. (2) Sarah.
[7c] Emma Robinson (Boulton), married
to Hon. William Cayley, of Toronto, barrister-at-law (2nd son of John Cayley, Esq., of St. Petersburgh, merchant, and afterwards of Beddington, Surrey, see Foster's *Baronetage*), and has 10 children, of whom are,
(1) John D'Arcy (Cayley), rector of St. George's, Toronto, born , 1837.
(2) Edward.
(3) Francis, born , 1845.
(4) Beverley, born , 1855.
(5) Hugh St. Quentin, born 1857.
(6) Harriet Anne, married to James Strachan Cartwright, barrister-at-law.
(7) Mary, married 23 Aug., 1866, to William Glascott, capt. late 30th regiment, and has two sons and three daughters,
William (Glascott), born 29 June, 1869.
Francis James. Ethel. Amy. Eva.
(8) Sophia Emma.
[8c] Sarah Anne (Boulton), married to Charles Wallace Heath, Esq., of Toronto, barrister-at-law, and has 5 sons.
Charles D'Arcy (Heath).
Stuart. Beverley. D'Arcy. William

HILLIARD, WILLIAM ROBERT, lieut. R.E., 19TH IN DESCENT FROM EDWARD III.; born 4 Jan., 1861; married 22 Nov., 1882, Lily, only daughter of Henry Mackinnon, Esq., of Mussourie, India.

THE DESCENT OF
WILLIAM ROBERT HILLIARD, LIEUT. R.E.,
FROM THE BLOOD ROYAL OF ENGLAND.

EDWARD III., KING OF ENGLAND, Earl of Chester 1320, Duke of Aquitaine, Count of Ponthieu and Montreuil, 1325; crowned at Westminster in his father's lifetime, 1 Feb., 1327; defeated the Scots at Halidon Hill, 1333. In 1339 he assumed the style of "King of France and England and Lord of Ireland," and quartered the arms of France in the first quarter; gained a great naval victory over the French off Sluys, 1340, and won the celebrated battle of Cressy 26 Aug., 1346; 17 Oct. following, the Scots were defeated at Neville Cross, and King David II. taken prisoner to London, where he remained nearly 11 years. Instituted the order of the Garter 1349. His son, the BLACK PRINCE, defeated the French at the battle of Poictiers, 19 Sept., 1356, and brought King John prisoner to London, where he remained nearly five years (for further particulars see *Royal Lineage* Foster's *Peerage*). The King died at Sheen, Surrey, 21 June, 1377, having had issue; their descendant

CATHERINE BLENNERHASSETT, (daughter of Robert Blennerhassett and Avice Conway, see page 566), married, 1st, to Richard MacLoughlin, of Ballydowney (son of Capt. Richard MacLoughlin by Elizabeth Pue, of Dublin); she re-married to John Conway and had a daughter, Mildred Conway, wife of Thomas Jeffcott, of Tonarigh. By her 1st husband she had 2 daughters.

[1] Elizabeth (MacLoughlin), married to Capt. Myles Martin, of Lurgan, co. Down, and of City of Cork, 1733; he died 1735, having had a son and 3 daughters.
- (1) Henry (Martin).
- (2) Eleanor, married 1744, to William Hilliard (son of Christopher Hilliard, of Baltygarron & Listrim); he was buried at Ballynahaglish Church, 18 Aug., 1747.
- (3) Catherine (Martin). (4) Agnes.

[2] Avice (MacLoughlin), married to John Mason, of Bally MacElligot (said to be great grandson of Sir John Mason, of Sion House, Middlesex, by Elizabeth, daughter of John Touchet, Lord Audley), and had 3 sons and 3 daughters.
- (1) James (Mason), married Catherine, daughter of Pierce Power, of Elm Grove (by Catherine O'Hara), and had, with other issue, a son and daughter.
  - [1] John (Mason), of Ballydowney, married 1764, Jane, youngest daughter of Thomas Hurly, Esq.
  - [2] Elizabeth (Mason), married 15 Nov., 1760, to Dr. Robert Emmett, and had 3 sons and a daughter.
    - (1) Christopher Temple (Emmett), died unmarried.
    - (2) Thomas Addis (Emmett), solicitor-general New York State, married, and had issue.
    - (3) Robert, "The Irish Patriot," hanged for treason 1803.
    - (4) ——— (daughter), grandmother of Viscountess Doneraile.
- (2) Richard (Mason), had at least a son and daughter.
  - [1] Richard, married Jane Gorham, and had a son, who married a Miss Sparks, and a daughter, Alice (see also p. 378).
  - [2] Avis or Alice, married to Walter Eagar, of Killarney (see page 593).
- (3) John (Mason), died unmarried.
- (4) Catherine, married to her cousin Francis Spring (see page 592).
- (5) **Barbara (Mason)**, married to William Hilliard, of whom immediately.
- (6) Ellen (Mason).

BARBARA MASON (2nd daughter of John Mason, aforesaid), married to William Hilliard, of Listrim, co. Kerry (great grandson of Capt. Robert Hilliard, of Baltygarron, co. Kerry); he died 1769, aged 29, having had 2 sons and 4 daughters.

[1] **Robert (Hilliard)**, of whom presently.
[2] Christopher (Hilliard), died 1806; married Ellen, daughter of Hilliard, of ; she died 1811, having had 4 sons and 2 daughters.
(1) William (Hilliard), capt. 89th regiment; died s.p.
(2) Robert, lieut., killed in the Peninsula; s.p.
(3) Morgan, lieut., killed in the Peninsula; s.p.
(4) Christopher, capt. 5th regiment; died in Canada.
(5) Harriet (Hilliard), married to James Royse Veilding, Esq., and has issue in America (see page 571).
(6) Barbara (Hilliard), married to Francis Twiss, and had 2 daughters, Ellen and Elizabeth Barbara.
[3] Avis (Hilliard), married 1st to her first cousin, John Mason (?), she re-married to John O'Connell, of Newtown, co. Cork (son of Morgan O'Connell, of Kiltannon, and Margaret Leppard); she married lastly to Major Henry Conyngham, 20th regiment of foot. By her 2nd husband she had at least a son and daughter.
(1) Morgan (O'Connell), married Christiana, daughter of Henry Stevens, Esq., of Winscot, Devon (niece of Henry, Lord Rolle).
(2) Mary (O'Connell), married to James Hickson (2nd son of John Hickson, of Tierbrim), and had a son and 2 daughters.
[1] John James (Hickson), died 1839; married Sarah, daughter of Rev. James Day, rector of Tralee and vicar-general of Ardfert (see p. 446), and had, with other issue, 2 sons and a daughter.
(1) James John (Hickson), of Hillville, co. Kerry, J.P.; died 19 Oct., 1865; married 4 Oct., 1841, his cousin, Deborah Godfrey, daughter of Rev. Edward Day, rector of Kilgobbin (see p. 446), and had a son and 5 daughters.
[1] Edward Day (Hickson), born 10 Jan., 1856.
[2] Deborah Margarette.
[3] Sarah Mary. [4] Lucy Eliza.
[5] Edwardina, married to Thomas A. Mulvany, C.E., and has a daughter, Isabel Day.
[6] Jane Maria, married 29 Nov., 1881, to John Spring, L.S.A. Lond., L.M., and has a son and daughter.
Arthur Day (Spring), born 4 July, 1883.
Eva Mary.
(2) John. (3) Mary Agnes (Hickson).
[2] Ellen (Hickson), died July, 1832; married 1818, to her cousin Morgan O'Connell Busteed, M.D., of Tralee; he died without issue 27 Jan., 1830.
[3] Maria, died 12 Sept., 1813; married 10 May, 1808, to her cousin, William Hilliard Busteed, of Castlebar (see below); he died 5 Feb., 1824, having had at least a son and 4 daughters.
(1) John William (Busteed), of Castle Gregory, Tralee, J.P., L.R.C.S.I., 1843; born 20 July, 1816, unmarried.
(2) Catharine.
(3) Frances, died unmarried.
(4) Barbara, died unmarried.
(5) Ellen, died unmarried.
[4] Mary (Hilliard), married to Major Richard Ellis, 66th regt., and had, with other issue, a son

THOMAS ELLIS, a master in Chancery, Ireland, M.P. Dublin (June) 1820-6; died 1832; married Dymphna, daughter of Col. Wm. Thomas Monsell, of Tervoe (see Foster's *Peerage*, B. EMLY), and had, with other issue, a son,
RICHARD ELLIS, of Glenasrone, co. Limerick, J.P., M.A. Trin. Coll., Dublin; born 1805; died 1879; married 1st, 1829, Frances Anne, 2nd daughter of Rev. Robert Conway Dobbs, of Castle Dobbs, co. Antrim; she died ; he married 2ndly, 1852, Mary, eldest daughter of Henry Chandler, Esq., of Buckingham; she died ; he married 3rdly, Louisa Theodora Blennerhassett, daughter of Edward Supple Eagar, Esq. (see page 568). By his 1st wife he had, with other issue, a son,
Thomas Ellis, of Glenasrone, co. Limerick, M.A. Trin. Coll., Dublin, 1879; incumbent of Killylea, co. Antrim, since 1858; born , 1830; married 1854, Louisa Jane, eldest daughter of John Echlin Mathews, lieut.-col. co. Down militia; and has, with other issue, a son,
Richard Ellis.
[5] Catherine (Hilliard), died Feb., 1830; married , 1780, to John Busteed; he died March, 1819, having had 5 sons and a daughter.
(1) Richard, 1782, died s.p.
(2) William Hilliard (Busteed), of Castlebar, died 5 Feb., 1824, aged 40; married 10 May 1808 Maria, daughter of James Hickson, Esq., of Fermoyle; she died 12 Sept., 1813, having had a son and 4 daughters (see above).
(3) George Washington Busteed, born 1788; married Anne Gale, and had at least 2 sons.
[1] Richard, a judge in Alabama (4th son).
[2] John, had at least 3 daughters.
(4) Morgan O'Connell (Busteed), M.D.; born 1789; died s.p. 27 Jan., 1830; married 1818, his cousin, Ellen, daughter of John James Hickson, Esq.; she died , July, 1832.
(5) John (Busteed), born , 1791; died 14 July, 1863; married 1st, his cousin, Mary Ellis, who died s.p. 1839; he married 2ndly, 1840, Isabella, daughter of Donald MacKay, of Newry; she died May, 1849; he married 3rdly, Mary Fitzgerald, who died s.p. 25 Dec., 1879; by his 2nd wife he had 3 daughters.
Anne, Mary, Isabella, all unmarried.
(6) Barbara, died s.p., married 1834, as 2nd wife, to her cousin, John Busteed Knox, Esq., of Ennis, co. Clare.
[6] Christina (Hilliard), died unmarried.

ROBERT HILLIARD, of Listrim; born 1742; died 1798; married 1764, Mary, daughter of Robert Hewson, of Castle Hewson, co. Limerick; she died 1814, having had 6 sons and 6 daughters.

[1] **William (Hilliard)**, of whom presently.
[2] Robert, died s.p. 1801.
[3] George, died s.p. 1869; married Mary, daughter of Giles, Esq.; she died 1860.
[4] John, of Ballydunled; died 1860; married (sett. 19 Jan., 1824) Anne, daughter of Robert Hickson, Esq., of Fermoyle, and had an only daughter,
Catherine (Hilliard), died 22 June, 1871; married 1843, as 1st wife to Major Oliver Day Stokes, of Castle Ballymalis and Carairaig, co. Kerry (see p. 438), and has had 3 sons and 3 daughters.
(1) Henry (Stokes), lieut. 38th regt.; died unmarried 26 Dec., 1872.

(2) William Edward, 14th Hussars; born Feb., 1852; died 27 Sept., 1878.
(3) Oliver Adrian, R.N.; born 14 Dec., 1854.
(4) Annie Jane.
(5) Elizabeth Emily.
(6) Kathleen Emily, married 3 Nov. 1883, to Capt. James White Thurburn, R.E.
[5] Christopher (Hilliard), died 1821; married Ellen, daughter of Thomas Collis, of Barrow; she died, having had 2 sons and 2 daughters.
(1) John (Hilliard), married , Elizabeth, daughter of John Creagh, of Dromartin, co. Kerry
(2) Robert, died s.p.
(3) Elizabeth, married 23 April, 1835, to Rev. John Kerin, rector of O'Brennan, &c.; he died 4 March, 1873, having had a son and 3 daughters.
[1] John (Kerin), born 10 Dec., 1837; died unmarried, 19 Jan. 1877.
[2] Ellen, died young, 1844.
[3] Elizabeth Avis.
[4] Catharine Collis (Kerin), married 8 July, 1874, to E C Morris, Esq.
(4) Mary.
[6] Henry (Hilliard), of Tubrid, captain 28th regiment; served in the Peninsula and at Waterloo; born ; died 27 Dec., 1874; married , 1836, Catherine, daughter of J Taylor, Esq., of ; she died April, 1841, leaving an only child.
JANE (HILLIARD), married 18 Sept., 1862, to John George Hewson, Esq., of Tubrid House, Ardfert, co. Kerry, and had 4 sons and a daughter.
Henry Hilliard (Hewson), born 9 July, 1863.
George Francis, born 30 Jan., 1868; died young.
John Alexander, twin with Thomas Vincent, born 29 Dec., 1869.
Laura Georgina.
[7] Barbara, married to Samuel Sealy, of Maglass, co. Kerry, and died s.p., 1832.
[8] Lilias, died s.p.
[9] Catherine, died ; married to Jeremiah Lawlor, Esq., of Tralee; he died having had, with other issue, 5 sons.
(1) Michael, of Tralee, born March, 1809, died s.p., 23 March, 1880; married , 1854, Lucinda, daughter of Capt. David Morphy, of Tralee (see Herbert, of Brewsterfield).
(2) Robert (Lawlor), died unmarried
(3) William, M.D., of Tralee, born 1 April, 1815; died s.p., 28 Aug., 1883; married Margaret Elmslie, daughter of Capt. James Aaron Roy.
(4) John, born 3 Oct., 1818; married 21 July, 1846, Catharine, elder daughter and co-heiress of Col. John Eliot Cairnes, K.H., J.P. Tyrone, and has had 7 sons and 4 daughters.
[1] John Elliot Cairnes (Lawlor), Royal Irish Constabulary, born 15 Oct., 1848.
[2] William Hamilton, born 15 Aug., 1850, married Mary Ellen 2nd daughter of Robert Martin of Kilbrony, co. Down, J.P., and has issue
[3] George Hilliard, born 26 January, 1857; died 26 March, 1858
[4] Hugh Jackson (Lawlor), in Ho., B.A., B.D., Trin. Coll., Dublin, born 11 Dec., 1860.
[5] Thomas Hamilton Jones, born
[6] Arthur Cairnes, born
[7] Henry Cairnes, born
[8] Catherine Hilliard, married to David Ellis of Creeve house, Newry, and has issue
[9] Susan May, married to Rev. J. N. Shearman, and has issue
[10] Annie Constance Gwynne, born 16 July, 1859; died, 22 Nov., 1875.
[11] Lucy Elizabeth Cairnes
(5) Edward (Lawlor), of Dublin, solicitor, born 16 March, 1820; married 8 Feb., 1847, his cousin Ellen, youngest daughter of William Lawlor, and has an only surviving daughter, Fanny.
[10] Ellen, died unmarried.
[11] Elizabeth, died 10 Feb., 1871; married 11 Feb., 1805, to Major the Hon. Edward de Moleyns (see page 662); he died 31 July, 1841, aged 63, having had 3 sons and 2 daughters.
[12] Mary, died unmarried.

WILLIAM HILLIARD, of Listrim, co. Kerry, J.P., capt. Limerick militia; died January, 1833; married 11 April, 1804, Margaret Agnes, daughter of Arthur Herbert, of Brewsterfield (see page 771); she died 19 April, 1862, having had 6 sons and 4 daughters

[1] Robert, born 21 Nov., 1805; died 11 Sept., 1824.
[2] Arthur Herbert, born 26 Nov., 1807; died 23 May, 1826.
[3] William (Hilliard), of Cahirslee, co. Kerry, J.P., born 24 Dec., 1811; died 29 Nov., 1879; married 14 Feb., 1860, Sarah Louisa, daughter of Frederick Nassau Alexander, Esq., and had 3 sons and 5 daughters.
(1) **William Robert** first named (see page 600).
(2) George, born 9 Oct., 1862.
(3) Arthur Herbert, born 18 June, 1872.
(4) Mary Elizabeth.
(5) Gertrude Anne.
(6) Margaret Herbert.
(7) Louisa Lilias Lees.
(8) Frances Trousdell.
[4] George (Hilliard), capt. 18th regt., born 11 April, 1814; died s.p. 16 Dec., 1871.
[5] Bastable Herbert (Hilliard), born 19 March, 1819.
[6] John Hewson, born 21 Sept., 1826; died 2 June, 1827.
[7] Barbara, died unmarried 9 Jan., 1828.
[8] Mary.
[9] Gertrude.
[10] Margaret, died unmarried 22 Aug., 1882.

BOURCHIER, MAJOR-GENERAL SIR GEORGE, R.A., K.C.B. 1872, served in Gwalior campaign, commanded field battery Indian mutiny, and a frontier district Bengal 1868-73; retired full-pay colonel Royal Artillery; 20TH IN DESCENT FROM EDWARD I.; born 23 Aug., 1821; married 1st, 16 July, 1854, Georgiana Clemenson, daughter of John Graham Lough, Esq., of London; she died 2 March, 1868, leaving 3 sons and a daughter.

(1) George Lough, born 29 July, 1855; married 11 Oct., 1879, Mary Catherine, daughter of late Rev. Barcroft Boake, principal Colombo academy.
[2] Edward Herbert, born 24 Nov., 1856.
[3] Arthur Charles Francis, born 15 April, 1864.
[4] Ina Maude Mary.

GEN. BOURCHIER married 2nd, 23 May, 1872, Margaret Murchison, daughter of Col. Bartleman; she died 13 July, 1881, having had a son,

[5] Herbert Eustace, born 13 Jan., 1874.

Bramfield Lodge, St. Margarets, Twickenham.

THE DESCENT OF
MAJOR-GENERAL SIR GEORGE BOURCHIER K.C.B.,
FROM THE BLOOD ROYAL OF ENGLAND.

EDWARD I., so named after Edward the Confessor; born at Westminster, 17 June, 1239; knighted at Burgos, 1254, created Earl of Chester; crowned at Westminster, 19 Aug., 1274, king of England, lord of Ireland, duke of Aquitaine; he subdued the principality of Wales 1283, claimed and exercised feudal superiority over Scotland; died at Burgh-on-the-Sands, Cumberland, 7 July, 1307, buried in Westminster Abbey; he married 1st, 1254, Eleanor, daughter of Ferdinand III., king of Castile; she died 27 Nov., 1290, leaving issue (see Foster's *Peerage*). The king married 2ndly, at Canterbury, 8 Sept., 1299, Margaret, daughter of Philip III. of France; she died 14 Feb., 1317, buried in Grey Friars, London, having had, with other issue, a son,

THOMAS, OF BROTHERTON (Yorks), where he was born 1 June, 1300; had a grant of the earldom of Norfolk, 16 Dec., 1312; marshal of England by patent 10 Feb., 1315, to him and the heirs male of his body; constable of Norwich Castle; died 1338, buried in St. Edmund Bury; married 1st, Alice, daughter of Sir Roger Haleys, of Harwich, Essex; and 2nd, Mary, widow of William, Lord Braose of Gower daughter of William, Lord Roos; (she re-married to Sir Ralph Cobham, Knt., and died 1362). By his 1st wife he had 2 daughters, of whom the elder,

MARGARET, created Duchess of Norfolk for life by charter dated 29 Sept., 1397 died 24 March, 1399; married 1st to John Lord Segrave; had summons to parliament 29 Nov. (10 Edw. III.), 1336, to 15 Nov. (25 Edw. III.), 1351; he made his will at Bretby, Palm Sunday, 1352; proved at Lambeth 20 July, 1353. The Duchess, re-married to Sir Walter Manny, K.G., lord of the town of Manny, in Cambray; he founded the Carthusian Monastery, now Charter House School, about 1371: he died 1372. The eldest daughter, viz.,

ELIZABETH SEGRAVE, died 1376; married to John, 4th Lord Mowbray, of Axholme: had summons to Parliament 14 Aug., 1362, to 20 Jan., 1366; he was slain near Constantinople on his way to the Holy Land 9 Oct., 1368, having had, with 2 sons, at least 4 daughters.

[1] Jane (Mowbray), married to Sir Thomas Grey, of Heton, Northumberland.
[2] Eleanor, married to John, Lord Welles, 5th baron; had summons to parliament from 20 Jan., 1376 to 26 Feb., 1421; was in the retinue of King John in the expedition to Flanders, 27 Edward III., &c., and had, with a son, 2 daughters, of whom the elder,
Margaret, see below.
[3] Margaret, married to Sir Thomas Lucy, Knt.
[4] Alianora, married to Roger, Lord Delawarr.

MARGARET WELLES, died 29 May, 1422; married 1st to John, Lord de Huntingfield, who had summons to parliament 14 Aug., 1362, to 6 April, 1369; she re-married before 1376 to Sir Stephen Scrope, 2nd Baron Scrope, of Masham; served in the French wars; went to the Holy Land, and was knighted at Alexandria 1365; summoned to parliament 1392-1406; died 25 Jan., 1405-6; buried in St. Stephen's Chapel in York Cathedral; will dated 5-7 Jan., 1405-6; proved 25 Jan., 1406-7; had, with other issue, a son,

SIR JOHN SCROPE, 4th Baron Scrope of Masham, heir to his brother Geoffrey; restored to the barony, and summoned to parliament from 7 Jan., 1426, to 26 May, 1455; sworn a privy councillor 28 Feb., 1424; ambassador to the King of Spain and the King of the Romans 1428; to Scotland 1429; treasurer of England 1432; died 15 Nov., 1455; buried in York Minster; married Elizabeth, daughter of Sir Thomas Chaworth, of Wiverton, Notts, Knt.; took the veil after her husband's death; she died 1466, leaving, with other issue, a daughter,

ELIZABETH SCROPE, married to Sir Henry Scrope, 4th Baron Scrope of Bolton; had summons to parliament 3 Dec., 1441, to May 1455; born at Bolton 4 June, 1418; died 14 Jan., 1459, having had, with other issue, a daughter,

ELIZABETH SCROPE, died 12 June, 1503; buried at Stoke Rochford, co. Linc., mon. inscription; married 1st to Sir John Bigod; 2nd, to Henry Rochford, Esq., of Stoke Rochford, co. Linc.; and lastly, to Oliver St. John, of Lydiard Tregoz, who made his will 2 March, proved 10 April, 1497; had, with 3 daughters, a son,

SIR JOHN ST. JOHN, knighted by Henry VII. in 1487 for his services in the battle of Stoke 16 June of that year, when Lambert Simnel and his adherents were defeated; died 1 Sept., 1512; married Johanna, daughter and heir of Sir John Iwardby, of Farley, Hants, and Ewell, Surrey (see p. 5), and had, with other issue, a son,

JOHN ST. JOHN, in ward to Sir Richard Carew, of Beddington, Surrey, who married him to his daughter Margaret, by whom he had a son, viz.,

NICHOLAS ST. JOHN, of Lydiard Tregoz, married Elizabeth, daughter of Sir Richard Blount, of Maple Durham, Oxon., lieut. of the Tower, and had, with other issue, 2 sons.

[1] Sir John (St. John), married Lucy, daughter and heir of Sir Walter Hungerford, of Farley, Wilts (she re-married to Sir Anthony Hungerford), and had, with other issue, a daughter,
Barbara (St. John), married to Sir Edward Villiers, of whom see below.
[2] Oliver St. John, knighted in Flanders, president of Munster, vice-president of Connaught, Master of the Ordnance, Ireland; lord deputy, 1616; created Viscount Grandison, of Limerick, 3 June following, with remainder to the issue of Sir Edward Villiers, high treasurer, Ireland, 1625, created Baron Tregoz, of Highworth, Wilts, 21 May, 1626; married Joan, granddaughter of Sir William Holcroft (or Rycroft), Knt., daughter and heir of Henry Roydon, of Battersea, and died s.p. 30 Dec., 1630.

BARBARA ST. JOHN, married to Sir Edward Villiers (youngest son of Sir George Villiers by Audrey, his wife), knighted at Windsor, 7 Sept., 1616, president and commander-in-chief of the forces in Munster; died 7 Sept., 1626, leaving, with other issue, a son.

GEORGE, 4th Viscount Grandison (on the death of his brother John), captain of a troop of horse, 1660; died 1699; married Mary Leigh, daughter and co-heir of Francis, Earl of Chichester; she died 7 July, 1671, having had, with other issue,

AUDREY VILLIERS (eldest daughter), married to Richard Harrison, of Balls, Herts (son of Sir John Harrison, Knt.), M.P. Lancaster, Oct. 1669-79; March to July, 1679; and had, with other issue, a son, John, and a daughter, viz.,

BARBARA HARRISON, died 27 Dec., 1719, aged 51; buried with her husband in the old parish church of Clontarf; married to Charles Bourchier, "a gent of the regiment of horse commanded by the Lord Windsor;" M.P.

Dungarvan, 1692-5, 1695-9; Armagh city, 1715, until his death, 18 May, 1716, aged 52; had 4 sons and 5 daughters (*a*).

[1*a*] Charles Bourchier, baptized at St. Michan's, Dublin, 3 April, 1695; died young.
[2*a*] Francis, baptized at St. Michan's, 22 Aug., 1696; died young.
[3*a*] Richard (Bourchier) was Resident at Surat, Governor of Bombay, 1718; married Sarah, daughter of George Hawkins, of Clay Hill, Epsom, Surrey, and had 2 sons and 2 daughters (*b*).
(1*b-3a*) Charles, (Bourchier), of Colney House, Shenley, Herts; high sheriff, 1788; governor of Madras; died s.p. 2 Feb., 1810, aged 82; married 6 May, 1776, Anne, daughter of Thomas Foley, Esq., M.P. co. Hereford (see Foster's *Peerage*, B. FOLEY); she died 14 May, 1814, aged 80.
(2*b-3a*) James, of Little Berkhamstead, Herts; high sheriff, 1792; died at Bath 5 Sept., 1816; married Eliza Diana, daughter and co-heir of Rev. Samuel Fowler, rector of Atcham, Salop; she died 8 March, 1837, aged 93, having had 2 sons and 2 daughters (*c*).
[1*c-2b*] Charles, of Christ Church Coll., Oxford, and of Lincoln's Inn, barrister-at-law, recorder of Hertford, assist. solicitor to the Treasury; born Mar., 1777, died unmarried, 1845.
[2*c-2b*] James Claud (Bourchier), K.H., lieut.-general in the army, col. 3rd dragoon guards and formerly of 11th and 22nd regiments of light dragoons; born 10 May, 1780; died 12 Feb., 1859, aged 79; married 3 Aug., 1821, Maria, 2nd daughter of George Caswall, of Sacomb Park, Herts; she died 14 Oct., 1850, having had 3 sons and 3 daughters (*d*).
(1*d-2c*) Charles John (Bourchier), of Speen Lodge, Newbury, Berks; served in the 8th Hussars, retired as a captain unattached; born 2 July, 1823; married 16 May, 1861, Fanny, eldest daughter of James Farr, and has a son,
Arthur, of Ch. Ch. Coll., Oxon.
(2*d-2c*) James Johnes (Bourchier), resides at Felthorpe Hall, Norfolk; major 52nd light infantry; born 25 Nov., 1826; married 18 May, 1864, Harriet Anne, 2nd daughter of Hon. Edward Cecil Curzon, 2nd son of Harriet Anne, Baroness de la Zouche, and has an only son,
Cecil Edward.
(3*d-2c*) Claud Thomas (Bourchier), V.C., knt. of the legion of honour, of the Medjidie, &c.; col. rifle brigade; served in the Caffre war, A.D.C. to the Queen, 1852-3, and in the Crimea at the battles of Alma, Balaklava, and Inkerman, and at the siege of Sebastopol; served throughout the Indian mutiny, 1857-8, and was at the siege and capture of Lucknow, &c.; born 26 April, 1851; died 19 Nov., 1877, aged 46.
(4*d-2c*) Maria Diana, married 8 Aug., 1849, to Rev. William James Stracey, M.A. Magdalen Coll., Camb., 1843, fellow 1846, rector of Buxton-with-Oxnead, Norfolk, since 1855 (see Foster's *Baronetage*), and has 3 sons and 5 daughters (*e*).
[1*e-4d*] John Bourchier (Stracey), lieut. Scots guards; born 31 May, 1853.
[2*e-4d*] Claud Edward, lieut 63rd regiment; born 29 March, 1855.
[3*e-4d*] Eustace William Clitherow, R.N., H.M.S. "Alexandra"; served in expedition to Egypt, 1882; 5th class Medjidie; born 29 March, 1864.
[4*e-4d*] Emma Maria, married 8 April, 1875, to Lieut.-col. Charles Birch-Reynardson, grenadier guards, A.D.C. to viceroy of India 1872-4, and has 2 daughters,
Miriam Anne; Alice Mary.
[5*e-4d*] Alice Harriet Argyll, married 17 Dec., 1872, to Sir Henry James Tufton, Bart., created Lord Hothfield (see Foster's *Peerage*), and has 3 sons and a daughter.
(1) Hon. John Sackville Richard (Tufton), born 8 Nov., 1873.
(2) Hon. Sackville Philip, born 5 May, 1875.
(3) Hon. Charles Henry, born 16 May, 1879.
(4) Hon. Rosamond.
[6*e-4d*] Evelyn, died 3 Dec., 1883; married 14 Aug., 1879, to Hon. Arthur Henry Chichester, only son of Henry Spencer, 2nd Baron Templemore, and had a son and daughter.
Arthur Claud (Chichester), born 12 Sept., 1880; Evelyn Laura Mary, died 20 Dec., 1883.
[7*e-4d*] Margaret Susan. [8*e-4d*] Ida Marion.
(5*d-2c*) Emma Monckton, died 12 March, 1838.
(6*d-2c*) Susan Ann, died 25 Nov., 1858; married 17 May, 1853, to Capt. Rowland Francis Walbanke Childers, of Cantley, Yorks, Scots fusilier guards; he died 12 Nov., 1855, leaving an only daughter, Rowlanda.
[3*c-2b*] Diana (Bourchier), died s.p., June, 1867; married , to John Newell Birch, of Henley Park, clerk of House of Lords.
[4*c-2b*] Emma Audrey, died unmarried.
(3*b-3a*) Sarah, died unmarried, 10 June, 1796, aged 67.
(4*b-3a*) Emilia, died unmarried, 1 Jan., 1800, aged 67.
[4*a*] **Edward,** of whom see below.
[5*a*] Mary.
[6*a*] Barbara, married to Richard Prittie, of Dunalley, co. Tipperary, and had, with other issue, a daughter,
Mary (Prittie), married to Major-gen. Robert Lewis, E.I.C.S., and had, with other issue, a daughter,
Harriet (Lewis), married to Samuel Bourchier, named below.
[7*a*] Catherine, wife of William, grandson of Sir Abraham Yarner, and had issue.
[8*a*] Anna Maria, died 12 Dec., 1725; married as 1st wife, to John, 6th Lord Ward, created Viscount Dudley and Ward, 1763; he died 6 May, 1774, leaving by her a son, John, 2nd viscount, married, and died s.p., 12 Oct., 1788.
[9*a*] Arabella, died unmarried, 1718.

EDWARD BOURCHIER, M.A., rector of Bramfield, 1740-75; vicar of All Saints and St. John, Hertford, 1741-71; J.P. Herts; born 7 April, 1707; died 17 Nov., 1775; married , Elizabeth, daughter of Rev. Edward Gattacre, rector of Mursley-cum-Salden, Bucks; she died 4 July, 1790, aged 75, having had 5 sons and 4 daughters(*f*).

[1*f*] **Edward,** of whom see page 609.
[2*f*] Charles Bourchier, a member of the council of Bombay; born 13 March, 1739; died 28 Nov., 1818; married 1st, 7 Oct., 1773, Barbara, daughter of James Richardson, of Knockshinnock, Dumfries; she died 18 Nov., 1784, having had 3 sons and a daughter (*g*).
(1*g-2f*) Charles, and (2*g-2f*) Edward, born in Bombay; died young.
(3*g-2f*) Samuel (Bourchier), H E.I.C.S.; born Oct., 1781; died at Bombay, 1813; married Harriet, daughter of Major gen. Robert Lewis, H.E.I.C.S. (by his wife, Mary Prittie, above named); she died 1850, having had 5 sons and 2 daughters (*h*).
[1*h-3g*] Robert Francis (Bourchier), capt. 4th Bombay native infantry; born ; died 1837; married 21 July, 1832, Antoinette Anna Louisa, 9th daughter of Hon. John Rodney (see

Foster's *Peerage*), capt. R.N., chief secretary to the government of Ceylon, and had a son and daughter.
(1) Robert Lennox (Bourchier), lieut.-col. R.M.A.; born 1838; died 12 May, 1882; married 14 Oct., 1859, Mary, elder daughter of Philip Hast, lieut. R.N., and left 3 sons and 2 daughters.
Philip Lennox Walter (Bourchier), born 13 Aug., 1870; Rodney Lewis, born 24 Jan., 1875; Raymond Walter Harry, born 26 Feb., 1880; Mary; Amabel.
(2) Harriet E. Lennox.
[2*h-3g*] Henry, E.I.C.S., died unmarried, in India.
[3*h-3g*] George, lieut. 36th regt.; died unm. 1837.
[4*h-3g*] John, lieut. 26th Cameronians; died unm.
[5*h-3g*] James, died young.
[6*h-3g*] Harriet, married , 1827, to John Burnett, Esq., Bombay civil service (a great nephew of Lord Monboddo of Session), and had a daughter,
Marianne.
[7*h-3g*] Jane, married , 1829, to Capt. William Chambers, Bombay native infantry, and has a daughter,
Jane, married 1853, to Capt. George Geach, and left a son, George Chambers Geach.
(4*g-2f*) Eliza, died , 1856; married 22 Oct., 1779, to her cousin, James Torkington, barrister-at-law, who died 6 Feb., 1852, having had 14 children (see p. 609).

CHARLES BOURCHIER married 2nd, 25 Jan., 1787, Elizabeth, daughter of Rev. Benjamin Preedy, D.D., rector of Brington, Northants; she died 27 April, 1822, having had 3 sons and 2 daughters (*g*).
(5*g-2f*) Charles Spencer (Bourchier), M.A., rector of Great Hallingbury, Essex, and vicar of Sandridge, Herts; born 22 Feb., 1791; died 22 July, 1872; married 13 April, 1814, Eliza, daughter of Samuel Harman, of Hadley, Barnet; she died 22 Jan., 1880, having had 2 sons and 3 daughters.
[1] Legendre Charles Bourchier, col. 98th regt.; provisional governor of Trinidad; served in Afghan war, at battle of Ghuznee 1839, storming and capture Khelat, twice wounded; commandant of Kurrachee during the Indian mutiny; born 13 March, 1815; died 27 April, 1866; married 22 Aug., 1850, Margaret, daughter of Rev. Thomas Beane Johnstone, rector of Chilton, Somerset, and had a son and 3 daughters.
(1) Charles Legendre Johnstone Bourchier, capt. Cape Colonial Forces, served Zulu war of 1879 (medal and clasp), and Basuto war 1881, late 35th and 65th regt., born 5 Aug., 1851; married 18 April, 1873, Annie Werge, widow of A. Kaye, Esq., daughter of E. W. Howey, Esq., of Tynemouth; she died 25 May, 1874, leaving an only son,
Charles Humphrey Johnstone, born 25 Mar., 1874.
(2) Helen Johnstone.
(3) Margaret Georgiana Johnstone, married 31 May, 1881, to Peter Purves, of Brampton, Hunts., and has a son and daughter.
Douglas Bourchier Johnstone (Purves), born 21 May 1883. Helen Georgiana Johnstone.
(4) Marianne, died young.
[2] John Henry James, died young.
[3] Georgiana Anne, married to Richard Weller Chadwick, Esq., and has with other issue,
Edward F. (Chadwick), late 33rd regt., married 20 Sept., 1882, Anna Louisa, daughter of Rev. Charles Torkington.
[4] Marianne Frances, twin with John Henry.
[5] Emilia Dorothy.
(6*g-2f*) Richard James (Bourchier), of the Island of Malta; born 16 June, 1793; married 1st, Miss Lander; 2nd, Dorothy, daughter of Capt. Darby, of Hadley, Barnet; by his 1st wife he had a son and 3 daughters; resident 67, Victoria Street, Westminster, S.W.
(7*g-2f*) Frederick, born 16 March, 1795; died unmarried at Malta 5 March, 1862.
(8*g-2f*) Georgiana, died 8 March, 1862, aged 75; married to James Garden Seton, of the Hanaper Office, in the Court of Chancery, and had issue.
(9*g-2f*) Caroline, born 16 Feb., 1792; died about 1820; married 31 March, 1814, as 1st wife to Rev. Theodore Dury, rector of Keighley, Yorks, and of Westmill, Herts, where he died 2 Oct., 1850, having had 2 sons and a daughter,
[1] Theodore (Dury) and [2] Charles, died young.
[3] Caroline (Dury), died s.p. 1877, married 1858, to Rev. W. H. Schwabe, rector of Copgrove, Yorks.
[3*f*] George, born 11 May, 1741.
[4*f*] John (Bourchier), capt. R.N., lieut.-governor of Greenwich Hospital; born 26 Sept., 1747; died 30 Dec., 1808; married 1st, Mary, daughter of Rev. Richard Walter, chaplain R.N.; she died 26 Nov., 1789, having had 2 sons and 2 daughters (*i*).
(1*i-4f*) George Pocock (Bourchier), died young.
(2*i-4f*) Henry (Bourchier), rear-admiral of the Blue; born Oct., 1787; died at Lille 14 Oct., 1852; married Mary, eldest daughter of Lieut.-col. John Macdonald; she died at Ostend 9 Feb., 1852, aged 62, leaving 2 sons.
[1] Macdonald, commr. R.N., born 6 Aug., 1814; married 5 Dec., 1843, Mary Eliza, eldest daughter of Rear-admiral John Hancock, C.B.; she died 19 June, 1872; he married 2nd, 12 May, 1874, Charlotte Brumby, youngest daughter of late John Holland, lieut. R.N., and by his first wife had 2 sons and 2 daughters.
(1) Macdonald Augustus Henry, born 9 Oct., 1844, died 28 April, 1850, twin with
(2) Seton Longuet, born 9 Oct., 1844, married 25 July, 1877, Georgiana Marian, daughter of late James N. Merriman, M.D., Apothecary Extraordinary to the Queen., and has had 3 daughters,
Olive Longuet; Emily Marion, a twin with May, who died in infancy.
(3) Mary Eliza Sophia.
(4) Alice Gertrude.
[2] Henry Prescott Pellew, capt. P. & O. service; born 9 Nov., 1816; died 1 Aug., 1856; married April, 1851, his cousin Mary Jane, only daughter of Rev. Edward Ince, vicar of Wigtoft with Quadring, co. Linc.; she died 13 March, 1856, leaving a son and 3 daughters.
(1) Henry Edward, lieut. R.N., born 5 Mar., 1852, married 16 Oct., 1878, to Jane Burnett, daughter of J. Williamson. (2) Mary Jane.
(3) Henrietta Catherine, married 21 Sept., 1881, to W. Booth Williamson, Esq. (4) Alice.
(3*i-4f*) Jane, died young.
(4*i-4f*) Mary Sophia, born 11 Aug., 1786; died 9 May, 1884; married 21 Aug., 1822, to Rev. Edward Ince, M.A., vicar of Wigtoft with Quadring, co. Linc.; he died 6 Aug., 1840, leaving a son and daughter.
[1] Edward Cumming (Ince), of Sunbury House, Watford, and Marrick Abbey, Yorks., M.A. Jesus Coll., Camb., vicar of Meltham Mills, Yorks, 1853-67; of Christ Church, Battersea, 1867-77; hon. sec. Church Missionary Society for West Herts; born 17 Mar., 1828; married 14 Aug., 1850, Elizabeth Margaret Caroline, daughter of Dr. John Gason, M.D., of co. Wicklow, and has had 5 sons and 2 daughters.
(1) Edward John Cumming (Ince), B.A. Corpus Christi Coll., Camb.; curate of Melcombe Regis, Dorset; born 4 Feb., 1852; married 23 Jan.,

THE DESCENT OF
Philip Lennox Walter Bourchier.

FROM THE

Blood Royal  **of England.**

EDWARD I., b. 17 June, 1239, crowned 19 Aug., 1274, d. 7 July, 1307. = Margaret (2nd wife), dau. of Philip III. of France, she died 14 Feb. 1317.

Thomas of Brotherton, where he was born 1 June, 1300, Earl of Norfolk 1312, Marshal of England 1315, d. 1338 = Alice (1st wife), dau. of Sir Roger Haleys.

Margaret, Duchess of Norfolk, 1397, d. 24 March, 1399. = John, Lord Segrave (1st husband), d. 1353.

Elizabeth, eventually sole heir. = John, 4th Lord Mowbray of Axholme, d. 9 Oct. 1368.

Eleanor Mowbray. = John, Lord Welles, sum. to parl. 1376 until his death, 1421.

Margaret Welles, d. 29 May, 1422. = Sir Stephen Scrope of Masham and Upsale, Yorks (2nd husband), sum. to parl. 1392 until his death 25 Jan. 1405-6.

Sir John Scrope, 4th Baron Scrope of Masham, sum. to parl. 1426 until his death, 15 Nov. 1455. = Elizabeth, dau. of Sir Thomas Chaworth of Wiverton, Notts, d. 1466.

Elizabeth Scrope. = Sir Henry Scrope, 4th Baron Scrope of Bolton, d. 14 Jan. 1459.

Elizabeth Scrope, d. 12 June, 1503. = Oliver St. John, of Lydiard Tregoz (3rd husband), d. 1497.

Sir John St. John of Lydiard Tregoz, d. 1 Sept. 1512. = Johanna, dau. and heir of Sir John Iwardby, of Farley, Hants.

John St. John, of Lydiard Tregoz. = Margaret, dau. of Sir Richard Carew, of Beddington, Surrey, Knt.

A

Continued above.

B

Continued from below.

John St. John. = Margaret Carew.

Nicholas St. John, of Lydiard Tregoz. = Elizabeth, dau. of Sir Richard Blount, of Maple-Durham, Oxon, Knt.

Sir John St. John of Lydiard Tregoz (1st husband). = Lucy, dau. and heir of Sir Walter Hungerford, of Farley, Wilts. — Sir Oliver St. John, cr. Visct. Grandison 3 June. 1616, d. s. p. 30 Dec. 1630.

Barbara St. John = Sir Edward Villiers, knted. 7 Sept. 1616, d. 7 Sept. 1626.

George Villiers, 4th Viscount Grandison, d. 1699. = Mary, 2nd dau. and co-heir of Sir Francis Leigh, Bart., cr. Earl of Chichester 1644.

Audrey Villiers. = Richard Harrison, of Balls, Herts, M.P. Lancaster 1669-79.

Barbara Harrison, d. 27 Dec. 1719, aged 51. = Charles Bourchier, M.P. Dungarvan 1692-5, 1695-9, Armagh City 1715 until his death, 18 May, 1716.

Edward Bourchier, M.A. rector of Bramfield, &c. b. 7 April, 1707, d. 17 Nov. 1775. = Elizabeth, dau. of Rev. Edw. Gattacre, rector of Mursley, Bucks, d. 4 July, 1790.

Barbara (1st wife), dau. of James Richardson, of Knockshinnock, N.B., m. 1773, d. 1784 = Charles Bourchier, a member of the Council of Bombay, b. 13 March, 1739, d. 28 Nov. 1818. = Elizabeth (2nd wife), dau. of Rev. Benjamin Preedy, D.D., m. 1787, d. 1822.

Samuel Bourchier, b. Oct. 1781, d. at Bombay, 1813. = Harriet, dau. of Major Gen. Lewis, H.E.I.C.S. d. 1850. — Eliza, m. 1799, to James Torkington.

Charles Spencer Bourchier, rector of Great Hallingbury, Essex, vicar of Sandridge, Herts, d. 1872. = Eliza, dau. of S. Harman, of Hadley, Barnet, m. 1814, d. 18[illegible]

Robert Francis Bourchier, capt. 4th Bombay N.I., d. 1837. = Antoinette, dau. of Hon. J. Rodney, capt. R.N., m. 1832. — Henry, E.I.C.S., d. unm. — George, lieut. 3[illegible]th regt., d. unm., 1837. — John, lieut. 26th Cameronians, d. unm. — James, d. young. — Harriett, m. 1827, to John Burnett, Esq., Bo. C.S. — Jane, m. [illegible], to Capt. W. Chambers, Bo. Native Inft.

Robert Lennox Bourchier, lieut.-col. R.M.A., b. 1838, d. 11 May, 1892. = Mary, elder dau. of Philip Hast, lieut. R.N., m. 14 Oct. 1859. — Harriet E. Lennox. — Marianne Burnett. — Jane, m. 1853, = Capt. George Geach.

Philip Lennox Walter, b. 1870. — Rodney Lewis, b. 24 Jan. 1875. — Raymond Walter Harry, b. 1880. — Mary. Amabel. — George Chambers Geach

K

1884, Annie Nora, daughter of Josceline F. Watkins, Esq., J.P., of Watford.
(2) Ralph Piggott, born 18 Aug. 1855; died young.
(3) Henry Gason (Ince), B.A. Oxon., curate of St. Andrew's, Watford; born 24 Sept., 1857.
(4) Charles Arthur Bourchier, born 16 Dec., 1859; died young.
(5) James Berkeley Cumming, born 26 Nov., 1862.
(6) Caroline Mary Elizabeth, died young.
(7) Anna Elizabeth.
[2] Mary Jane (Ince), died 13 Mar., 1856; married April, 1851, to her cousin, Henry Prescott Pellew Bourchier, who died 1 Aug., 1856, leaving issue.
Capt. JOHN BOURCHIER married 2nd, at St. James', Westminster, Dec., 1790, Charlotte, 2nd daughter of Thomas Corbett, Esq., of Darnhall, Cheshire, of Elsham, co. Linc., and of Lincoln's Inn, barrister-at-law; she died 5 Jan., 1839, having (re-married, 27 Feb., 1810, to Captain Platt, of royal So Linc. Militia; and lastly, to J. Z. Sandars Lang, of Keaton, Devon), had 5 sons and 5 daughters (*i*).
(5*i-4f*) William (Bourchier), commr. R.N.; born 1791; died in Canada 22 Jan., 1844; married 1st in Canada, 8 April, 1821, Amelia, daughter of John Mills Jackson, of Downton, Wilts; and had an only son(*j*).
[1*j-5i*] Eustace Fane (Bourchier), lieut.-gen. in the army, R.E., C.B., knight of the legion of honour, of the Medjidie, &c.; served throughout the Kaffir campaign, 1846, and the Eastern campaign, 1854-5, including the battle of the Alma, Inkermann, and Tchernaya, and as brigade major to the royal engineers at the siege and fall of Sebastopol; born 25 Aug., 1822; married 1st, Anne Jane, daughter of Charles Stuart Pillans, merchant, of Rosebank, Rondebosch; she died 6 April, 1868; he married 2nd, 25 Aug. 1869, Maria, relict of Wilmot Seton, of the Treasury; she died 6 Feb., 1882; by his 1st wife he had with 5 daughters 2 sons.
(1) Charles Edward (Bourchier).
(2) Alfred Heseltine.
Commr. WILLIAM BOURCHIER married 2ndly Laura, (1st married to Robert Wrangham Luk'n, lieut. Bombay army), daughter of Richard Preston, of London, and had with 4 daughters a son (*j*).
[2*j-5i*] Henry Seton (Bourchier), major R.M.L.I., instructor of musketry, British resident at Lukoja on the Niger; born 17 Feb., 1842; married 28 May, 1868, Jessie Caroline, daughter of Robert Hawkes, col. 80th regiment, and has a daughter.
(6*i-4f*) Thomas Bourchier (a twin with James), by his wife Anne, daughter of Morris Graham, of Deal, had 3 sons.
[1] Edward, lost at sea.
[2] William Sutherland Bourchier, staff-commr. R.N., capt.-supt. of the Metropolitan training ship Exmouth, commr. training ship Goliath, destroyed by fire, Dec., 1875, born 15 Nov., 1823; married 1st, 8 Sept., 1850, Mina Glover, daughter of John Aldrich, master R.N.; she died leaving 2 daughters,
(1) Mina Mary (Bourchier), married to Fred. D'Iffanger, Esq.
(2) Florence Anne, married , to William Cooper Keates, L.R.C.P., M.R.C.S.
Capt. Bourchier, married 2ndly, 1 May, 1856, Mary, daughter of Isaac Halse, of Sloane Street, Chelsea, and has also 2 daughters,
(3) Emily Halse. (4) Ethel Annie.
[3] Thomas (Bourchier), navigating-lieutenant R.N., employed in the searches for Sir John Franklin's expedition; born 10 Sept., 1827; died 9 July, 1866; married 22 Jan., 1853, Anne Bourchier, daughter of J. Aldrich, master R.N., and had 6 children.
(7*i-4f*) James O'Brien (Bourchier), settled in Canada, where he was a justice of the peace (twin with Thomas), born ; died 28 Aug., 1872, aged 75; married Jeanne, daughter of James Lyall, of Canada West, and had with 6 daughters 2 sons.
[1] William (Bourchier), married, and has issue.
[2] John Raines (Bourchier), married, and has issue.
(8*i-4f*) John, M.D., born 4 March, 1802; died 11 Feb., 1842; married 23 April, 1836, Sophia, daughter of Edward Phillips, M.D., of Winchester; she died 18 April, 1859, having had an only son,
Walter Bourchier, M.A. (fellow) New Coll., Oxon., 1863; vicar of Steeple Morden 1874; of Sibford, 1864-74; born 20 Dec., 1837; married 20 April, 1876, Harriet Louisa Eliza, daughter of late John Peach MacWhirter, Bengal C.S., and has 2 sons and 2 daughters,
Walter John Majendie (Bourchier); Basil Graham; Constance Corbett; Sybil Audrey.
(9*i-4f*) Julius, clerk in Privy Seal office, born 1 March, 1803; died, 1818.
(10*i-4f*) Charlotte Margaret, died 21 July, 1852; married 1819, to Edward Parke, capt. and paymaster R.M., who died 14 Nov., 1835, having had 2 sons and 3 daughters.
[1] Richard (Parke), R.M., C.B., colonel in the army; born 21 March, 1821; married 8 May, 1862, Louisa, daughter of the Rt. Rev. and Hon. Edward Grey, lord bishop of Hereford (see Foster's *Peerage*), and has a son and daughter.
[2] Frederick (Parke), capt. R.N., married Lucy Anne, daughter of William John Wickham, of Fareham.
[3] Caroline Mary (Parke), married 6 Jan., 1842, to Rev. Isaac Philip Prescott, M.A. Oriel Coll., Oxon., 1840, rector of Kelly, Devon, since 1882, of Willingale-Doe, 1856-61, vicar of Priors Marston, Warwickshire, 1862-78 (son of Admiral Sir Henry Prescott, G.C.B.), and has 2 sons and 4 daughters.
(1) Henry (Prescott), born 7 July, 1843.
(2) Arthur Edward (Prescott), born 8 March, 1852; married 20 Nov., 1877, Kathleen, daughter of late Rev. Henry Clarke, rector of Guisborough, and has a son and 2 daughters,
Henry Cecil, born 1 March, 1882; Kathleen Mary; Constance Alice.
(3) Charlotte Alice, died 20 Aug., 1865; married 25 July, 1864, to Joseph Kaye, Esq., a master of Supreme Court of Judicature (formerly Court of Common Pleas), and had a daughter,
Alice Mary.
(4) Mary, married 25 July, 1877, to Capt. Hardy McHardy, R.N., chief constable Ayrshire, and has had 2 sons and 3 daughters.
Robert Prescott (McHardy) Hardy, died 1884.
(5) Jane, died 21 March, 1850. (6) Beatrice Jane.
[4] Charlotte, died unmarried 5 Nov., 1851.
[5] Mary, died unmarried 3 Jan., 1847.
(11*i-4f*) Anne, died 29 April, 1877; married 5 July, 1826, to John Spice Hulbert, of Stakes Hill Lodge, Hants, J.P.; he died 21 Feb., 1844, having had 3 sons and 3 daughters (*k*).
[1*k-11i*] George Alexander (Hulbert), M.A. Oxon., born 2 May, 1827; unmarried.
[2*k-11i*] John Henville (Hulbert), born 2 June, 1831; married 1st, 20 June, 1854, Anna Mary, daughter of late David John Day, Esq., of Rochester; she died 22 Sept., 1864, having had 3 sons and 4 daughters,
Walter, born 4 June, 1856; Henry, born 5 June, 1858; Charles, born 5 Feb., 1860; Agnes, Ethel, Anna, Ella.
Mr. JOHN HENVILLE HULBERT married 2nd, 26 Oct., 1865, Harriet, daughter of Rev. Joseph Carson, D.D.; she died 14 Dec., 1884, having had 4 sons and 5 daughters.
John, born 12 Sept., 1866; Joseph George, born

14 Sept., 1867; William Henville, born 29 Aug., 1869; Thomas Ernest, born 13 July, 1879; Harriet Ann, died 23 March, 1873; Fanny, Eleanor, Caroline Edith, Olivia Mary.

[3k-11i] Charles Curtis (Hulbert), born 28 March, 1833; drowned at Sandhurst, June, 1846.

[4k-11i] Mary (Hulbert), married 21 Aug., 1850, to Henry Geldart Metcalfe, M.A., Oxon, of Ringwood Hants, and has had 5 sons and 4 daughters.

(1) Henry Hulbert Metcalfe, of New Zealand, born 30 Oct., 1851; married 25 March, 1879, Jessie Alexandra, 2nd daughter of late M. Hamilton, of Cheltenham, and has a son and 2 daughters.
(2) John Greetham, born 8 Jan., 1855.
(3) Arthur Henry, born 31 March, 1859.
(4) Edward, born 21 Feb., died 6 March, 1861.
(5) Charles Ernest, born 16 March, 1864.
(6) Mary Georgina. (7) Clara Warren.
(8) Constance Alice. (9) Florence Charlotte.

[5k-11i] Anne Caroline (Hulbert), died 6 Aug., 1857; married 21 March, 1855, as 1st wife, to Henry Leslie Hunt, formerly of 67th regiment, and afterwards capt. royal Wilts militia, late major and adjutant of the West York Rifle V.C. (for his 2nd marriage see Foster's *Peerage*, M. TWEEDDALE); he died 17 Dec., 1880, leaving by her an only son.

(1) Henry de Vere (Hunt), B.A. Clare Coll., Camb., in holy orders, born 12 March, 1856; married 20 July, 1882, Mary Catherine Caroline, daughter of late Rev. P. William Browne, of Blackrod, co. Lanc., and has a daughter,
Alice Kathleen (Hunt).

[6k-11i] Fanny (Hulbert), unmarried.

(12i-4f) Caroline, married , to George Lamburn Greetham, deputy judge advocate at Portsmouth, who died s.p. 10 Oct., 1866.

(13i-4f) Susanna, born 13 April, 1800; died 9 Nov., 1875; married at Waltham Abbey, 24 March, 1827, to John Cole, of Easthorpe Court, co. Linc.; he died 12 April, 1855, leaving 2 sons and a daughter.

[1] John Charles (Cole), of Easthorpe.
[2] James Edwin (Cole), of Swineshead Hall, co. Linc., J.P., and of the Inner Temple, barrister-at-law, married 7 Dec., 1880, Mary Barbara, 2nd daughter of late Gent. Huddleston, of Lincoln.
[3] Mary Ann, married 12 Oct., 1859, to Hugh Williams, Esq. (2nd son of Henry Williams, Esq., of Tre'Jarddur and Tre'r Castell, co. Anglesey); he died 1860.

(14i-4f) Frances, born 13 Dec., 1807; married to John Overington, who died s.p. 1873.

[5f] Richard (son of Edward), born 11 May, 1749.

[6f] Mary, born 1 Oct., 1737; married to Rev. James Torkington, D.D., of Stukeley Hall, and rector of Little Stukeley, Hunts, and had 2 sons and 2 daughters (*l*).

(1l-6f) JAMES TORKINGTON, of Great Stukeley, Hunts; died 7 June, 1828; married 22 Oct., 1799, his cousin, Elizabeth, daughter of Charles Bourchier, Esq., aforesaid, and had 14 children, of whom only 2 sons married (*m*),

[1m-1l] Laurence John (Torkington), of Great Stukeley, lieut. 4th light dragoons; born 27 Sept., 1809; died 7 May, 1874; married 26 Sept., 1839, Mary Anne, daughter of Lieut.-col. Walker, R.A., and had 2 sons and 4 daughters.

(1) John (Torkington), born 8 Sept., 1840; died unm.
(2) Charles, of Stukeley, The Leven, Tasmania, late capt. 41st regiment; born 20 July, 1847; married 3 Aug., 1875, Florence Elizabeth Caroline, 3rd daughter of Richard George Coke, Esq., of Brimington Hall, co. Derby, and has 4 sons and a daughter.
Laurence John, born 6 July, 1877; Gerard Stukeley, born 24 Sept., 1878; Charles Coke, born 7 March, 1880; son born 19 Nov., 1884; Dorothy Mary.
(3) Mary Dorothy. (4) Alice. (5) Isabella.
(6) Gertrude, married 1 Oct., 1868, to Rev. John Allen, M.A. Exeter Coll., Oxon., 1861, D.D. 1876, vicar of St. Mary's, Lancaster, since 1871, rural dean, 1871, hon. canon of Manchester, 1878.

[2m-1l] Charles (Torkington), rector of Almer, Dorset, since 1871; born 13 Dec., 1817; married 1st, , 1842, Anna, daughter of James Powell, Esq., of Clapton, Middlesex; she died 8 Nov., 1847, having had a son and 3 daughters (*n*).

(1n-2m) Henry, major R.A., adjutant 3rd brigade, born 26 May, 1843; married Oct., 1875, Annie Ibbetson, daughter of William J Browne, Esq., and has 2 sons and a daughter,
Richard Humphrey, born 1 May, 1878; Oliver Miles, born 27 April, 1880; Mary Catherine.
(2n-2m) Catharine. (3n-2m) Edith, d. 14 Jan., 1847.
(4n-2m) Anna Louisa, died 26 May, 1871.

Rev. Charles Torkington, married 2ndly, Nov., 1848, Ellen Eliza, daughter of Rev. W Cookson, and had 3 sons and 2 daughters (*n*).

(5n-2m) James, b. 23 Nov., 1852; d. 2 July, 1873.
(6n-2m) Edward, born 15 Jan., 1856.
(7n-2m) Charles Richard, born 26 March, 1860.
(8n-2m) Georgina.
(9n-2m) Amy, married 20 Sept., 1882, to Col Edward F. Chadwick, of Chetnole, Sherborne, Dorset, late 33rd regt.

(2l-6f) Edward (Torkington).
(3l-6f) Mary. (4l-6f) Dorothy.

[7f] Frances (Bourchier), born 6 June, 1745; married to Rev. William Lloyd, preacher of the Charter House, and of Much Hadham, and had issue.

[8f] Elizabeth, born 6 Sept., 1746; married to—Howell

[9f] Julia Charlotte; born 11 Feb., 1752; married to—Tonge, of London.

EDWARD BOURCHIER, M.A., vicar of All Saints and St. John's, Hertford, 1771-85; rector of Bramfield, 1775-85; born 6 Sept., 1738; died 14 Dec., 1785; married Catherine, 2nd daughter of William Wollaston, of Finborough, Suffolk, M.P. Ipswich; she died 4 Feb., 1801, having had a son and 4 daughters.

[1] **Edward** (see below).
[2] Catherine, [3] Mary, and [4] Elizabeth, died in infancy. [5] Blanch Maria.

EDWARD BOURCHIER, M.A., rector of Bramfield; born 13 July, 1776; died 21 April, 1840; married 7 Feb., 1804, Harriet, youngest daughter of Robert Jenner, Esq., of Lincoln's Inn Fields; she died 18 Jan., 1864, having had 4 sons and 5 daughters.

[1] Edward, born 6 July, 1810.
[2] Francis, born 10 Aug. 1812.
[3] Robert James, born 2 Oct., 1818; died 1 Oct., 1883.
[4] **Sir George,** named on page 603.
[5] Harriet Jenner, born 29 Nov., 1804; married , to Rev. W Harris; died 11 April, 1883.
[6] Catherine Anne Jenner, died 7 Aug., 1849.
[7] Elizabeth Jenner, died 7 June, 1860; married to Rev. J. North, who died
[8] Louisa Jenner, born 26 Jan., 1809.
[9] Emma Jenner, born 9 April, 1814.

→ THE ✣ DESCENT ✣ OF ←

Edmund Anderson Shuldham, Esq.,

Of Dunmanway, Co. Cork,

FROM THE

Blood Royal of England.

EDWARD I., crowned 19 Aug. 1274, b. 17 June, 1239, d. 7 July, 1307. = Eleanor (1st wife) dau. of Ferdinand III., King of Castile, d. 27 Nov. 1290.

Joan of Acre, b. there 1272, d. 10 May, 1305, 2nd wife. = Gilbert de Clare, Earl of Gloucester, etc., d. 7 Dec. 1295.

Margaret de Clare, m. 1st to Sir Piers Gaveston, Earl of Cornwall. = Hugh de Audley (2nd husband), cr. Earl of Gloucester, d. 1347.

Margaret de Audley, d. 7 Sept. 1349. = Ralph de Stafford, K.G., cr. Earl of Stafford, d. 31 Aug. 1372.

Hugh, 2nd Earl of Stafford K.G., d. Oct. 1386. = Philippa, dau. of Thomas Beauchamp, Earl of Warwick.

Katherine de Stafford = Sir Michael de la Pole, cr. Earl of Suffolk 1399, d. 18 Sept. 1415.

Isabel de la Pole = Thomas Morley, 5th Baron Morley, d. 1435.

Anne Morley = Sir John Hastings, of Fenwick, Yorkshire.

Elizabeth Hastings = Sir Robert Hildyard, of Winestead, Yorkshire, d. 29 Aug. 1489.

Margery or Mary Hildyard = Sir William Ayscough, of Stallingborough, co. Linc., Knt., d. 26 March, 1509.

Sir William Ayscough, of Stallingborough, d. 1540-1. = Elizabeth (1st wife), dau. of Thomas Wrottesley, of Wrottesley, co. Staff.

A. continued above.

A. continued from below.

Sir William Ayscough = Elizabeth Wrottesley.

Sir Francis Ayscough, of South Kelsey, co. Linc., d. 19 Oct. 1564. = Elizabeth (1st wife), dau. and co-heir of William Hansard, Esq., of South Kelsey, co. Linc., she d. 29 Sept. 1558.

Faith Ayscough, m. about 1550. = Edward Maddison, of Fonaby, co. Linc.

Edward Maddison, of Fonaby, d. 1619. = Katherine, dau. of Ralph Bosvile, of Bradborne, Kent.

Sir Ralph Maddison, of Fonaby, knighted 23 July 1603. = Mary, dau. of Robert Williamson, of Walkeringham, Notts.

Humphrey Maddison, of Coningsby, co. Linc. = Cornelia (1st wife), dau. and co-heir of Rev. John Duport, D.D.

Ralph Maddison, of Stamford, co. Linc. High Sheriff 1679. = Theodosia, dau. and co-heir of Nicholas Newcomen, of Theddlethorpe, co. Linc.

John Maddison, of Stamford, co. Linc. High Sheriff 1719. = Katherine, dau. of George Whichcote, of Harpswell, co. Linc., m. 9 July, 1723.

Anne Maddison, m. 7 Aug. 1747, d. 31 Aug. 1783. = Rev. Sir William Anderson, of Broughton, co. Linc., Bart., d. 9 Mar. 1785.

Catherine Maria Anderson (1st wife), m. 31 July, 1777, buried 17 Nov. 1788. = Arthur Lemuel Shuldham, of Dunmanway, co. Cork, &c. lt.-col. E. Devon yeo. cavlry., d. Aug. 1839.

- Edmund William Shuldham, of Dunmanway, co. Cork, lieut.-gen. H.E.I.C.S., b. 1 Dec. 1778, d. 17 Nov. 1852. = Harriet Eliza Bonar, dau. of Dr. Rundell, of Bath, m. 3 Dec. 1817, d. 31 July, 1847.
- Molyneux Shuldham, com. R.N., m. his ccs. Frances, dau. of Rev. T. N. O. Leman, and d. 23 Feb. 1866.
- Arthur Shuldham, m. 2nd 20 Jan. 1823 Charlotte, dau. of Major Delamain, and d. 23 Feb. 1835.
- Maria Lucy Eliza, m. 3 Sept. 1801, d. 26 Oct. 1817. = Rev. Joseph Guerin, rec. Bagborough and Norton Fitzwarren, Somerset, d. 12 Nov. 1863.
- Emily, d. 1877

- Edmund Anderson Shuldham, of Dunmanway, co. Cork, J.P., D.L., High Sheriff 1871, M.A., Hon. lt.-col. South Cork Militia, b. 12 May, 1826.
- Leopold Arthur Francis, of Coolkelan, co. Cork, J.P., b. 25 July, 1828.
- Harriet Maria Catherine, m. 1852, d. 1884 = George Patrick 7th Lord Carbery.

Hon. Georgiania Dorothea Harriet (Evans Freke) m. 22 June, 1876. = James Francis, 4th Earl of Bandon.

SHULDHAM, EDMUND ANDERSON, of Dunmanway, co. Cork, J P., D.L.; high sheriff, 1871; M.A. Ch. Ch., Oxon. 1853; late major and hon. lieut.-col. South Cork militia; late A.D.C. to Lord Lieut. of Ireland; 21ST IN DESCENT FROM EDWARD I.; born 12 May, 1826.

THE DESCENT OF
EDMUND ANDERSON SHULDHAM, ESQ.,
OF DUNMANWAY, CO. CORK,
FROM THE BLOOD ROYAL OF ENGLAND.

EDWARD I., so named after Edward the Confessor; born at Westminster, 17 June, 1239, knighted at Burgos, 1254, created Earl of Chester; crowned at Westminster, 19 Aug. 1274, king of England, lord of Ireland, duke of Aquitaine; he subdued the principality of Wales 1283, claimed and exercised feudal superiority over Scotland; died at Burgh-on-the-Sands, Cumberland, 7 July, 1307, buried in Westminster Abbey; by his 1st wife, Eleanor, daughter of Ferdinand III., king of Castile, who died 27 Nov., 1290, he had

JOAN OF ACRE, born there 1272; died 10 May, 1305, having married 1st, 2 May, 1290, as 2nd wife to Gilbert de Clare (surnamed "The Red"), Earl of Gloucester and Hertford; he died at Monmouth Castle, 7 Dec., 1295, she re-married, 1296, to Ralph de Monthermer, who had summons to parliament as Earl of Gloucester and Hertford, in right of his wife 1299-1306, and had issue. JOAN OF ACRE had by her 1st husband, with other issue, a daughter,

MARGARET DE CLARE, 2nd sister and co-heir of Gilbert de Clare, Earl of Gloucester and Hertford (who fell at Bannockburn, 24 June, 1314, s.p.); she married 1st to Sir Piers Gaveston, Earl of Cornwall, to whom Edward II. granted the county of Cornwall by charter, dated at Dumfries, 6 Aug., 1307, summoned to parliament 19 Jan. following; beheaded without form of trial, 1314, leaving an only daughter, who was betrothed to John Moulton, Margaret, Countess of Cornwall, married 2ndly to Hugh de Audley; he had summons to parliament in the lifetime of his father, 1317-21, and 1326-36, and was created Earl of Gloucester by patent, 16 March, 1337; he died without male issue in 1347, and the dignity which was to him and his heirs appears to have been considered extinct; he left an only child,

MARGARET DE AUDLEY, died 7 Sept., 1349, having married to Ralph de Stafford, K.G. (son and heir of Edmund de Stafford, a lord of parliament); summoned to parliament 14 Jan., 10 Edward III., 1337, to 25 Nov., 24 Edward III., 1350; created Earl of the County of Stafford, 5 March, 1351, to hold to him and his heirs; served in the wars in Scotland and in Britany; taken prisoner at the siege of Nantes; seneschal of Aquitaine, 20 Edward III.; had a principal command at the battle of Cressy; one of the founders of the Order of the Garter; lieutenant and captain-general of the duchy of Aquitaine; he died 31 Aug., 1372, having had with other issue, a son,

HUGH DE STAFFORD, K.G., 2nd Earl of Stafford and 3rd baron; was in the retinue of the Black Prince in the French wars; made his will 6 April, 1385; died at Rhodes, on his return from a pilgrimage to Jerusalem, Oct., 1386; married Philippa, daughter of Thomas Beauchamp, Earl of Warwick, and had with other issue, a daughter,

KATHERINE DE STAFFORD, married to Sir Michael de la Pole (son of Michael, attainted earl of Suffolk); on the accession of Henry IV. he was restored to the lands and earldom of his father; he fell at the siege of Harfleur, 18 Sept., 1415 (on Wednesday next after the feast of the Holy Cross); made his will on the preceding 1 July; he had, with other issue, a daughter,

ISABEL DE LA POLE; her will dated 1464, proved 1466; married to Thomas Morley, 5th Baron Morley, heir of his grandfather; had summons to parliament, 15 July, 1427, to 5 July, 1435, in which year he died, leaving an only son and 2 daughters.

[1] Robert Morley, 6th baron; had summons to parliament, 3 Dec., 1441; married Elizabeth de Roos, daughter of William, Lord Roos, and died 1442, leaving an only daughter,
[2] Elizabeth, married to Sir John Arundel.
[3] Anne (Morley), married to Sir John Hastings, of Fenwick-juxta-Ardsley, Yorkshire (see *Herald's Visitation*, ed. Foster), and had at least 3 sons and 2 daughters.
(1) Sir Hugh Hastings, of Fenwick, high sheriff Yorks 1480; died 7 June, 1489; married Anne, daughter of Sir William Gascoigne, of Gawthorpe, Yorks, knt. (grandson of the Chief Justice, see Foster's *Yorkshire collection*); she re-married to Christopher Dransfield, of Stubbs Walden, and had issue.
(2) Sir Edward Hastings, married Eleanora, daughter of Edward Wodehouse, of Kimberley, Norfolk, and had issue; she re-married 1st, to John Bozun, of Wetheringsett, Suffolk; and lastly, to Cressener; she died 1487, leaving issue by her 1st husband.
(3) Robert Hastings, of Elsing, Norfolk; married Isabela, sister of John Thwaites, of Hardingham, Norfolk, and had issue.
(4) Isabel (Hastings), married to Thomas Bosvile, of Ardsley and Newhall, Yorkshire, and had issue (see Foster's *Yorkshire collection*).
(5) Elizabeth, married to Sir Robert Hildyard, of Winestead, Yorkshire, called "Robin of Redesdale;" knighted at the coronation of Richard III.; defeated the Earl of Pembroke at Dane's Moor near Edgecote, Oxford, and took him prisoner; he died 29 Aug., 1489, having had, with other issue (see Foster's *Yorkshire collection*), a daughter, viz.:—

MARGERY, or Mary Hildyard; married as 1st wife, to Sir William Ayscough, of Stallingborough, co. Linc., knt.; sheriff 1500, 1505, 1508; died 26 March (1 Henry VIII.), 1509; mon. inscription at Stallingborough; and had, with other issue, a son.

SIR WILLIAM AYSCOUGH, of Stallingborough, co. Linc.; sheriff, 1521; knighted, 1513; made his will, 6 Aug., 1540; proved, 28 May, 1541; married 1st, Elizabeth, daughter of Thomas Wrottesley, of Wrottesley, co. Staff.; he married 2nd, Elizabeth, daughter of John Strelley, of Strelley, Notts; she died s.p.; he married 3rdly, Elizabeth, widow of Sir William Hansard, daughter of John Hutton, of Teddone; she was buried at St. Martin's, Lincoln, 12 May, 1550; by his 1st wife Sir Francis had, with other issue, a son.

SIR FRANCIS AYSCOUGH, of South Kelsey, co. Linc.; sheriff 1545, 1549, 1554; knighted "at the winning of Boulogne," 3 Henry VIII.; died 19, buried 21 Oct., 1564, at St. Mary's, South Kelsey; he married 1st, Elizabeth, daughter and co-heir of William Hansard, Esq., of South Kelsey; she died 29 Sept., 1558; he married 2nd, Elizabeth, widow of William Dallison, daughter of Robert Dighton, of Sturton, co. Linc.; she died 6 Dec., 1570; buried at Clerkenwell, leaving by him a son and daughter, of whom the eldest,

FAITH AYSCOUGH, married about 1550 to Edward Maddison, of Fonaby, co. Linc., and had, with other issue, a son.

EDWARD MADDISON, of Fonaby, died 1619, leaving by Katherine, his wife, daughter of Ralph Bosvile, of Bradbourne. Kent, with other issue, a son,

SIR RALPH MADDISON, of Fonaby, knighted at Whitehall, 23 July, 1603; author of *Great Britain's Remembrances*, published 1650; married Mary, daughter of Robert Williamson, of Walkeringham, Notts (ancestor of Sir Hedworth Williamson, Bart.), and had, with other issue, a son,

HUMPHREY MADDISON, of Coningsby, co. Linc.; married 1st, Cornelia, daughter and co-heir of Rev. John Duport, D.D., master of Jesus Coll., Camb., and had issue. He

married 2nd, Helen, sister of Henry Wagstaffe, of Hasland, co. Derby, and had issue. By his 1st wife he had a son,

RALPH MADDISON, of Stamford, co. Linc., high sheriff 1679; married Theodosia, daughter and co-heir of Nicholas Newcomen, of Theddlethorpe, co. Linc., and had a son.

JOHN MADDISON, of Stamford, co. Linc., high sheriff 1719; married 9 July, 1723, Katherine, daughter of George Whichcote, Esq., of Harpswell, co. Linc., and had, with a son, 3 daughters, of whom the youngest, viz.—

ANNE MADDISON, died 31 Aug., 1783, aged 56; buried at Lea, co. Linc., 5 Sept.; married at Little Grimsby 7 Aug., 1747, to Rev. Sir William Anderson, of Broughton, co. Linc., 6th bart., rector of Epworth, Isle of Axholme, 1757-84, baptised at St. Giles'-in-the Fields, 31 March, 1721; died at Bell Hall, near York, 9 March, 1785; buried at Lea, 15th, aged 63, and had 5 sons and 6 daughters (*a*),

[1*a*] William (Anderson), baptised 21 March, 1749-50; buried at St. Margaret's, Lincoln, 3 April following.

[2*a*] John (Anderson), buried at St. Margaret's, Lincoln, 17 Jan., 1754.

[3*a*] Sir Edmund (Anderson), Bart., of Broughton, born 11 Sept., 1758; died 30 May, 1799; buried at Lea, co. Linc., 9 June; married 11 Sept., 1784, Catherine, daughter of Thomas Plumer, Esq., of Lilling Hall, Yorks; she was buried at Lea 8 Dec., 1798.

[4*a*] George William (Anderson), B.A., rector of Epworth and of Lea; born 10 Nov., 1759; died s.p. 16 April, 1785; buried in York Minster; married 11 Sept., 1784, Lucy, eldest daughter of Thomas Plumer, Esq., of Lilling Hall, Yorks.

[5*a*] Sir Charles John (Anderson), 8th Bart., of Broughton, prebendary of Thorngate in Lincoln cathedral, rector of Lea; born 5 Oct., 1767; died 24 March, 1846; married 15 Dec., 1802, Frances Mary, youngest daughter of Sir John Nelthorpe, Bart., of Scawby (extinct); she died 17 Aug., 1836, having had 2 sons and 2 daughters (*b*).

(1*b*-5*a*) Sir Charles Henry John Anderson (9th bart.), of Broughton, born 25 Nov., 1804; married 11 Sept., 1832, Emma, youngest daughter of John Savile Foljambe, Esq., of Osberton, Notts; she died 8 Aug., 1870, having had 3 sons and 3 daughters (*c*).

[1*c*-1*b*] Edmund Willoughby (Anderson), born 27 July, 1837; died 27 Aug., 1839.

[2*c*-1*b*] Francis Foljambe (Anderson), of Knaith, co. Linc., J.P., lieut. Notts yeomanry, born 19 Aug., 1841; died 15 Sept., 1881; married 14 July, 1874, Anne Louisa, only daughter of late Benjamin Heywood Jones, Esq., of Larkhill, co. Lanc., and had 3 daughters.

Margaret Louise (Anderson); Katherine Helen; Frances Olive.

[3*c*-1*b*] Charles Whichcott, capt. N. Linc. militia, born 10 May, 1845; died 7 Sept., 1877.

[4*c*-1*b*] Charlotte Arabella, married 26 April, 1862, to Col. George Phipps Prevost (brevet 1875), ass. adj. and quarter-mast.-general Home district, 1880-5, lieut.-col. Royal Welsh fusiliers, 1870; half-pay, 1880; eldest son of Ven. Sir George Prevost, Bart., M.A. (see Foster's *Baronetage*). He died s.p. 27 March, 1885.

[5*c*-1*b*] Emma Theodosia.

[6*c*-1*b*] Frances Mary, died s.p. 21 Oct., 1870; married 23 June, 1863, as 1st wife, to Rev. Ernest Roland Wilberforce, afterwards bishop of Newcastle-upon-Tyne (1882); M.A. Ex. Coll., Oxon., 1865; D.D., 1882; rector of Middleton Stoney, Oxon., 1866-9; sub-almoner 1871-82; canon of Winchester, 1878-82; 2nd son of late bishop of Winchester.

(2*b*-5*a*) William Edmund, died 31 May, 1815.

(3*b*-5*a*) Fanny Maria (Anderson), died 12 Nov., 1883; married 24 June, 1838, to Sir John Nelthorpe, Bart., of Scawby (extinct); he died 22 Nov., 1865.

(4*b*-5*a*) Emily Margaret Charlotte (Anderson), a nurse in the Crimea with Miss Stanley; died unmarried 30 Aug., 1870, aged 53.

[6*a*] Anne (Anderson), died 12 July, 1830, aged 77; married 1st, 30 Aug., 1771, to Samuel Thorold, Esq., of Harmston co. Linc.; he died 19 Jan., 1820; she re-married to Rosser alias Roys; by her 1st husband she had, with other issue, 3 daughters,

(1) Ann Eliza (Thorold), married 29 June, 1797, to Benjamin Hart, of the Middle Temple, barrister-at-law, and had an only son,

Benjamin Hart Thorold, of Harmston Hall, born 1798, died 1883.

(2) Louise, married 28 Feb., 1796, to Capt. Simpson, 2nd regt.

(3) Theodosia, married Sept., 1800, to Lieut. Gibbons, 37th regt., died 1806.

[7*a*] **Catherine Maria**, buried at Lea, 17 Nov., 1788; married 31 July, 1777, to Arthur Lemuel Shuldham (whom see next page).

[8*a*] Theodosia Dorothy, died 3 May, 1831; married 1 Jan., 1778, to Rev. Richard Vevers (see page 651).

[9*a*] Henrietta Jane, died 9 March, 1843; married 3 Dec., 1783, to Rev. Naunton Thomas Orgill Leman, of Brampton Hall, Suffolk (son of William Orgill, Esq., of Beccles, and Sarah his wife, 3 daughter of Thomas Leman, Esq., of Brampton); he died 31 Jan., 1837, having had 7 sons and 8 daughters (*e*),

(1*e*-9*a*) Leman Orgill (Leman), born 5, died 12 Feb., 1787.

(2*e*-9*a*) George Orgill (Leman), of Brampton Hall, M.A. (incumbent and patron of Stoven); born 4 June, 1789; died unmarried 14 Dec., 1867.

(3*e*-9*a*) Naunton Orgill, born 20 March, 1792; died in Africa 21 May, 1818.

(4*e*-9*a*) Robert Orgill (Leman), of Brampton Hall, Suffolk, B.A. of Balliol Coll., Oxon; in holy orders: born 12 April, 1799; died 24 Feb., 1869; married 1st, 25 March, 1824, Isabella Camilla, daughter of Sir William Jervis Twysden, Bart. (see Foster's *Baronetage*); she died 7 March, 1850, having had 3 sons and a daughter (*f*),

[1*f*] Naunton Robert Twysden Orgill (Leman), of Brampton Hall, Suffolk, lord of the manor; born 12 Sept., 1825; married 11 Aug., 1869, Rose Elizabeth, daughter of late Rev. John Alexander Ross, vicar of Westwell, Kent, and has a son,

Robert Naunton Orgill (Leman), born 2 Oct., 1870.

[2*f*] Twysden George, born 9 June, 1833; died 14 March, 1834.

[3*f*] John Thomas Twysden, born 26 March, 1836; died April, 1857.

[4*f*] Frances Henrietta Eliza Flora.

REV. ROBERT ORGILL-LEMAN, married 2nd, 29 March, 1859, Ellen Maria, 4th daughter of Rev. John Alexander Ross, vicar of Westwell, aforesaid, and has a son and 3 daughters,

[5f] Anderson Thomas John Orgill (Leman), born 31 Jan. 1862.
[6f] Beatrice Amelia Ellen.
[7f] Maud Henrietta Emily, died 24 Dec., 1876.
[8f] Ethel Helena Mary.
(5e-9a) Charles Orgill (Leman), born 11 March, 1801; died unmarried 25 Jan., 1845.
(6e-9a) William Orgill (Leman), born 24 Dec., 1802; died 7 March, 1848.
(7e-9a) Thomas Orgill (Leman), rector of Brampton; born 31 March, 1804; died s.p. 7 June, 1873; married 27 Feb., 1838, Emily Antonia, daughter of Rev. Joseph Guerin, of Bagborough and Norton Fitzwarren, Somerset (see page 616).
(8e-9a) Elizabeth Mary, died unmarried 16 April, 1842.
(9e-9a) Susan Leman, died unmarried 26 Oct., 1856.
(10e-9a) Harriet, died unmarried 15 Oct., 1834.
(11e-9a) Maria, died 5 May, 1796; aged 2.
(12e-9a) Charlotte Catherine, died 4 May, 1796.
(13e-9a) Frances, died 22 Jan., 1866; married 3 Dec., 1820, to her cousin, Molyneux Shuldham, Esq., commr. R.N.; he died 25 Feb., 1866 (see below).
(14e-9a) Anne, died 27 May, 1878; married 26 March, 1822, to Thomas Gee, Esq., of Brothertoft Hall, Lincolnshire, banker (son of Henry Gee, Esq.); he died s.p. 3 Sept., 1871; aged 87.
(15e-9a) Charlotte, died Aug., 1868; married 25 Sept., 1821, to George Barlee, attorney-at-law (2nd son of Rev. William Barlee, rector of Wrentham, Suffolk); he died , 1866, having had a son,
Naunton Dalling (Barlee), born 13 June, 1829; died 7 Nov., 1838.
[10a] Charlotte, died s.p. 9 Oct., 1822; married to Robert Rede, Esq.
[11a] Frances Maria, died unmarried Oct., 1846.

CATHERINE MARIA ANDERSON (2nd daughter of Rev. Sir William Anderson, 6th Baronet, of Broughton), buried at Lea, 17 Nov., 1788; married 31 July, 1777, as 1st wife, to Arthur Lemuel Shuldham, Esq., of Dunmanway, co. Cork, and Pallas Green, co. Limerick, lieut.-col. East Devon yeomanry cavalry, D. L. Devon; he died Aug., 1839, having had 5 sons and 2 daughters. (g)

[1g] **Edmund William (Shuldham)**, of whom see page 616.
[2g] John George Evelyn, lieut. R.N.; born 24 Jan., 1780; died in the West Indies.
[3g] Molyneux (Shuldham), commr. R.N.; lieut. H.M.S. Edgar at battle of Copenhagen; 8 years prisoner of war at Verdun; born 27 April, 1781; died 23 Feb., 1866; married 3 Dec., 1820, his cousin Frances, daughter of Rev. Thomas Naunton Orgill Leman, of Brampton Hall, Suffolk (named above); she died 22 Jan., 1866, having had 4 sons and 3 daughters (h),
(1h-3g) Arthur James (Shuldham), lieut.-col. 108th foot (retired 1869); served in Burmah 1852-3 (medal), and with Turkish contingent in Crimea 1855-6 (Turkish medal); born 13 Sept., 1823; married 1st, 8 Jan., 1857, Katharine Dora, daughter of Rev. C E Dukinfield; she died 19 Aug., 1865, having had 3 sons and 4 daughters,
[1] Edmond Dukinfield (Shuldham), born 29 Nov., 1857.
[2] Molyneux Charles Dukinfield, born 13 Aug., 1861
[3] Herbert Leman Dukinfield, born 17 Feb., 1863.
[4] Margaret Evelyn. [5] Geraldine Maud.
[6] Eleanor Maria.
[7] Dora Frances Mary Blanche.
LIEUT.-COL. ARTHUR JAMES SHULDHAM married 2nd, 14 Sept., 1869, Lucy Elizabeth, daughter of Sir William Sidney Thomas, 5th bart.; capt. R.N. (see Foster's *Baronetage*), and has 3 sons and a daughter,
[8] Sidney Arthur Naunton (Shuldham), born 27 June, 1870.
[9] Harry George, born 16 Sept., 1871.
[10] Victor Lemuel, born 23 Oct., 1872.
[11] Violet Lucy Hester.
(2h-3g) Naunton Lemuel (Shuldham), born 24 Sept., 1831; died 14 July, 1874; married 9 Aug., 1866, Sophia Frances, daughter of John Quantock, Esq., of Norton, Somerset; she died 14 April, 1874, having had, with twin daughters who died in infancy, a son,
Frank Naunton Quantock (Shuldham), lord of the manor of Norton-sub-Hamdon, a ward in Chancery, born 25 March, 1868.
(3h-3g) Molyneux Alfred Chesney, died young Nov., 1837.
(4h-3g) Henrietta Emily.
(5h-3g) Maria Harriet Susannah.
(6h-3g) Catherine Leman, married 5 July, 1849, to Rev. William Wrighte Gilbert Cooper, M.A. Magdalen Hall, Oxon, 1853; vicar of Burwash, Weald, Sussex, 1877; chaplain on Madras ecclesiastical establishment 1855-77, and has had 3 sons and 4 daughters.
[1] Cecil Molyneux (Gilbert-Cooper), lieut. H.M.S. Vulture, born 19 Oct., 1851; died 3 Jan., 1874.
[2] Arthur Edward, born 4 Oct., 1853.
[3] William Naunton Roger, born 14 Sept., 1867.
[4] Mary Frances.
[5] Fanny Catherine Alice, married 27 Dec., 1876, to Ralph Sillery Benson, Madras C.S.
[6] Edith Shuldham, married 9 April, 1885, to Alfred, youngest son of late Commander Holland, R.N. (see Foster's *Baronetage*).
[7] Amy Dora.
(7h-3g) Frances Molyneux (Shuldham), died 27 Aug., 1854; married 1853, to Lieut.-col. Lye, 13th Bombay native infantry; he died , 1872, leaving a son,
Harry Shuldham (Lye), capt. Royal Irish regiment 1881 (Afghan and Tel-el Kebir medals); born 15 July, 1854.
[4g] Henry George (Shuldham), midshipman R.N.; killed at taking of Surinam, 1804; unmarried.
[5g] Arthur (Shuldham), lieut.-col. H.E.I.C.S., born 1790; died 23 Feb., 1835; married 1st daughter of — Sibley, Esq.; she died s.p. he married 2nd, 20 Jan., 1823, Charlotte (sister of Col. Delamain), and daughter of Major Innis Delamain, H.E.I.C.S.; she died 23 Jan., 1867, having had a son and 2 daughters (j),
(1j-5g) Arthur Innis (Shuldham), late lieut.-col. Indian army, born 30 April, 1830; married 5 Nov., 1871, Julia, daughter of Thomas Barnes, Esq.
(2j-5g) Charlotte Katherine, married 4 April, 1843, to Major-Gen. Robert Unwin; served with Major-Gen. Notts' force in 1842; in Gwalior campaign, 1843; Sutlej campaign, at Moodkee, Ferozeshah, and Sobraon, 1845-6; in Punjaub, 1848-9; and in Indian mutiny at Lucknow and Bareilly, 1857-8; cantonment magistrate and J P. at Bareilly, 1858-74; and has had 5 sons and 4 daughters,
[1] Robt. Henry (Unwin), born 21 Dec., 1843; died 7 Oct., 1845.
[2] Herbert, born 30 July, 1845; died 24 Aug. 1846.
[3] Edmund, born 7, died 23 Jan., 1847.
[4] Alfred Cawthorne, born 17 Sept., 1848; died 15 July, 1849.
[5] Frederick Augustus, born 5 Dec., 1849; died 5 June, 1855.

THE DESCENT OF

Charlotte Katherine,

Wife of Major-General Robert Unwin,

FROM THE

Blood Royal  **of England.**

EDWARD I., crowned 19 Aug. 1274, b. 17 June, 1239, d. 7 July, 1307. = Eleanor (1st wife) dau. of Ferdinand III., King of Castile, d. 27 Nov. 1290.

Joan of Acre, b. there 1272, d. 10 May, 1305, 2nd wife. = Gilbert de Clare, Earl of Gloucester, etc., d. 7 Dec. 1295.

Margaret de Clare, m. 1st to Sir Piers Gaveston, Earl of Cornwall. = Hugh de Audley (2nd husband), cr. Earl of Gloucester, d. 1347.

Margaret de Audley, d. 7 Sept. 1349. = Ralph de Stafford, K.G., cr. Earl of Stafford, d. 31 Aug. 1372.

Hugh, 2nd Earl of Stafford K.G., d. Oct. 1386. = Philippa, dau. of Thomas Beauchamp, Earl of Warwick.

Katherine de Stafford = Sir Michael de la Pole, cr. Earl of Suffolk 1399, d. 18 Sept. 1415.

Isabel de la Pole = Thomas Morley, 5th Baron Morley, d. 1435.

Anne Morley = Sir John Hastings, of Fenwick, Yorkshire.

Elizabeth Hastings = Sir Robert Hildyard, of Winestead, Yorkshire, d. 29 Aug. 1489.

Margery or Mary Hildyard = Sir William Ayscough, of Stallingborough, co. Linc., Knt., d. 26 March, 1509.

Sir William Ayscough, of Stallingborough, d. 1540-1. = Elizabeth (1st wife), dau. of Thomas Wrottesley, of Wrottesley, co. Staff.

A, *continued above.*

A, *continued from below.*

Sir William Ayscough = Elizabeth Wrottesley.

Sir Francis Ayscough, of South Kelsey, co. Linc., d. 19 Oct. 1564. = Elizabeth (1st wife), dau. and co-heir of William Hansard, Esq., of South Kelsey, co. Linc., she d. 29 Sept. 1558.

Faith Ayscough, m. about 1550. = Edward Maddison, of Fonaby, co. Linc.

Edward Maddison, of Fonaby, d. 1619. = Katherine, dau. of Ralph Bosvile, of Bradborne, Kent.

Sir Ralph Maddison, of Fonaby, knighted 23 July, 1603. = Mary, dau. of Robert Williamson, of Walkeringham, Notts.

Humphrey Maddison, of Coningsby, co. Linc. = Cornelia (1st wife), dau. and co-heir of Rev. John Duport, D.D.

Ralph Maddison, of Stamford, co. Linc. High Sheriff 1679. = Theodosia, dau. and co-heir of Nicholas Newcomen, of Theddlethorpe, co. Linc.

John Maddison, of Stamford, co. Linc. High Sheriff 1719. = Katherine, dau. of George Whichcote, of Harpswell, co. Linc., m. 9 July, 1723.

Anne Maddison, m. 7 Aug. 1747, d. 31 Aug. 1783. = Rev. Sir William Anderson, of Broughton, co. Linc., Bart., d. 9 Mar 1785.

Catherine Maria Anderson (1st wife), m. 31 July, 1777, buried 17 Nov. 1788. = Arthur Lemuel Shuldham, of Dunmanway, co. Cork, &c. lt.-col. E. Devon yeo. cavlry., d. Aug. 1839.

- Edmund William Shuldham, of Dunmanway, co. Cork, lieut.-gen. H.E.I.C.S., b. 1 Dec. 1778, d. 17 Nov. 1852. = Harriet Eliza Bonar, dau. of Dr. Rundell, of Bath, m. 3 Dec. 1817, d. 31 July, 1847.
- Molyneux Shuldham, com. R.N., m. his cos. Frances, dau. of Rev. T. N. O. Leman, and d. 23 Feb. 1866.
- Arthur Shuldham, m. 2nd 20 Jan. 1823 Charlotte, dau. of Major Delamain, and d. 23 Feb. 1835.
- Maria Lucy Eliza, m. 3 Sept. 1801, d. 26 Oct. 1817. = Rev. Joseph Guerin, rec. Bagborough and Norton Fitzwarren, Somerset, d. 12 Nov. 1863.
- Emily, d. 1877

- Arthur Ionis Shuldham, late lt.-col. Indian Army, b. 30 April, 1830. = Julia, dau. of Thomas Barnes, Esq., m. 5 Nov. 1871.
- Charlotte Katherine, m. 4 April, 1843. = Major-Gen. Robert Unwin, served in Indian Mutiny.
- Amelia Ward, m. 28 Feb. 1854. = Fitz-Edward Hall, C.E., D.C.L.

Children of Major-Gen. Robert Unwin and Charlotte Katherine:

- Robert Henry. Herbert. Edmund. Alfred Cawthorne. Frederick Augustus. — All died unmarried.
- Emily Constance, m. 31 Dec., 1874, to Augustus Lawrence Francis, Head Master Blundell's School, Tiverton.
- Margaret Gertrude and Amy Grace, both died young.
- Mabel Unwin.

Children of Fitz-Edward Hall and Amelia Ward: Richard. Katharine.

[6] Emily Constance, married 31 Dec., 1874, to Augustus Laurence Francis, fellow of Jesus Coll., Camb., head master of Blundell's School, Tiverton, and has 2 sons and 2 daughters,

Augustus Claude (Francis), born 22 Feb., 1878; Harold Vansittart, born 25 Sept., 1883; Constance Amy, Hilda.

[7] Margaret Gertrude, died 7 July, 1855.

[8] Amy Grace, died 19 Nov., 1861.

[9] Mabel (Unwin).

(3*j*-5*g*) Amelia Ward (Shuldham), married 28 Feb., 1854, to Fitzedward Hall, C.E., D.C.L. Oxon. (son of Daniel Hall), Esq., and has had (with 2 other daughters who died young) 2 sons and a daughter.

(1) Arthur Molyneux (Hall), born 7 Dec., 1854; died 7 Feb., 1855.

(2) Richard Daniel, born 18 Feb., 1863.

(3) Katharine Frances.

[6*g*] Maria Lucy Eliza (Shuldham), died 26 Oct., 1817; married 3 Sept., 1801, to Rev. Joseph Guerin, rector of Bagborough and Norton Fitzwarren, Somerset, J.P., D.L.; he died 12 Nov., 1863, having had 2 sons and 5 daughters (*k*).

(1*k*-6*g*) Edmund Arthur (Guerin), col. Indian army (retired 1861); served in Persian campaign, 1856-7 (medal), and in Indian mutiny (Indian mutiny clasp); born 22 April, 1804; married 20 Sept., 1836, Louisa, youngest daughter of Joseph Gilbert, Esq., and has a son and 2 daughters.

[1] Joseph Arthur (Guerin), E.I.C.S. deputy district collector, Belgaum, Bombay; born 12 July, 1837; married July, 1871, Elizabeth Walker, youngest daughter of Rev. John Dudley Oland Crosse, vicar of Pawlett, Somerset, and has a son and daughter.

Joseph (Guerin), born 25 Jan., 1875.
Emily Maud.

[2] Emily Louisa, died 9 May, 1865; married 10 Sept., 1856, to Charles Frederic Keays, major-gen. Bombay army (retired 1881), (son of late Ven. Robert Young Keays, Archdeacon of Bombay (see page 850), and has 3 sons and 2 daughters.

(1) Frederic Edmund (Keays), born 25 Oct., 1857.

(2) Henry Guerin, born 9 April, 1862, married 17 Aug., 1884, Edith, 2nd daughter late George Jinman, M.R.C.S.

(3) Arthur Maitland, born 14 April, 1865.

(4) Evelyn Louisa Frances, married 16 Feb., 1878, to Newton P. Fowell, capt. R.H.A. (see p. 734).

(5) Maude Emily.

[3] Matilda Jemima, died unmarried 27 Aug., 1861.

(2*k*-6*g*) Arthur Joseph (Guerin), born and died 6 July, 1803.

(3*k*-6*g*) Catherine Maria, died s.p. April, 1874; married 5 July, 1843, to Rev. Richard Thos. Lowe, rector of Lea, Lincoln; both lost at sea, April, 1874.

(4*k*-6*g*) Emily Antonia, married 27 Feb., 1838, to her cousin, Rev. Thos. Orgill Leman, rector of Brampton; he died s.p. 7 June, 1873 (see p. 614).

(5*k*-6*g*) Lucy Frances.

(6*k*-6*g*) Jemima Caroline, died 25 March, 1882.

(7*k*-6*g*) Elizabeth Sophia.

[7*g*] Emily Anne (Shuldham), died 8 Feb., 1877, aged 95.

EDMUND WILLIAM SHULDHAM, of Dunmanway, co. Cork; lieut.-gen. H.E.I.C.S.; quartermaster-general Bombay; born 1 Dec., 1778; died 17 Nov., 1852; married 3 Dec., 1817, Harriet Eliza Bonar, daughter of Dr. Thomas Rundell, of Bath; she died 31 July, 1847, having had 2 sons and a daughter.

[1] **Edmund Anderson** (Shuldham), first-named (see page 611).

[2] Leopold Arthur Francis, of Coolkelan, co. Cork, J.P., born 25 July, 1828.

[3] Harriet Maria Catherine, died 19 Aug., 1884, married 5 Aug., 1852, to George Patrick, 7th Lord Carbery (see Foster's *Peerage*), and has a daughter,

Hon. Georgiana Dorothea Harriet (Evans-Freke), married 22 June, 1876, to James Francis, 4th Earl of Bandon (see Foster's *Peerage*), a representative peer of Ireland since 1881; late State steward to Lord Lieut. of Ireland; colonel royal Cork artillery militia since 1876; lord lieut. and cus. rot. Cork; s.p.

THE DESCENT OF
Col. Edmund Arthur Guerin
AND
Frederic Edmund Keays, Esq.
FROM THE

Blood Royal of England.

EDWARD I., crowned 19 Aug. 1274, b. 17 June, 1239, d. 7 July, 1307. = Eleanor (1st wife) dau. of Ferdinand III., King of Castile, d. 27 Nov. 1290.

Joan of Acre, b. there 1272, d. 10 May, 1305, 2nd wife. = Gilbert de Clare, Earl of Gloucester, etc., d. 7 Dec. 1295.

Margaret de Clare, m. 1st to Sir Piers Gaveston, Earl of Cornwall. = Hugh de Audley (2nd husband), cr. Earl of Gloucester, d. 1347.

Margaret de Audley, d. 7 Sept. 1349. = Ralph de Stafford, K.G., cr. Earl of Stafford, d. 31 Aug. 1372.

Hugh, 2nd Earl of Stafford K.G., d. Oct. 1386. = Philippa, dau. of Thomas Beauchamp, Earl of Warwick.

Katherine de Stafford = Sir Michael de la Pole, cr. Earl of Suffolk 1399, d. 18 Sept. 1415.

Isabel de la Pole = Thomas Morley, 5th Baron Morley, d. 1435.

Anne Morley = Sir John Hastings, of Fenwick, Yorkshire.

Elizabeth Hastings = Sir Robert Hildyard, of Winestead, Yorkshire, d. 29 Aug. 1489.

Margery or Mary Hildyard = Sir William Ayscough, of Stallingborough, co. Linc., Knt., d. 26 March, 1509.

Sir William Ayscough, of Stallingborough, d. 1540-1. = Elizabeth (1st wife), dau. of Thomas Wrottesley, of Wrottesley, co. Staff.

A. continued above.

A. continued from below.

Sir William Ayscough = Elizabeth Wrottesley.

Sir Francis Ayscough, of South Kelsey, co. Linc., d. 19 Oct. 1564. = Elizabeth (1st wife), dau. and co-heir of William Hansard, Esq., of South Kelsey, co. Linc., she d. 29 Sept. 1558.

Faith Ayscough, m. about 1550. = Edward Maddison, of Fonaby, co. Linc.

Edward Maddison, of Fonaby, d. 1619. = Katherine, dau. of Ralph Bosvile, of Bradborne, Kent.

Sir Ralph Maddison, of Fonaby, knighted 23 July, 1603. = Mary, dau. of Robert Williamson, of Walkeringham, Notts.

Humphrey Maddison, of Coningsby, co. Linc. = Cornelia (1st wife), dau. and co-heir of Rev. John Duport, D.D.

Ralph Maddison, of Stamford, co. Linc. High Sheriff 1679. = Theodosia, dau. and co-heir of Nicholas Newcomen, of Theddlethorpe, co. Linc.

John Maddison, of Stamford, co. Linc. High Sheriff 1719. = Katherine, dau. of George Whichcote, of Harpswell, co. Linc., m. 9 July, 1723.

Anne Maddison, m. 7 Aug. 1747, d. 31 Aug. 1783. = Rev. Sir William Anderson, of Broughton, co. Linc., Bart., d. 9 Mar. 1785.

Theodosia Dorothy Anderson, m. 1 Jan., 1778, d. 3 May, 1831. = Rev. Richard Vevers, rector of Saxby, co. Leicester, etc.

Theodosia Anne Vevers, eldest dau., m. 18 Oct., 1804, d. 28 June, 1852. = Thomas, Lord Denman, so created 28 March, 1834, Lord Chief Justice 1832-50, d. 22 Sept., 1854.

- Edmund William Shuldham, of Dunmanway, co. Cork, lieut.-gen. H.E.I.C.S., b. 1 Dec. 1778, d. 17 Nov. 1852. = Harriet Eliza Bonar, dau. of Dr. Rundell, of Bath, m. 3 Dec. 1817, d. 31 July, 1847.
- Molyneux Shuldham, com. R.N., m. his cos. Frances, dau. of Rev. T. N. O. Leman, and d. 23 Feb. 1866.
- Arthur Shuldham, m. 2nd 20 Jan. 1823 Charlotte, dau. of Major Delamain, and d. 23 Feb. 1835.
- Maria Lucy Eliza, m. 3 Sept. 1801, d. 26 Oct. 1817. = Rev. Joseph Guerin, rec. Bagborough and Norton Fitzwarren, Somerset, d. 12 Nov. 1863.
- Emily, d. 1877.

Children of Maria Lucy Eliza and Rev. Joseph Guerin:

- Edmund Arthur Guerin, col. Indian army, retired 1861, served in Indian Mutiny, b. 22 April, 1804. = Louisa, youngest dau. of Joseph Gilbert, Esq., m. 20 Sept., 1836.
- Catherine, m. to Rev. R. T. Lowe, and d. s.p. 1874.
- Emily, m. [illegible], to Rev. T. O. Leman.
- Lucy.
- Jemima, d. 18[illegible].
- Elizabeth.

Children of Edmund Arthur Guerin and Louisa:

- Joseph Arthur Guerin, E.I.C.S., deputy collector of Belgaum, Bombay, b. 12 July, 1837. = Elizabeth Walker, youngest dau. of the Rev. John Dudley Oland Crosse, vicar of Pawlett, Somerset, m. July, 1871.
- Emily Louisa, m. 15 Sept., 1856, d. 9 May, 186[illegible]. = Charles Frederic Keays, Maj.-Gen., Bom. army, retired 18[illegible].
- Matilda, d. unm. 18[illegible].

Children of Joseph Arthur Guerin and Elizabeth Walker:

- Joseph Guerin, b. 25 Jan. 1875.
- Emily Maud.

Children of Emily Louisa and Charles Frederic Keays:

- Frederick Edmund Keays, b. 25 Oct. 1857.
- Henry Guerin, b. 9 April, 1862, m. 17 Aug. 18[illegible], Edith, 2nd dau. of late George Jinman, M.R.C.S.
- Arthur Maitland, b. 14 April, 1865.
- Evelyn Louisa Frances, m. to Newton P. Fowell, R.H.A.
- Maude Emily.

HORNBY, EDMUND GEOFFREY STANLEY, of Dalton Hall, Westmoreland, LL.B., J.P., D.L. Lancashire; capt. (hon. major) 3rd battalion King's Own Royal Lancaster regiment 1858-83, 19TH IN DESCENT FROM EDWARD I.; born 2 Jan., 1839.

Dalton Hall, Burton, Westmoreland.

THE DESCENT OF
MAJOR HORNBY, OF DALTON HALL,
FROM THE BLOOD ROYAL OF ENGLAND.

EDWARD I., so named after Edward the Confessor; born at Westminster 17 June, 1239; knighted at Burgos, 1254; created Earl of Chester; crowned at Westminster, 19 Aug., 1274, King of England, Lord of Ireland, Duke of Aquitaine; he subdued the principality of Wales 1283, claimed and exercised feudal superiority over Scotland; died at Burgh-on-the-Sands, Cumberland, 7 July, 1307; buried in Westminster Abbey; by his 1st wife, Eleanor, daughter of Ferdinand III., King of Castile, who died 27 Nov., 1290, he had, with other issue, a daughter,

ELIZABETH, died 5 May, 1316, aged 32; she married 1st to John, Count of Holland and Zealand, and Lord of Friesland, who died s.p.; she re-married to Humphrey de Bohun, Earl of Hereford and Essex, Lord of Brecknock, and constable of England; served in the wars against Scotland; taken prisoner at the battle of Stryvelin, 7 Edward II., was exchanged for the wife of Robert Bruce; he fell at the battle of Boroughbridge, Yorks. 16 March, 1321, leaving, with other issue, a son,

WILLIAM DE BOHUN, K.G., created Earl of Northampton 17 March, 1337; one of the heroes of Cressy; served also in the wars with Scotland; married Elizabeth, widow of Edmund de Mortimer, daughter of Bartholomew, —and co-heir of her brother, Giles—de Badlesmere, and had, with other issue, a daughter,

ELIZABETH DE BOHUN, died 3 Feb., 1385; buried at Lewes; married 1359, as 1st wife to Richard, Earl of Arundel and Surrey, K.G., admiral of the west and south 1377, and of England 1386; beheaded in Cheapside 21 Sept., 1397, buried in the Church of the Augustine Friars, in Bread Street; his will dated 4 March, 1392; and had a daughter.

ELIZABETH FITZALAN, (elder sister and co-heir of her brother, Thomas FitzAlan, Earl of Arundel); died 8 July, 3 Henry VI., 1425; married, 1st, to Thomas de Mowbray, created Duke of Norfolk, 1397, and died 27 Sept., 1400, leaving a son and 2 daughters; the Duchess of Norfolk re-married to Sir Robert Goushill, Knt., and had 2 daughters, viz.:—

[1] Elizabeth Goushill, elder daughter and co-heir, married to Sir Robert Wingfield, Knt., and had issue.
[2] Joan Goushill, younger daughter and co-heir; married to Sir Thomas Stanley, K.G., lord-deputy of Ireland 1429, and lord.-lieut. 1430-1; was many times in the commissions to treat for peace, &c., with the Scots; knight of the shire for Lancashire 1447-51, and 1453-4; summoned to Parliament as Baron Stanley 20 Jan., 1456; died 1459, having had, with 2 daughters, 4 sons.
(1) **Sir Thomas**, K.G., created Earl of Derby, of whom presently.

(2) Sir William, of Holt Castle, Denbigh, K.G.; beheaded as an adherent of Perkin Warbeck, 16 Feb., 1495, having married Joyce, widow of John Lord Tiptoft, daughter of Edward Charlton, Baron of Powis, and had issue.
(3) Sir John, of Weever, Cheshire, in right of his wife, Elizabeth, daughter and heir of Sir Thomas Weever, Knt., of Weever, ancestor of Lord Stanley of Alderley.
(4) James, archdeacon of Carlisle.

SIR THOMAS, 2ND LORD STANLEY, K.G. 1483; justice of Chester 1463-85; steward of the household 1474, and constable of England for life; and in consideration of his services at the victory of Bosworth Field was created Earl of Derby 27 Oct., 1485; died 1504; will dated 28 July, 1504; proved 9 Nov. following; buried at Borough Priory; he married 1st, Eleanor, daughter of Richard Nevil, Earl of Salisbury, and sister to Richard, Earl of Warwick, "the King maker;" he married 2ndly, Margaret, daughter and heir of John, Duke of Somerset, widow of Edmund Tudor, Earl of Richmond, and mother of Henry VII.; by his 1st wife he had, with 2 daughters, 6 sons, of whom the eldest,

SIR GEORGE STANLEY, K.B., K.G. 1487, P.C.; died 5 Dec., 1848, having been summoned to Parliament as Baron Strange, of Knockyn, 1482 to 1497, in right of his wife Joan, daughter and heir of John, Lord Strange, of Knockyn; and had, with other issue, 2 sons,

[1] Thomas, Baron Strange, of Knockyn, on the death of his father 1488, and succeeded his grandfather as 2nd Earl of Derby, 1504; died 24 May, 1522, having married Anne, daughter of Edward Hastings, and sister of George Hastings, 1st Earl of Huntingdon, and relict of John Radcliffe, Lord Fitzwalter, and left issue, extinct in the male line on the death of James, 10th Earl, 1 Feb., 1735-6 (see Foster's *Peerage*, D. ATHOLE).
[2] Sir James Stanley, of Cross Hall, co. Lanc., marshal of Ireland, married Anne, widow of Edmund Talbot, of Bashall, Yorks, and daughter of John and sister of Sir Percyvall Hart, of Lullingstone, Kent, and had 2 sons and 4 daughters.
(1) Sir George Stanley, Knt., marshal of Ireland; married Isabel Dukinfield, of Dukinfield, Cheshire, and had 2 sons, who died s.p.
(2) Henry Stanley, of Bickerstaffe, in right of his wife, May, sole daughter and heir of Peter Stanley, of Bickerstaffe (by Elizabeth, daughter of James Scarisbrick, of Bickerstaffe; he died 23 July, 1597, having had a son and 2 daughters.
[1] **Sir Edward,** of whom hereafter.
[2] Jane, married to Gabriel Hesketh, of Aughton, co. Lanc.
[3] Dorothy, married to Henry Butler, of Rawcliffe, co. Lanc.
(3) Anne, wife of Ralph Ryshton, of Dunkenhalgh, Cheshire.
(4) Jane, wife of Ashley, of Lancashire.
(5) Margaret, wife of Edward Stanley, of Flintshire.
(6) Eleanor, wife of Gilbert Langtree, of Langtree, Herts, and had a son and 2 daughters.

SIR EDWARD STANLEY, of Bickerstaffe, co. Lanc. (son of Henry), was created a baronet 26 June, 1627; buried at Arley 4 May, 1640, having married 1st, Catherine, daughter of Sir Randle Mainwaring, of Peover, Cheshire; she buried at Arley, 27, Nov., 1613, leaving 3 daughters; he married 2ndly, Isabella, daughter and co-heir of Peter Warburton, of Arley, Cheshire, and had, with other issue, 2 sons.

[1] Sir Thomas, 2nd Bart., baptized at Ormskirk, 22 Oct., 1616; died May, 1653, having married Mary, daughter of Peter Egerton, of Shaw, co. Lanc. (she re-married to Henry, 6th son of Sir Gilbert Hoghton, of Hogton Tower, Lanc., Bart., see Foster's *Baronetage*) and had 2 sons and a daughter.
(1) Sir Edward, 3rd Bart., died 16 Oct., 1671, aged 28, having married 25 Dec., 1663, Elizabeth, daughter and co-heir of Thomas Bosvile, of Warmsworth, Yorks (see Foster's *Yorkshire Collection*), and had, with other issue, a son and daughter.
(1) **Sir Thomas Stanley**, 4th Bart., of whom see page 621.
(2) Barbara, married to Rev. Zachary Taylor.
(2) Peter, buried at Ormskirk, 27 Jan., 1686, having married, 19 April, 1683, Catherine, daughter and co-heir of Col. Alexander Rigby, of Middleton, in Goosnargh, Lanc.; she buried 26 Feb., 1732 (having re-married 2 Nov., 1689, to Paul Amyas, gentleman), and had a son.
THOMAS STANLEY, of Cross Hall, co. Lanc., sheriff 1718; buried at Ormskirk, 10 April, 1733; married Catherine, daughter of Anthony Parker, Esq., of Bradkirk, co. Lanc.; and had, with other issue, a son and daughter.
(1) Thomas Stanley, D.D., rector of Winwick, baptized at Clitheroe, 2 Jan., 1717; buried at Ormskirk, 30 June, 1764; married Betty, daughter and co-heir of John Shaw, of York; she buried with her husband, 4 Dec., 1780, having had issue; their grandson,
EDWARD STANLEY, of Cross Hall, Lanc., J.P. and D.L (son of James Stanley, of Cross Hall, whose brother Thomas was M.P. Lancashire, 1780-1818); born 1789; died 8 March, 1870; having married 3 Sept., 1819, Lady Mary Maitland, 2nd daughter of James, 8th Earl of Lauderdale; she died 8 Nov. 1877, having had a son and 2 daughters.
(1) Edward James, of Cross Hall, co. Lanc., J.P., D.L., and of Quantock Lodge, Somerset, J.P.; high sheriff 1880, and of Cumberland 1883; M.A. Christ Church, Oxon; M.P. West Somerset, 1882; born 16 Dec., 1826; married 19 Sept., 1872, Hon. Mary Dorothy Labouchere, eldest daughter and co-heir of Henry, Lord Taunton (extinct), and has 2 sons and a daughter.
Henry Thomas, born 20 Aug., 1873.
Edward Arthur Vesey, born 30 Aug., 1879.
Evelyn Mary.
(2) Eleanor Julian (Hon.), late maid of honour to

the Queen; married 11 Dec., 1866, as 4th wife, to Lieut.-col. Samuel Long, of Bromley Hill, Kent, who died 31 Aug., 1881 (see page 625).
(3) Augusta, married 12 July, 1841, to Richard, Earl of Dartrey, so created 12 July, 1866, a lord in waiting 1857-8, 1859-66; lord-lieut. co. Monaghan, 1871, and has 4 sons and a daughter.
(1) Vesey, Baron Cremorne, lieut.-col. late Coldstream guards; M.P. co. Monaghan 1865-8; born 22 April, 1842; married 29 Aug., 1882, Julia Georgina Sarah, eldest daughter of Sir George Orby Wombwell, Bart.
(2) Hon. Edward Stanley, capt. R.N. 1882; born 16 Aug., 1843.
(3) Hon. Richard Maitland Westenra (Dawson), capt. late 92nd regiment; born 30 Jan. 1845; married 20 Aug., 1878, Jane Emily, eldest daughter and co-heir of Lieut.-col. Samuel Long, of Bromley Hill, Kent, and has a son and daughter.
Richard Long, born 23 June, 1879.
Emily Mary, born 30 Dec., 1881.
(4) Hon. Anthony Lucius, late lieut. Coldstream guards, born 12 May, 1855; married 2 Oct., 1878, Hon. Mary Frances Fitzgerald de Ros, only child of Dudley Charles, 24th Baron de Ros, and has 2 daughters.
Una Mary, born 5 Oct., 1879.
Maude Elizabeth, born 21 Jan., 1882.
(5) Lady Mary Eleanor Anne, married 8 Feb., 1872, to Henry Edward, 4th Earl of Ilchester, and has 2 sons and a daughter.
(1) Giles Stephen Holland, BARON STAVORDALE; born 3 May, 1874.
(2) Hon. Denzil Vesey, born 26 Feb. 1879.
(3) Lady Muriel Augusta.
[2] Mary (Stanley), buried at Winwick 22 June, 1778; married about 1745, to Rev. John Lowe, M.A., rector of Much Hoole, co. Lanc., and P.C. Winwick 56 years, and had (with an only daughter, Catharine, died young) an only son,
THOMAS LOWE, married Ellen, daughter of John Higginbotham, of Manchester, merchant; and died in the lifetime of his father, having had 2 sons and 2 daughters.
(1) Higginbotham Lowe, captain 33rd regiment, died unmarried.
(2) John (Lowe), of Glazebrooke House, Devon; D.L.; captain 3rd Royal Lanc. militia; died 1843; married Catherine, eldest daughter and co-heiress of Peter Tonkin, of Plymouth; she died 1869, having had an only son,
PETER STANLEY LOWE of Whitehall, Churchstow, Devon; capt. 1st Royal Lanc. militia; born 23 Jan., 1809; married , 1832, Anne Elizabeth, daughter of Admiral Searle, C.B., she died 5 July, 1884, having had 5 sons and 3 daughters.
[1] Stanley John (Lowe), major in the service of the Cape Government; married Annie, 2nd daughter of Francis William Dobson, Esq., LL.D., and has a son.
Francis Stanley, born Sept., 1868.
[2] George Tonkin Shortland, married Harriett, 2nd daughter of Edward Younge, Esq., barrister-at-law.
[3] Charles Henry.
[4] John, died s.p. in Australia, 23 June, 1879; married Lilian, daughter of Dr. Large.
[5] Frederick Carnegie, married Eleanor FitzGerald, only daughter of Rev. Isaac Litchfield, of and has 2 sons and a daughter.
William Frederick Litchfield (Lowe), George Stanley, Elinor Mabel Rose.
[6] Annie Kathleen; married 4 Jan., 1870, to Rev. George Marie Capell, B.A., rector of Passenham since 1870 (see Foster's *Peerage*, E. ESSEX), and has a son and 5 daughters.
Arthur George Coningsby (Capell), Dora Amy Isabel, Marie Kathleen, Leonie Annie, Hilda Amelie, Violet Bertha Sybil.
[7] Amy Elizabeth.
[8] Bertha Violet, married 1st, to Sir William West Turner, K.C.S.I.; and 2ndly, to Col. George Scougall Macbean, B.S.C., served in Indian Mutiny, dep. commissary general at Lucknow since 1875, and has issue.
(3) Betty (Lowe), married , to Thomas Chadwick, major 22nd light dragoons; served at the storming of Seringapatam, in the Mahratta war, and at the taking of Java; he died 18 May, 1818, leaving an only child,
Catherine Morritt (Chadwick), died 8 Feb., 1854; married 15 May, 1826, to Rev. Thomas Hinde, M.A., Jesus Coll., Camb., head master Winwick Grammar School; he died 5 July, 1851, having had 6 sons and 6 daughters.
[1] Thomas Chambre (Hinde), of Trin. Hall, Camb.; born 31 March, 1827; died 19 April, 1847.
[2] Henry John (Hinde), lieut. 24th regiment; present at Chillianwallah; born 25 Sept., 1828; died 24 Oct., 1854.
[3] Hugh Alan, lieut. H.M.S. Winchester; born 9 Jan., 1830; died of wounds received in Burmah, 24 March, 1853.
[4] Walter James Stanley, born 28 Nov., 1832; died 15 Feb., 1834.
[5] Arthur Richard, born 15 March, 1834; married 24 Sept., 1874 his cousin Elizabeth Jane, only daughter of Thomas Mason, Esq., and has had 2 sons and a daughter.
Thomas Stanley (Hinde), born 9 March, died 18 July, 1877.
Arthur Geoffrey Wynewic, born 25 July, 1878.
Bessie Kathleen.
[6] Charles Leonard Morland (Hinde), B.A. Trin. Coll., Dublin, 1864; vicar of Flockton-cum-Denby-Grange since 1881; born 1 Dec., 1843.
[7] Catherine Margaretta Jane; died unmarried 29 Jan., 1853.
[8] Eleanor Mary, died 24 Oct., 1836.
[9] Dora Elizabeth.
[10] Mary Anna. [11] Ellen Anne.
[12] Blanche Susan, died 3 Feb., 1842.
(4) Catherine (Lowe), married , to Mr. Foden, of Manchester; she died s.p.
(3) Mary, married to John Bradshaw, of Pennington, co. Lanc.
[2] Henry (Stanley), baptized at Ormskirk, 3 Sept., 1617; buried there 16 Oct., 1658; married 1st, Eleanor Dutton, and had a daughter; he married 2ndly, Mary, daughter of Hamlet Cropper, Esq., of Bickerstaffe, and had a son,
EDWARD STANLEY, of Preston; died there, 1755, aged 103, having had 8 children, of whom a daughter, —(Anne, born 1703, married to Capt. Richard Tyldesley, of the Priory, Castletown, Isle of Man, and had issue)—and a son,
CHARLES STANLEY (captain), of Ballacaigan, &c., in right of his wife; receiver general of the Isle of Man; baptized at Preston 16 Sept., 1702; buried 8 March, 1749-50; married 30 Dec., 1728, Elizabeth, daughter and heir of Christopher Parker, Esq. (by his wife, Catherine, daughter of John Stanley of the

Isle of Man); she buried with her husband at Kirk Arbory, 11 Jan., 1759, having had, with other issue, a son and daughter.

(1) Charles (Stanley), born 3 April, and baptized at Kirk-Malen, 17 April, 1745; died at Manchester, 10 June, 1805; married Martha, daughter of Henry Rawsthorn, of Manchester; she born 8 Sept., 1744; buried at Ormskirk, 7 March, 1805, having had a son and 3 daughters.

[1] James, of Peter House, Cambridge; vicar of Ormskirk, 1800-12; born 30 Oct., 1768; buried there 17 June, 1812, having married 11 July, 1797, Sarah, daughter of John Edleston, Esq.; she died 12 Feb., 1856, aged 91, having had 4 sons and 3 daughters.

(1) Edward, vice-admiral R.N.; born 10 May, 1798; died 19 Feb., 1878, having married 1st, 5 July, 1834, Elizabeth, daughter of John Snell; she died s.p. 20 April, 1848; he married 2ndly, 13-18 Oct., 1855, Caroline Cordelia, daughter of Edward Hancorne, of Hendon, Middx.; she died 4 Oct., 1876, leaving 5 sons and 2 daughters.

Edward James, born 12 Dec., 1857.
Montague Neville, born 5 Sept., 1861.
Henry Harrington, born 14 Dec., 1862.
Ferdinand Charles Nelson, born 11 April, 1865.
Alphonso Frederick, born 28 Oct., 1869.
Rosamond Jane. Emma Cordelia.

(2) Frederick, R.N., born 10 May, 1799; lost in H.M.S. *Drake*, 23 June, 1822, unmarried.

(3) Henry, born 11 Sept., 1800; died s.p. 24 May, 1877, having married 1st, 4 Feb., 1847, Charlotte Fuller; she died 23 April, 1849; he married 2ndly, 25 April, 1854, Eliza, only daughter of Edward Charles, Esq.; she died 11 Sept., 1868.

(4) Charles Thomas, born 28 Sept., 1806; died s.p. 23 Sept., 1883, having married 8 June, 1841, Elizabeth Rosamond, eldest daughter of James Ward, Esq., of Willey Place, Surrey; J.P. Hants; gent. commoner of Wadham College, and widow of Robert Henry Stanhope, com. R.N. (nephew of Charles, 3rd Earl of Harrington).

(5) Jane, died 11 Sept., 1873, having married 1 Aug., 1825, to Richard Bayly Bowden, com. R.N., who died s.p. 12 Aug., 1861.

(6) Caroline, died 4 Jan., 1877, having married 28 July, 1827, to Henry Robert Crozier, Esq., and had, with 2 daughters died young, 5 sons.

[1] Henry Edward (Crozier), capt. R.N., born 2 Feb., 1830.

[2] Frederick William (Crozier), born 14 June, 1832; died .

[3] Stanley, lieut.-col. 1st Oxford. L.I.; born 12 Aug., 1834; married 11 Dec., 1866, Ellen Harriette, 2nd daughter of Lieut.-col. Highmoor, Madras cavalry, and has had 2 daughters.

(1) Emmeline Stanley (Crozier), died 3 Feb., 1872.

(2) Constance Stanley.

[4] Walter James, twin with Charles, born 14 July, 1844; died .

[5] Charles, born 14 July, 1844; died

(7) Harriet, unmarried.

[2] Catherine, born 15 Aug., 1770; married 2 Mar. 1793, to Capt. Henry M'Kittrick.

[3] Margaret Rawsthorn, born 1 Aug., 1773; married 25 Aug., 1792, to John, brother of Capt. Henry M'Kittrick.

[4] Mary Jane, born 8 May, 1777; married 27 Oct., 1798, to Thomas Johnson, of Liverpool.

(2) Katherine, born 6, baptized at Kirk Arbory, 18 Oct., 1732; married to John Allen or Allan, of Liverpool, and had at least a daughter,

Elizabeth Allen or Allan, married to her cousin, Stanley Tyldesley, Esq., eldest son of Capt. Richard Tyldesley aforesaid.

SIR THOMAS STANLEY, 4th Bart.; M.P. Preston, 1695; born 27 Sept., 1670; died 7 May, 1714; married 1st, , 1688, Elizabeth, only daughter and heir of Thomas Patten, of Preston, co. Lanc.; she died 1694; he married 2ndly, Margaret, widow of Sir Richard Standish, of Duxbury, co. Lanc., Bart., daughter of Thomas Holcroft, of Holcroft; she died 14 Oct., 1735, aged nearly 100; by his 1st wife he had 4 sons, of whom the eldest.

SIR EDWARD, 5th Bart., succeeded as 11th Earl of Derby, 1 Feb., 1735-6, and took his seat 13 April, 1736; M.P. Lancashire 1727-36 and 1735; lord-lieut. and custos rotulorum 1742; born 17 Sept., 1689; died 23 Feb., 1776, having married , 1714, Elizabeth, only daughter and heir of Robert Hesketh, of Rufford, co. Lanc.; she died 25 Feb., 1776, having had, with other issue, a son and 2 daughters,

[1] **James**, Lord Strange, of whom presently.

[2] Elizabeth, died 2 Sept., 1780; married 1 March, 1745-6, to Sir Peter Warburton, of Arley, Cheshire, Bart.; he died

[3] Jane, died s.p. 9 June, 1776; married . to Gen. John Burgoyne, P.C., M.P., of Lambert's Oak, Surrey; he died s.p.l.

JAMES, LORD STRANGE, assumed the additional surname and arms of Smith, by Act of Parliament, 1749; died in his father's lifetime, May, 1771; married 17 March, 1747, Lucy, daughter and co-heir of Hugh Smith, of Weald Hall, Essex; she died 5 Feb, 1759, having had, with other issue, 2 sons and 3 daughters.

[1] Edward, 12th Earl of Derby, left by his 1st wife, Elizabeth, only daughter of James, 6th Duke of Hamilton and Brandon, a son and 2 daughters,

(1) Edward Smith, 13th Earl of Derby (see Foster's *Peerage*, and page 624 of this work).

(2) Lady Charlotte, died 25 Nov., 1803; married 22 Aug., 1796, to her cousin, Edmund Hornby, Esq. (see page 626).

(3) Lady Elizabeth Henrietta, died ; married 15 Jan., 1795, to Stephen Thomas Cole, Esq., of Twickenham, Middx., and Stoke Lyne, Dorset; he died 6 Sept., 1835.

[2] Hon. Thomas (Stanley), major in the army; M.P. Lancashire 1776; died in Jamaica, Nov., 1779.

[3] Elizabeth, married 28 July, 1779, to Rev. Sir Thomas Horton, Bart. (see page 634).

[4] **Hon. Lucy Stanley,** married to Geoffrey Hornby, next named.

LUCY STANLEY (2nd daughter of James Lord Strange), died 10 Feb., 1833; married, by special licence, at Knowsley, 25 April, 1772, to Geoffrey Hornby, of Scale Hall, co. Lanc.; D L., and high sheriff 1774; lieut.-colonel Lanc. militia, 1776; M.A.; took holy orders; rector of Winwick, 1781-1812 (son of Edmund Hornby, of Poulton and Scale Hall; and see Foster's *Lancashire Collection*); born at Layton Hall; baptized at Bispham, co. Lanc., 14 Aug., 1750; died 31 July, 1812; buried at Winwick 5 Aug., 1812, having had 7 sons and 6 daughters.

[1] **Edmund Hornby,** of whom see page 626.
[2] James John (Hornby), rector of Winwick, co. Lanc.; born 27 Aug., 1777; died 14 Sept., 1855; married 1st, 14 Oct., 1800, Hester, youngest daughter and co-heir of Robert Vernon Atherton, Esq., of Atherton; she died 30 June, 1830; he married 2ndly, Catherine, daughter of Alexander Boyle, Esq.; she died 12 May, 1859; by his 1st wife he had 2 sons.
(1) James John (Hornby), born 4 July, 1801; died 1818.
(2) Robert Vernon Atherton (Hornby), born 6 Nov., 1805; died s.p. Sept., 1857.
[3] Geoffrey (Hornby), rector of Bury, Lanc.; born 4 April. 1780; died 4 March, 1850; married 12 April, 1810, Hon. Georgiana Byng, sister of John, 5th Viscount Torrington; she died 23 July, 1856, having had 4 sons and a daughter.
(1) William Windham (Hornby), admiral R.N. (retired 1864); commissioner of prisons since 1877; J.P., D.L. Lanc.; born 23 July, 1812; married 17 Jan., 1849, Augusta, widow of Charles Dacres Paterson, Esq., daughter of Sir William Pratt Call, Bart.
(2) Stanley Byng (Hornby), lieut. R.A.; born 15 Nov., 1814; died 21 Nov., 1843; married 8 July, 1836, Caroline Sarah, daughter of Joseph Thompson, Esq., of New Providence, Barbadoes, and had a son and daughter.
[1] Stanley Edward (Hornby), born 31 July, 1842.
[2] Georgiana Elizabeth, died s.p. 14 Oct., 1858; married to Rev. Robert Swann, rector of Christchurch Cathedral, Nassau, Bahamas.
(3) Edward James Geoffrey (Hornby), M.A. Merton Coll., Oxon., 1844; rector of Bury, Lanc., since 1850, and rural dean 1855; hon. canon Manchester Cathedral 1855; born 9 Nov., 1816; married 19 Aug., 1841, Elizabeth, only daughter of Hornby Roughsedge, Esq., of Foxghyll, Westmoreland, and has 2 sons.
[1] Cecil Roughsedge (Hornby), born 29 Dec., 1842.
[2] Geoffrey Edward, born 10 July, 1844.
(4) Frederick John, lieut. R.N.; born 1 July, 1819; died unmarried, in Sir John Franklin's Polar expedition, about 1845.
(5) Georgina Lucy Cecilia (Hornby), married 2 June, 1863, to Admiral Sir Henry Leeke, K.C.B., who died s.p. March, 1870.
[4] Edward Thomas Stanley (Hornby), M.A. (and fellow) Caius Coll., Camb., 1809; in holy orders; died unmarried, 25 March, 1825, aged 43.
[5] Sir Phipps (Hornby), G.C.B., of Little Green, Sussex; admiral R.N.; supdt. of Royal Naval Hospital and Victualling Yard, Plymouth 1832; supdt. Woolwich Dockyard 1838; controller-gen. of coastguard 1841-6; com.-in-chief on Pacific station, 1848-51; a lord of the Admiralty 1852; C.B. 1815; K.C.B. 1852; G.C.B. 1861; born 27 April, 1785; died 19 March, 1867; married 22 Dec., 1814, Maria Sophia, sister of F. M. Sir John Fox Burgoyne, Bart.; she died 25 Dec., 1860, having had 3 sons and 5 daughters.
(1) Phipps John (Hornby), capt. R.E., born 10 April, 1820; died in Canada 18 April, 1848; married 7 March, 1844, Frederica, daughter of Capt. Breton, and had 2 daughters.
[1] Frederica Lucy Phipps (Hornby), married 30 July, 1874, to Lieut.-col. Charles Edward Henry Stanley, late grenadier guards, grandson of Edward Smith, 13th Earl of Derby, K.G. (see Foster's *Peerage*), and has 2 sons and 2 daughters.
Son, born 9 April, 1878; a son born 1880; a daughter, born 1 May, 1882; a daughter born June 1884.
[2] Lina Mary Phipps (Hornby), married Oct., 1869, to John Lambert Ovans, Esq., who died 1883.
(2) Sir Geoffrey Thomas Phipps (Hornby), G.C.B., of Littlegreen and Lordington, Suffolk, admiral R.N., com-in-chief West African Station 1865-8, of flying squadron 1869-70; senior officer of Channel squadron 1871-4; a junior lord of the admiralty 1874-6; com.-in-chief Mediterranean squadron 1876-80; at Portsmouth since 1882; president Royal Naval College since 1881; born 20 Feb., 1825; married 27 April, 1853, Emily Frances, only daughter of Rev. John Coles, of Ditcham Park, Hants (sister of late Cowper Coles, capt. R.N., C.B.), and has 3 sons and 3 daughters.
[1] Geoffrey Stanley Phipps (Hornby), capt. rifle brigade, born 15 Dec., 1856; married 21 Feb., 1884, Jessie Wilson, 2nd daughter of T. B. Gunston, Esq., of London, and has a daughter born 26 Feb., 1885.
[2] Edmond John Phipps (Hornby), born 31 Dec., 1857
[3] Robert Stewart (Hornby), born 9 July, 1866.
[4] Emily Frances Phipps.
[5] Mary Augusta Phipps, married 5 Nov., 1879, to Frederick William Egerton, capt. R.N., 1881 (see Foster's *Peerage*, B. EGERTON).
[6] Ethel Mary Phipps.
(3) James John (Hornby), M.A. Balliol Coll., Oxon, 1852; D.D. 1869; D.C.L. (Durham) 1882; provost of Eton Coll. 1884; head-master 1868-84; hon. chaplain in ordinary to the Queen, 1882; fellow Brasenose Coll., Oxon, 1851-68; principal of Bishop Cosin's Hall, Durham, 1854-64; senior proctor of Oxford 1866; 2nd master of Winchester Coll. 1867-8; born 18 Dec., 1826; married 5 Aug., 1869, Augusta Eliza, daughter of Rev. J. C. Evans, of Stoke Poges, Slough, and has 3 sons and 2 daughters.
James John, born 14 March, 1871; Robert Phipps, born 9 June, 1876; William, born 4 Aug., 1878; Mary Sophia; Eveline Augusta.
(4) Maria Elizabeth.
(5) Caroline Lucy (C.I.), married 29 Nov., 1838, to Lieut.-gen. Sir William Denison, K.C.B. 1856; governor of Madras, 1861-6; acting governor-gen. of India, Jan., 1864; governor-gen. of New South Wales, 1854-61; governor of Tasmania, 1846-54; and knighted 1846; colonel R.E.; (brother of late Viscount Ossington); he died 19 Jan., 1871, having had 8 sons and 6 daughters.
[1] William Evelyn (Denison), J.P., D.L., Notts.; capt. R.A.; M.P. Nottingham 1874-80; born 25 Feb., 1843; married 25 Oct., 1877, Lady Elinor Amherst, daughter of William Pitt, 2nd Earl Amherst, and has a son, born 22 Dec., 1878.
[2] Frank George (Denison), born 22 Dec., 1844; died unmarried 3 Feb., 1869.
[3] Henry Phipps (Denison), B.A., Christ Church, Oxon., 1871; curate of East Brent, Somerset, since 1876; born 3 June, 1848.
[4] James Edward (Denison), M.A., Christ Church, Oxon. 1884; vice-principal Cuddesdon College, 1884; born 22 July, 1853.

Rev. James John Hornby, D.D.,

D.C.L., Provost of Eton College.

FROM THE

Blood Royal  **of England.**

EDWARD I., crowned 19 Aug., 1274, b. 17 June, 1239, d. 7 July, 1307. = Eleanor (1st wife), dau. of Ferdinand III., King of Castile, d. 27 Nov. 1290.

John, Count of Holland, etc. (1st husband), d. s.p. = Elizabeth, d. 5 May, 1316, aged 32. = Humphrey de Bohun, Earl of Hereford, etc. (2nd husband), fell at Boroughbridge, 16 March, 1321.

William de Bohun, K.G., Earl of Northampton (2nd husband). = Elizabeth, widow of Edmund de Mortimer, dau. of B. de Badlesmere.

Elizabeth de Bohun (1st wife) d. 3 Feb., 1385. = Richard, Earl of Arundel and Surrey, K.G., beheaded 21 Sept., 1397.

Thomas de Mowbray Duke of Norfolk (1st husband). = Elizabeth Fitz Alan, d. 8 July, 1425. = Sir Robert de Goushill (2nd husband).

Joan Goushill, younger dau. and co-heir. = Sir Thomas Stanley, K.G., Baron Stanley by summons, 1456.

Sir Thomas Stanley, K.G., created Earl of Derby, 1485, d. 1504. = Eleanor (1st wife), sister of Richard, Earl of Warwick, "the king-maker."

Sir George Stanley, K.B., K.G., P.C., sum. to Parlt. as Baron Strange, d. 5 Dec., 1488. = Joan, dau. and heir of John, Lord Strange, of Knockyn.

Sir James Stanley, of Cross Hall, co. Lanc., marshal of Ireland (2nd husband). = Anne, widow of Edmund Talbot, of Bashall, dau. of John Hart, of Lullingstone.

Henry Stanley, of Bickerstaffe. = Mary, dau. and heir of Peter Stanley, of Bickerstaffe.

A, continued above.

A, continued from below.

Henry Stanley = Mary Stanley.

Sir Edward Stanley, of Bickerstaffe, Bart., d. 1640. = Isabella (2nd wife) dau. and co-heir of Peter Warburton, of Arley, Cheshire.

Sir Thomas Stanley, 2nd bart (1st husband), baptised 22 Oct., 1616, d. May, 1653. = Mary, dau. of Peter Egerton, of Shaw, co. Lanc.

Sir Edward Stanley, 3rd bart., d. 16 Oct., 1671. = Elizabeth, dau. and coheiress of Thomas Bosvile, of Warmsworth, Yorks., m. 25 Dec., 1663.

Sir Thomas Stanley, 4th bart., M.P., b. 27 Sept., 1670, d. 7 May, 1714. = Elizabeth (1st wife), only dau. and heir of Thomas Patten, of Bold, co. Lanc., m. 1688, d. 1694.

Sir Edward Stanley, 5th bart. and 11th Earl of Derby, b. 17 Sept., 1689, d. 23 Feb., 1776. = Elizabeth, only dau. and heir of Robert Hesketh, of Rufford, co. Lanc., m. 1714, d. 25 Feb., 1776.

James, Lord Strange, d. May, 1771. = Lucy, dau. and co-heiress of Hugh Smith, of Weald Hall, Essex, m. 1747, d. 1759.

Hon. Lucy Stanley, younger dau., m. 25 April, 1772, d. 10 Feb., 1833. = Rev. Geoffrey Hornby of Scale Hall, co. Lanc., rector of Winwicke, d. 31 July, 1812.

Sir Phipps Hornby, G.C.B., admiral R.N., a lord of the Admiralty, b. 27 April, 1785, d. 19 March, 1867. = Maria Sophia, sister of F.M. Sir John Fox Burgoyne, bart., m. 22 Dec., 1814, d. 25 Dec., 1860.

Children:

- Phipps John Hornby, capt. R.E., d. 1848.
- Sir Geoffrey Thomas Phipps Hornby, G.C.B., Admiral R.N., b. 20 Feb., 1825.
- James John Hornby, M.A., Balliol, D.D., D.C.L., Provost of Eton Coll., b. 11 Dec., 1826. = Augusta Eliza, dau. of Rev. J. C. Evans, m. 5 Aug., 1869.
- Maria.
- Caroline Lucy (C.I.), m. 1838, to Lieut.-Gen. Sir William Denison, K.C.B., Gov. of Madras, who d. 1871.
- Susan, m. to Ven. Archd. Hornby.
- Lucy Hester, m. to Vice-Admiral Stopford.
- Elizabeth, m. to Rev. J. E. Cross.

Children of James John Hornby:

- James John Hornby, b. 14 March, 1871
- Robert Phipps, b. 9 June, 1876
- William, b. 4 Aug. 1878.
- Mary Sophia.
- Eveline Augusta.

[5] Charles (Denison), born 15 April, 1855; died 4 Oct., 1858.
[6] Alfred John, born 8 April, 1857.
[7] Arthur Geoffrey, born 17 Feb., 1859; died 23 Aug., 1876.
[8] George Charles, born 5 Jan., 1861.
[9] Mary Charlotte, died unmarried 12 May, 1861.
[10] Susan Maria, married 19 Feb., 1863, to James Wilkinson Breeks, Esq., of Warcop, Penrith, he died 6 June, 1872, leaving issue.
[11] Lucy Emily. [12] Caroline Elizabeth.
[13] Ellen Matilda died 10 Sept., 1858.
[14] Katharine Mary.

(6) Susan Charlotte Margaret, married 18 April, 1844, as 2nd wife to the Ven. William Hornby, M.A. Christ Church, Oxon., 1833; vicar of St. Michael-on-Wyre since 1847; hon. canon of Manchester Cathedral, 1850; archdeacon of Lancaster, 1870; rural dean of Preston, 1850-78; and has had 5 sons and 2 daughters,
[1] William (Hornby), died 25 March, 1858, aged 13.
[2] Hugh Phipps (Hornby), born 10 March, 1849.
[3] Phipps John (Hornby), M.A. Balliol Coll., Oxon., 1879, in holy orders; born 10 Jan., 1853.
[4] James John (Hornby), born 18 Dec., 1854.
[5] William Starkey (Hornby), born 2 Sept., 1861.
[6] Susan.
[7] Anne Lucy, married 9 April, 1885, to Richard Heywood, 4th son of S. H. Thompson, Esq., of Thingwall, Liverpool.

(7) Lucy Hester, married 1 June, 1865, as 2nd wife to Vice-Admiral Robert Fanshawe Stopford, R.N. (see Foster's *Peerage*, E. COURTOWN).

(8) Elizabeth (Hornby), married 22 June, 1854, to Rev. John Edward Cross, M.A. Christ Church, Oxon, 1846; vicar of Appleby, co. Linc., 1856; prebendary of Lincoln 1880; rural dean 1880 (brother of Rt. Hon. Sir Richard Assheton Cross, P.C., G.C.B.)

[6] George (Hornby), D.D., and fellow of Brasenose Coll., Oxon; born 10 Jan., 1790; died unmarried at Naples, 3 Nov. 1872.

[7] Charles (Hornby), lieut.-col. Scots fusilier guards; born 31 Jan., 1791; died 1865.

[8] Lucy, died Nov. 1849; married 3 May, 1796, to Rev. Henry William Champneys, of Westenhanger, Kent, rector of Badsworth, Yorks; assumed the surname and arms of Champneys, in lieu of Burt, by royal licence, 10 Nov., 1778; he died 18 Feb., 1845, having had 5 sons and 6 daughters.

(1) Henry William Justinian (Champneys), born 12 Dec., 1798; died in Paris 16 Nov. 1819.

(2) Thomas Phipps Amyan (Champneys), B.A. Merton Coll., Oxon, 1833; rector of Badsworth 1859-79; vicar of Owston 1850-9; born 3 Sept., 1808; died 16 Jan., 1879.

(3) Edward Geoffrey John (Champneys), E.I.C.S., born 19 Feb., 1813; died unmarried 22 April, 1884.

(4) Maximilian Hugh Stanley (Champneys), M.A. Brasenose Coll., Oxon, 1841; rector of Epperstone, co. Linc., since 1853; born 13 Feb., 1816; married 9 May, 1854, Frances Anne, daughter of Rev. Francis Bickley Astley, rector of Manningford Abbots and Bishopstrow, Wilts (see Foster's *Baronetage*); she died 13 Jan., 1882, having had a son and 4 daughters.
[1] Edward Hugh Stanley (Champneys), born 24 July, 1861.
[2] Lucy Dorothea. [3] Mary Margaret.
[4] Frances Millesent. [5] Susan Edith.

(5) Charles James Hornby (Champneys), born 5 Nov. 1817, died in Australia about 1840.

(6) Lucy Henrietta, died 9 Oct., 1875; married 15 Sept., 1836, to Rev. William Hastings Kelke, rector of Drayton Beauchamp, Bucks; he died 22 April, 1864, leaving an only son,
William Henry Hastings (Kelke), M.A., Brasenose Coll., Oxon, barrister-at-law, Lincoln's Inn, 1879; born 26 Feb., 1839; married 25 Aug., 1880, Frances Mary, daughter of late John Sparrow, J.P., of Blackburn.

(7) Frances Susanna, died unmarried 31 May, 1878.

(8) Louisa Charlotte Margaret, died unmarried 13 April, 1883.

(9) Harriet Mary, born 9 April, 1805; died 31 Jan., 1808.

(10) Emily Catherine, died 27 Feb., 1875; married 8 Sept., 1825, to Adam Hodgson, Esq., of Scarthwaite, co. Lanc., and of Liverpool, merchant, who died Dec., 1862, having had 11 sons and 3 daughters.
[1] Thomas Edward (Hodgson), M.A. Trin. Coll., Camb., 1853; vicar of Darlington since 1873; rural dean of Darlington 1880; surrogate, 1874; born 23 Sept., 1827; married 1 Oct., 1864, Maria Theodosia, daughter of William Light, Esq., of Clifton, Bristol; she died 22 Jan., 1875, leaving a son and daughter.
Cecil Ernest Champneys (Hodgson), born 3 July, 1870. Ethel Mary.
[2] Adam Henry (Hodgson), born 11 Nov., 1828.
[3] Francis, born 11 June, 1831; died 16 Oct. following.
[4] Frederick, born 22 June, 1832; died unmarried 23 Feb., 1884.
[5] Wilberforce, born 30 July, 1833; died unmarried 23 March, 1861.
[6] Alfred, born 15 Jan., 1835; died 20 Aug. following.
[7] Edward Hornby, born 8 July, 1836.
[8] Albert Champneys, born 9 July, 1838; died 5 April, 1840.
[9] Reginald, born 27 May, 1840.
[10] Herbert, born 3 Dec., 1841; died 13 Feb. following.
[11] Evelyn Gisborne, born 1 April, 1846.
[12] Emily Lucy.
[13] Elizabeth Tylston.
[14] Katharine Gertrude, died 17 July, 1845.

(11) Mary Sophia, married 7 Oct., 1845, to Benjamin Haigh Allen, Esq., of Clifford Priory, Herefordshire; J.P., D.L.; high sheriff 1875, and has 2 daughters,
[1] Mary Lucy, married 27 Feb., 1878, to John Knowles, Esq., of Darnhall Hall, Cheshire, only son of late Thomas Knowles, M.P., Wigan.
[2] Emily Kate (Allen).

[9] Charlotte Margaret, died 16 June, 1817; married 30 June, 1798, to her cousin, Edward Smith, 13th Earl of Derby, K.G.; lord-lieut. and custos rotulorum co. Lanc.; colonel Lanc. militia; vice-admiral of coast of Lancashire; president of Linnæan and Zoological societies; M.P. Preston 1796-1812, Lancashire 1812-32; created Baron Stanley, of Bickerstaffe, co. Palatine of Lanc., by letters patent, 22 Dec., 1832; born 21 April, 1775; died 30 June, 1851, having had 3 sons and 3 daughters.

(1) Edward Geoffrey, 14th earl; K.G., G.C.M.G., P.C., D.C.L., F.R.S.; chancellor of the university of Oxford; M.P. Stockbridge 1822-6, Preston 1826-30, Windsor 1831-2, and North Lancashire 1832-44; summoned to the House of Lords 4 Nov., 1844, in his father's Barony of Stanley of Bickerstaffe; and was elected K.G. 28 June, 1849; chief secretary for Ireland 1830-33; secretary of state for the colonies 1833-4, 1841-5; and first lord of the treasury in 1852, 1858, and 1866; born 29 March, 1799; died 23 Oct., 1869, having married 31 May, 1825, Hon. Emma Caroline Wilbraham, 2nd daughter of Edward, 1st Lord Skelmersdale (E. LATHOM); she died 26 April, 1876, having had 2 sons and a daughter.
[1] Edward Henry Stanley, K.G., 15th Earl of Derby (1485, E.), Baron Stanley (1832, U.K.), and a Baronet (1627, E.); P.C.; trustee British Museum;

M.P. King's Lynn 1848-69; a member of Universities committee, 1881; lord rector Edinburgh University 1875; under-secretary of state for foreign affairs 1852; secretary of state, colonies, 1858, 1884-5; president board of control 1858; secretary of state, India, 1858-9; secretary of state, foreign affairs, 1866-8, 1874-8; born 21 July, 1826; married 5 July, 1870, Lady Mary Catherine, 2nd daughter of George John, 5th Earl Delawarr, and widow of James Brownlow William, 2nd Marquis of Salisbury, K.G.

[2] Right Hon. Frederick Arthur Stanley, M.P.; secretary of state for war 1878-80; financial secretary to the treasury 1877-8; a lord of admiralty 1868; M.P. Preston 1865-8, North Lancashire, 1868-85; Blackpool Division, N.W. Lancashire, Dec., 1885; lieut.-col. 1st royal Lanc. militia since 1874; capt. late grenadier guards; militia A.D.C. to the Queen; heir presumptive to the peerage; born 15 Jan., 1841; married 31 May, 1864, Lady Constance Villiers, eldest daughter of George, 4th Earl of Clarendon, and has had, with other issue, 7 sons and a daughter.

Edward George Villiers, born 4 April, 1865.
Albert Victor (H.M. the Queen sponsor), born 16 Jan., 1867.
Arthur, born 18 Nov., 1869.
Ferdinand Charles, born 28 Jan., 1871.
George Frederick, born 14 Oct., 1872.
Algernon Francis, born 8 Jan, 1874.
Frederick William, born 27 May, 1878.
Isobel Constance Mary.

[3] Lady Emma Charlotte, married 11 Oct., 1860, to Lieut.-col. Hon. Wellington Patrick Manvers Chetwynd-Talbot, of Honeybourne, Worc.; hon lieut.-col. 1st (King's Own) Staffordshire militia; capt. late 7th regt.; comptroller of household 1845-6; British resident at Cephalonia 1855-60; a governor and vice-president of Wellington College since 1873; serjeant-at-arms to House of Lords since 1858 (see Foster's *Peerage*, E. SHREWSBURY), and has 5 sons and 3 daughters.

Charley Stanley, born 31 Jan., 1862.
Frederick Gilbert, born 1 May, 1868.
Walter Stanley, born 4 Nov., 1869.
Henry Arthur, born 23 Aug., 1872.
Gilbert Edward, born 4 Sept., 1876.
Cecil Emma.
Edith Constance Louisa.
Helen Ivory, born 14 April, 1880.

(2) Hon. Henry Thomas (Stanley), of Stanley Hall, co. Lanc.; M.P. Preston 1832-7; born 9 March, 1803; died 2 April, 1875, having married 1 Sept., 1835, Anne, daughter of Richard Woolhouse, Esq., and had 3 sons and a daughter.

[1] Edward Henry (Stanley), of Stanley Hall, born 5 Jan., 1838.

[2] Charles Geoffrey (Stanley), capt. 32nd regt.; born 5 Sept., 1839; died 22 April, 1877, having married 11 April, 1861, Agnes Nina, youngest daughter of late Honoratus Leigh Rigby, Esq., of Hawarden, Flint, (see Foster's *Peerage*, B. Teynham), and has 3 sons and a daughter.

Charles Henry, born 25 March, 1862.
Henry Edmund, born 8 July, 1863.
A son, born 6 March, 1871.
Mary Kathleen Fanny.

[3] Henry Edmund (Stanley), capt. 23rd regt.; born 27 Dec., 1840; died 15 Nov., 1867, having married 15 Oct., 1863, Ida Emily, eldest daughter of Thomas Allen Brown, of Agra, India, and has a son and daughter.

Henry Edmund Thomas, born 30 Sept., 1864.
Isabell Clayton.

(3) Hon. Charles James Fox (Stanley), colonel 7th Lanc. militia; lieut.-col. late grenadier guards; born 25 April, 1808; died 13 Oct., 1884; married 10 Dec., 1836, Frances Augusta, daughter of Gen. Sir Henry Frederick Campbell, K.C.B. (E. Cawdor); she died 29 May, 1878, having had 4 sons and 4 daughters.

[1] Charles Edward Henry (Stanley), late capt. and lieut.-col. grenadier guards; born 28 April, 1843; married 30 July, 1874, Frederica Lucy, daughter of Capt. Phipps John Hornby, R.E. (named above); and has a son, born 9 April, 1878, and a daughter born 1 May, 1882.

[2] Douglas James George, born 8 March, 1847; died 10 July, 1877.

[3] Albert Hamilton, capt. late 68th regt.; born 9 July, 1849.

[4] Edmund Phipps, B.A. Brasenose Coll., Oxon, 1878; rector of Wootton Courtenay, Somerset; incumbent Prestbury-cum-Lower Withington, 1883; curate of Crosthwaite, Cumberland, 1879; born 13 Oct., 1855; married 9 Sept., 1885, Catherine Stewart, eldest daughter of John Stewart Browne, Esq., of Port Lincoln, South Australia.

[5] Evelyn Emma. [6] Margaret Alice.
[7] Mary Louisa. [8] Constance Emily.

(4) Lady Charlotte Elizabeth, died 15 Feb., 1853, having married 16 Dec., 1823, to Edward (Leycester), Penrhyn, Esq., of East Sheen, Surrey; he died 6 March, 1861, having had 2 sons and 2 daughters.

[1] Edward Hugh Leycester Penrhyn, of East Sheen, Surrey; J.P., D.L., Hants; born 7 June, 1827; married 21 April, 1853, Vere, daughter of Robert Gosling, Esq., of Botleys Park, Surrey, and of Hassiobury, Herts, and has 2 sons and 6 daughters.

(1) Arthur Leycester (Penrhyn), born 10 March, 1866.
(2) George Leycester, born 25 April, 1871.
(3) Charlotte Georgiana. (4) Constance Vere.
(5) Agnes Eleanor. (6) Amy Gertrude.
(7) Maud Lina. (8) Cecil Mary.

[2] Oswald Henry Leycester (Penrhyn), M.A. Balliol Coll., Oxon, 1852; vicar of Huyton, Liverpool, 1869; hon. canon Liverpool, 1880; perp. curate Bickerstaffe 1858-69; born ; married 24 April, 1862, Charlotte, daughter of Edmund Hornby, Esq., of Dalton Hall (see next page), and has a son and 3 daughters.

Charles Windham Leycester (Penrhyn), born 5 Nov., 1873.
Ethel Frances. Mary Charlotte.
Elizabeth Gertrude.

[3] Mary Charlotte, married 1 Oct., 1850, to Morgan Yeatman, Esq., of Shawfield, Bromley, Kent, and has had 5 sons and 5 daughters.

(1) Morgan Edward (Yeatman), M.A. Trin. Coll., Camb., born 8 Aug., 1851.
(2) Harry Oswald, born 19 Nov., 1856.
(3) Charles Leycester, born 17 Nov., 1858; died 6 April, 1884.
(4) Arthur William, B.A., Pembroke Coll., Camb., 1884; born 5 May, 1862.
(5) Frank Pym Stanley, born 12 Oct., 1869.
(6) Ellinor Mary. (7) Lucy Emma.
(8) Florence Charlotte.
(9) Alice Maud, died 1880.
(10) Edith Vere.

[4] Emma Catherine Leycester (Penrhyn).

(5) Lady Louisa Emily, died s.p. 11 Dec., 1825, having married, as 1st wife, 18 April, 1825, to Lieut.-col. Samuel Long, of Bromley Hill, Kent, high sheriff 1863; late grenadier guards; brother of Lord Farnborough (extinct); he died 31 Aug., 1881 (see page 620).

(6) Lady Ellinor Mary, married 11 June, 1835, to Rev. Frank George Hopwood, M.A. Christ Church Coll., Oxon, 1840; rector of Winwick, Lanc., 1855, hon.

canon of Chester 1866, (see page 633) and has (to survive) 3 sons and 2 daughters.

[1] Frank Edward (Hopwood), M.A. Christ Church Coll., Oxon, 1868; rector of Badsworth, Yorks, since 1819; born 19 April, 1843.

[2] Arthur Robert, born 19 March, 1845.

[3] Charles Augustus, born 27 Dec., 1847.

[4] Susan.

[5] Cecilia Catherine, married 4 May, 1871, to Ven. John Lionel Darby, M.A. Trin. Coll., Dublin, 1865; archdeacon of Chester since 1877; hon. canon Chester Cathedral 1873; rector of St. Bridget with St. Martin's, Chester, since 1875.

[10] Georgiana (Hornby), died unmarried 16 March, 1861, aged 78.

[11] Frances Susanna. [12] Louisa.

[13] Henrietta Elizabeth, died unmarried 29 Oct., 1859, aged 66.

EDMUND HORNBY, of Dalton Hall, co. Lanc., J.P., D.L.; high sheriff 1828; M.A. Trin. Coll., Camb., 1797; M.P. Preston in 3 Parliaments, 1812, 1818, 1820; baptized 16 June, 1773; died 18 Nov., 1857; married 22 Aug., 1796, Lady Charlotte Stanley, daughter of Edward, 12th Earl of Derby, K.G. (see page 621); she died 25 Nov., 1805, having had an only son,

EDMUND GEORGE HORNBY, of Dalton Hall, J.P., D.L.; M.P. Warrington 1832; constable of the Castle of Lancaster; born 16 Nov., 1799; died 26 Feb., 1865; married 30 Jan., 1827, Sarah, 2nd daughter and co-heir of Thomas Yates, Esq., of Irwell House, co. Lanc., and had a son and 6 daughters.

[1] **Edmund Geoffrey Stanley Hornby,** 1st named (see page 618).

[2] Elizabeth Sarah (Hornby), died 27 Sept., 1884; married 21 Feb., 1865, to Rev. Henry Ware, M.A. Trin. Coll., Camb., 1856; vicar of Kirkby Lonsdale since 1862; rural dean; chaplain to the Bishop of Carlisle; hon. canon Carlisle since 1883; canon residentiary 1879-83; hon. canon 1870-9; fellow and assistant tutor Trin. Coll., Camb., 1854-62; s.p.

[3] Lucy Francesca, married 29 July, 1851 to Charles Samuel Bagot, barrister-at-law, Inner Temple, 1853; a commissioner in lunacy; principal secretary to Lord Hatherley, Lord Chancellor of England; B.A. Trin. Coll., Camb. (2nd son of Charles Harvey Bagot, of South Australia).

[4] Ellinor Georgina Katherine, married 18 Aug., 1857, to Rev. Henry Arbuthnot Feilden, B.A. St. Alban Hall, Oxon, 1871; chaplain of St. Raphael's Convalescent Home, Torquay, 1873-84 (see Foster's *Baronetage*), and has 2 daughters.

Helen Arbuthnot. Katherine Maud.

[5] Charlotte Louisa Jane, married 24 April, 1862, to Rev. Oswald Henry Leycester Penrhyn, M.A. Balliol Coll., Oxon, 1852; vicar of Huyton, co. Lanc., since 1869; perp. curate Bickerstaffe 1858-69; hon. canon Liverpool; and has a son and 3 daughters (see preceding page).

[6] Victoria Susan, married 22 Jan., 1861, to Rev. Charles James Satterthwaite, M.A. Jesus Coll., Camb., 1860; vicar of Disley, Cheshire, since 1859, and has 2 sons and a daughter.

Edmund James (Satterthwaite), born 1 March, 1866

Charles Geoffrey, born 15 April, 1873.

Gertrude Mary Charlotte.

[7] Gertrude Mary Augusta.

M'GILLICUDDY, DENIS CHARLES, "The M'Gillicuddy of the Reeks," 17TH IN DESCENT FROM EDWARD III.; born 14 May, 1852; married 24 Oct., 1881, Gertrude Laura, daughter of E. H. Miller, Esq., of Ringwood, near New York, and has a son.

[1] —— born 26 Oct., 1882.

THE DESCENT OF
"THE M'GILLICUDDY OF THE REEKS"
FROM
THE BLOOD ROYAL OF ENGLAND.

EDWARD III., KING OF ENGLAND, Earl of Chester 1320, Duke of Aquitaine, Count of Ponthieu and Montreuil, 1325; crowned at Westminster in his father's lifetime, 1 Feb., 1327; defeated the Scots at Halidon Hill, 1333. In 1339 he assumed the style of "King of France and England, and Lord of Ireland," and quartered the arms of France in the first quarter; gained a great naval victory over the French off Sluys, 1340, and won the celebrated battle of Cressy 26 Aug., 1346; 17 Oct. following the Scots were defeated at Neville Cross, and King David II. taken prisoner to London, where he remained nearly 11 years. Instituted the order of the Garter 1349. His son, the BLACK PRINCE, defeated the French at the battle of Poictiers, 19 Sept., 1356, and brought King John prisoner to London, where he remained nearly five years (for further particulars, see *Royal Lineage*, Foster's *Peerage*). The King died at Sheen, Surrey, 21 June, 1377, having had issue; their descendant

ANNE BLENNERHASSETT (eldest daughter of Capt. John Blennerhassett, of Castle Conway, co. Kerry, known as Black Jack (see page 593B), born 24 Jan., 1694; married 1st, to Denis M'Gillicuddy, of Carrabeg, who died 1730; she re-married, Jan, 1731, to Thomas Herbert, of Currens; by her 1st husband she had 4 sons and 3 daughters.

[1] Denis M'Gillicuddy, born 15 Nov., 1718; died s.p.
[2] **Cornelius**, of whom presently.
[3] John, born 26 Jan., 1727; died s.p.
[4] Philip, born 10 Feb., 1729; died s.p.
[5] Avice Catherine.
[6] Mary.
[7] Elizabeth.

CORNELIUS M'GILLICUDDY, born 1720; died ; married 16 July, 1745, Catherine, 5th daughter of Richard Chute, Esq., of Tulligaron, co. Kerry (by his wife Charity Herbert), and had 6 sons and 6 daughters.

[1] Denis, born 31 Oct., 1747; died unmarried.
[2] Richard, "The M'Gillicuddy of the Reeks," born 30 May, 1750; died s.p. 19 Nov., 1826; married Feb., 1780, Hon. Arabella Mullins, daughter of Thomas, 1st Lord Ventry; she died Dec., 1821 (see page 664).
[3] Francis M'Gillicuddy, born 17 Aug., 1751; died 6 April, 1820; married 1788, Catherine, relict of Darby M'Gill, Esq., daughter of Denis Mahony, Esq., of Dromore, co. Kerry, and had 3 sons and 2 daughters.
(1) **Richard**, of whom see page 629.
(2) Francis, died unmarried.
(3) Denis, died s.p., April, 1843; married Mary Kirwan.
(4) Mary.
(5) Catherine, married 17 June, 1827, to Montgomery Agnew Martin, Esq., and had 3 sons and 5 daughters (see page 596).
[4] Daniel, born Feb., 1753; died ; married 1st Elizabeth, daughter of Conway Blennerhassett, Esq. (see page 594); she died s.p.; he married 2ndly, 26 Aug., 1811, Sophia, daughter of Sir

Barry Denny, Bart. (see page 724); she died 1832, having had a son and 2 daughters.

(1) Daniel de Courcy (M'Gillicuddy), of Day Place, Tralee, co. Kerry, J.P., born 18 Aug., 1815; died 4 Oct., 1882; married 24 Sept., 1839, Lucinda Margaret, daughter of Richard Morphy, Esq., of Tralee; she died 16 May, 1878, having had 6 sons and 2 daughters.

[1] Daniel de Courcy (M'Gillicuddy), of Tralee, sessional crown solicitor, co. Kerry; born 20 July, 1840; married 10 June 1880, Jemima Maria, youngest daughter of late Henry Samprey, Esq., of Ballyglass House, co. Roscommon.

[2] Richard Edward, born May, 1850.

[3] Henry Arthur, born Nov., 1852.

[4] Edward Abram, born Nov., 1854; married 14 April, 1880, Annabella Charlotte, only child of Townsend Blennerhassett, capt. Kerry militia (see pages 567 and 574); she died 1 May, 1882, leaving a son,

Townsend Blennerhassett (M'Gillicuddy), born 27 April, 1882.

[5] Arthur Orpen, born Nov., 1856.

[6] Francis John, born June, 1860.

[7] Sarah Lucinda, married 1 Oct., 1867, to Rev. Raymond de Audemer Orpen, rector of Tralee (son of Sir Richard John Theodore Orpen, Knt.), and has 3 sons and a daughter.

Richard Theodore (Orpen), born 13 Oct., 1869

Charles William M'Gillicuddy, born 11 June, 1871; Henry Arthur Herbert, born 12 May, 1874; Lucinda Elizabeth.

[8] Sophia Elizabeth.

(2) Arabella (M'Gillicuddy), died 21 Dec., 1881; married Aug., 1843, to Edward Morphy, Esq., of Tralee; she died 1878, having had 4 sons and a daughter.

(3) Sophia Catherine, married 22 Nov., 1834, to her cousin, Rev. Henry Denny, rector of Ballynahaglish, &c. (see page 725); he died 25 Sept., 1877, having had 9 sons and 4 daughters.

[1] Edward (Denny), M.A. Trin. Coll., Dublin, rector of Laracor, co. Meath; born 17 Aug., 1835; married 18 Oct., 1877, Marion Georgina, daughter of Lyttelton Henry Lyster, Esq., of Dublin, and has a son.

Henry Lyttelton Lyster, born 10 Sept., 1878.

[2] Henry, born 1 Jan., 1837; died 9 Nov., 1872, having married 1 Dec., 1864, Jane, daughter of Joseph Armstrong, Esq., of Coote Hill, Cavan (she re-married 18 May, 1875, to Joseph Keatinge, of Lismore), and had 2 sons and a daughter.

(1) Henry Arthur Francis, born 8 March, 1868.

(2) Edward Ernest Armstrong, born (posth.) 21 July, 1873.

(3) Kathleen Elizabeth.

[3] Arthur M'Gillycuddy, hon. lieut.-col., late major on reserve; formerly capt. 13th L.I.; born 3 March, 1838.

[4] De Courcy Daniel, born 24 Dec., 1840; died 16 Dec., 1875, having married 17 April, 1873, Clementina, daughter of late Richard Leahy, Esq., of Tralee, and had a son.

Henry de Courcy, born 28 May, 1874.

[5] Robert, born 5 June, 1843.

[6] William, born 28 Feb., 1847.

[7] Richard, capt. R.M.L.I; born 8 Aug., 1848; married 24 Aug., 1881, Mary, eldest daughter of T S Guppy, M.D., Falmouth, and has a daughter,

Eileen, born 10 Feb., 1883.

[8] Roland John, born 30 Sept., 1849.

[9] Edmund Barry, born 29 Nov., 1860.

[10] Sophia. [11] Elizabeth.

[12] Arabella Jane, married 16 Feb., 1874, to Richard Hungerford Townsend, M.D., and has 3 sons and 8 daughters (see Denny pedigree, page 725).

[13] Diana (Denny).

[5] Eusebius (M'Gillicuddy), born May, 1754; married Anne, daughter of James FitzGerald, of Bally-Ellen, co. Carlow, and had 5 sons and 4 daughters.

(1) Richard.

(2) Daniel.

(3) Francis Chute, had a daughter , Ursula, married to George Mahony Mayberry, M.D., J.P., of Riversdale, co. Kerry; and has, with other issue, a son,

Francis George (Mayberry), of Riversdale, B.A., Trin. Coll., Dublin, 1868; born , 1847.

(4) Eusebius.

(5) James. (6) Ellen.

(7) Catherine, married to James Morphy, and had at least a son,

Eusebius M'Gillicuddy (Morphy), born died ; married , Dorcas, daughter of James Hilliard, Esq., of Ballyhorgan (see p. 514), and had an only daughter,

Gertrude Margaret (Morphy), married Jan., 1874, to Shubrick Martin, who died at Burton-on-Trent, 19 April, 1879, leaving a son,

William Herbert (Martin), born 16 Nov., 1874.

(8) Charity.

(9) Margaret, died July, 1849; married 1817, to Alexander Eagar, county inspector Irish constabulary, some time lieut. 57th regt.; he died Sept., 1855, having had 4 sons and 2 daughters.

[1] Thomas (Eagar), died unmarried, 8 July, 1847, aged 26.

[2] Eusebius M'Gillicuddy (Eagar), of Lickeen, and of Clifton Cottage, J.P. co. Kerry born 16 Sept., 1820.

[3] Francis M'Gillicuddy (Eagar), of Philipstown, King's co.; born ; married , 1855, Frances Margaret, daughter of Holden, and has 2 sons and a daughter—Alexander Richard, James, Anne.

[4] James.

[5] Rosanna Catherine.

[6] Margaretta M'Gillicuddy (Eagar).

[6] Cornelius (M'Gillicuddy), born July, 1762.

[7] Charity, married , to Edward Collis, Esq., of Lismore, co. Kerry; he died , having had a son and 2 daughters.

(1) William Collis, of Lismore, co. Kerry, high sheriff, died ; married , 1806, his cousin Catherine, eldest daughter of Rev. Samuel Collis, of Fort William, co. Kerry; she died , having had 4 sons and 4 daughters.

[1] Edmund (Collis), born 1810.

[2] Samuel, captain of Kerry militia.

[3] William.

[4] Richard.

[5] Charity, died 5 Nov., 1847; married Sept., 1837, to Richard Townsend de Moleyns, Esq. (see page 661), who died , 1850, leaving a son,

Guiscarde Henry, died 26 March, 1859.

[6] Anne. [7] Frances. [8] Catherine.

(2) Arabella (Collis), married , to David Fitzgerald, Esq., and has a son,

Thomas (Fitzgerald), C.E., of 3, Beresford-place, Dublin.

(3) Margaret Ruth (Collis), married , to Francis Twiss, Esq., and had a son and 5 daughters (see p. 514).

[8] Mary Anne, died unmarried.

[9] Margaret, married , to Rev. James Day, rector of Tralee, vicar-general of Ardfert and Aghadoe, and had 4 sons and 4 daughters (see page 446).

[10] Ruth, and [11] Avis, both died unmarried.

[12] Agnes Ruth Herbert, married , to

Maurice Leyne, M.D., J.P., Tralee; he died Jan., 1833, having had 4 sons and 4 daughters.

(1) Richard (Leyne), captain 58th and 73rd regiments; born 1 Jan., 1790; died 3 Jan., 1864; married , 1817, Elizabeth, daughter of James O'Connor, of Tralee, and had, with other issue, 8 sons and 2 daughters.

[1] Maurice Richard (Leyne), 11th Hussars; died 29 June, 1854; married , Ellen, daughter of Richard Kehoe, Esq., of Carlow, and had a son, Maurice.

[2] James (Leyne), major 59th regiment and 14th regiment.

[3] Jeremiah (Leyne), of Dublin; born ; married 26 June, 1862, Alexis, daughter of John Balfour, of Edinburgh, and has had 2 sons and 5 daughters.

(1) Richard Fitz-Jerome Alexis (Leyne), born Feb., 1866.

(2) Jerome John Mercer, born 21 Aug., 1867; died 9 Sept. following.

(3) Marguerite Alexis Elizabeth Mary.

(4) Elizabeth Agnes Mary.

(5) Agnes Mary Aloysia.

(6) Alexis Mary Clare, died 14 Dec., 1868.

(7) Avice Alexis Mary, died 5 May, 1884.

[4] Edward (Leyne), died 19 April, 1861.

[5] O'Connell (Leyne), born ; married , 1881, Frances, daughter of Richard Sullivan, Esq., of Kilkenny.

[6] Richard (Leyne).

[7] John Gerald (Leyne), born ; married , 1871, Margaret Wilkinson, of Bermuda.

[8] Charles Joseph (Leyne), died March, 1873.

[9] Elizabeth Mary Clare, a nun of the presentation order.

[10] Agnes Teresa, married 1 Aug., 1866, to her 2nd cousin, Christopher O'Connell Fitz-Simon, Esq., of Glancullen, co. Dublin, J.P., D.L. (see page 591), he died 16 Nov., 1884, having had 4 sons and a daughter.

(2) Maurice (Leyne), of Dublin, barrister-at-law, died unmarried, , 1865.

(3) Jeremiah (Leyne), M.D., married 1st, , 1819, Mary, daughter of Robert Christopher Hickson, Esq., of Fermoyle and Tralee; she died ; he married 2ndly, , Margaret, widow of Rev. James Chute, rector of Ballyheigue, daughter of . By his 1st wife he had an only daughter.

Mary (Leyne), married , to Thomas Stewart, Esq., of .

(4) James (Leyne), died unmarried , 1819.

(5) Catherine (Leyne), died 17 May, 1858; married , 1811, to John Spotswood, captain Valencia yeomanry corps, who died 2 April, 1859, having had 6 sons and 6 daughters.

[1] Theobald (Spotswood), born , 1812; died unmarried, 19 Oct., 1844.

[2] Maurice (Spotswood), of Cahirceveen, M.R.C.S. England, 1841; born 19 Sept., 1814; married 18 Dec., 1862, Therisa, daughter of W. F. de Bentley, Esq., and has had a son and 5 daughters.

John Theobald, born 10 March, 1870.

Edith Butler, died 21 Sept., 1881.

Kathleen Agnes; Myra Leyne; John Theobald; Bessie Ethel.

[3] John, died s.p.

[4] Richard, married Miss Minshull, of Tiff, and died s.p., 27 Jan., 1877.

[5] James.

[6] Robert, married

[7] Agnes, married O'Connell.

[8] Mary, died unmarried, 5 March, 1871.

[9] Elizabeth, married 1856, to Francis Twiss, and had a daughter, Kathleen (see page 512).

[10] Cherry.

[11] Christina, died June, 1848.

[12] Louisa, died 8 April, 1854.

(6) Agnes (Leyne), died ; married , to Thomas Day, of Miltown (son of Rev. John Day, of the Manor and Keelballylahavic, co. Kerry, and had issue (see page 724).

(7) Charity (Leyne), married , to Capt. Samuel Collis, R.N., and died s.p.

(8) Elizabeth (Leyne), married , 1821, to Thomas Hannigan, of Woodford, co. Cork, and had, with other issue, a son and 2 daughters.

[1] Anthony (Hannigan), of Lockington House, Bray, died .

[2] Agnes, unmarried. [3] Maria.

RICHARD, "The M'Gillicuddy of the Reeks," J.P., D.L. co. Kerry, high sheriff 1823-4; born 1 Jan., 1790; died 6 June, 1866; married 1st, 9 Nov., 1814, Margaret, only daughter of James Bennett, M.D., of Cork; she died 2 Feb., 1849, having had 2 sons and 2 daughters.

[1] Francis, born 25 Dec., 1819; died unmarried 3 Nov., 1841.

[2] Robert, born 29 Dec., 1823; died unmarried.

[3] Arabella, died unmarried.

[4] Dorothea, married 29 June, 1847, to William Leader, Esq., of Rosnake, co. Cork, J.P.; he died, 1861, having had 2 sons and 2 daughters.

(1) William Nicholas (Leader), born 1853.

(2) Francis Henry Mowbray, born 1855.

(3) Dora Margaret. (4) Margaret.

"THE M'GILLICUDDY" married 2ndly, 6 Nov., 1849, Anna, daughter of John Johnstone, Esq., of Mainstone Court, co. Hereford (see Foster's *Peerage*, B. DERWENT), and had 5 sons and 4 daughters.

[5] Richard Patrick, "The M'Gillicuddy," born 15 July, 1850; died 28 Nov., 1871.

[6] **Denis Charles**, "The M'Gillicuddy" (see page 627).

[7] John, born 24 March, 1855.

[8] Charles, born 8 Nov., 1857.

[9] Neill, born 22 July, 1860.

[10] Agnes, married 28 Oct., 1882, to George Stoker, M.R.C.S. (5th son of the late Abraham Stoker, Esq., of Dublin).

[11] Anna Catherine, married 1 Jan., 1878, to Thomas Wells, Esq., of Moxley, Staffordshire.

[12] Mary Ruth. [13] Sylvia Emily.

THE DESCENT OF

Joshua Thomas Horton, Esq.,

Of Howroyde, Yorks., J.P., D.L.,

FROM THE

Blood Royal  **of England.**

EDWARD I., crowned 19 Aug., 1274, b. 17 June, 1239, d. 7 July, 1307. = Eleanor (1st wife) dau. of Ferdinand III., King of Castile, d. 27 Nov., 1290.

Joan of Acre, b. there 1272, d. 10 May, 1305, 2nd wife. = Gilbert de Clare, Earl of Gloucester, &c., d. 7 Dec., 1295.

Margaret de Clare, m. 1st to Sir Piers Gaveston, Earl of Cornwall. = Hugh de Audley (2nd husband), cr. Earl of Gloucester, d. 1347.

Margaret de Audley, d. 7 Sept., 1349. = Ralph de Stafford, K.G., cr. Earl of Stafford, d. 31 Aug., 1372.

Beatrix Stafford = Thomas, 5th Lord Roos of Hamlake (2nd husband).

William de Roos, 7th Baron, K.G., Lord Treasurer of England, 1404. = Margery, yr. dau. of Sir John de Arundel, Knt., Marshal of England.

Margaret de Roos (1st wife) = James Touchet, Lord Audley, lord almoner, slain at Blore Heath, 1458.

John, Lord Audley, had summons to Parliament 1461-83, d. 26 Sept., 1491. = Anne, dau. of Sir Thomas Itchingham.

Joan (1st wife) dau. of Fulke Bourchier, Lord FitzWarren. = James, Lord Audley, Knt., beheaded 28 June, 1497, attainted and forfeited. = Margaret (2nd wife) dau. of Richard Dayrell, of Lillingston.

John, Lord Audley, restored in blood and honour 1512, and to his father's lands 1533. = Mary, dau. of John Griffin, of Braybrooke, Northants.

A, *continued above.*

A, *continued from below.*

John, Lord Audley = Mary Griffin

George, Lord Audley, took his seat in the House of Lords 20 Jan., 1558, d. 1560. = Elizabeth, dau. of Sir Bryan Tuke, Knt., treasurer of the Chamber, Henry VIII.

Henry, Lord Audley, Knight Banneret, never sat in Parliament, d. 1595. = Elizabeth, dau. of Sir William Sneyd, of Bradwall, Staffordshire, buried at Thelwall, 4 Jan., 1610.

Anne Touchet = Thomas Brooke, of Norton, Cheshire, Sheriff 1578, 1592.

Christian Brooke = Richard Starkey, Esq., of Stretton, Cheshire, b. 1568.

Anne Starkey = Ralph Gregge, of Bradley, Cheshire.

Edward Gregge, of Hapsford, buried in St. Michael's, Chester, 13 Nov. 1665. = Elizabeth, dau. of Chr. Lightfoot, of Barrow, d. 3 May, 1659.

Robert Gregge, d. Feb., 1661-2. = Elizabeth, buried in St. Michael's, 18 Oct. 1658.

Robert Gregge, buried at St. Michael's, Chester, 19 June, 1673. = Jane, dau. of —— Holt, of Bridge Hall, co. Lanc., buried 17 July, 1689.

Mary Gregge, b. 9 June, 1658, m. 27 Feb., 1678, d. 27 Dec., 1708. = Joshua Horton, of Chadderton, co. Lanc., d. 15 Dec., 1708.

Thomas Horton, of Chadderton, co. Lanc., governor of the Isle of Man, d. 18 March, 1757. = Anne, dau. and co-heir of Richard Mostyn, of London, merchant, d. 17 June, 1725, aged 39.

Sir William Horton, of Chadderton, Bart., so created 1764, d. 25 Feb. 1774. = Susanna, only dau. and heir of Francis Watts, Esq., of Barn Hall, Yorks, m. 23 Aug. 1751, d. 19 May, 1778.

2. Joshua Horton, of Howroyde, Yorks, b. 12 May, 1720, d. 29 Jan., 1793. = Mary Bethia (2nd wife), dau. of Rev. J. Woolen, A.M., rector of Emley, Yorks, &c., d. 8 Feb. 1806.

Susanna, m. 24 March, 1742, d. 16 March, 1797. = George Lloyd, of Hulme, co. Lancashire.

Thomas Horton, of Howroyde, Yorks, b. 26 Aug. 1766, d. 22 Dec., 1829. = Lady Mary Gordon, ygst. dau. of George, 3rd Earl of Aberdeen, m. 12 March, 1789, d. 7 Aug. 1852.

Joshua Sydney Horton, adml. R.N., b. 7 March, 1768, d. 24 Nov., 1835. = Grace, wid. of Henry Whorwood, of Headington, Oxon., d. 8 Nov., 1845.

William Horton, incumbt. of St. Mary's, Rochdale b. 5 May, 1769, d. 13 Aug. 1817. = Elizabeth, eld. dau. of John Lyon, M.D. m. 7 Nov., 1793, d. 24 Oct., 1835.

Other issue, see page 636.

Joshua Horton, of Howroyde, vicar of Ormskirk, co. Lanc. b. 12 Nov. 1790, d. 21 Nov. 1845. = Harriet, eld. dau. of Sir Thomas Dalrymple Hesketh, Bart., m. 6 Nov., 1832, d. 10 May, 1836.

George William, of Embsay Kirk, Yorks, col. in the army, b. 3 Nov., 1792, d. 1 May, 1877. = Frances Esther, 2nd dau. of Rev. William Garnier, of Rookesbury, Hants., m. 1 Aug., 1826, d. March, 1861.

Mary, m. 26 June, 1816, d. 28 Dec., 1881 = Francis Beynon Hacket Esq. of Moor Hall, co. Warwick, m. 26 June, 1816, d. 14 Oct., 1863.

Joshua Thomas Horton, of Howroyde, Yorks, J.P., D.L., late capt. 2nd West York Yeomanry cavalry, b. 10 May, 1836. = Elizabeth Blackie, dau. of John Robertson, Esq., of Edenmouth, Kelso, N.B.

George William Horton, M.A., vicar of Wellow since 1859, b. 17 Dec., 1830. = Annie Elizabeth, dau. of late Le Gendre Nicholas Starkie, of Huntroyde, co. Lanc., m. 19 Aug., 1858, d. 24 Jany., 1869.

William Thomas, b. 1838, m. 1866, Elizabeth, dau. of J. Waterhouse, Esq.

Fanny Laura.

Joshua Thomas, b. 12 June, 1860.
William Theodore, b. 7 Aug. 1874.

George Herbert, b. 14 Sept., 1877.
Harriet, b. 1858.

Le Gendre George Horton, in H.O., b. 12 July, 1859.

Anne Frances.

HORTON, JOSHUA THOMAS, of Howroyde, Yorkshire, J.P., D.L., West Riding, Yorks; late capt. 2nd W. York yeomanry cavalry; 23RD IN DESCENT FROM EDWARD I.; born 10 May, 1836; married 18 Nov., 1857, Elizabeth Blackie, daughter of John Roberton, Esq., of Edenmouth, Kelso, and has had at least 4 sons and 2 daughters,

[1] Joshua Thomas, born 12 June, 1860.
[2] John, born 15 Feb., 1865; died 25 Dec., 1870.
[3] William Theodore, born 7 Aug., 1874.
[4] George Herbert, born 14 Sept., 1877.
[5] Harriet, born 24 Oct., 1858.
[6] Margaret Elizabeth Jane, died 3 Dec., 1870.

THE DESCENT OF
JOSHUA THOMAS HORTON, ESQ.,
OF HOWROYDE, YORKSHIRE,
FROM THE BLOOD ROYAL OF ENGLAND.

EDWARD I., so named after Edward the Confessor; born at Westminster, 17 June, 1239, knighted at Burgos, 1254, created Earl of Chester; crowned at Westminster, 19 Aug. 1274, king of England, lord of Ireland, duke of Aquitaine; he subdued the principality of Wales, 1283, claimed and exercised feudal superiority over Scotland; died at Burgh-on-the-Sands, Cumberland, 7 July, 1307, buried in Westminster Abbey; by his 1st wife, Eleanor, daughter of Ferdinand III., king of Castile, who died 27 Nov., 1290, he had, with other issue, a daughter,

JOAN OF ACRE, born there 1272; died 10 May, 1305, having married 1st, 2 May, 1290, as 2nd wife to Gilbert de Clare (surnamed "The Red"), Earl of Gloucester and Hertford; he died at Monmouth Castle, 7 Dec., 1295; she re-married, 1296, to Ralph de Monthermer, who had summons to Parliament as Earl of Gloucester and Hertford, in right of his wife, 1299-1306, and had issue. JOAN OF ACRE had by her 1st husband, with other issue, a daughter

MARGARET DE CLARE, 2nd sister and co-heir of Gilbert de Clare, Earl of Gloucester and Hertford (who fell at Bannockburn, 24 June, 1314, s.p.); she married 1st to Sir Piers Gaveston, Earl of Cornwall, to whom Edward II. granted the county of Cornwall by charter, dated at Dumfries, 6 Aug., 1307; summoned to Parliament 19 Jan. following; beheaded without form of trial, 1314, leaving an only daughter, who was betrothed to John Moulton Margaret, Countess of Cornwall, married 2ndly to Hugh de Audley; he had summons to Parliament in the lifetime of his father, 1317-21, and 1326-36, and was created Earl of Gloucester by patent, 16 March, 1337; he died without male issue in 1347, and the dignity which was to him and his heirs appears to have been considered extinct; he left an only child,

MARGARET DE AUDLEY, died 7 Sept., 1349, having married to Ralph de Stafford, K.G. (son and heir of Edmund de Stafford, a lord of Parliament); summoned to Parliament 14 Jan., 10 Edward III., 1337, to 25 Nov., 24 Edward III., 1350; created Earl of the County of Stafford, 5 March, 1351, to hold to him and his heirs; served in the wars in Scotland and in Brittany; taken prisoner at the siege of Nantes; seneschal of Aquitaine, 20 Edward III.; had a principal command at the battle of Cressy; one of the founders of the Order of the Garter; lieutenant and captain-general of the duchy of Aquitaine; he died 31 Aug., 1372, having had, with other issue, a daughter,

BEATRIX STAFFORD, married 1st to Maurice Oge, 2nd Earl of Desmond, and had a daughter; she re-married 1368, to Thomas, 5th Lord Roos, of Hamlake, who had summons to Parliament 24 Aug., 1362, to 3 March, 1384, in which year he died, leaving, with other issue, a son,

WILLIAM DE ROOS, 7th Baron, K.G. (on the death of his brother John at Paphos, in the Isle of Cyprus, in 1393); had summons to Parliament 20 Nov., 1394, to 24 Dec., 1413; Lord Treasurer of England, 1404; he married Margaret, younger daughter of Sir John de Arundel, Knight, Marshal of England; he died Sept., 1414, having had, with other issue, a daughter,

MARGARET DE ROOS, married as 1st wife to James Touchet, Lord Audley, who had summons to Parliament as "Jacobo de Audley," from 26 Feb., 1421, to 26 May, 1455; served in the French wars, at the siege of Molyn, on the Seine; lord almoner at the coronation of the King and Queen; at the siege of Meaux, 9 Henry V.; in 8 Henry VI. he had a chief command of some forces in the war with France; he encountered the forces under Richard Nevil, Earl of Salisbury, at Blore Heath, with about 10,000 men, and was there slain, 1458, leaving by his 1st wife a son,

JOHN, LORD AUDLEY; had sum mons to Parliament 26 May, 1461, to 9 Dec., 1483; had a grant of the stewardship of all the King's manors and lands lying in the county of Dorset, and warden of his forests, chaces, and parks in that county, and of the castle of Wardour, &c.; a commander of the forces in Brittany, 15 Edward IV., and an ambassador to treat for peace; he attended among the barons at the coronation of Richard III.; married Anne, daughter of Sir Thomas Itchingham, and died 26 Sept. (or Dec.), 1491, having had, with 3 daughters, a son,

JAMES, LORD AUDLEY, Knight of the Bath at the creation of Edward, Prince of Wales; had summons to Parliament 12 Aug., 1492, to 16 Jan., 1497; at the siege of Boulogne; he joined the Cornishmen in their insurrection, and was taken prisoner at the battle of Blackheath, 24 June, 1497; he was drawn from Newgate to Tower Hill in his own coat-of-arms, painted on paper, but reversed and torn, and there beheaded, 4 days after; buried in the Blackfriars, near Ludgate; attainted and forfeited; he married 1st, Joan, daughter of Fulke Bourchier, Lord FitzWarren; he married 2ndly, Margaret, daughter of Richard Dayrell, of Lillingston Dayrell, Bucks; his son,

JOHN, LORD AUDLEY, was restored to his father's honours in 4 Henry VIII., 1512; had summons to Parliament 23 Nov., 1514, to 21 Oct., 1556, in 5 Henry VIII.; he was at the taking of Therouenne; had restitution of his father's lands 25 Henry VIII.; he married Mary, daughter of John Griffin, of Braybrooke, Northants, and had a son,

GEORGE, LORD AUDLEY; had summons to Parliament, and took his seat 20 Jan., 1558; married Elizabeth, daughter of Sir Bryan Tuke, Knt.; treasurer of the chamber to Henry VIII.; he died 1560, leaving 2 sons, of whom the elder,

HENRY, LORD AUDLEY, never sat in Parliament; was made a Knight Banneret, 7 Oct., 1586, for his distinguished services at the fight before Zutphen, 22 Sept.; he died , 1595; married Elizabeth, daughter of Sir William Sneyd, of Bradwell, Staff.; she was buried at Thelwall, 4 Jan., 1610, having had, with 2 sons, 2 daughters, of whom the elder,

ANNE TOUCHET, married to Thomas Brooke, of Norton, Cheshire, sheriff 1578, 1592, and had, with other issue, a daughter,

CHRISTIAN BROOKE, married to Richard Starkey, Esq., of Stretton, Cheshire; he was 12 years of age in 1580, and had, with a son an only daughter,

ANNE, married to Ralph Gregge, of Bradley, Cheshire, and had, with other issue, a son,

EDWARD GREGGE, of Hapsford, examiner in the Court of Exchequer, Chester; buried in St. Michael's, Chester, 13 Nov., 1665; he married , Elizabeth, daughter of Christopher, Lightfoot, of Barrow; she died 3 May, 1659, having had, with other issue, a son,

ROBERT GREGGE; died in the life-time of his father, Feb., 1661-2; buried in St. Michael's, Chester, with his wife, Elizabeth, who was buried there 18 Oct., 1658; had a son,

ROBERT GREGGE, barrister-at-law; examiner in the Court of Exchequer, Chester; buried, in St. Michael's, 19 June, 1673; married , Jane, daughter of Holt, of Bridge Hall, in Bury, co. Lanc.; buried 17 July, 1689, having had 2 sons and 2 daughters (*a*).

[1*a*] Edward Gregge, buried at St. Michael's, Chester, 1689, his wife, Abigail, buried with her husband, 27 Feb. 1716; had a son and 2 daughters.

(1*a*) Peter (Gregge), only son and heir apparent; baptized April, 1687, and buried 18 Dec., 1694.

(2) Jane (Gregge), buried at St. Michael's, Chester, 22 Nov., 1720; married there 22 April, 1707, to Roger Barnston, of Churton, and had issue (see page 776).

(3) Mary, married to Francis Jodrell, Esq., of Yeardsley, Cheshire, and died s.p.

[2*a*] Joseph (Gregge), admitted to Gray's Inn 7 July, 1674, and then called son and heir; baptized 16 June, 1657; married , Mary, daughter and heir of Henry Wrigley, Esq., of Chamber Hall, near Oldham, and had a son,

BENJAMIN GREGGE, of Chamber Hall, Lancashire; admitted to Gray's Inn 28 Nov., 1699; married Elizabeth Gill, of Carr House, Yorkshire, and had with other issue a son.

EDWARD GREGGE-HOPWOOD, of Hopwood Hall, co. Lanc.; assumed the additional surname of Hopwood; married Judith, daughter of John Sunderland, Esq., of Whittington Hall, co. Lanc., and had with 3 daughters an only son.

ROBERT GREGGE-HOPWOOD, of Hopwood Hall, Lanc., J.P., D.L.; high sheriff 1802; born 30 Nov., 1773; died 19 July, 1854; married 31 Dec., 1805; Hon. Cecilia Byng, daughter of John, 5th Viscount Torrington; she died July, 1843, leaving 2 sons and 2 daughters (*b*).

(1*b*) Edward John Gregge-Hopwood, Hopwood Hall, co. Lanc., J.P., D.L.; capt. in the army; 22ND IN DESCENT FROM EDWARD I.; born 27 April, 1810; married 20, April, 1840, Susan Fanny, daughter of John Baskervyle Glegg, Esq., of Old Wilthington and Gayton, Cheshire, and has a son and 4 daughters.

[1] Edward Robert (Gregge-Hopwood), born 6 Feb., 1846; married 23 June, 1875, Mary Brenda Madeleine, youngest daughter of George Beauchamp Cole, Esq., of Heatham House, Twickenham.

[2] Cecilia, married 20 April 1864, to Shallcross Fitzherbert Widdrington, Esq., of Newton Hall, Northumberland, J.P.; high sheriff 1874; major Northumberland militia, and has 2 sons and 2 daughters.

Gerard (Widdrington), born , 1871.
Bertram FitzHerbert, born , 1873.
Frances Dorothea. Idonea.

[3] Lucy, died 14 Oct., 1882; married 14 Jan., 1874, to Henry Crossley, Esq. (see Foster's *Baronetage*), and had a son and daughter.

Gilbert St. Andrew (Crossley), born 30 Nov., 1876; died 7 Oct., 1882. Mabel.

[4] Mary Rose, married 7 May, 1867, to James Pender, Esq., formerly 25th regiment.

[5] Evelyn, married 20 April, 1869, to Richard John Lloyd Price, Esq., of Rhiwlas, and has at least a son,

Robert Kenrick.

(2*b*) Frank George (Hopwood), M.A., Christ Church, Oxon, 1840; rector of Winwick since 1855; hon. canon Chester Cathedral 1866; perp. curate Knowsley, co. Lanc. 1840-55; born 2 Aug., 1810; married 11 June, 1835, Lady Ellinor Mary Stanley, daughter of Edward, 13th Earl of Derby, K.G., (see page 625), and has 3 sons and 2 daughters.

( ) Frank Edward (Hopwood), M.A., Christ Church, Oxon, 1868; rector of Badsworth, Yorks, since 1879; born 19 April, 1843.

(2) Arthur Robert, born 19 March, 1845.

(3) Charles Augustus, born 27 Dec., 1847.

(4) Susan.

(5) Cecilia Catherine, married 4 May, 1871, to Ven. John Lionel Darby, M.A. Trin. Coll., Dublin, 1865; Archdeacon of Chester since 1877; hon. canon Chester Cathedral, 1873; rector of St. Bridget with St. Martin's, Chester, since 1875.

[3*b*] Hervey (Hopwood), lieut.-col. grenadier guards; born 9 Aug., 1811; married 8 July, 1852, Lucy, daughter of Edmond Wodehouse, Esq., M.P., of Sennow Lodge, Norfolk (see Foster's *Peerage*, E. KIMBERLEY).

[4*b*] Mary Augusta (Hopwood), married 18 June, 1834, to Charles William, 3rd Earl of Sefton, M.P. South Lancashire 1832-5, lord-lieut. Lancashire (see Foster's *Peerage*); he died 2 August, 1855, having had 4 sons and a daughter (*c*).

(1*b*-4*c*) Sir William Philip Molyneux, 4th Earl of Sefton; capt. late grenadier guards; grand cross of the Tower and Sword of Portugal; lord-lieut. Lancashire since 1858; born 14 Oct., 1835; married 18 July, 1866, Hon. Cecil Emily Hylton-Jolliffe, 5th daughter of Sir William George, 1st Baron Hylton, and has 3 sons and 2 daughters.

[1] Charles William Hylton, VISCOUNT MOLYNEUX, born 25 June, 1867.

[2] Hon. Osbert Cecil, born 20 Feb., 1871.

[3] Hon. Richard Frederick, born 24 March, 1873.

[4] Lady Gertrude Eleanor.

[5] Lady Rose Mary.

(2*b*-4*c*) Hon. Caryl Craven, lieut.-col. late 10th hussars, born 4 Oct., 1836; married 21 April, 1870,

Hon. Caroline Elizabeth Lawley, eldest daughter of Sir Beilby Richard, 2nd Baron Wenlock, and has a son,

Caryl Richard, born 10 Feb., 1871.

(3*b*-4*c*) Hon. Henry Hervey, com. R.N., born 18 April, 1842; married 23 Oct., 1873, Alice Catherine, daughter of late Humphrey St. John Mildmay, Esq., (see Foster's *Baronetage*).

(4*b*-4*c*) Hon. Roger Gordon, lieut. Duke of Lancaster's Own yeomanry cavalry 1881; lieut. late 1st dragoons; born 4 Jan., 1849

(5*b*-4*c*) Lady Cecilia Maria Charlotte, hon. lady in waiting to H.R.H. the Duchess of Connaught and Strathern 1883; married 12 July, 1869, to Hugh Richard, 8th Viscount Downe; major 2nd life guards; A.D.C. to H.R.H. the Duke of Connaught in India 1884; served in Zulu war 1879, and has 2 sons and 3 daughters.

[1] Hon. John (Dawnay), born 23 May, 1872.
[2] Hon. Hugh, born 19 Sept., 1875.
[3] Hon. Beryl. [4] Hon. Norah. [5] Hon. Faith.

[3*a*] **Mary Gregge**, of whom presently.

[4*a*] Elizabeth (Gregge), baptized 20 May, 1656; buried 20 July, 1657.

MARY GREGGE (elder daughter of Robert Gregge aforesaid), born 9 June, 1658; died 27 Dec., 1708; married 27 Feb., 1678, to Joshua Horton, of Chadderton, co. Lanc., by purchase (son of Joshua Horton, of Sowerby, Yorks, J.P., see Foster's *Yorkshire Collection*); he died 15 Dec., 1708, having had, with other issue, 2 sons and 4 daughters.

[1] **Thomas** (Horton), of whom presently.

[2] James, receiver general or treasurer in the Isle of Man; baptized 18 April, 1695; died unmarried 14 Dec., 1734.

[3] Sarah, baptized 6 Jan., 1687; married , to Thomas Williamson, of Liverpool, merchant.

[4] Elizabeth, baptized 28 May, 1689; married , to William Williamson, of Liverpool, merchant.

[5] Martha, born 30 Nov., 1697; married , to Richard Clayton, of Adlington, co. Lanc

[6] Jane, married at St. Michael's Church, Liverpool, 10 June, 1713, to John Parr, of Liverpool, merchant.

THOMAS HORTON, of Chadderton, co. Lanc., J.P.; governor of the Isle of Man for the Earl of Derby; born at Chester 4 May, 1685; died at Manchester 18 March, 1757; married Anne, daughter and co-heir of Richard Mostyn, of London, merchant; died at Chadderton, co. Lanc., 17 June, 1725, aged 39, having had (with other issue, all died unmarried) 2 sons and a daughter (*c*).

[1*c*] Sir Willliam (Horton), of Chadderton, co. Lanc., J.P., D.L., and high sheriff; Baronet, so created 14 Jan., 1764; died 25 Feb., 1774; married at Tankersley, 23 Aug., 1751, Susannah, only daughter and heir of Francis Watts, of Barns Hall, Yorks; she died 19 May, 1778, leaving 3 sons (*d*).

(1*d*-1*c*) Sir Watts Horton, 2nd Bart., born 17 Nov., 1753; died 15 Nov., 1811; married 3 June, 1778 Harriet, daughter of James, Lord Stanley, eldest son of Edward, 11th Earl of Derby; she died 15 Oct., 1830, having had an only child,

HARRIET SUSANNAH ANNE (HORTON), only daughter and sole heir, born 4 Jan., 1790; died at Bath 29 Dec., 1827; married at Bath 22 July, 1813-14, to Charles Rees, major 53rd foot (younger brother of John Rees, Esq., of Killymaenllyd); he died 6 Aug., 1852, having had a son and 2 daughters.

[1] Charles Horton Rhys, of Chadderton Hall, co. Lancs. (? Morton Price of the stage); married Agnes Cuthbert, daughter of Brig.-general Cureton, C.B., A.D.C. to the Queen; she died a widow 7 Feb., 1884, having had 2 sons and a daughter.

(1) C. Cureton (Rhys).
(2)
(3) daughter, married to Armitage.

[2] Harriet, died unmarried.

[3] Caroline (Rees), married to Fitzmaurice Parry Okeden (son of David Okeden Parry Okeden, Esq., of More Critchill and Turnworth, Dorset; he died 1869, leaving a son and daughter.

(1) Algernon Fitzmaurice.
(2) Grace Harriett, married Dec., 1880 to Ernest King, Esq., of Wimbleton.

(2*d*-1*c*) Sir Thomas Horton, 3rd Bart., vicar of Badsworth; born 21 July, 1758; died 2 Mar., 1821; married 28 July, 1778-9, Elizabeth, daughter of James, Lord Stanley (see page 621); she died 3-13 April, 1796, leaving an only daughter,

Charlotte (Horton), only daughter and sole heir; born 21 Oct., 1784; died at Lyons 25 Dec, 1842; married , 1805, to George Pollard, Esq., of Stannary Hall, Yorks; J.P., D.L., West Riding, lieut.-col. command. West Riding yeom. cavalry; he died 26 May, 1866, aged 84, having had a son and 3 daughters.

[1] George Thomas (Pollard), of Hundhill, Yorks, born 1 Aug., 1809; died 3 Dec., 1876, and having married 31 Aug, 1835, Clara, eldest daughter of James Royds, Esq., of Woodlands, Cheshire, and had 3 daughters.

(1) Clara Louisa Elizabeth (Pollard), married 5 Aug., 1873, as 2nd wife, to Rev. Wm. Bishop de Moleyns, M.A., Prebendary of Wells and Vicar of Burrington (see page 662).

(2) Julia Frances (Pollard), married 30 Jan, 1866, to Joseph Armitage-Armitage, Esq., J.P., of Milnsbridge House, Yorks, and has a son and daughter.

George Pollard (Armitage), born 21 April, 1867.
Julia Ethel.

(3) Georgina (Pollard), married 17 April, 1866, to T. Maitland Reid, capt. R. Monmouthshire Engineers (son of John Reid, of Alloa, N.B., and governor Bank of England, Manchester), and had a son and 2 daughters.

George Maitland (Reid), born 19 July, 1867;
Clara Adelaide, Beatrice Maitland.

[2] Elizabeth (Pollard).

[3] Henrietta (Pollard), married 30 Oct., 1830, to Robert Bell, Esq., of Sculcoates, Hull.

[4] Fanny (Pollard), died unmarried 14 Feb, 1832.

(3*d*-1*c*) William (Horton), lieut.-col. 2nd Lanc. militia, born 21 Oct., 1767; died 15 April, 1816.

[2*c*] **Joshua (Horton)**, of whom presently.

[3*c*] Susanna, died 16 March, 1797; married 24 March, 1742, to George Lloyd, Esq., of Hulme, co. Lanc., and had issue (see page 654).

JOSHUA HORTON, of Howroyde, Yorks, born 12 May, baptized 1 June, 1720; died 29 Jan., 1793; he married 1st, Anne, daughter

THE DESCENT OF

Sydney George Horton,

Lieut., R.A.,

FROM THE

Blood Royal  **of England.**

EDWARD I., crowned 19 Aug., 1274, b. 17 June, 1239, d. 7 July, 1307. = Eleanor (1st wife) dau. of Ferdinand III., King of Castile, d. 27 Nov., 1290.

Joan of Acre, b. there 1272, d. 10 May, 1305, 2nd wife. = Gilbert de Clare, Earl of Gloucester, &c., d. 7 Dec., 1295.

Margaret de Clare, m. 1st to Sir Piers Gaveston, Earl of Cornwall. = Hugh de Audley (2nd husband), cr. Earl of Gloucester, d. 1347.

Margaret de Audley, d. 7 Sept., 1349. = Ralph de Stafford, K.G., cr. Earl of Stafford, d. 31 Aug., 1372.

Beatrix Stafford = Thomas, 5th Lord Roos of Hamlake (2nd husband).

William de Roos, 7th Baron, K.G., Lord Treasurer of England, 1404. = Margery, yr. dau. of Sir John de Arundel, Knt., Marshal of England.

Margaret de Roos (1st wife) = James Touchet, Lord Audley, lord almoner, slain at Blore Heath, 1458.

John, Lord Audley, had summons to Parliament 1461-83, d. 26 Sept., 1491. = Anne, dau. of Sir Thomas Itchingham.

Joan (1st wife) dau. of Fulke Bourchier, Lord FitzWarren. = James, Lord Audley, Knt., beheaded 28 June, 1497, attainted and forfeited. = Margaret (2nd wife) dau. of Richard Dayrell, of Lillingston.

John, Lord Audley, restored in blood and honour 1512, and to his father's lands 1533. = Mary, dau. of John Griffin, of Braybrooke, Northants.

A.
Continued above.

B.
Continued from below.

John, Lord Audley = Mary Griffin

George, Lord Audley, took his seat in the House of Lords 20 Jan., 1558, d. 1560. = Elizabeth, dau. of Sir Bryan Tuke, Knt., treasurer of the Chamber, Henry VIII.

Henry, Lord Audley, Knight Banneret, never sat in Parliament, d. 1595. = Elizabeth, dau. of Sir William Sneyd, of Bradwall, Staffordshire, buried at Thelwall, 4 Jan., 1610.

Anne Touchet = Thomas Brooke, of Norton, Cheshire, Sheriff 1578, 1592.

Christian Brooke = Richard Starkey, Esq., of Stretton, Cheshire, b. 1568.

Anne Starkey = Ralph Gregge, of Bradley, Cheshire.

Edward Gregge, of Hapsford, buried in St. Michael's, Chester, 13 Nov. 1665. = Elizabeth, dau. of Chr. Lightfoot, of Barrow, d. 3 May, 1659.

Robert Gregge, d. Feb., 1661-2. = Elizabeth, buried in St. Michael's, 18 Oct. 1658.

Robert Gregge, buried at St. Michael's, Chester, 19 June, 1673. = Jane, dau. of —— Holt, of Bridge Hall, co. Lanc., buried 17 July, 1689.

Mary Gregge, b. 9 June, 1658, m. 27 Feb., 1678, d. 27 Dec., 1708. = Joshua Horton, of Chadderton, co. Lanc., d. 15 Dec., 1708.

Thomas Horton, of Chadderton, co. Lanc., governor of the Isle of Man, d. 18 March, 1757. = Anne, dau. and co-heir of Richard Mostyn, of London, merchant, d. 17 June, 1725, aged 39.

Sir William Horton, of Chadderton, Bart., so created, 1764, d. 25 Feb., 1774. = Susanna, only dau. and heir of Francis Watts, Esq., of Barn Hall, Yorks, m. 23 Aug., 1751, d. 19 May, 1778.

2. Joshua Horton, of Howroyde, Yorks, b. 12 May, 1720, d. 29 Jan., 1793. = Mary Bethia (2nd wife), dau. of Rev. J. Woolen, A.M., rector of Emley, Yorks, &c., d. 8 Feb., 1806.

Susanna, m. 24 March, 1742, d. 16 March, 1797. = George Lloyd, of Hulme, co. Lancashire.

Thomas Horton, of Howroyde, Yorks, b. 26 Aug. 1766, d. 22 Dec., 1829. = Lady Mary Gordon, yngst dau. of George, 3rd Earl of Aberdeen, m. 12 March, 1789, d. 7 Aug., 1852.

Joshua Sydney Horton, admrl., R.N., b. 7 March, 1768, d. 24 Nov. 1835. = Grace, wid. of Henry Whorwood, of Headington, Oxon., d. 8 Nov., 1845.

William Horton, incumbt. of St. Mary's, Rochdale b. 5 May, 1769, d. 13 Aug., 1817 = Elizabeth, eld. dau. of John Lyon, M.D. m. 7 Nov., 1793, d. 24 Oct., 1835.

Other issue, see page 636

Sydney Lloyd Horton, lieut. 14th dragoons, d. unm. 1844.

Agnes Jane (1st wife), dau. of J.J. Fisher, Esq. of Ealing Park, m. 1846, d. 1853. = William Horton, rear-adml. R.N., C.B., b. 22 Aug., 1820, d. 22 March, 1853. = Mary (2nd wife), widow of Capt. Chas. Acton Broke, R.E., m. 8. Dec., 1859.

Mary Emily, b. 4 Feb., 1818, m. 11 July, 1854. = Rev. Herbert James, M.A., rector of Great and Little Livermere.

Agnes Mary, m. 22 Feb., 1876. = Arthur Craigie Oliphant, of Condie, N.B.

Sydney George Horton, lieut. R.A., b. 25 Feb., 1862.

Sydney Rhodes James, b. 1855.
Herbert Ellison, b. 1857.
Montague, b. 1862.
Grace Constance.

Arthur. Lawrence. Launcelot.

of George Clarke, governor of New York; she died s.p. 25 May, 1764; he married, 2nd, Mary Bethia, daughter of Rev. John Woolen, A.M., rector of Emley, Yorks, 1742-72, and vicar of Blackburn, co. Lanc.; she died 8 Feb., 1806, having had 4 sons and 4 daughters (*e*).

[1*e*] **Thomas**, of whom (see page 638).
[2*e*] Joshua Sydney (Horton), admiral R.N., born 7 March, 1768; died 24 Nov., 1835; married Grace, widow of Henry Whorwood, of Headington House, Oxon, daughter of James Treacher, Esq.; she died 8 Nov., 1845, having had 2 sons and a daughter (*f*).
(1*f*-2*e*) Sydney Lloyd (Horton), lieut. 14th dragoons; born 3 Feb., 1816; died unmarried at Bombay 1844.
(2*f*-2*e*) William (Horton), rear-admiral R.N., C.B., served at St. Jean d'Acre 1840, in Black Sea and Azoff expedition 1855, knight legion of honour, 5th class medjidie; J.P. Suffolk; born 22 Aug., 1820; died 22 March, 1883; married 1st, 18 Feb., 1846, Agnes Jane, daughter of Jacob Jeddere Fisher, Esq., of Ealing Park, Middx.; she died 25 July, 1853, leaving a daughter.
[1] Agnes Mary (Horton), married 22 Feb., 1876, to Arthur Cragie Oliphant, of Condie, N.B., and has 3 sons,
Arthur (Oliphant), born 8 Nov., 1876.
Laurence Richard, born 16 Dec., 1877.
Launcelot, born 8 Oct., 1881.
Adl. Horton married, 2ndly, 8 Dec., 1859, Anna Maria, widow of Capt. Charles Acton Bro e, R.E. (see Foster's *Baronetage*), daughter of John Hamilton, Esq., of Sundrum, co. Ayr, and had a son.
[2] Sydney George (Horton), lieut. R.A., born 25 Feb., 1862.
(3*f*-2*e*) Mary Emily, born 4 Feb., 1818; married 11 July, 1854, to Rev. Herbert James, M.A. King's Coll., Camb., 1849, some time fellow; rector of Great and Little Livermere since 1865, and has 3 sons and a daughter,
Sydney Rhodes (James), born 30 May, 1855.
Herbert Ellison Rhodes, born 20 Oct., 1857.
Montague Rhodes, born 1 Aug., 1862.
Grace Caroline Rhodes.
[3*e*] William (Horton), incumbent of St. Mary's, Rochdale; J.P. and D.L. cos. Lanc. and Yorks, West Riding; born 5 May, 1769; died 13 Aug., 1817; married 7 Nov., 1793, Elizabeth, eldest daughter of John Lyon, M.D., of Liverpool; she died 24 Oct., 1835, having had (with numerous children who died young) a son and 3 daughters (*g*).
(1*g*-3*e*) Richard George (Horton), of Leeds, 5th son, born 8 March, 1806; died 12 May, 1875; married 1st, at Leeds, 3 April, 1828, Emily, 2nd daughter of Robert Boulton, Esq., of Great Driffield, Yorks; she died 4 Sept., 1855; he married 2ndly, Oct., 1857, Elizabeth, 4th daughter of late John Fawsett, M.D., of Horncastle; by his 1st wife he had a son and 3 daughters.
[1] Richard George (Horton), of Darley, M.D., born 14 April, 1829; died 25 Jan., 1861; married Mary Hargreave, youngest daughter of Edward Taylor, Esq., and had 2 sons and 3 daughters.
(1) William (Horton), born 14 April, 1853; died 2 March, 1869.
(2) Edward Sydney, born 18 June, 1856; married 3 June, 1881, Elizabeth, daughter of Hall, of Manchester.
(3) Mary, married 30 Oct., 1883, to Frederick Brewster, of Middlesbrough, solicitor.
(4) Emily.
(5) Edith.
[2] Emily, died 14 Aug., 1879.
[3] Margaret Frances, died 14 Jan., 1879.
[4] Ellen, married 6 May, 1862, to Rev. Adam Clarke Smith, M.A., Worcester College, Oxon, Vicar of St. John, Crowborough, Sussex, 1879-84; of St John, Middlesbrough, Yorks, 1859-78.
(2*g*-3*e*) Mary Anne, born 23 June, 1797; married to Robert Sutcliffe, of Rochdale, surgeon.
(3*g*-3*e*) Charlotte, born 15 Nov. 1802; died 11 Nov., 1871; married 12 May, 1830, to Stephen Davey, Esq., of Redruth and Bochym, Cornwall, J.P., D.L.; he died 16 Nov., 1864, having had 2 sons and 2 daughters (*h*).
[1*h*-3*g*] William Horton (Davey), of Redruth, J.P., M.A. Brasenose Coll., Oxon, born 15 Oct., 1835; died unmarried, 13 April, 1871.
[2*h*-3*g*] Joshua Sydney (Davey), of Bochym and Redruth, J.P., born 28 April, 1842; married 2 Aug., 1871, Julia, daughter of late William Watt, Esq., of Ticton Grange, Yorks, and has 2 daughters.
Aimée Sydney Horton (Davey).
Alice Millicent.
[3] Elizabeth Maria, died 24 May, 1884; married 24 Feb., 1852, to John Michael Williams, Esq., of Caerhays Castle, and of Burncoose, Cornwall, and Gnaton Hall, Devon, D.L.; high sheriff 1865; special deputy warden of the Stannaries; a partner in Williams, Foster & Co. (elder son of Michael Williams, of Scorrier House, see Foster's *Baronetage*); he died 16 Feb., 1880, having had 3 sons and 4 daughters.
(1) Michael (Williams), of Gnaton Hall, Devon; J.P., M.A., Trin. Hall., Camb. from Eton, born 2 June, 1857; married 2 March, 1882, Dorothea Mary, 2nd daughter of E. S. Carus-Wilson, Esq., of Penmount, Truro.
(2) John, died young.
(3) John Charles, born 30 Sept., 1861; married 15 Oct., 1884, Mary Christian, daughter of Sir Frederick Martin Williams, 2nd Bart.
(4) Elizabeth, married 12 Dec., 1872, to John Borlase Bolitho, Esq., lieut. Royal miners art. mil.; he died 20 Aug., 1876, having had 2 sons.
John Williams Horton (Bolitho), born 25 Sept., 1873. Thomas Robins Evelyn, born 2 Sept. 1875.
(5) Charlotte, married 17 Nov., 1881, to Edward Powys, 2nd son of late Rev. John Rogers, of Stanage Park, co. Hereford, and has a son and daughter.
Charles Michael (Rogers), born 1 March, 1884.
Charlotte Harriett.
(6) Clara, died 3 Oct., 1884, married 7 Aug., 1884, to Rev. Walter Raleigh Gilbert, Chaplain R.N.
(7) Florence.
[4*h*-3*g*] Charlotte Mary Horton (Davey), married 29 March, 1859, to George Williams, Esq., J.P., D.L., of Scorrier House and Lanarth, high sheriff Cornwall 1875 (youngest brother of John Michael Williams aforesaid), and has had 3 sons and a daughter.
(1) John (Williams), born 7 Sept., 1861.
(2) George, died young.
(3) Percival Dacres, born 22 April, 1865.
(4) Mabel Claudia Susan.
(4*g*-3*e*) Elizabeth Maria (Horton), born 8 July, 1807; died s.p. 6 May, 1869; married to William Lloyd, M.D.
[4*e*] Richard Henry (Horton), major 84th regt.; born 6 May, 1777; died 20 April, 1813; married 12 Jan., 1808, and had a daughter Frances, who died unmarried.
[5*e*] Anna Maria, born 22 Oct., 1770; died unmarried 19 July, 1831.
[6*e*] Jane, born 22 Feb., 1773; died 11 Aug., 1829.

Elizabeth, Widow of John Borlase Bolitho, Esq.,

FROM THE

Blood Royal  of England.

EDWARD I., crowned 19 Aug., 1274, b. 17 June, 1239, d. 7 July, 1307. = Eleanor (1st wife) dau. of Ferdinand III., King of Castile, d. 27 Nov., 1290.

Joan of Acre, b. there 1272, d. 10 May, 1305, 2nd wife. = Gilbert de Clare, Earl of Gloucester, &c., d. 7 Dec., 1295.

Margaret de Clare, m. 1st to Sir Piers Gaveston, Earl of Cornwall. = Hugh de Audley (2nd husband), cr. Earl of Gloucester, d. 1347.

Margaret de Audley, d. 7 Sept., 1349. = Ralph de Stafford, K.G., cr. Earl of Stafford, d. 31 Aug., 1372.

Beatrix Stafford = Thomas, 5th Lord Roos of Hamlake (2nd husband).

William de Roos, 7th Baron, K.G., Lord Treasurer of England, 1404. = Margery, yr. dau. of Sir John de Arundel, Knt., Marshal of England.

Margaret de Roos (1st wife) = James Touchet, Lord Audley, lord almoner, slain at Blore Heath, 1458.

John, Lord Audley, had summons to Parliament 1461-83, d. 26 Sept., 1491. = Anne, dau. of Sir Thomas Itchingham.

Joan (1st wife) dau. of Fulke Bourchier, Lord FitzWarren. = James, Lord Audley, Knt., beheaded 28 June, 1497, attainted and forfeited. = Margaret (2nd wife) dau. of Richard Dayrell, of Lillingston.

John, Lord Audley, restored in blood and honour 1512, and to his father's lands 1533. = Mary, dau. of John Griffin, of Braybrooke, Northants.

A, continued above.

A, continued from below.

John, Lord Audley = Mary Griffin

George, Lord Audley, took his seat in the House of Lords 20 Jan., 1558, d. 1560. = Elizabeth, dau. of Sir Bryan Tuke, Knt., treasurer of the Chamber, Henry VIII.

Henry, Lord Audley, Knight Banneret, never sat in Parliament, d. 1595. = Elizabeth, dau. of Sir William Sneyd, of Bradwall, Staffordshire, buried at Thelwall, 4 Jan., 1610.

Anne Touchet = Thomas Brooke, of Norton, Cheshire, Sheriff 1578, 1592.

Christian Brooke = Richard Starkey, Esq., of Stretton, Cheshire, b. 1568.

Anne Starkey = Ralph Gregge, of Bradley, Cheshire.

Edward Gregge, of Hapsford, buried in St. Michael's, Chester, 13 Nov. 1665. = Elizabeth, dau. of Chr. Lightfoot, of Barrow, d. 3 May, 1659.

Robert Gregge, d. Feb., 1661-2. = Elizabeth, buried in St. Michael's, 18 Oct. 1658.

Robert Gregge, buried at St. Michael's, Chester, 19 June, 1673. = Jane, dau. of —— Holt, of Bridge Hall, co. Lanc., buried 17 July, 1689.

Mary Gregge, b. 9 June, 1658, m. 27 Feb., 1678, d. 27 Dec., 1708. = Joshua Horton, of Chadderton, co. Lanc., d. 15 Dec., 1708.

Thomas Horton, of Chadderton, co. Lanc., governor of the Isle of Man, d. 18 March, 1757. = Anne, dau. and co-heir of Richard Mostyn, of London, merchant, d. 17 June, 1725, aged 39.

Sir William Horton, of Chadderton, Bart., so created 1764, d. 25 Feb. 1774. = Susanna, only dau. and heir of Francis Watts, Esq., of Barn Hall, Yorks, m. 23 Aug. 1751, d. 19 May, 1778.

2. Joshua Horton, of Howroyde, Yorks, b. 12 May, 1720, d. 29 Jan., 1793. = Mary Bethia (2nd wife), dau. of Rev. J. Woolen, A.M., rector of Emley, Yorks, &c., d. 8 Feb. 1806.

Susanna, m. 24 March, 1742, d. 16 March, 1797. = George Lloyd, of Hulme, co. Lancashire.

Thomas Horton, of Howroyde, Yorks, b. 26 Aug. 1766, d. 22 Dec., 1829. = Lady Mary Gordon, ygst. dau. of George, 3rd Earl of Aberdeen, m. 12 March, 1789, d. 7 Aug. 1852.

Joshua Sydney Horton, adml. R.N., b. 7 March, 1768, d. 24 Nov., 1835. = Grace, wid. of Henry Whorwood, of Headington, Oxon., d. 8 Nov., 1845.

William Horton, incumbt. of St. Mary's, Rochdale b. 5 May, 1769, d. 13 Aug. 1817. = Elizabeth, eld. dau. of John Lyon, M.D. m. 7 Nov., 1793, d. 24 Oct., 1835.

Other issue, see page 63[illegible].

Richard George Horton (5th son), b. 8 Mar. 1806, d. 12 May, 1875. = Emily (1st wife), 2nd dau. of Robert Boulton, Esq. of Great Driffield, Yorks, m. 1828, d. 1855.

Mary Anne, b. 23 June, 1797. = Robert Sutcliffe, of Rochdale, surgeon.

Charlotte, b. 15 Nov. 1802, m. 12 May, 1830, d. 11 Nov., 1871. = Stephen Davey, of Redruth and Bochym, Cornwall, J.P., D.L., d. 16 Nov., 1864.

William Horton Davey, of Redruth, J.P., M.A., b. 1835, died unm. 1871.

Joshua Sydney Davey, of Bochym and Redruth, J.P., b. 28 April, 1842. = Julia, dau. of late William Watt, Esq., of Tickton Grange, Yorks, m. 2 Aug., 1871

Elizabeth Maria, m. 24 Feb., 1852, d. 24 May, 1884. = John Michael Williams, Esq., of Caerhays Castle, and of Burncoose, Cornwall, and Gnaton Hall, Devon, D.L., High Sheriff, d. 16 Feb., 1880.

Charlotte Mary Horton, m. 1859, to George Williams, Esq. of Scorrier Ho. and Lanarth, High Sheriff Cornwall, 1875.

Aimée.
Alice.

Michael Williams, of Gnaton, b. 1857, m. 1882, Dorothea Mary, 2nd dau. of E. S. Carus-Wilson, Esq., of Truro.

John Charles Williams, b. 1861, m. 1884, Mary Christian, dau. of Sir F. M. Williams, 2nd Bart.

Elizabeth, m. 12 Dec., 1872, to John Borlase Bolitho, who died 20 Aug. 1876. =

Charlotte, m. 1881, to E. P. Rogers, Esq.
Clara, m. to Rev. W. R. Gilbert, and d. 1884.
Florence.

John, born 1861.
Percival, b. 1865.
Mabel

John Williams Horton Bolitho, b. 25 Sept., 1873.

Thomas Robins Evelyn Bolitho, b. 2 Sept., 1875.

[7*i*] Charlotte, born 26 Feb., 1776; died 18 May, 1839; married to Rev. William Richardson, of Ferry Fryston, Yorks, he died 26 Feb., 1852, having had 2 sons and 3 daughters.

(1) William (Richardson), in holy orders, died unmarried.

(2) Joshua Thomas, father of William Edmund.

(3) Charlotte (Richardson), married 20 Oct., 1834, to Rev. Henry Linton, M.A. Magdalen Coll., Oxon, 1827, sometime fellow; hon. canon Christ Church, Oxon, 1871; vicar of Diddington, Hunts, 1835-56; vicar of St. Peter-le-Bailey, Oxford, 1856-77, and had 6 sons and 3 daughters.

[1] Henry, born 11 Jan., 1838, died unmarried, 24 Aug., 1866.

[2] John, born 20 Jan., 1840, married Mary, daughter of Rev. R. Gatty.

[3] Sydney, bishop of Riverino, N. S. Wales, born 2 July, 1841; married Isabella, daughter of Dr. Heurtley.

[4] Edward Francis, born 16 March, 1848.

[5] William Richardson, born 2 April, 1850.

[6] Arthur, born 4 July, 1853.

[7] Charlortte Isabella, married to Rev. Allen Smith, canon.

[8] Jane, married to Rev. W. M. Myres.

[9] Harriet Louisa, married to Rev. G. F. W. Mumby.

(4) Jane Annabella (Richardson), married to Rev. Joseph Bradshaw,

(5) Elizabeth Mary (Richardson), married to John Hill, Esq.

[8*k*] Henrietta Horton, born 20 June, 1783; died unmarried 25 April, 1871.

THOMAS HORTON, of Howroyde, Yorks, J.P., D.L. Lancashire; born 26 Aug., 1766; died 22 Dec., 1829; married 12 March, 1789, Lady Mary Gordon, youngest daughter of George, 3rd Earl of Aberdeen; she died 7 Aug., 1852, having had 2 sons and 2 daughters (*i*).

[1*i*] Joshua (Horton), of Howroyde, Yorks, J.P., D.L.; vicar of Ormskirk, co. Lanc.; born 12 Nov., 1790; died 21 Nov., 1845; married 6 Nov., 1832, Harriet, eldest daughter of Sir Thomas Dalrymple Hesketh, Bart.; she died 10 May, 1836, leaving an only son.

Joshua Thomas (Horton), first-named (see page 631).

[2*i*] George William (Horton), of Embsay Kirk, Yorks, colonel in the army; served with 71st light infantry in the Peninsula and at Waterloo; born 3 Nov., 1792; died 1 May, 1877; married 1 Aug. 1826, Frances Esther, 2nd daughter of Rev. William Garnier, of Rookesbury, Hants (by Lady Harriet North, daughter of the Bishop of Winchester); she died March, 1861, leaving (surviving) 2 sons and 2 daughters.

(1) George William (Horton), M.A. Trin. Coll., Camb. 1856; vicar of Wellow, Somerset, since 1859; born 17 Dec., 1830; married 19 Aug., 1858, Annie Elizabeth, daughter of late Le Gendre Nicholas Starkie, of Huntroyde, co. Lanc.; she died 24 Jan., 1869, having had a son and daughter.

[1] Le Gendre George (Horton), in holy orders, born 12 July, 1859.

[2] Anne Frances.

(2) William Thomas (Horton), born 9 April, 1838; married 16 Dec., 1866, Elizabeth, daughter of late John Waterhouse, C.E., of York.

(3) Lucy (Horton), died 3 Feb., 1885.

(4) Fanny Laura.

[3*i*] Mary (Horton), died 28 Feb., 1881, aged 91; married 26 June, 1816, to Francis Beynon Hacket, Esq., of Moor Hall, co. Warwick; he died 14 Oct., 1863, having had 4 sons and 6 daughters (*k*).

(1*k*-3*i*) Andrew (Hacket), died , aged 18.

(2*k*-3*i*) John George (Hacket), lieut. 91st regt., born ; died ; married Susan Hussey, daughter of Henry Disney Roebuck, Esq., of Ingress Abbey, Kent, and had 3 sons and a daughter.

[1] George Algernon Beynon Disney (Hacket), of Moor Hall, co. Warwick, J.P., born 6 June, 1844; married 12 Dec., 1867, Adela, 2nd daughter of Charles Rowland Palmer Morewood, Esq., of Alfreton Park, co. Derby, and of Ladbroke, co. Warwick (see Foster's *Peerage*, E. SELBORNE), and has 4 sons and a daughter.

John Lisle (Hacket), born 10 Sept., 1869; George Lisle, born 22 March, 1872; Charles Lisle, born 21 Oct., 1874; Andrew Lisle, born 24 July, 1877; Adela Mary.

[2] Charles (Hacket).

[3] Andrew Henry, died in infancy, 29 March, 1848.

[4] Constance Helena Mary, married to Capt. Richard Young, 2nd son of Alan Young, Esq., of Orlingbury, Northants.

(3*k*-3*i*) Charles (Hacket), died unmarried , 1848.

(4*k*-3*i*) Frederick, lieut. 59th regt., killed at Canton 28 Dec., 1857, aged 29.

(5*k*-3*i*) Frances Mary, died 28 Dec., 1879; married 18 April, 1843, to Childers Henry Thompson, late 11th light dragoons, and formerly capt. 7th dragoon guards (see Foster's *Baronetcy*), and has had 6 sons and 4 daughters.

[1] Frank Childers (Thompson), born 16 Mar., 1847.

[2] Stephen Henry, lieut. R.N., born 16 May, 1849; married , and has issue.

[3] Leonard Walbanke, born 31 Oct., 1851.

[4] Gerald Charles, M.A. Keble Coll., Oxon., rector of Offord Cluny, Hunts, 1881, born 8 Mar., 1853.

[5] Charles Edward, born 27 April, 1855.

[6] Frederick Hacket, born 1 July, 1858.

[7] Mary Frances.

[8] Alice Harriot, married 17 Dec., 1867, to Rev. John Bedford, curate of Scarborough 1865-72, s.p.

[9] Emma Mildred, married 17 Dec., 1867, to George Hall Ringrose, capt. late 4th dragoon guards.

[10] Laura Emilia, married 23 Aug., 1870, to Samuel Barrett, capt. late 3rd (K.O.) hussars and 14th King's hussars, also Royal South Down militia, and has a son and 2 daughters.

Gerald Edwin Hamilton (Barrett), born 18 May, 1871. Ethel Maud Hamilton. Ada Violet Hamilton, born 22 Oct., 1879.

(6*k*-3*i*) Katherine Alicia, died s.p. 19 Mar., 1878; married to Col. Bertie Edward Murray Gordon, 91st Highlanders; he died 27 July, 1870 (see *Our Noble and Gentle Families*).

(7*k*-3*i*) Elizabeth Anne, married 27 Mar., 1841, to Thomas William Lloyd, Esq., of Cowesby Hall, Yorks, and had an only daughter,

Gertrude Elizabeth; died young (see page 655).

(8*k*-3*i*) Mary.

(9*k*-3*i*) Charlotte Sarah.

(10*k*-3*i*) Harriet Jane (Hacket), married 20 April, 1864, to William Roundell, Esq., of Gledstone, Yorks (see Foster's *Yorkshire Collection*); he died 21 Sept., 1881, having had at least 3 sons.

Richard Foulis, twin with Charles Selborne (Roundell), born 4 Nov., 1872.

A son, born and died 21 July, 1875.

(4*i*) Georgiana Henrietta Catherine Anne (Horton), born 19 and died 30 Oct., 1791.

RAYMOND, GEORGE, of Dublin, barrister-at-law, King's Inns, 1841, 17TH IN DESCENT FROM EDWARD III., born 11 Sept., 1817; married 20 Oct., 1858, Martha Jane, relict of Maurice Collis, Esq., daughter of Richard Montgomery, Esq., of Coote Hill.

THE DESCENT OF
GEORGE RAYMOND, OF DUBLIN,
BARRISTER-AT-LAW,
FROM THE BLOOD ROYAL OF ENGLAND.

EDWARD III., KING OF ENGLAND, Earl of Chester, 1320, Duke of Aquitaine, Count of Ponthieu and Montreuil, 1325; crowned at Westminster in his father's lifetime, 1 Feb., 1327; defeated the Scots at Halidon Hill, 1333. In 1339 he assumed the style of "King of France and England, and Lord of Ireland," and quartered the arms of France in the first quarter; gained a great naval victory over the French off Sluys, 1340, and won the celebrated battle of Cressy, 26 Aug., 1346; 17 Oct. following, the Scots were defeated at Neville Cross, and King David II. taken prisoner to London, where he remained nearly 11 years. Instituted the order of the Garter, 1349. His son, the BLACK PRINCE, defeated the French at the battle of Poictiers, 19 Sept., 1356 and brought King John prisoner to London, where he remained nearly five years (for further particulars, see *Royal Lineage*, Foster's *Peerage*). The King died at Sheen, Surrey, 21 June, 1377, having had issue; their descendant

THOMAS BLENNERHASSETT, of Littur, co. Kerry (3rd and youngest son of John Blennerhassett, of Ballyseedy, by his wife, Martha Lynn, see p. 566), married Ellen, daughter of Anthony Stoughton, of Rattoo, co. Kerry, clerk of the Court of Castle Chamber (by Honora, his wife, daughter of Dermot O'Brien, Lord Inchiquin), and had 6 daughters (*a*).

[1*a*] Martha (Blennerhassett), married 1st, 1685, to Frederick Mullins, Esq., of Ventry, who died 30 Oct., 1695 (see page 660). She re-married to Henry Parr, of Tralee, and had 2 daughters,
 Theodora (Parr). Anne.

[2*a*] Honora (Blennerhassett), married to Joseph Morris, of Urlee, and left 4 daughters.
 (1) Honora (Morris), married to Valentine Elliott, Esq. ,and had issue.
 (2) Ellen (Morris), married to Michael Madden, and had issue.
 (3 Jane, married to Maron.
 (4)

[3*a* Ellen (Blennerhassett), married to her cousin Charles, only son of Capt. Thomas Wren.

[4 Elizabeth, married to Capt. Arthur O'Lavery, of Moira, co. Down, and had 3 sons and 4 daughters.
 (1) Eugene (O'Lavery), attorney-at-law, died , 1733; married , Elizabeth, 4th daughter of Robert Blennerhassett, Esq., and Alice Osborne, and had a son and daughter.
 [1] Eugene (O'Lavery), posthumous son.
 [2] Alice, died young.
 (2) Arthur (O'Lavery), died unmarried , 1733.
 (3) Charles.
 (4) **Ellen**, married 23 June, 1714, to Samuel Raymond, Esq., of Ballyloughrane, and had 4 sons and 3 daughters (see next page).
 (5) Elizabeth (O'Lavery). (6) Honora.
 (7) Martha, married 1730, to Jemmett, brother of Samuel Raymond aforesaid, and had 2 sons and 2 daughters,
 [1] Samuel. [2] Arthur.
 [3] Elizabeth, married to Kerry Moore, Esq.
 [4] Mary, married 1st to James Fitzgerald, Esq.; and 2ndly to Maurice O'Connor, Esq.

[5*a*] Margaret (Blennerhassett), married to Lancelot Glanville, and had a son and 3 daughters (*b*).
 (1*b*-5*a*) Nicholas Glanville, married.
 (2*b*-5*a*) Mary, married , to William Harnett, of Ballyhenry, and had 2 sons,

Lancelot and William (Harnett).

(3*b 5a*) Ellen (Glanville), married , to Alexander Elliott, of Dowhill, co. Limerick, and had at least 2 sons and a daughter, viz., Thomas Blennerhassett Elliott, Alexander, and Margaret; the younger son, viz.,

ALEXANDER (ELLIOTT), of , married Mary, daughter of John Hewson, Esq., of Ennismore (by his wife, Margaret, daughter of Maurice Fitzgerald, Knight of Kerry (see page 490), and had 3 sons and 5 daughters (*c*).

(1*c*) Thomas (Elliott), of Garrynthenavally, co. Kerry, shot during the disturbances of 1808; married Ruth, daughter of Francis Chute, Esq., of Chute Hall, and had an only son,

Alexander (Elliott), of Tanavalla, J.P.; born 6 July, 1798; died 16 March, 1873; married 3 Jan., 1826, Meliora Southwell, daughter of Capt. John Brown, of 19th regt., and of Mount Brown, co. Limerick (by Meliora, daughter and coheir of Hon. Henry Southwell); she died 28 Jan., 1882, having had an only child,

MARY GORDON (Elliott), of Tanavalla, married 6 July, 1876, to Henry Cooke, J.P., only surviving son of William Cooke, of Retreat, co. Westmeath, J.P. (by Catherine, only child of Capt. F. Chute, of Chute Hall); he died s.p., 24 Oct., 1882.

(2*c*) Alexander (Elliott), married Alice, daughter of John Hurly and Mary Conway, and had 2 sons and a daughter.

[1] Alexander, and [2] Thomas; both died unmarried.

[3] Lucy Hurly (Elliott), died ; married , to Charles Newburgh Tisdall, Esq., of Castle Shane, co. Monaghan, and had a son,

Charles Elliott (Tisdall), born 5 Nov., 1848; married 25 July, 1876, Louisa, daughter of late Captain John Dynon, 5th R.I. Lancers, and had a son and 2 daughters,

Ernest Newburg (Tisdall), died an infant 23 Dec., 1878, Louisa Mary Lucy Elliott, Grace Marianmissa, died an infant 26 May, 1883.

(3*c*) John (Elliott), physician, married daughter of Lancelot O'Brien, of Tarmons co. Kerry, and had 4 sons and a daughter.

[1] Alexander (Elliott), of Tarmons, married his cousin Harriet, daughter of Edward Carte, Esq. (named below), and left, with other issue, a son and daughter.

(1) John Elliott, of Tarmons.

(2) Annie, married 18 Aug., 1860, as 2nd wife to William Carte, Esq., J.P. (see p. 514).

[2] Glanville. [3] Francis. [4] John.

[5] Marion, married Lysaght, and died s.p.

(4*c*) Margaret (Elliott), died Oct., 1822; married as 1st wife to Edward Carte, Esq., of the Castle, Newcastle, co. Limerick, and had 5 son and 4 daughters.

[1] William (Carte), E.I.C.S., died in India.

[2] Edward, in holy orders, married Miss Wyatt, and died s.p.

[3] Alexander (Carte), M.D., F.L.I., F.R.C.S.; born ; married , Ellen daughter of Thomas Dixon, Esq., barrister-at-law, and died s.p., Sept., 1881.

[4] Thomas, of Limerick, solicitor; born ; died , 1883; married Emily, daughter of Parker, Esq., and had issue.

[5] John Elliott (Carte), C.B.; deputy surgeon-gen., inspector gen. of hospitals; born ; died 19 April, 1876; married , 1857, Harriett, daughter of Thomas MacMahon, of Dublin, solicitor, and had 2 sons.

(1) Edward, born 1 Jan., 1860; died 10 Sept., 1874.

(2) Thomas Elliott (Carte), lieut. R.A.; born 23 Feb., 1861.

[6] Marion, died s.p., Feb., 1884; married to John Lysaght, Esq., who died

[7] Anne, died unmarried.

[8] Harriett, married , to her cousin, Alexander Elliott, of Tarmons, aforesaid.

[9] Frances (Carte), died unmarried.

(5*c*) Elizabeth (Elliott), married to Pierce Chute, Esq., of O'Brenan, and had 4 sons and 5 daughters.

[1] Eusebius (Chute), and [2] Alexander (Chute), died unmarried.

[3] Charles (Chute), of Tralee, married 1 July, 1869, Alice, daughter of Rowland Blennerhassett, Esq., of Tralee and Kells, &c. (see Foster's *Baronetage*); he died s.p. 24 May, 1884 (see page 575).

[4] Francis Elliott (Chute), major Kerry militia.

[5] Jane, married , to Richard Poole, surgeon 32nd regiment; he died s.p.

[6] Arabella. [7] Kate.

[8] Matilda Elliott (Chute).

[9] Anne, married to Thomas Goodman, late R.N.; and has a son, Thomas.

(6*c*) Mary, married to her cousin, William Day, and died s.p.

(7*c*) Dora, died unmarried.

(8*c*) Kate (Elliott), married to Frederick Usher Mullins Mason, of Kilmore, co. Kerry; and had, with 4 sons, who died unmarried, an only daughter.

Marion (Mason), married to Richard Huggard of Tralee, solicitor, and had 2 daughters.

[1] Katharine Wilhelmina (Huggard), married 16 Oct., 1877, as 2nd wife, to Lieut.-col. William Rowan, of Belmont, Tralee, J.P. co. Kerry, major and hon. lieut.-col. 4th R.M. fusiliers (see page 590), and has a daughter,

Marion Annie (Rowan).

[2] Anne (Huggard), died unmarried.

(4) Martha (Glanville).

[6*a*] Mary (Blennerhassett), married to John Sandes, Esq., M.A., ancestor of the Sallow Glen family (see page 824).

ELLEN (daughter of Capt. Arthur O'Lavery) married 23 June, 1714, to Samuel Raymond (son of Samuel Raymond, by his wife Maria Tennison, daughter of the Lord Bishop of Killala), and had 4 sons and 3 daughters.

[1] **Samuel (Raymond)**, of whom presently.

[2] Arthur (Raymond), of Kilferghrig.

[3] Anthony. [4] Eugene.

[5] Elizabeth (Mrs. Gregory).

[6] Mary, married 8 May, 1742, to Dominick Ferriter, Esq., and had a daughte, Ellen, married to Eraneis Giles.

[7] Ellen, married to Ambrose Madden, of Derryhoran, and had 3 daughters,

(1) Mary, married to James More, of Balyna, co. Kildare, who made his will 13 Dec. 1778, and had an only daughter,

Letitia, married to Richard O'Ferrall, Esq., and had at least 3 sons and 5 daughters.

(2) Ellen, married 2 Dec., 1771, to William Connor.
(3) Catherine.

SAMUEL RAYMOND, of Ballyloughrane, J.P., High Sheriff, 1773, married, 4 Jan., 1759, Frances, daughter of John Harnett, Esq., of Ballyhenry (and his wife Frances Nash), and had 4 sons and 3 daughters (*d*).

[1*d*] Anthony Samuel, of Ballyloughrane, married 1 Jan., 1785, Jane, daughter of Rev. William Maunsell, D.D., of Limerick, and had 3 sons and 6 daughters (*e*).
(1*e*-1*d*) Samuel (Raymond), of Ballyloughrane, died 27 Jan., 1822; married 25 May, 1815, Catherine Frances, daughter of George Rowan, Esq., of Rathany, co. Kerry; she re-married to Rev. A. Mackintosh, of Kilmurry, near Castle Island, by whom she had 3 sons and 2 daughters; by her 1st husband she had 3 sons.
[1] Anthony, of Kilmurry, co. Kerry, born 14 March, 1816, died 30 Oct., 1864.
[2] **George Raymond**, first named (see page 639).
[3] Samuel (Raymond), late 9th regt. foot, born 13 Aug., 1820; married , his cousin Frances, daughter of Thomas Ledman, Esq., died s p.
(2*e*-1*d*) William, 39th regt., died s.p.
(3*e*-1*d*) Anthony, died s.p.
(4*e*-1*d*) Eliza (Raymond), married 2 Nov., 1808, to George Rowan, Esq., of Rathany, and had 3 sons and 3 daughters,
[1] Maurice. [2] Thomas. [3] Samuel.
[4] Jane, married to W. Ormsby.
[5] Elizabeth (Rowan), married to Richard Chute, M.D., (2nd son of Richard Chute, of Chute Hall, by his 2nd wife, Elizabeth, daughter of Rev. William Maunsell, D.D.); he died 14 Sept., 1866, having had a son and daughter.
[1] Richard (Chute), lieut. 8th regt.; married 3 wives, s.p.
[2] Rowena (Chute), married first to Arthur Crispe, who divorced her; she re married to John Atkinson, Q.C.
[6] Dora, died unmarried.
(5*e*-1*d*) Frances, married 11 Feb. 1811, to Thomas Ledman, Esq., and had, with other issue, 2 daughters,
[1] Frances, married to Samuel Raymond, Esq., named above.
[2] Cherry, married, as 2nd wife, to Alexander Mason (see page 573).
(6*e*-1*d*) Ellen, died s.p.
(7*e*-1*d*) Jane, married 25 Nov., 1812, to William Marchant Ardagh, Esq.
(8*e*-1*d*) Anne, and (9*e*-1*d*) Dorothea, both died s.p.
[2*d*] John, died young.
[3*d*] Richard (Raymond) married Arabella, daughter of John S. Giles, of Castle Drum, by Anne Eagar, and had 2 sons and 2 daughters.
(1) Richard Horatio Nelson (Raymond), born married Grace Dunfey, and had 2 sons and 2 daughters.
[1] Richard William, married Ellen Hall, and has 2 sons and a daughter,
Fred, Richard Horatio Nelson, and Grace.
[2] Charles, married 1883, Amelia Bomford.
[3] Grace.
[4] Arabella, married 1822, to James Fidden.
(2) John.
(3) Maria (Raymond), married to Jeffcott.
(4) Frances Giles, married to Frederick Henry West, and had a son and daughter.
[1] Raymond West, a judge in India, who married Clementina Ferguson, only daughter of William Maunsell Chute, younger son of Richard Chute, of Chute Hall.
[2] Ann West, married to Capt. Thomas Thring.
[4*d*] James.
[5*d*] Elizabeth, married 24 Dec., 1785, to Samuel Sealy, Esq., and had a son and 3 daughters.
(1) John Sealy, of Ballymalis, sold Maglass.
(2) Agnes, died Jan., 1872, having married John Weekes, Esq., of the Limerick militia, she died Jan., 1872, leaving issue (see page 572).
(3) Eliza, married to Capt. Richard Quill, and had a son, Richard, who died s.p., and an only daughter, Maria, married to Abraham Goff, of Enniscorthy.
(4) Jane, married to John Crump, M.D., and had several sons, who died unmarried, and 2 daughters.
[1] Elizabeth Aphia (Crump), died 21 July, 1874; married 5 Nov., 1855, to George, 2nd son of Capt. John Massy, of Glenville, co. Limerick (see B. CLARINA, in Foster's *Peerage*), and had 4 daughters.
Ida Jane Elizabeth (Massy), Elize Crumpe, Georgiana Travers, Geraldine Ellinor Orpen.
[2] Jane (Crump), married to David E. Young, and has issue.
[6*d*] Frances, married, 1st, to Rev. James Raymond, who died s.p., she re-married to Neville Bath, Esq., and had a daughter,
ELIZA BATH, died 25 Feb., 1878; married 3 Sept., 1828, to Edward Richard Townsend, of Cork, he died 6 July, 1878, having had 2 sons and 5 daughters.
[1] Samuel Philip (Townsend), capt. R.N.; born 30 July, 1831; married 24 April, 1860, Emma Maria, daughter of John William Bridges, Esq., and has 5 sons and a daughter,
Edward Bridges, born 30 May, 1861; Neville Frederic, born 7 July, 1863; Ernest Horace, born 9 Jan. 1865; Cuthbert Hanson, born 5 April, 1872; Cyril Samuel, born 28 June, 1875; Constance Emma.
[2] Edward Richard, M.D., Dublin, 1861; M.B., 1857; L.K.Q.C.P., Ireland, 1859; M.R.C.S., England, 1858; born ; married Elizabeth, daughter of W. Humphrey, Esq.
[3] Helena, married , to William Penrose, Esq.
[4] Fanny, died 31 Dec., 1859.
[5] Mary, married , to Lieut. Pemberton Harrison, R.A., and died s.p.
[6] Eliza, married 29 Oct., 1872, to Rev. Robert Cooper Wills, M.A., Trin. Coll., Dublin, 1865, rector of Mallow since 1873, canon of Cloyne and rural dean of Buthon, and has 2 daughters,
Mary Townsend (Wills), Elizabeth Lucy.
[7] Lucy Cuthbert, married 28 March, 1865, to John Chetwood Aiken, Esq., of Bristol, banker, and has had 8 sons,
Walter Chetwode (Aiken), born 9 Feb., 1866; Edward Hamilton Chetwode, born 3 April, 1867; Harold Frederick Chetwode, born 1 Dec., 1868; Knightley Chetwode, born 11 Oct., 1870; Chetwode, born and died 26 Dec., 1871; John Chetwode, born 25 April, 1873; Cuthbert Chetwode, born 1 June, 1879, died 17 April following; Hugh Chetwode, born 3 July, 1882.
[7*d*] Mary, married 25 Nov., 1801, to Thomas Spring Eagar, of Cottage, J.P., who died 1808 (see page 592), having had a son and 2 daughters.
(1) James Raymond (Eagar), of Tralee, sold "Cottage," died unmarried.
(2) Frances, died unmarried.
(3) Catherine, married 1824, to William Fitz-Maurice Sealy, Esq., and had issue.

JEBB, JOSHUA GLADWYN, of Barnby Moor House, Notts; formerly capt. 54th regiment; 20TH IN DESCENT FROM EDWARD I.; born 16 March, 1839; married 7 June, 1870, Alice Caroline, 7th and youngest daughter of Rev. and Hon. Charles Dundas, rector of Epworth, and granddaughter of Robert, 2nd Viscount Melville (see Foster's *Peerage*), and has 3 sons and a daughter.

[1] Sydney Gladwyn (Jebb), born 26 Feb., 1871.
[2] Joshua Henry Miles, born 12 Feb., 1875.
[3] A son, born 29 March, 1877.
[4] Mary Mabel.

THE DESCENT OF
JOSHUA GLADWYN JEBB, ESQ.,
OF BARNBY MOOR HOUSE, NOTTS,
FROM THE BLOOD ROYAL OF ENGLAND.

EDWARD I., so named after Edward the Confessor; born at Westminster, 17 June, 1239, knighted at Burgos, 1254, created Earl of Chester; crowned at Westminster, 19 Aug. 1274, king of England, lord of Ireland, duke of Aquitaine; he subdued the principality of Wales 1283, claimed and exercised feudal superiority over Scotland; died at Burgh on-the-Sands, Cumberland, 7 July, 1307, buried in Westminster Abbey; by his 1st wife, Eleanor, daughter of Ferdinand III. king of Castile, who died 27 Nov., 1290, he had issue; their descendant

DIONIS HILDYARD (see Chart pedigree, page 645), married to Charles Barnby, of Barnby Don, Yorkshire, and had a daughter,

MURIEL BARNBY, married to John Bosvile, of Gunthwaite, Yorks., who died 12 Feb., 33 Hen. VIII., leaving with, other issue,

GODFREY BOSVILE, of Gunthwaite, eldest son and heir, aged 23, 33 Hen. VIII.; died 23 July, 1580; made his will the day before; married Jane, daughter of John Hardwick, of Hardwick, Derbyshire (sister of Elizabeth, Countess of Shrewsbury), and had, with other issue (see Foster's *Yorkshire Collection*), a daughter,

DOROTHY BOSVILE, married to John Lacy, of Brearley, who recorded his pedigree at the Visitation of Yorkshire, 1585, and had, with other issue (see *Visitation*, ed. Foster), a daughter,

ELIZABETH LACY (add. MS. 26,739, p. 223), married to Arthur Dakyns, of Stubbing Edge, Derbyshire, and had, with other issue, a son,

HENRY DAKYNS, of Stubbing Edge, married Elizabeth, daughter of Gregory Walker, of Mansfield, Notts, and had, with other issue, a son,

DIGBY DAKYNS, of Stubbing Edge; married Dorothy Sherratt, and had a daughter,

MARY DAKYNS, married to Henry Gladwin, of Stubbing Edge, in right of his wife, and had 2 sons and 2 daughters.

[1] **Henry Gladwin**, of whom presently.
[2] John (Gladwin), in holy orders, had 4 daughters.
(1) Dorothy, married to Francis Eyre, of Hassop, who with his sons erroneously assumed the title of Earl of Newburgh; all died s.p.
(2) Mary, married to Robert Cloves, of London.
(3) Jane, married to Gen. William Wynyard, Cold-

stream guards; col. 5th regiment; equerry to George III., and deputy adjt.-gen. (son of Lieut.-gen. William Wynyard, grandson of Lieut.-Gen. John Wynyard, descended from John Wynyard, groom of the wardrobe to Queen Elizabeth and James I.); born 20 June, 1759; died 11 July, 1819, having had 2 sons and 2 daughters.

[1] William Clinton (Wynyard), lieut. and capt. Coldstream guards; born 21 May, 1789; died s.p. 27 April, 1814; married E , daughter of Col. Sowerby; she died Feb., 1812.

[2] Robert Henry (Wynyard), lieut.-gen. in the army; C.B.; col. 98th regiment; born 24 Dec., 1802; died 6 Jan., 1864; married 12 Aug., 1826, Ann, daughter of H. Macdonell, Esq., and had 4 sons and 2 daughters.

(1) George Henry (Wynyard), major 58th regiment, born 3 Oct., 1827; died July, 1861.

(2) Gladwin John Richard (Wynyard), born 12 Jan., 1831.

(3) Henry John, capt. 58th regt., died at sea 1863.

(4) Robert Macdonnell (Wynyard), born Aug., 1844; married 29 April, 1865, Gertrude Maria, 3rd daughter of Major J H England, 75th regiment.

(5) Maria Theresa, died young, 5 Jan., 1830.

(6) Louisa Mary, died 14 April, 1838.

[3] Anna Maria, died young.

[4] Frederica Wynyard, born 11 Dec., 1792; died 18 Dec., 1824; married to Samuel B Hurd, grenadier guards.

(4) Helen, married to Sampson Coleclough, Esq., of Brecon Hill, Notts.

[3] Mary, married to Benjamin Brocklehurst, Esq.

[4] Dorothy, died s.p. 4 June, 1792; married as 1st wife to Rev. Basil Bury Beridge, rector and patron of Algarkirk; prebendary of Sleaford; he died 22 Feb., 1808, leaving issue by his second wife.

HENRY GLADWIN, of Stubbing Court, Derby, major-gen. in the army; fought under Gen. Woolf, in Canada, and was left for dead on the field of battle, but recovered; died at Stubbing 22 June, 1791, aged 61; married 30 March, 1772, Frances, daughter of Rev. John Beridge (and co-heir of her half brother, John Beridge, of Derby); she died at Exeter 16 Oct., 1817, having had 2 sons and 9 daughters *(a)*.

[1a] Charles Dakeyne (Gladwin), of Belmont and Stubbing, lieut.-col. Derbyshire militia; born 22 March, 1775; married Miss Stringer, and had an only child, Frances (Gladwin), married to Melland, Esq., and died s.p.

[2a] Henry, died in infancy.

[3a] Frances (Gladwin), died at Mapleton 25 Oct., 1841; married 9 June, 1801, to Francis Goodwin, Esq., of Mapleton; capt. Derbyshire militia (son of John Goodwin, Esq., by Mary, his wife, daughter and co-heir of Francis Ridgway, Esq., of Nottingham); he died 26 Aug., 1836, having had a son and 3 daughters *(b)*.

(1b-3a) Henry John (Goodwin), of Hinchleywood, Derby, in holy orders; born 21 Nov., 1803; died 24 May, 1863; married 11 Oct., 1832, Frances Eleanora, daughter and heir of Rev. Richard Burrow Turbutt, B.A., and had a son and 2 daughters.

[1] Richard Henry (Goodwin-Gladwin), of Belmont, Stubbing, and Hinchleywood House, Derby, capt. 6th foot; educated at Rugby; assumed the additional surname, together with the arms of Gladwin, under the will of his great uncle, C. D. Gladwin; born 15 Sept., 1833.

[2] Frances Isabella Turbutt (Goodwin), married 9 Feb., 1860, to Rev. John Launcelot Errington, M.A. Brasenose Coll., Oxon, 1857; vicar of Midgham, Berks, since 1867 (2nd son of George H. Errington, Esq., of Lexden Park, Essex), and has a son and 4 daughters.

A son, born 29 Dec., 1876.

Fanny Isabella (Errington). Frances Evelyn.

Florence Emilia. Helen Muriel.

[3] Helen Emilia (Goodwin), married 27 Nov., 1878, to Arthur Finch Dawson, Esq., of Barrow Hill, co. Staff.

(2b-3a) Frances (Goodwin).

(3b-3a) Mary Ridgway, died unmarried 1859.

(4b-3a) Martha Elizabeth (Goodwin), died s.p. 27 Dec., 1873; married 2 Aug., 1842, to John Goodwin Johnson, Esq., of Bentley; he died 21 Oct., 1871.

[4a] **Dorothy** (Gladwin), of whom (see next page).

[5a] Mary (Gladwin), died 28 June, 1837; married 29 Nov., 1800, to Baldwin Duppa-Duppa, Esq., of Hollingbourne House, Kent, J.P., D.L.; he died 5 April, 1847, having had 6 sons and 5 daughters *(c)*.

(1c-5a) Baldwin Francis (Duppa), barrister-at-law of Lincoln's Inn, 7 June, 1833, commoner of Brasenose Coll., Oxon, J.P. Kent; born ; died 5 Jan., 1840; married 12 Sept., 1826, Catherine, daughter and co-heir of Philip Darell, Esq. (brother to Henry Darell, of Calehill, Kent), and had 4 sons and 3 daughters.

(1) Baldwin Francis (Duppa), of Hollingbourne House, Kent, J.P., and Trinity Hall, Camb., F.R.S., F.C.S.; born 18 Feb., 1828; died 10 Nov., 1873; married 26 Aug., 1869, Adeline Frances Mary, only surviving child of John Henry Dart, Esq., barrister-at-law, of Lincoln's Inn, and of Beech House, Hants, has an only daughter,

Catherine Mary (Duppa).

[2] Brian Philip Darell (Duppa).

[3] Euston Whitney.

[4] Chicheley, born 1838; died unmarried at Boulogne, 26 Nov., 1861.

[5] Catherine Mary (Duppa), died at Boulogne 22 July, 1861; married 16 April, 1860, to William Chambers, Esq. (son of Osborn W Chambers, Esq., and Elinor Darell, and grandson of Sir Samuel Chambers, of Bredgar House, Kent), and had a son.

Osborn Augustine (Chambers), born 9 Feb., 1861.

[6] Ellen Harriett.

[7] Blanche Florence, died unmarried.

(2c-5a) Brian Edward (Duppa), B.A., born 24 Feb., 1804; died s.p. 14 Feb., 1866; married 26 Sept., 1844, Mary Anne Catherine, daughter of Walter Long Esq., M.P., of Rood Ashton, Wilts; she remarried 31 Oct., 1868, to John Philip Green Esq., of the Temple Trees, Colombo, Ceylon.

(3c-5a) Henry Clarke (Duppa), of Malmayes Hall, Kent; born 6 April, 1805; died s.p., 21 Sept., 1865; married 12 July, 1840, Julia Ann, only daughter Major-Gen. Thorndike, R.A. (by Frances, his wife, daughter of Col. Edmund Faunce).

(4c-5a) Charles Gladwin (Duppa), of Jersey, born 8 Feb., 1808; married 6 Dec., 1843, Ellen Pincke, daughter of Major-Gen. Alured Dodsworth Faunce, C.B., of Bath, and has 2 sons and 2 daughters.

[1] Alured Lloyd (Duppa), born 27 June, 1846.

[2] Henry Charles de Malmeynes, born 29 July, 1849.

[3] Edith Ellen.

[4] Maud Henrietta.

(5c-5a) Richard Beridge, R.N., of H.M.S. *Rattlesnake*: drowned at sea.

(6c-5a) George (Duppa), high sheriff Kent, 1875; one of the founders of the colony of New Zealand; born 21 Dec., 180 ; married 17 Dec. 1870, Alice Catherine, eldest daughter of Sir Philip John William Miles, Bart., of Leigh Court, Bristol (see Foster's *Baronetage*), and has had 3 sons.

Bryan Baldwin George (Duppa), born 17 Nov., 1871.
Gladwin Archibald Euston Whitney George, born 7 Sept., 1873; died 19 March, 1883.
Beridge Greville George, born 14 Jan., 1883.

(7*c*-5*a*) Mary Dorothy (Duppa), married 31 Dec., 1840, to Capt. Edmund Barrell Faunce, E.I.C.S., of Sharsted, Kent, and Newington, Surrey, D.L.; he died 17 Dec., 1861, having had 2 sons and a daughter.

[1] Chapman Delaune Faunce-Delaune, of Sharsted, Kent, J.P.; born 7 May, 1843; married 29 Dec., 1868, Annie, 2nd daughter of late George Stoddart, Esq., of Ballendrick, Perth, some time H.M.'s consul at Madeira, and has 3 sons.

Alured Delaune (Faunce-Delaune), born 14 June, 1870.
Edmund, born 31 Dec., 1870.
Hubert, born 14 Nov., 1874.

[2] Edmund Gladwin (Faunce), of Merton Coll., Oxon; born 13 April, 1846; died unmarried.

[3] Anne Isabella Mary (Faunce), died unmarried 8 May, 1866.

(8*c*-5*a*) Frances Anne (Duppa), married 14 Aug., 1860, to William, 2nd son of late Sir William Marjoribanks, Bart., of Lees (see Foster's *Baronetage*), s.p.

(9*c*-5*a*) Sarah Charlotte (Duppa), died s.p., 19 May, 1873; married 15 Sept., 1842, to John Savage, Esq., of St. Leonard's, Maidstone, late master of H.M.'s Supreme Court at Madras; he died 21 May, 1868.

(10*c*-5*a*) Harriet (Duppa), married 4 April, 1846, to Archibold Impey Lovibond, Bengal engineers; field engineer in Indian mutiny at Cawnpore; chief engineer Central Provinces (son of Edward Impey, B.C.S., and Julia de L'Etang, eldest daughter of Chevallier de L'Etang, page to Mary Antoinette, peer of France), and has 2 daughters.

[1] Marion Harriot (Impey), married 15 Dec., 1870, to Capt. Albert Elias Pearse, 76th regt.

[2] Julia Blanche, married 3 Jan., 1875, as 1st wife to Benjamin Edward Somers, Esq., of Mendip Lodge, Somerset, J.P., D.L., barrister-at-law, of Lincoln's Inn, 1877; M.A., Oxon.

(11*c*-5*a*) Ellen (Duppa), died 28 March, 1878; married 30 May, 1850, to Gladwin Turbutt, Esq., of Ogston Hall, Derby, and Arnold Grove, Notts, J.P., L.D.; high sheriff, 1858 (see below); he died 3 Sept., 1872, leaving 2 sons.

[1] William Gladwin (Turbutt), born 7 Feb., 1853.
[2] Richard Duppa, born 8 Jan., 1855.

[6*a*] Ann (Gladwin), died 7 Sept., 1855; married 22 June, 1814, to William Turbutt, of Ogston Hall, Derby, and Arnold Grove, Notts, Esq., barrister-at-law; he died 25 Oct. or Dec., 1836, having had a son and 4 daughters.

(1) Gladwin (Turbutt), born 31 March, 1823; died 3 Sept., 1872; married 30 May, 1850, Ellen, 5th daughter of Baldwin Duppa-Duppa, Esq.; she died 28 Mar. 1878, leaving 2 sons named above.
(2) Ann (Turbutt), died unmarried July, 1835.
(3) Lucy, died unmarried Oct., 1838.
(4) Hellen, died unmarried April, 1839.
(5) Maria (Turbutt).

[7*a*] Charlotte (Gladwin), died s.p. married 23 April, 1805, to Rev. George Hutton, D.D. vicar of Sutterton; he died

[8*a*] Martha, died unmarried, 22 Oct., 1812.

[9*a*] Harriet, [10*a*] Ellen, [11*a*] Susannah, all died unm.

DOROTHY GLADWIN, died 15 July 1825; married 4 Jan., 1792, to Joshua Jebb, of Walton Lodge, Derbyshire, J.P. and D.L.; capt. Derbyshire militia, and lieut.-col. of the Scarsdale regt. of volunteers; he died 19 Aug., 1845, having had 6 sons and 3 daughters (*d*).

[1*d*] **Sir Joshua** (Jebb), K.C.B., of whom (see p. 646).

[2*d*] Samuel Henry (Jebb), of Boston, Linc.; born 21 April, 1796; died 7 Feb., 1875; married 2 Nov., 1822, Fanny, daughter of John Straw, Esq., of Lincoln; she died 2 July, 1873, having had 7 sons and 5 daughters (*e*).

(1*e*-2*d*) Charles William (Jebb), born 4 April, 1824; died unmarried, 20 May, 1870.

(2*e*-2*d*) Henry Gladwin (Jebb), F.S.A., of Firbeck Hall, Rotherham, J.P. W.R. Yorks; M.A. St. John's Coll., Camb., 1872; rector of Fontmel Magna, 1870-3; of Chetwynd, Salop, 1873-8; born 6 May, 1826; married 29 Sept., 1853, Emma Louisa, 4th daughter of Robert Ramsden, Esq., of Carlton Hall, Notts, (see Foster's *Baronetage*), and has (with other issue, who died young) a son and 2 daughters.

Henry Scrope Frescheville (Jebb), born 17 July, 1867.
Florence Emma Dorothy. Edith Fanny Maud.

(3*e*-2*d*) John Joshua (Jebb), of Norton House, Lincolnshire; born 1 Nov. 1830; married 14 June, 1860, Georgiana Hutton, daughter of Rev. William Roy, D.D., rector of Skirbeck, and has a son.

George Samuel William (Jebb), born 5 Sept., 1861.

(4*e*-2*d*) Richard George (Jebb), lieut. 23rd light infantry E.I.C.S.; born 13 Sept., 1832; died unmarried in Bombay, 10 June, 1857.

(5*e*-2*d*) Frederick William (Jebb), brig.-gen. and adjt.-g.n. of Madras army, lieut.-col. command. 67th regiment; born 1 Dec., 1835; died s.p. 20 Feb., 1880; married 21 Dec., 1869, Mary Charlotte, daughter of Rev. John Chancourt Girardot, of Car-Colston Hall, Notts, rector of Screveton, Notts (she remarried 1 June, 1881, to Major Francis Montgomery Onslow, squadron commander 2nd Madras Cavalry (see E. Onslow, Foster's *Peerage*).

(6*e*-2*d*) Arthur (Jebb), late major 31st regt.; born 1 July, 1838.

(7*e*-2*d*) Avery (Jebb), capt. Royal South Linc. regt. of militia, late lieut. 85th light infantry; born 13 April, 1842; married 19 Dec., 1872, Susan Clara, daughter of late Col. Boddam-Whetham, of Kirklington Hall, Notts, and has a son and daughter.

Avery Gladwin (Jebb), born 19 March, 1878.
Agatha Frances Whetham (Jebb), died 1880.

(8*e*-2*d*) Susan Gladwin.

(9*e*-2*d*) Frances Dorothy (Jebb), married 21 Aug., 1856, to Thomas Laurence Kington Oliphant, Esq., of Gask, Perthshire; D.L., M.A., Balliol Coll. Ox. (son of Thomas Kington, Esq., of Charlton House, Somerset, by his wife Margaret Oliphant, of Gask).

(10*e*-2*d*) Marianne.

(11*e*-2*d*) Charlotte, died unmarried, 7 June, 1861.

(12*e*-2*d*) Harriet Ellen, died 28 Mar., 1857.

[3*d*] Charles Anthony (Jebb), R.N., born 31 Jan., 1802; died at sea, 16 Oct., 1814.

[4*d*] John Beridge (Jebb), of Walton Lodge, Derbyshire, incumbent of St. Thomas Brampton, Chesterfield; born 9 Dec., 1808; died at Nice, 27 Jan., 1863; married 1st, 30 July, 1839, Charlotte, daughter of Richard Dunn, Esq.; she died 7 Dec., 1860, having had a son,

(1) John Beridge Gladwyn (Jebb), formerly lieut. 88th regt.; born 30 Dec., 1841; married 18 Feb., 1876, Bertha Helen, youngest daughter of (Hon.) William MacDougall, of Toronto, Canada, and since divorced; had a daughter, Isabel Muriel.

REV. J. B. JEBB married 2nd, 27 Nov., 1861, Mary Frances, eldest daughter of Rev. John Simon Jenkinson (and Harriet Caroline Augusta Grey, 3rd daughter of

THE DESCENT OF

John Joshua Jebb, Esq.,

Of Norton House, Lincolnshire,

FROM THE

Blood Royal  **of England.**

EDWARD I., crowned 19 Aug. 1274, b. 17 June, 1239, d. 7 July, 1307. = Eleanor (1st wife) dau. of Ferdinand III., King of Castile, d. 27 Nov., 1290.

Joan of Acre, b. there, 1272 d. 10 May, 1305, 2nd wife. = Gilbert de Clare, Earl of Gloucester, etc., d. 7 Dec., 1295.

Margaret de Clare, m. 1st to Sir Piers Gaveston, Earl of Cornwall. = Hugh de Audley (2nd husband), cr. Earl of Gloucester, d. 1347.

Margaret de Audley, d. 7 Sept. 1349. = Ralph de Stafford, K.G., cr. Earl of Stafford, d. 31 Aug., 1372.

Hugh, 2nd Earl of Stafford K.G., d. Oct. 1386. = Philippa, dau. of Thomas Beauchamp, Earl of Warwick.

Katherine de Stafford = Sir Michael de la Pole, cr. Earl of Suffolk 1399, d. 18 Sept., 1415.

Isabel de la Pole = Thomas Morley, 5th Baron Morley, d. 1435.

Anne Morley = Sir John Hastings, of Fenwick, Yorkshire.

Elizabeth Hastings = Sir Robert Hildyard, of Winestead, Yorkshire, d. 29 Aug., 1489.

Dionis Hildyard = Charles Barnby, of Barnby Don.

A

Continued above.

A

Continued from below.

Dionis Hildyard = Charles Barnby.

Muriel Barnby = John Bosvile, d. 12 Feb., 33 Henry VIII.

Godfrey Bosvile, of Gunthwaite, d. 23 July, 1580. = Jane, dau. of John Hardwick, of Hardwick, Derbyshire.

Dorothy Bosvile = John Lacy, of Brearley, Yorks.

Elizabeth Lacy = Arthur Dakyns, of Stubbing Edge, Derbyshire.

Henry Dakyns, of Stubbing Edge. = Elizabeth, dau. of Gregory Walker, of Mansfield, Notts.

Digby Dakyns, of Stubbing Edge. = Dorothy Sherratt.

Mary Dakyns = Henry Gladwin, of Stubbing Edge, in right of his wife.

Henry Gladwin, of Stubbing Court, major-gen. in the army, d 22 June, 1791. = Frances, dau. of Rev. John Beridge, m. 30 March, 1772, d. at Exeter, 16 Oct., 1817.

Dorothy Gladwin, m. 4 Jan. 1792, d. 15 July, 1825. = Joshua Jebb, of Walton Lodge, co. Derby, J.P., D.L., lieut.-col. of volunteers, d. 19 Aug., 1845.

Samuel Henry Jebb, of Boston, co. Lincoln, b. 21 April, 1796, d. 7 Feb., 1875. = Fanny, dau. of John Straw, Esq., of Lincoln, m. 2 Nov. 1822, d. 2 July, 1873.

- Charles William Jebb, d. unmard. 1870.
- Henry Gladwin Jebb, of Firbeck Hall, Yorks, in H.O. m. 1853, Emma, dau. of R. Ramsden, Esq.
  - Henry, b. b. 18[illegible]7.
  - Florence.
  - Edith.
- John Joshua Jebb, of Norton House, Lincolnshire, b. 1 Nov., 1830, m. 14 June, 1860, Georgiana Hutton, dau of Rev. William Roy, D.D. rector of Skirbeck.
  - George Samuel William Jebb, b. 5 Sept., 1861.
- Richard George, lt. 23rd Foot, d. unm. 1857.
- Frederick William, lt.-col. com. 67th regt. d. s.p. 1880.
- Arthur Jebb, late maj. 31st regt., b. 18[illegible].
- Avery Jebb, cap. mil. m. Susan, dau. of Col. Boddam-Whetham.
  - Avery, b. 18[illegible].
- Susan Gladwin.
- Frances Dorothy, m. 18[illegible], to Thomas L. K. Oliphant, Esq., of Gask, N.B.
- Marianne.
- Charlotte, d. 18[illegible].
- Harriet d. 18[illegible].

Hon. Sir George Grey—see Foster's *Peerage*, E. GREY), and had a daughter.

(2) Annie Beridge Jebb, born (posthumous) 16 April, 1863; married June, 1882, to Rev. Herbert Leigh Mallory.

[5*d*] Richard Gladwyn, born 6 Jan., 1812, supposed to have died in 1832.

[6*d*] Charles William, major 1st Glouc. volunteer artillery; formerly lieut. 60th rifles; born 14 Oct., 1814; married 12 May, 1841, Eliza, one of the daughters and co-heirs of late John Yerbury, Esq., of Shirehampton, Gloucestershire; she died 8 Sept., 1857, having had a son and 5 daughters.

(1) John de Witt (Jebb), major on reserve of officers 1883; major 3rd batt. (Lanark militia) Scottish rifles; late of Scottish rifles (26th foot); b. 21 Nov., 1847; married 5 Dec., 1885, Edith Victoria, youngest daughter of late Mr. W. Murphy, of Mount Merrion, co. Dublin.

(2) Francesca Romana Maria (Jebb), married 31 May, 1871, to Robert Henry Ramsden, Esq. (eldest son of Robert John Ramsden, Esq., M.A., J.P., of Carlton Hall, Notts, see Foster's *Baronetage*); he died 19 May, 1874, having had a son and daughter.

Robert Charles Plumptre (Ramsden), born 9 Feb., 1874. Frances Mary Alice.

(3) Alice Eliza (Jebb), married 16 Nov., 1867, to Bartlet Span, Esq., of Clifton, Bristol, and has 3 sons and a daughter.

Reginald Bartlet (Span), born 6 Sept., 1868.
Oliver William Bartlet, born 27 July, 1869.
Henry John Bartlet, born 9 Sept., 1870.
Alice Ethel Bartlet.

(4) Mary Edith. (5) Amy Louisa.

[7*d*] Dorothy (Jebb), died unmarried, May, 1865.

[8*d*] Frances Harriott, married 5 June, 1823, to William Miles, Esq., of Manilla Hall, Clifton (son of Philip Miles, Esq.); he died s.p., 13 Nov., 1844, see Foster's *Baronetage*.

[9*d*] Marianne (Jebb), married 17 Sept., 1824, to Rev. Francis Sharpe, vicar of Tibshelt, Derbyshire; he died, 1873, leaving 3 sons.

(1) Granville William (Sharpe).

(2) John Henry, colonel (retired), late capt. 55th foot; served in the Crimea 1855 (medal with clasp, and Turkish medal); born 2 July, 1837.

(3) Charles Babington (Sharpe).

SIR JOSHUA JEBB, K.C.B., major-general in the army; lieut.-col. R.E.; surveyor-general of convict prisons and inspector of military prisons; born 8 May, 1793; died 26 June, 1863; married 1st, 14 June, 1830, Mary Legh, daughter of William Burtinshaw Thomas, Esq., of Highfield; she died 6 April, 1850. He married 2nd, 5 Sept., 1854, Lady Amelia Rose Pelham, 2nd daughter of Thomas, Earl of Chichester; by his 1st wife he had a son and 3 daughters. (*f*).

[1*f*] **Joshua Gladwyn** (Jebb), first-named, see p. 642.

[2*f*] Mary Dorothy (Jebb), married 27 April, 1854, to Rev. Henry John Ellison, M.A. Trin. Coll., Camb., 1838; rector of Great Haseley, Tetsworth, Oxon., since 1875; hon. canon Ch. Ch., Oxon., 1873; chaplain in ordinary to the Queen, 1879; formerly vicar of Edensor, Derbyshire, 1845-55; prebendary of Dassett Parva in Lichfield Cathedral, 1854-73; vicar of New Windsor, 1855-75; reader at Windsor Castle, 1856-75; hon. chaplain in ordinary to the Queen, 1875-9; she died 29 June, 1870, and had 4 sons and 3 daughters.

(1) John Henry Joshua (Ellison), M.A. Merton Coll., Oxon., 1881; curate of Kensington, London, since 1883; chaplain to Archbishop (Tait) of Canterbury, 1881-2; born 18 March, 1855.

(2) Gerald Francis, born 18 Aug., 1861.

(3) Douglas, born 27 Jan., 1863.

(4) Henry Blomfield, born 3 June, 1868.

(5) Constance Margaret. (6) Mary Beatrice.

(7) Dorothy Frances.

[3*f*] Emily (Jebb), married 28 Jan., 1860, to Basil Charles Boothby, Esq., assistant-commissary-general eastern district (ranking with lieut.-col.), 1880; formerly captain 95th regt., and barrack master; served in the Crimea in 1854, and was severely wounded at the battle of Alma—foot amputated (medal with clasp, Sardinian and Turkish medals), (4th son of Rev. Charles Boothby, see Foster's *Baronetage*), and has had 5 sons and 2 daughters.

(1) Beridge Gladwyn (Boothby), born 8 Aug., 1861; died 23 Nov., 1863.

(2) Hubert Basil, born 4 March, 1863.

(3) Walter Ralph Jebb, born 26 June, 1865.

(4) Francis Stuart Evelyn, born 23 April, 1867.

(5) Evelyn Leonord Beridge, born 4 March, 1876.

(6) Marion Agnes Serena Penelope.

(7) Mary Dorothy Cecilia.

[4*f*] Frances Beatrice (Jebb), married 11 April, 1861, to Rev. William Edmund Batty, M.A., Queen's Coll., Oxon., 1848; vicar of St. John's, Walham Green, London, since 1862; lecturer at Butcher's almshouses, Walham Green, 1883; and has had 7 sons and 4 daughters.

(1) William Joshua (Batty), born 29 Nov., 1863; died March, 1864.

(2) Laurence Joshua, born 31 May, 1867; died 21 Feb., 1876.

(3) Arthur Montague, born 11 July, 1868.

(4) Henry Edmund, born 6 Jan., 1872.

(5) Basil Staunton, born 12 May, 1873.

(6) William Gladwyn, born 21 Nov., 1874.

(7) Francis de Witt, born 10 Jan., 1879.

(8) Adelaide Emily. (9) Agnes Mary.

(10) Alice Beatrice, died 30 Jan., 1876

(11) Rose Amelia, born 7 Aug., 1876.

FITZMAURICE, MAURICE, of Duaghnafealy, co. Kerry, 18TH IN DESCENT FROM EDWARD III., born 7 May, 1853; married 30 April, 1878, Anabella Rollstein, 2nd daughter of John Palmer, Esq., of Banmore, co. Kerry, and has a son and 3 daughters.

[1] Maurice, born 3 Feb., 1883.
[2] Kathleen Honoria.
[3] Mary Lydia Jeanne.
[4] Anabella Studdert Dymphna.

THE DESCENT OF
MAURICE FITZMAURICE, ESQ.,
FROM THE BLOOD ROYAL OF ENGLAND.

EDWARD III., KING OF ENGLAND, Earl of Chester 1320, Duke of Aquitaine, Count of Ponthieu and Montreuil, 1325; crowned at Westminster in his father's lifetime, 1 Feb., 1327; defeated the Scots at Halidon Hill, 1333. In 1339 he assumed the style of "King of France and England, and Lord of Ireland," and quartered the arms of France in the first quarter; gained a great naval victory over the French off Sluys, 1340, and won the celebrated battle of Cressy 26 Aug., 1346; 17 Oct. following the Scots were defeated at Neville Cross, and King David II. taken prisoner to London, where he remained nearly 11 years. Instituted the Order of the Garter 1349. His son, the BLACK PRINCE, defeated the French at the battle of Poictiers, 19 Sept., 1356, and brought King John prisoner to London, where he remained nearly five years (for further particulars, see *Royal Lineage*, Foster's *Peerage*). The King died at Sheen, Surrey, 11 June, 1377, having had issue; his descendant

TRYPHENA BLENNERHASSETT (3rd daughter of Capt. John Blennerhassett, of Castle Conway, "Black Jack," see page 593*b*) married (settlement dated 8 Jan., 1723) to Ulick FitzMaurice, of Duaghnafealy, co. Kerry (eldest son of Garrett FitzMaurice, see note *); made his will 10 Aug., 1738; had at least 4 ons and 2 daughters.

[1] Garrett (FitzMaurice), born 7 Oct., 1724; died young
[2] **John,** of whom presently.
[3] Ulick, and [4] Henry, named in their father's will, 1738.
[5] Elizabeth, born 9 June, 1726; living 1738.
[6] Clifford, born 9 July, 1727; living 1738.

JOHN FITZMAURICE, of Duaghnafealy, named in his father's will, 1738; married Margaret, daughter of John Stack, of Ballyconry, co. Kerry (by his wife Anne, 4th daughter of Maurice FitzGerald, Knight of Kerry), and had at least 2 sons.

[1] **Ulick,** of whom presently.
[2] John (FitzMaurice), had 3 sons and 2 daughters (*a*).
(1*a*) Ulick (FitzMaurice), capt. R.N., had a grant of land in Canada; married Mary, youngest daughter of James Eagar, Esq., of Dingle.
(2*a*) John (FitzMaurice), a major.-gen. in the army 1861, K.H. 1831, lieut. of the royal body guard; joined the 95th regt. (rifle brigade) at Torres Vedras in 1811 as a volunteer, served at the battle of Fuentes d'Onor, siege, &c., of Ciudad Rodrigo, and Badajoz (wounded), battle of Vittoria, and of the Pyrenees, of the Nivelle, Nive, and Toulouse; Peninsula medal; led the

* Garrett FitzMaurice, of Duaghnafealy, made his will 30 April, 1738; in the marriage settlement of his son John above named, in 1723, his younger sons are named—viz., Raymond (who married Mary, sister of Tryphena Blennerhassett), Garrett, Kerry, and Henry; in his will, 1738, he names his daughter Susannah, and appoints Hon. John FitzMaurice, of Lixnaw, and Harman FitzMaurice executors.

advanced guard at Quartre Bras, and wounded; Waterloo medal; born at Knockavillig, co. Kerry 24 June, 1793; died at Drayton Green, Middlesex, 24 Dec., 1865; married 3 Nov., 1824, Frances Maria, daughter of Rev. Henry Watkins, vicar of Silkstone, Yorkshire, and vicar of Beckingham, Notts., (see BOWER, Foster's *Yorkshire Collection*); she died 9 June, 1877, having had 2 sons and 6 daughters.

[1] Maurice Henry, capt. and adjt., 11th brigade R.A., served in Indian campaign 1857-8, relief of Lucknow, battle of Cawnpore, capture of Lucknow, &c., born 9 June, 1833; died 3 Aug., 1865.

[2] John Gerald (FitzMaurice), inspector of schools since 1874; undergraduate St. Mary's Coll., Oxon, barrister-at-law of the Inner Temple; born 21 July, 1837; married 15 July, 1869, Florence Augusta Marian, only daughter of Thomas Adolphus Boyrenson, Esq., H.E.I.C.S., and has had 4 sons and a daughter.

Maurice Swinfen, born 12 Aug., 1870.

Gerald Vere, born 13 June, died 19 Aug., 1872

Desmond, born 27 Nov., 1873; Raymond, born 7 Aug., 1878; Geraldine Augusta.

[3] Anna Maria, married 10 April, 1850, to Benjamin Huntsman, Esq., of West Retford Hall, Notts, J.P., and of Attercliffe, Yorks, lord of the manor of Wadworth, and has, with other issue, a son.

Francis (Huntsman), born , 1852.

[4] Emma. [5] Geraldine Elizabeth.

[6] Frances Mary. [7] Mary Frances.

[8] Gertrude.

(3a) Robert Day (FitzMaurice), married Miss Shannon, and had a son and daughter.

[1] Robert (FitzMaurice), of Glenvile, Dublin. married eldest daughter of — Hickman, of Nottingham, and had a son and daughter.

Robert. Frances.

[2] Mildred.

(4a) Margaret, died ; married to George Pinchin, an inspector royal Irish constabulary; he died , having had 3 sons and 3 daughters.

[1] John FitzMaurice (Pinchin), born 4 April, 1824; married 24 Dec., 1841, Harriet Rosini, daughter of Joseph Lennard, Esq.; she died 18 Dec., 1876, having had 4 sons and 3 daughters.

(1) Richard Pennefather (Pinchin), of Texas; born 2 May, 1843.

(2) John FitzMaurice, of Monaghan, born

(3) Maurice FitzMaurice (Pinchin) of Texas.

(4) George FitzMaurice, born ; died .

(5) Margaret Ellen (Pinchin), married , to Stack, M.D., surgeon, &c., of Listowel, co. Kerry; he died .

(6) Dora Mary, died unmarried. (7) Emily Mary.

[2] George Wallis (Pinchin), M.D., &c., and has, with other issue, a daughter, Agnes, of Liverpool.

[3] Blennerhassett, died .

[4] Emily, married 8 Jan., 1854, to William Lowth, Esq., who died s.p., 17 Nov., 1869.

[5] Maria, married , to William Everett, of Skibbereen, and has issue in New York.

[6] Agnes (Pinchin), died ; married to Capt. Clyde, who died 1860, leaving a son,

John Clyde.

(5a) Mary (FitzMaurice), died , 1850; married , to Patrick McKenna, of Dingle, agent to Lord Ventry; he died 13 Jan., 1839, having had 3 sons and 3 daughters.

[1] Thomas FitzMaurice (McKenna), born 1822; died , 1858.

[2] James FitzMaurice (McKenna), of Dingle; born 20 Dec., 1825; unmarried.

[3] Patrick John (McKenna), in holy orders; bursar S. V. C. Coll., Castleknock; late professor of history, Irish College, Paris; born, 16 Aug., 1829; unmarried.

[4] Mary, died unmarried, 1850.

[5] Ellen, married 8 Sept., 1853, to Dr. Patrick Murphy, of Dingle, who died there 1 Feb., 1869, leaving 4 sons and a daughter.

(1) Thomas Patrick (Murphy), born 11 Jan., 1858, married 24 Oct., 1883, Julia, daughter of David Dillon, of Herbert's town, co. Limerick.

(2) Patrick, born 15 April, 1862.

(3) Eugene, born 1 Feb., 1864.

(4) James, born 9 April, 1867.

(5) Mary, born 12 July, 1860; died 30 May, 1876.

[6] Kate (McKenna) a nun.

ULICK FITZMAURICE, of Duaghnafealy, co. Kerry; born died married 1778, Agnes Elizabeth Anne, elder daughter of Maurice Studdert, Esq., of Elm Hill, co. Limerick; she died having had a son and daughter.

[1] **Maurice** (FitzMaurice), of whom presently.

[2] Elizabeth Agnes (FitzMaurice), died married to Richard FitzGerald, Esq., of Listowel, co. Kerry; he died having had (with other issue, who died unmarried) 3 daughters.

(1) Maria, married to Adam Murray, Esq.

(2) Catherine Jane (FitzGerald), married 27 Dec., 1858, to Nathaniel Massy Stack, major-gen. in the army, served with 71st Highland light infantry; (see Day pedigree, page 434), he died 18 Feb., 1874, having had 2 sons and 2 daughters.

[1] George FitzGerald (Stack), born 10 Sept., 1860,

[2] Eyre Massy John, born 7 Nov., 1863.

[3] Agnes Elizabeth, died 27 Dec., 1877.

[4] Maria Catherine Jane.

(3) Georgina, married to FitzGibbon, Esq.

MAURICE FITZMAURICE, of Duaghnafealy; born 1782; died 24 June, 1843; married 1812, Margaret, daughter of Oliver Stokes, Esq., J.P., barrack master Tralee (see page 440); she died April, 1877, having had 9 sons and 3 daughters (*b*).

[1*b*] Oliver (FitzMaurice), of Duagh, co. Kerry, J.P. born 8 Feb., 1818; died ; married 24 April, 1859, Alicia, daughter of Richard Gabbett, Esq., of Caherline (she remarried to Matthew Blood Smyth, Esq., Q.C.), and had a son and 2 daughters.

(1) Maurice, of Duagh died 1862.

(2) Deborah Olivia (FitzMaurice).

(3) Margaret Elizabeth.

[2*b*] Maurice (FitzMaurice), of Duagh, J.P.; born 21 Jan., 1821; died 6 Jan., 1881; married 24 June, 1851, Mary Leadbeater, daughter of James Fisher, Esq., of Limerick, and had 2 sons.

(1) **Maurice (FitzMaurice)**, first-named (see preceding page).

(2) William Henry, born 27 July, 1855.

[3*b*] George (FitzMaurice), B.A. Trin. Coll., Dublin, 1844; in holy orders; born 20 May, 1822; married April, 1861, Winifred, daughter of John O'Connor, Esq., of Kilcara, co. Kerry, and has had 5 sons and 7 daughters.

Maurice Rowland (FitzMaurice), born 3 Jan., 1866.
Oliver, born 28 March, 1867.
George, born 28 Jan., 1877.
Henry, born 16 May, 1879.
Ulysses, born 15 June, 1881.
Elizabeth, died unmarried. Margaret. Una.
Mary Georgina. Agnes Amelia. Honoria.
Eleanor, died unmarried.

[4*b*] Henry (FitzMaurice), born ; married Honoria, daughter of O'Connor, Esq.; she died having had 2 children.

[5*b*] Robert (FitzMaurice), physician co. Kerry Fever Hos. and co. Kerry Infir.; L.K.Q.C.P. Irel. 1857; L R.C.S.I. 1851; L.M. Rotunda Hosp., Dublin, 1851 (R.C.S. Irel.); contrib. to *Dublin Quarterly* and *Monthly;* born 15 April, 1827; married 17 July, 1860, Thomasine, widow of Richard Stephens, Esq., of Calcutta, and daughter of William Taylor, Esq., of Dublin, and has had 4 sons and 3 daughters.

(1) Maurice (FitzMaurice), B.A. Trinity Coll., Dublin, 1883, born 11 May, 1861.
(2) John Day Stokes (FitzMaurice), Bombay Civil Service, born 4 Jan., 1863.
(3) William Herbert, born 13 March, 1864.
(4) Robert, born 7 Jan., 1866. (5) Thomasine.
(6) Frances Margaret, died Aug., 1874.
(7) Honoria.

[6*b*] John

[7*b*] Edward, F.R.C.S.I. 1874; L. & Lic. Med. 1856; L.M. Coombe Hosp., Dublin, 1856 (Meath Hosp.); 1st prizeman; born 12 May, 1832; married 5 Jan., 1865, Constance Wilhelmina, daughter of William Odell, M.D., dep. insp. army; she died , leaving a daughter,
Edina (FitzMaurice).

[8*b*] Ulysses, physician to R.I. constabulary; L.K.Q.C.P. Irel. 1857; L.M. Coombe Hosp., Dublin, 1857; obtained clinical prize of Meath Hosp., Dublin, 1852, and med. prize 1853, also med. prize at Peter Street School of Med. 1853; contrib. to *Dublin Medical Journal;* born 22 Oct., 1831; married 10 December, 1862, Lucy, daughter of William Seely, Esq., of Magh, co. Kerry, and has had, with other issue who died in infancy, 4 sons and 2 daughters.

(1) Maurice Otho (FitzMaurice), born 20 Sept., 1863.
(2) Francis Crump, born 13 Dec., 1865.
(3) William Edward, born 25 Dec., 1874.
(4) John, born 2 July, 1878.
(5) Margaret. (6) Mary.

[9*b*] Julian Patrick, born 3 Dec., 1833; married 13 Aug., 1868, Amelia Mary, daughter of Francis Peet, Esq., of Arabella, co. Kerry, and has a son and 3 daughters.

(1) Maurice Raymond (FitzMaurice), born 7 Dec., 1873.
(2) Selina Francis. (3) Margaret Honoria.
(4) Elizabeth Amelia.

[10*b*] Elizabeth (FitzMaurice), married 1st, 2 Aug., 1830, to James Eidingtoun, Esq., D.L., of Gargunnock, co. Stirling; he died Nov., 1838, leaving a son and daughter (*c*).

(1*c*-10*b*) Fitzmaurice (Eidingtoun), died young.
(2*c*-10*b*) Margaret (Eidingtoun), married 1861, to Richard Rowland Chute, Esq., of Lee Brook, Tralee, co. Kerry (son of Capt. Rowland Chute), and had 3 sons and 3 daughters.

Rowland Eidingtoun (Chute), born .
Fitzjames, born .
Richard Crosbie, born .
Elise Bateman.
Frances Ethel. Rosamond Margaret.

[10*b*] Mrs. Eliz. Eidingtoun remarried , to Rev. Rowland Bateman, of Abbey Feale, co. Kerry (2nd son of Colthurst Bateman, Esq., of Bedford House, Listowel, co. Kerry (see page 440); he died 1854, having had 3 sons and 3 daughters (*c*).

(3*c*-10*b*) Rowland (Bateman), M.A., Magd. Coll., Oxon, 1867; C.M.S. missionary in the Punjab since 1868; born 14 Jan., 1842; died 9 Feb., 1881; married Oct., 1870, Elizabeth Bridget, daughter of Edward Day Stokes, of Farranakilla, co. Kerry (see p. 440), and had a son.

Rowland, born 1871.

(4*c*-10*b*) Maurice, born 30 April, 1845; married Mary, daughter of John Hancock, Esq., of co. Limerick, and has 2 daughters,
Elizabeth. Georgina.

(5*c*-10*b*) Colthurst, Capt. Kerry regt., born 23 May, 1848; married 1873, Louisa Anne, daughter of Lieut.-col. Patrick Day Stokes (see Day pedigree, page 440), and has 2 sons and a daughter.

Rowland Colthurst (Bateman), born 20 June, 1874; Edmund, born 1 Oct. 1880; Edith.

(6*c*-10*b*) Agnes, married 1st, , to Capt. Dickson Davenport, J.P., of Ballynacourty, co. Limerick; he died 20 March, 1872, leaving a son and 2 daughters.

[1] Rowland Bateman (Davenport).
[2] Elizabeth Agnes. [3] Jane Dickson.

Mrs. Agnes Davenport re-married 13 Feb, 1877, to Leslie Wren Crosbie (see Foster's *Baronetage*), of Ardfert, co. Kerry; L.K.Q.C.P. Irel., 1872; L.R.C.S.I., 1865; L.M., 1871; and has 3 sons.

[4] Pierse Leslie (Crosbie), born 19 March, 1878.
[5] Douglas. [6] FitzGeorge.

(7*c*-10*b*) Elizabeth, married , to her cousin, Frederick Bateman, Esq., of Bertholey, co. Monmouth, and Bellford, co. Kerry, and has a son and daughter.

Frederick Francis (Bateman). Dora Coningsby.

(8*c*-10*b*) Dora Calza (Bateman).

[11*b*] Agnes Elizabeth Ann (FitzMaurice), married 6 Oct., 1836, to William Hutton, Esq., of Headview, Lismore, and has had 5 sons and 3 daughters.

(1) Andrew (Hutton), of Clanloghlin, co. Cork, born 6 Dec., 1838.
(2) Maurice FitzMaurice, major 3rd batt. Black Watch, 1881; born 13 Dec., 1840; married 13 Dec., 1876., Mary, daughter of late James McKay, of Thurso, N.B., and has a son and daughter.

Maurice FitzMaurice (Hutton), born 4 Dec., 1877.
Geraldine Mary Fitzmaurice.

(3) William McGregor, born 4 March, 1845; died unmarried 22 Nov., 1846.
(4) Oliver FitzMaurice, born 4 June, 1847; died unmarried 27 Nov., 1883.
(5) Rowland Bateman Fullton, born 11 July, 1853.
(6) Margaret Elizabeth Agnes, married 7 July, 1857, to John Wyld, Esq., late 3rd light dragoons, and has had 2 sons and 2 daughters.

[1] William George (Wyld), lieut. 1st Hampshire regiment, 1881; born 3 Dec., 1859.
[2] Henry Granby Lockwood, born 22 March, 1868.
[3] Agnes Cecil, died 18 July, 1866. [4] Milward.

(7) Elizabeth McGregor, married 7 April, 1869, to Richard Fitzjohn Aldworth, Esq., royal Irish constabulary (see Foster's *Peerage*, V. Doneraile), and has a son,

Oliver FitzMaurice (Aldworth), born 5 Mar. 1870.

(8) Honoria Agnes (Hutton).

[12*b*] Honoria (FitzMaurice), married 14 Dec., 1851, to Francis C. Peet, Esq., of Rathany, co. Kerry, and has 4 sons.

Francis FitzMaurice (Peet), born 9 Oct., 1862.
FitzMaurice, born 3 May, 1865.
John St. Leger, born 17 July, 1866.
Robert FitzMaurice, born 9 Feb., 1868.

THE DESCENT OF

Charles Ichabod Wright,

Of Stapleford Hall, Notts., and of Watcombe Park, near Torquay.

FROM THE

Blood Royal  of England.

Edward I., crowned 19 Aug. 1274, b. 17 June, 1239, d. 7 July, 1307. = Eleanor (1st wife) dau. of Ferdinand III., King of Castile, d. 27 Nov. 1290.

Joan of Acre, b. there 1272, d. 10 May, 1305, 2nd wife. = Gilbert de Clare, Earl of Gloucester, etc., d. 7 Dec. 1295.

Margaret de Clare, m. 1st to Sir Piers Gaveston, Earl of Cornwall. = Hugh de Audley (2nd husband), cr. Earl of Gloucester, d. 1347.

Margaret de Audley, d. 7 Sept. 1349. = Ralph de Stafford, K.G., cr. Earl of Stafford, d. 31 Aug. 1372.

Hugh, 2nd Earl of Stafford K.G., d. Oct. 1386. = Philippa, dau. of Thomas Beauchamp, Earl of Warwick.

Katherine de Stafford = Sir Michael de la Pole, cr. Earl of Suffolk 1399, d. 18 Sept. 1415.

Isabel de la Pole = Thomas Morley, 5th Baron Morley, d. 1435.

Anne Morley = Sir John Hastings, of Fenwick, Yorkshire.

Elizabeth Hastings = Sir Robert Hildyard, of Winestead, Yorkshire, d. 29 Aug. 1489.

Margery or Mary Hildyard = Sir William Ayscough, of Stallingborough, co. Linc., Knt., d. 26 March, 1509.

Sir William Ayscough, of Stallingborough, d. 1540-1. = Elizabeth (1st wife), dau. of Thomas Wrottesley, of Wrottesley, co. Staff.

A, *continued above.*

A, *continued from below.*

Sir William Ayscough = Elizabeth Wrottesley.

Sir Francis Ayscough, of South Kelsey, co. Linc., d. 19 Oct. 1564. = Elizabeth (1st wife), dau. and co-heir of William Hansard, Esq., of South Kelsey, co. Linc., she d. 29 Sept. 1558.

Faith Ayscough, m. about 1550. = Edward Maddison, of Fonaby, co. Linc.

Edward Maddison, of Fonaby, d. 1619. = Katherine, dau. of Ralph Bosvile, of Bradborne, Kent.

Sir Ralph Maddison, of Fonaby, knighted 23 July, 1603. = Mary, dau. of Robert Williamson, of Walkeringham, Notts.

Humphrey Maddison, of Coningsby, co. Linc. = Cornelia (1st wife), dau. and co-heir of Rev. John Duport, D.D.

Ralph Maddison, of Stamford, co. Linc. High Sheriff 1679. = Theodosia, dau. and co-heir of Nicholas Newcomen, of Theddlethorpe, co. Linc.

John Maddison, of Stamford, co. Linc. High Sheriff 1719. = Katherine, dau. of George Whichcote, of Harpswell, co. Linc., m. 9 July, 1723.

Anne Maddison, m. 7 Aug. 1747, d. 31 Aug. 1783. = Rev. Sir William Anderson, of Broughton, co. Linc., Bart., d. 9 Mar. 1785.

Theodosia Dorothy Anderson, m. 1 Jan., 1778, d. 3 May, 1831. = Rev. Richard Vevers, rector of Saxby, co. Leicester, etc.

Theodosia Anne Vevers, eldest dau., m. 18 Oct., 1804, d. 28 June, 1852. = Thomas, Lord Denman, so created 28 March, 1834, Lord Chief Justice 1832-50, d. 22 Sept., 1854.

Thomas, 2nd Lord Denman, b. 30 July, 1805, married twice.
Hon. Joseph, vice-admiral, m. and died s.p. 1674.

Hon. Richard, m. and has issue.
Hon. George, a justice of High Court, m. and has is.
Rev. and Hon. Lewis, m. and has issue.

Hon. Theodosia Denman, m. 21 Nov., 1825. = Ichabod Wright, of Mapperly Hall Notts, d. 14 Oct. 1871.

Hon. Elizabeth, m. to Rev. F. Hodgson, and d. 1880.
Hon. Frances, m. to Adml. Sir R. L. Baynes, K.C.B., who died 1869.

Hon. Margaret Owen, m thrice.
Hon. Anne, m. to F. Holland, Com., R.N.
Hon. Caroline, m. to Rev. J. G. Beresford, M.A.

Charles Ichabod Wright, of Stapleford Hall, Notts, etc., b. 19 Sept., 1828. = Blanche Louisa, dau. of late Hy. Corles Bingham, Esq., of Wartnaby Hall, co. Lincoln, m. 9 June, 1852.

Henry Smith Wright, of Park Hill, Hants, m. 1st, Mary Jane, dau. of late W. Cartledge, Esq. she died 1866. = Josephine (2nd wife), only dau. of late Rev. J. A. Wright. m. 1869.

Frederick, of Lenton Hall, Notts, b. 1840, m. 1865, Ada, dau. of Rev. J. Bateman.

Rev. George H., m. 1870, Anne, dau. of Rev. E. R. Larken M.A.

Theodosia, m. to W H. Sinclair, Esq.
Frances, m. to E. W. Cropper, Esq.
Neville Sophia, d 1853.

Ichabod, R.A., killed in Afghanistan, 29 Dec., 1879.

Charles Bingham b. 19 Nov., 1854.
Nevill, b. 26 Nov. 1857.

Blanche.
Rosamond, m. 1883, to E. J. Webb, Esq.
Grace m. to Col. Campbell-Davys.

Edith.

Henry, b. 1869.
George, b. 1872.
Edward, b. 1875.

John, b. 1882.
Alice.

Frederick.
Emily.
Mary.
Florence.

Margaret.
Hilda.
Maud.

George.
Eric.
Theodosia.

WRIGHT, CHARLES ICHABOD, of Stapleford Hall, Notts, and Watcombe Park, near Torquay, and of Nottingham, banker; J.P.; M.P. Nottingham, 1868-70; lieut.-col. Robin Hood Rifle Volunteers, 1861-75; 22ND IN DESCENT FROM EDWARD I.; born 19 Sept., 1828; married 9 June, 1852, Blanche Louisa, daughter of late Henry Corles Bingham, Esq., of Wartnaby Hall, co. Leic.; and has had 3 sons and 3 daughters.

[1] Ichabod Denman (Wright), lieut. R.A.; born 4 April, 1853; killed at Gandamak, Affghanistan, 29 Dec., 1879.
[2] Charles Bingham (Wright), born 19 Nov., 1854.
[3] Nevill, born 26 Nov., 1857.
[4] Blanche Theodosia.
[5] Rosamond Frances, married, 15 Aug., 1883, to Elias John Webb, of Tiddington, co. Warwick.
[6] Grace Henrietta, married 7 Nov., 1885, to Col. Richard Campbell Davys, of Neuaddfaur, Llandovery, and Askomel, Argyllshire.

THE DESCENT OF
CHARLES ICHABOD WRIGHT, ESQ.,
FROM THE BLOOD ROYAL OF ENGLAND.

DWARD I., so named after Edward the Confessor; born at Westminster, 17 June, 1239, knighted at Burgos, 1254, created Earl of Chester; crowned at Westminster, 19 Aug. 1274, king of England. lord of Ireland, duke of Aquitaine; he subdued the principality of Wales 1283, claimed and exercised feudal superiority over Scotland; died at Burgh-on-the-Sands, Cumberland, 7 July, 1307, buried in Westminster Abbey; by his 1st wife, Eleanor, daughter of Ferdinand III., king of Castile, who died 27 Nov., 1290, he had issue; their descendant

THEODOSIA DOROTHY ANDERSON (3rd daughter of Sir William Anderson, Bart., see p. 613), died 3 May, 1831; married 1 Jan., 1778, to Rev. Richard Vevers, rector of Saxby, co. Leic., of Stoke Albany, and of Kettering; he died , having had 4 sons and 7 daughters.

[1] Richard William (Vevers), M.A. Trin. Coll., Camb. 1816; rector of Cubley, Derbyshire, 1832-58; rector o Marton, Linc.; J.P. Derbyshire; died s.p. 24 Jan., 1858, aged 80; married *circa* 1817, Frances Darby, *fil. nat.* Philip, 5th Earl of Chesterfield, K.G.; she died 1860.
[2] Edmund (Vevers), H.E.I.C.S.; born 1783; died in India.
[3] Charles, killed 31 Aug., 1813, in the forlorn hope at the siege of St. Sebastian.
[4] Thomas, R.N., died 1807.
[5] George, lieut. R.N., died 1873.
[6] **Theodosia Anne**, died 28 June, 1852; married 18 Oct., 1804, to Thomas, afterward Lord Denman. (See below.)
[7] Emily, born 1780.
[8] Maria, died 1870.
[9] Anne, died 1874.
[10] Charlotte.
[11] Elizabeth.
[12] Catherine.

THEODOSIA ANNE VEVERS (eldest daughter of Rev. Richard Vevers), died 28 June, 1852; married 18 Oct., 1804, to Thomas Denman, barrister-at-law, Lincoln's Inn; M.P. Wareham, 1818-20; Nottingham, 1820-6 and 1830-2; Solicitor-General to the Queen, 1820-1; common serjeant of the city of London, 1822-30; knighted 1 Dec., 1830; Attorney-General, 1830-2; Lord Chief Justice of England, 1832-50; created Baron Denman, 28 March, 1834; he died 22 Sept., 1854, having had 5 sons and 6 daughters.(*a*)

[1*a*] **Thomas Aitchison - Denman,** 2nd Baron Denman, assumed the additional prefix surname of Aitchison by Royal Licence 20 Dec., 1876, barrister-at-law, 1830; marshal of Queen's Bench, 1832-50; born 30 July, 1805; married 1st, 12 May, 1829, Georgiana, eldest surviving daughter of Rev. Thomas Roe; she died s.p. 25 April, 1871; he married 2nd, 10 Oct., 1871,

Marion, eldest daughter of James Aitchison, Esq., of Alderston Haddington, and niece of Gen. Sir J. Aitchison, G.C.B.

[2a] Hon. Joseph, vice-admiral, R.N.; born 23 June, 1810; died s.p. 26 Nov., 1874, having married, 12 Feb., 1844, Grace, younger daughter of Jesse Watts Russell, Esq., of Ilam House, co. Stafford, and Biggin House, Northants.

[3a] Hon. Richard, M.A. Trin. Coll., Camb.; barrister-at-law, L.I., 1838; member of council University Coll., London; heir-presumptive to Lord Denman; born 13 Jan., 1814; married 28 Oct., 1840, Emma, youngest daughter of Hugh Jones, Esq., of Larkhill, co. Lancashire, and has 2 sons and 4 daughters (*b*).

(1*b*-3*a*) Richard, born 3 Jan., 1842; died 5 April, 1883; married 31 May, 1871, Helen Mary (she divorced him April, 1878), eldest daughter of Gilbert Mac-Micking, of Liverpool (she re-married 16 April, 1879, to James Montgomery, 3rd son of William Stuart Walker, C.B., of Bowland, N.B.), had 2 sons and a daughter.

Thomas, born 16 Nov., 1874.

Richard Douglas, born 24 Aug., 1876.

Anne Maria Heywood.

(2*b*-3*a*) Thomas Hugh Anderson, born 16 Jan., 1855.

(3*b*-3*a*) Emma Sophia Georgiana, married 31 Oct., 1872, to Oswin Cumming Baker-Cresswell, of Harehope, Alnwick; high sheriff 1882; M.A. Ch. Ch., Oxon.; late major Northumb. militia; formerly capt. 3rd hussars (see Gordon-Cumming in Foster's *Baronetage*), and has 2 sons and 2 daughters.

Addison Francis (Baker-Cresswell), born 8 Nov., 1874.

Henry, born 17 March, 1876.

A daughter born 19 March, 1877.

A daughter born 28 Oct., 1878.

(4*b*-3*a*) Elizabeth Margaret, married 20 Jan., 1870, to Sir Peniston Milbanke, Bart. (see Foster's *Baronetage*), and has 2 sons.

John Peniston (Milbanke), born 9 Oct., 1872.

Mark Richard, born 17 March, 1875.

(5*b*-3*a*) Anna Maria, married 16 July, 1867, to Reginald Garton Wilberforce, of Lavington House, Sussex; J.P.; D.L.; barrister-at-law, the Inner Temple, 1870; late 52nd light infantry (eldest son of late Bishop of Winchester), and brother of Bishop of Newcastle-upon-Tyne, and had 4 sons and 3 daughters.

Reginald William (Wilberforce), born 28 Mar., 1868.

Ernest John, born 8 April, 1869.

Francis Richard, born 2 Jan., 1871.

Samuel, born 19 Feb., 1874.

Dorothy Mary, born 28 Sept., 1875.

Anna Barbara, born 14 Aug., 1879.

Emily Susan, born 17 Feb., 1881.

(6*b*-3*a*) Eleanora.

[4a] Hon. George, M.A., barrister-at-law, L.I., 1846, Q.C. and a bencher, 1861, judge of Court of Common Pleas 1872-5, judge of Common Pleas div. High Court of Justice 1876-80, judge of Queen's Bench div. High Court of Justice 1880, M.P. Tiverton 1859-65, 1866-72; born 23 Dec., 1819; married 19 Feb., 1852, Charlotte, 5th daughter of Samuel Hope, Esq., of Liverpool, and has 4 sons and 2 daughters.

(1) George Lewis, LL.M., barrister-at-law, L.I., 1877; recorder of Queenborough since 1882; born 5 May, 1854.

(2) Arthur, M.A., barrister-at-law, born 1 May, 1857.

(3) Lancelot Baillie, R.N.; born 15 Jan., 1861.

(4) Francis Richard Amory, born 5 Dec., 1862.

(5) Charlotte Edith, married 19 June, 1883, to Rev. Wm. Henry Draper, vicar of Alfreton, Derbyshire, 1883.

(6) Grace.

[5a] Hon. Lewis William, M.A. Magd. Coll., Camb 1844, rector of Willian, Herts, since 1861, of Washington, co. Durham, 1848-61; born 23 March, 1821; married 1st, 18 June, 1850, Frances Marianne, daughter of Thomas Eden, Esq., of The Bryn, Swansea (see Foster's *Peerage*, B. Auckland); she died 25 April, 1862. He married, 2ndly, 22 Aug., 1865, Frances Starkie Mary, eldest daughter of Col. Henry Armytage, Coldstream guards (see Foster's *Baronetage*). By his 1st wife he had a son and 3 daughters.

Lewis William Eden, born 9 May, 1857; Frances Emily; Theodosia Louisa; Caroline Annie.

[6a] Hon. **Theodosia** married to Ichabod Wright, Esq., of whom (see next page).

[7a] Hon. Elizabeth, died 5 Aug., 1880, having married, 3 May, 1838, to Rev. Francis Hodgson, B.D. (son of Rev. James Hodgson), provost of Eton, archdeacon of Derby, incumbent of Edensor, and vicar of Bakewell; he died 29 Dec., 1852, having had, with other issue, a son and 3 daughters.

(1) James Thornton Hodgson, M.A. Univ. Coll., Oxon.; born 4 Oct., 1845; died 1880; married 15 June, 1872, Marie Blanche, only sister of Harry William Verelst, Esq., of Aston Hall, Yorks, and had 2 sons and 3 daughters.

Francis Coke Denman (Hodgson), born 10 Dec. 1874.

James Vaughan, born 3 July, 1878.

Maud Vevers. Sybil Blanche. Lilian Verelst.

(2) Elizabeth Denman, married 17 April, 1882, to Herbert Charles, 4th son of Rev. Francis Michael MacCarthy, M.A.

(3) Matilda Frances. (4) Jane Theodosia.

[8a] Hon. Frances, married 8 July, 1846, to Adm. Sir Robert Lambert Baynes, K.C.B., who died 7 Sept., 1869, having had, with other issue, 2 sons,

(1) Denman Lambert Baynes, capt. Gordon Highlanders (75th regt.), employed on special service Zulu war 1879; served in campaign in Egypt 1882; born 8 Sept., 1851; died in Egypt Aug., 1882.

(2) Henry Compton Anderson, lieut. R.N.; born 13 Oct., 1852; married, 21 Aug., 1884, Isabel, 2nd daughter of late Admiral Sir Joseph Nias, K.C.B.

[9a] Hon. Margaret married 1st, 23 Nov., 1841, to Henry William Macaulay, H.M.'s Commissary Judge, Sierra Leone (3rd son of Zachary Macaulay and brother of Lord Macaulay); he died 24 Sept., 1846, having had 2 sons. (*d*)

(1*d*-9*a*) Henry Denman Macaulay, lieut. R.N. (retd.) late capt. 1st Warwick mil.; born 10 Aug., 1843; married 18 Feb., 1868, Selina, daughter of Sir Joseph Needham, chief justice of Trinidad, and has 3 sons,

William Edward Babington Macaulay, cadet R.N., born 2 Feb., 1869.

Arthur James Denman, born 14 May, 1870.

Thomas Cary Elwes Cropper, born 15 Aug., 1871.

(2*d*-9*a*) Joseph Babington Macaulay, born 17 Oct., 1846; married 8 July, 1869, Eleanor, daughter of Henry Studdy, of Waddeton Court, Devon, commr. R.N. (retd.), and has had 3 sons and 3 daughters.

Robert Holdsworth Babington Macaulay, born 2 Feb., 1871, died an infant; Aulay Babington, born Nov., 1876; Edward, born 3 Nov., 1877; Eleanor Josephine; Maud Olive; Lois Theodosia, born 12 Jan., 1882.

HON. MARGARET MACAULAY, re-married 10 Aug., 1848, as 3rd wife, to Edward Cropper, of Swaylands, Kent, J.P. for that co. and Lanc.; he died 23 May, 1877. She re-married 22 April, 1879, to Col. John Owen-Owen (see Foster's *Baronetage*). By her 2nd husband she had a son and 3 daughters (*a*).

(3*d*-9*a*) Edward Denman Thornburgh-Cropper, of Ovenden House, Kent, assumed by R.L., 14 Nov., 1874, the surname and arms of Thornburgh in addition to and before that of Cropper; lieut. on reserve of officers 1882, capt. W. Kent L.I. mil., capt. 4th brigade

Welsh div. R.A. 1881; born 23 May, 1854; married 4 June, 1874, Minnie Virginia, only child and heir of William Butler Thornburgh, of San Francisco.

(4*d-9a*) Amelia Margaret Elizabeth Cropper, married 1st, 4 June, 1867, to Henry Studdy, of Waddleton Court, Devon, commr. R.N. (retd.); he died 13 Sept., 1880, she re-married, , to William Summers, Esq., of Milton, Pembrokeshire; by her 1st husband she had a son and 2 daughters.

Henry Edward Macaulay Studdy, born 19 March, 1868; Eleanor Margaret; Anita Georgina Edith.

(5*d-9a*) Florence Anne Cropper, married 1 July, 1873, to Arthur Frederick Holdsworth, of Widdicombe, Devon, J.P., capt. late Devon mil. and royal N. Linc. mil., midshipman Baltic and Black Sea 1853 and 1859, and has had 2 sons and a daughter.

Arthur Mervyn Holdsworth, born 5 Nov., 1875; Edward Denman, born 28 May, 1877, died young; Margaret Annie, died young.

(6*d-9a*) Marian Eliza Blanche Cropper, married 5 March, 1878, to Lieut.-col. Rowley Richard Conway-Hill, lieut.-col. in the army, major in reserve of officers (see Foster's *Baronetage*), and has 4 sons.

Rowley Arthur Edward (Hill), born 3 Jan., 1879; Hugh Rowley, born 18 Feb., 1880; Conway Rowley, born 16 Sept., 1881; son, born 22 Nov., 1883.

[10*a*] Hon. Anne, married 18 Aug., 1846, to Frederick Holland, commr. R.N. (see Foster's *Baronetage*); he died 21 July, 1860, having had 4 sons and 3 daughters.

(1) Edward Holland, born 30 Aug., 1850.
(2) Frederick Arthur, born 17 Oct., 1853.
(3) Richard Lancelot, born 24 April, 1858.
(4) Alfred, born 14 Aug., 1859; married 9 April, 1885, Edith Shuldham, 3rd daughter of Rev. W. W. Gilbert Cooper, vicar of Burward Weald, Sussex, see page
(5) Annie Susan. (6) Charlotte and
(7) Theodosia Caroline (twins).

[11a] Hon. Caroline Amelia, married 3 Feb., 1846, to Rev. John George Beresford, M.A., vicar of St. Andrews, Whittlesey, 1846-9; rector of Wymondham, Leic., 1849-61; rector of Bedale, Yorks, since 1861 (see Foster's *Baronetage*), and has 5 sons and 6 daughters (*e*).

(1*e-11a*) John Peirse de la Poer (Beresford), lieut. South Wales Borderers, 1881; born 2 Dec., 1846; married 25 Aug., 1881, Mary Elizabeth Thomasina, eldest daughter of Lieut.-col. Henry Stewart Beresford Bruce, of Ballyscullion House, co. Londonderry (see Foster's *Baronetage*), and has a daughter.

A daughter, born 3 April, 1883.

(2*e-11a*) Charles Windham de la Poer, lieut. R.N., born 2 June, 1858.

(3*e-11a*) Henry William de la Poer, born 27 April, 1862.

(4*e-11a*) Walter Vevers de la Poer, born 22 June, 1864.

(5*e-11a*) Caroline Theodosia, married 3 Dec., 1866, as 2nd wife, to Thomas Hood Cockburn-Hood, Esq., formerly a member of the Legislative Council in Sydney, N. S. Wales (eldest son of late John Cockburn-Hood, Esq., of Stoneridge, Berwickshire).

(6*e-11a*) Marion Harriet.

(7*e-11a*) Gertrude Georgina, married 19 April, 1876, to Rev. John Shapland Elliot Cockburn-Hood, vicar of Kirkby Fleetham, Yorks, and has a son and 4 daughters.

Claude Beresford (Cockburn-Hood), born 5 Aug., 1878; Marion; Gertrude Cecilia; Caroline Charlotte; Mary Margaret.

(8*e-11a*) Frances Anne.

(9*e-11a*) Elizabeth Margaret, married 31 Jan., 1877, to Rev. Ernest Henry Kellett Long, M.A. Ch. Ch., Oxon., 1882; rector of Tickencote, Stamford, since 1880 (see page 15); and has 5 sons and a daughter.

Basil Kellett (Long), born 28 Feb., 1878.
John Beresford, born 20 Feb., 1879.
William Fortescue, born 24 May, 1880.
Walter Denman, born 22 Sept., 1881.
Charles Ernest, born 21 Nov., 1882.
Margaret Marie, born 27 Feb., 1884.

(10*e-11a*) Catherine Emily (Beresford).

HON. THEODOSIA DENMAN, married 21 Nov., 1825, to Ichabod Wright, Esq., of Mapperley Hall, Notts; he died 14 Oct., 1871, having had 5 sons and 3 daughters.

(1) **Charles Ichabod (Wright)**, of whom (see page 651).

(2) Thomas Denman (Wright), born 22 March, 1833; died unmarried 14 Feb., 1871.

(3) Henry Smith (Wright), of Park Hill, Lyndhurst, Hants; B.A. Trin. Coll., Camb. 1862; barrister-at-law, I. T 1866; born 27 June, 1839; married 1st, 17 Oct., 1865, Mary Jane, only daughter of late William Cartledge, Esq., of Woodthorpe, Notts; she died 4 Dec., 1866, having had a daughter.

(1) Edith Mary Smith Wright.

HENRY SMITH WRIGHT, married 2nd, 6 Feb., 1869, Josephine Henrietta, only daughter of late Rev. John Adolphus Wright, rector of Ickham, Kent; and has (with 2 other daughters, who died in infancy) 4 sons and a daughter.

[2] Henry Adolphus Smith (Wright), born 13 Dec., 1869.
[3] George Lewis Smith, born 30 Jan., 1872.
[4] Edward Henry Smith, born 4 Sept., 1875.
[5] John Harold Smith, born 18 Aug., 1882.
[6] Alice Dorothea Smith.

(4) Frederick (Wright), of Lenton Hall, Notts, banker; born 12 Aug., 1840; married 12 Feb., 1863, Ada Joyce, daughter of Rev. John Bateman, of East and West Leake, Notts, and has a son and 6 daughters,

Frederick Denman (Wright), born 17 Dec., 1872.
Emily Theodosia. Mary Neville.
Florence Ada. Margaret Joyce.
Hilda Dorothy. Maud Frances Bateman.

(5) George Howard (Wright), Rev., born 1 June, 1845; married 12 July, 1870, Anne Frances, 2nd daughter of Rev. Edmund Roberts Larken, M.A., rector of Burton, co. Linc., and has 2 sons and daughter,

George Denman Larken (Wright), born 31 Aug., 1872. Eric James, born 12 Nov., 1880.
Theodosia Anne Emily.

(6) Theodosia Harriet (Wright), married 8 Sept., 1863, to William Houston Sinclair, Esq., of Morton Manor, Brading, Isle of Wight, and has 3 sons and a daughter,

Charles George (Sinclair), born 5 Jan., 1865.
William Frederick, born 26 April, 1867.
John Houston, born 6 Dec., 1869.
Theodosia Agnes.

(7) Frances (Wright), married 30 May, 1861, to Edward William Cropper, Esq., of Great Crosby, co. Lanc., and has had 5 sons and 5 daughters,

James Cropper, B.A., Trin Coll., Camb., 1884; born 2 May, 1862. John, born 17 Sept., 1864. Charles Henry Edward, born 25 Jan., 1866. Edward Neville, died young. Frederick William, born 1 Feb., 1871. Frances Mildred Theodosia. Mary Isabella, died young. Anne Wakefield. Emily Mabel. Eveline Wright.

(8) Neville Sophia (Wright), died 23 June, 1853.

LLOYD, GEORGE WHITELOCKE, of Strancally Castle, co. Waterford, J.P.; High Sheriff 1859; also of Calton, Yorks; D.L. West Riding, 23RD IN DESCENT FROM EDWARD I., born 30 May, 1830, married 1st, 14 Sept., 1854, Selina Jane, daughter of late Arthur Henry, Esq., of Lodge Park, co. Kildare; she died 11 Jan., 1860; he married 2ndly, 7 Feb., 1861, Lady Anne Margaret Butler, 2nd daughter of Somerset Richard, 3rd Earl of Carrick. By his first wife he had a son and 3 daughters.

[1] William Whitelocke (Lloyd), born 5 May, 1856.
[2] Eveline Selina.
[3] Augusta Frances Jane.
[4] Selina Mary.

THE DESCENT OF
GEORGE WHITELOCKE LLOYD, ESQ.,
OF STRANCALLY CASTLE, CO. WATERFORD,
FROM THE BLOOD ROYAL OF ENGLAND.

EDWARD I., so named after Edward the Confessor; born at Westminster, 17 June, 1239, knighted at Burgos, 1254, created Earl of Chester; crowned at Westminster, 19 Aug. 1274, king of England, lord of Ireland, duke of Aquitaine; he subdued the principality of Wales 1283, claimed and exercised feudal superiority over Scotland; died at Burgh-on-the-Sands, Cumberland, 7 July, 1307, buried in Westminster Abbey; by his first wife, Eleanor, daughter of Ferdinand III., king of Castile, who died 27 Nov., 1290, he had issue; their descendant

SUSANNAH, daughter of Thomas Horton, of Chadderton (see page 634); married 24 March, 1742, as 2nd wife to George Lloyd, F.R.S., of Hulme Hall, Lancashire (which he sold to the Duke of Bridgewater), M.B. Camb., D.L. Yorks., West Riding (for his ancestry and second marriage, see Foster's *Yorkshire Collection*); he died at Barrowby, near Leeds, 4 Dec., 1783, and had 3 sons and 3 daughters (*a*).

[1*a*] **Gamaliel Lloyd**, of whom (see page 657).
[2*a*] George (Lloyd), barrister-at-law, resided at Manchester, and lastly at York; born 30 Oct., 1748, died 12 Oct., 1804; married 1780, Elizabeth, daughter of Jeremiah Naylor, of Wakefield; she died 30 Oct., 1847, having had 2 sons and 3 daughters (*b*).

(1*b*-2*a*) George (Lloyd), of Stockton Hall, Yorks; born 21 May, 1787; died 12 March, 1863; married 17 May, 1810, Alicia Maria, daughter and eventual heiress of John Greame, Esq., of Sewerby House, Yorks (by his wife Sarah Yarburgh); she died 3 Jan., 1867, having had 4 sons and a daughter (*c*).

(1*c*-1*b*) George John (Yarburgh), of Heslington Hall, Yorks., assumed the surname of Yarburgh, in lieu of his patronymic; born 28 July, 1811; died 1874; married 23 July, 1840, Mary Antonia, daughter of Samuel Cheetham Hilton, Esq., of Pennington, co. Lanc., and had 2 daughters.

(1) Mary Elizabeth (Yarburgh), married 8 May, 1862, to her cousin George William Bateson, Esq., heir presumptive to Lord Deramore, and has issue (see page 656).

(2) Susan Anne, married 25 Jan., 1865, to Charles Lethbridge, Esq., J.P. Somerset (see Foster's *Baronetage*), and has 2 sons and 5 daughters,

Ambrose Yarburgh (Lethbridge), born 2 Nov., 1874; Bertram Escott, born 5 June, 1878; Mary; Dorothea; Elinor; Ruth; Susan.

(2*c*-1*b*) Yarburgh Gamaliel Lloyd-Greame, of Sewerby House, Yorks, J.P.; M.A. Trin. Coll., Camb., 1842; vicar of Dunston, co. Linc. 1847-56; on his mother's death he assumed the additional surname of Greame; born 18 July, 1813; married 7 May, 1839, Editha Christian, 5th daughter of William Augustus Le Hunte, Esq., of Artramount, co. Wexford, and has had a son and 3 daughters.

[1] Yarburgh George Lloyd-Greame, born 15 June, 1840; married, 1 Aug., 1869, Dora, daughter of Right Rev. James Thomas O'Brien, D.D., bishop of Ossory, Ferns, and Leighlin, and has 3 sons and 2 daughters,

Yarburgh, born 19 May, 1872; Francis, born Aug., 1873; Philip, born 1 May, 1884; Editha; Dora.

[2] Pattie Warburton, died 9 May, 1870.

[3] Edith Henrietta, died 20 April, 1859.

[4] Maria (Lloyd-Graeme).

(8c-1b) Henry (Lloyd), in holy orders, born 31 May, 1815; died 17 Nov, 1862; married 30 Sept., 1857, Anne Eliza, daughter of Rev. Wm. Roy, D.D., rector of Skirbeck, co. Linc., and had 2 sons and a daughter.

[1] George William (Lloyd), born 3 March, 1861.

[2] Henry John Graeme, born 10 June, 1862.

[3] Alicia Margaret.

[4c-1b] Edward (Lloyd), of Lingcroft, Yorks, born 27 May, 1823; drowned when out hunting, in the ferry-boat accident at Newby Ferry, Yorks, 4 Feb., 1869; married 21 Sept., 1854, Rosabelle Susan, daughter of George Lloyd, Esq., of Cowesby Hall (see below), and had 3 daughters.

(1) Georgina Rosabelle (Lloyd), married 15 July 1879, to Guy St. Maur Palmes, 14th hussars, and has 2 sons and a daughter.

Geoffrey St. Maur, born 26 Dec., 1881; Guy Roger, born 24 June, 1883; Cecil Muriel.

(2) Edith Maria Greame, married 22 April, 1879, to Frederick Reynard, Esq., of Sunderlandwick, and has 2 sons,

Claude Edward, born 9 Feb. 1880. Algernon Horner, born 1884.

(3) Cecil Mary.

[5c-1b] Alicia Maria (Lloyd).

(2b-2a) Edward Jeremiah (Lloyd), of Oldfield Hall, Cheshire, barrister-at-law, born 22 June, 1790; died s.p.s., 3 July, 1850: married 17 Nov., 1828, Eliza, 2nd daughter and co-heir of William Rigby, Esq., of Oldfield Hall, aforesaid; she died 1859.

(3b-2a) Elizabeth (Lloyd), married 1st, , to William Butler Laird, of Strathmartin, Dundee, capt. 17th dragoons; he died 26 August, 1810, leaving issue; she re-married to Robert Alison, of Dundee, and had further issue.

(4b-2a) Susannah Georgiana, died Jan., 1873, aged 89.

(5b-2a) Mary Ann (Lloyd), married 4 Aug., 1831, as 2nd wife to her cousin, Rev. Cecil Daniel Wray (see below).

[3a] Thomas (Lloyd), of Horsforth Hall, Yorks, lieut.-col.-commandant Leeds volunteers; born 17 July, 1750; died at Kingthorpe House, Yorks, 7 April, 1828; married 27 March, 1783, Ann, daughter of Walter Wade, Esq., of New Grange, Leeds, she died 21 Jan., 1830, having had a son and daughter *(d)*.

(1d-3a) George (Lloyd), of Cowesby Hall, Yorks, born 25 May, 1786; died 25 July, 1844; married 1st, 2 Dec., 1820, Marion Christina, 5th daughter of Alexander Maclean, Esq., of Coll, Argyllshire; she died s.p., 16 June, 1821; he married 2ndly, 7 June, 1825, Elizabeth Henrietta, 2nd daughter of William Rookes Leeds Serjeantson, Esq., of Camp Hill, Yorks; she died 10 April, 1881, aged 79, having had 5 sons and 8 daughters.

[1] Thomas William (Lloyd), of Cowesby Hall, Yorks, and of Spotland, co. Lanc., J.P., D.L.; born 8 Mar., 1826; married 27 Mar., 1849, Elizabeth, Anne, 3rd daughter of Francis Beynon Hacket, Esq., of Moor Hall, Warwickshire (see page 638), and had a daughter.

Gertrude Elizabeth, born 9 Sept., 1850; died 22 May, 1851.

[2] George Walter Edward (Lloyd), capt. R.N.; born 10 May, 1828; married 17 Oct., 1876, Fannie, daughter of William Henry Powell, Esq., of New York, and has had 2 sons: a son born in Paris, 11 June, 1878, died 29 Feb., 1880; William Alexander Charles, born 8 May, 1885.

[3] John George, died 13 Oct., 1856.

[4] Alexander Ogilvie, died 24 Oct., 1865.

[5] Alfred Hart (Lloyd), born 28 Aug., 1837; married at Port Mackay, Queensland, 28 Mar., 1883, Maria, sister of late Charles Walker, Esq., of Dumbleton, Port Mackay, and has a daughter.

Mary Eleanor Susan.

[6] Caroline Anne.

[7] Marianne Jane, married 9 April, 1863, to Edward Bowen Cooke, major 83rd regt. (see Foster's *Baronetage*); he died 11 April, 1877, leaving 2 daughters,

Rosabelle Juliana, and Evelyn Mary (Cooke).

[8] Elizabeth Juliana.

[9] Rosabelle Susan, married 21 Sept., 1854, to Edward Lloyd, of Lingcroft, who died 4 Feb., 1869, leaving 3 daughters, named above.

[10] Cecilia Amy. [11] Lucy Emma.

[12] Isabella Harriet, died, 29 Nov. 1877.

[13] Eleanor.

(2d-3a) Marianne (Lloyd), died 24 Dec., 1823; married 16 Nov., 1815, to John Priestley, Esq., of Thorpe, Halifax; he died 1858, leaving 2 daughters.

[1] Elizabeth Marianne (Priestley), married 2 July, 1840, to John Rawson, of Brockwell, Yorkshire, and of Fallbarrow, Westmorland, and had an only child.

Gertrude Elizabeth (Rawson), born 19 June, 1843; died 23 Dec., 1859.

[2] Harriet Susanna (Priestley), married 12 Oct., 1843, to Frederick Edward Rawson, of Thorpe, Yorks (see Foster's *Yorkshire Collection*); he died 16 May, 1879, having had 2 sons and a daughter.

(1) Frederick Gerald Selwyn (Rawson), born 10 Aug., 1851.

(2) John Selwyn (Rawson), born 20 March, 1858.

(3) Florence Harriet Marianne (Rawson), born 1 Feb., 1853; died 21 Oct., 1861.

[4a] Anne (Lloyd) died 1830, aged 85.

[5a] Susannah, born 2 April, 1747; buried at St. Martin's, Micklegate, York, 25 Nov., 1830; married 15 Oct., 1776, to Rev. Henry Wray, of Brogden House, and of Kelfield, Yorks; D.L. West Riding; A.M. Trin. Coll., Camb.; rector of Newton Kyme, Yorks; vicar of Hatfield-Broad-Oak, Essex; he died 3 March, 1814, having had 2 sons and a daughter.

(1) Cecil Daniel (Wray), of Kelfield, 1815; M.A. Oxon; canon of Manchester Cathedral, and rector of Runcton, Norfolk; born 25 Jan., 1778; died ; married 1st, 4 April, 1804, Elizabeth, 2nd daughter of Joseph Thackeray, Esq., of Manchester; she died , 1825; he married 2ndly, 4 Aug., 1831, his cousin, Marianne, 3rd daughter of George Lloyd, Esq., barrister-at-law; by his 1st wife he had 3 sons and 4 daughters.

[1] Cecil (Wray), incumbent of St. Martin-in-the-Fields, Liverpool; born 4 Jan., 1805; died, leaving issue.

[2] George (Wray), born 9 Sept., 1814; died 1882, leaving issue.

[3] Henry, born 11 June, 1823; married and died, s.p., 1879.

[4] Eliza, died 1817. [5] Harriet.

[6] Susanna Mary. [7] Louisa Georgiana.

(2) George (Wray), A.M., rector of Leven, Yorks; born 30 Oct., 1781; died 26 June, 1878, aged 96; married , 1816, Caroline, daughter of William Wainman, Esq., of Carr Head, Yorks; she died Dec., 1824; buried at Bentley, leaving an only son,

William Henry (Wray), in holy orders; born 14 Oct., 1817; died Trinity Sunday, 1863; married 18 June, 1851, Mary, daughter of Charles Heaton Ellis, Esq., and had 2 sons and a daughter.

(1) Herbert George (Wray), of Wadworth Hall, Yorks., born 22 Nov., 1853.

(2) Cecil Henry (Wray), of Thurlby Hall, co. Lincoln; born 1 Aug., 1855; married 21 Feb., 1878, Edith Catherine, daughter of Rev. George Clifford Pease (see Foster's *Yorkshire Collection*), and has 2 sons.

Henry Cecil, born 11 Dec., 1878; Gerald Christopher, born 7 Sept., 1881.

(3) Alice Emma (Wray) died

(3) Harriet (Wray), born 2 April, 1786.

[6a] Elizabeth (Lloyd), died 2 Jan., 1840; married April, 1779, to Thomas Bateson, Esq., of Belvoir Park, co. Down (son of Thomas Bateson who sold the family property in Lancashire); he died 15 May, 1811, leaving an only son,

Sir Robert Bateson (descended in the 6th generation from Thomas Bateson, of Garstang, Lancashire), high sheriff co. Down 1809; created a baronet 18 Dec., 1818; M.P. co. Londonderry 1830-42; born 13 March, 1780; died 21 April, 1863, having married 27 April, 1811, Catherine youngest daughter of late Samuel Dickson, Esq., of Ballynaguile, co. Limerick; she died 23 Dec., 1873, having had 6 sons and 2 daughters *(e)*.

(1e) Robert, born 29 March, 1816; died unmarried 23 Dec., 1843.

(2e) Sir Thomas Bateson, of Belvoir Park and Moira Park, both co. Down, J.P., D.L.; 2nd Bart., created Baron Deramore, of Belvoir, co. Down, Nov. 1885, capt. late 13th light dragoons; M.P. co. Londonderry 1843-57, J.P., D.L., Devizes since 1864; a junior lord of the treasury in 1852; born 4 June, 1819; married 24 Feb., 1849, Hon. Caroline Elizabeth Anne Rice-Trevor, 2nd daughter of George, 4th Lord Dinevor, and has 2 daughters.

[1] Eva Frances Caroline, married 4 March, 1871, to David Alfred Ker, of Montalto, co. Down capt. 12th lancers, who died 8 Dec., 1877, leaving 4 daughters.

Sybil Anna (Ker), Eva Winifrid Selina, Kathleen Eleanor Mary, Eva Cecil Violet.

[2] Kathleen Mary, married 29 May, 1877, to Walter Randolph, 2nd son of Sir Walter Rockliff Farquhar, Bart., and has a son,

Walter Randolph FitzRoy (Farquhar), born 31 May, 1878.

(3e) Samuel Stephen, of Cambusmere, Sutherlands. N.B., barrister-at-law; contested Ipswich, 1852; born 13 Oct., 1821; died s.p. 9 March, 1879, having married 25 July, 1854, Hon. Florinda Handcock, eldest daughter of Richard, 3rd Lord Castlemaine.

(4e) George William Bateson de Yarburgh, of Heslington Hall, Yorks, J.P., D.L.; he assumed the additional name and arms of de Yarburgh by royal licence 15 April, 1876; heir presumptive to his brother's peerage; born 2 April, 1823; married 8 May, 1862, Mary Elizabeth, elder daughter and co-heir of late George John Yarburgh, Esq., of Heslington Hall, Yorks (see page 654); she died 22 Oct., 1884, having had with other issue 2 sons and 2 daughters.

Robert Wilfrid, born 5 Aug., 1865, George Nicholas, born 25 Nov., 1870, a son born 13 Oct., 1884. Mary Lilla. Katharine Hylda.

(5e) Richard, colonel 1st life guards; A.D.C. to F.M. H.R.H. Duke of Cambridge; born 18 Dec., 1828.

(6e) John, born 8 July, 1832; married 27 June, 1868, Edith Elizabeth, 4th daughter of Charles John Pearse, Esq., s.p.s.

(7e) Maria Catherine, died 6 Aug., 1876, having married 4 Jan., 1838, to Sir Beresford Burston McMahon, Bart., capt. Scots guards, who died 11 Jan., 1873, having had 5 sons and 3 daughters.

[1] Sir William Samuel McMahon, of Faccary House, co. Tyrone, 3rd Bart; capt. 2nd life guards 1869-80; attaché to British Legation at Florence, Munich, and Constantinople, 1858-62; born 9 Nov., 1839.

[2] Robert Bateson (McMahon) heir presumptive to the baronetcy; born 5 Nov., 1840.

[3] Beresford Burston, born 26 July, 1849; married

[4] Gerald Charles, born 3 Sept., 1851.

[5] Lionel, barrister-at law, Inner Temple, 1883, late 58th regt. of foot, born 30 June, 1856.

[6] Catherine Charlotte, married 27 July, 1867, to Sir Edward Grogan, Bart., of Ballintyre Hall, co. Dublin; D.L.; admitted to King's Inns, Hilary, 1839; called to the bar 1840; M.P. city of Dublin, 1841-65, and has a son and 3 daughters.

(1) Edward Ion Beresford (Grogan), born 29 Nov., 1873.

(2) Maria Katharine Nina.

(3) Sarah Madeleine.

(4) Aileen Edward Sybil Teresa.

[7] Frances Tomasine, married 3 Sept., 1863, to Joseph Gubbins, Esq., of Kilfrush, co. Limerick, and has at least 5 sons,

Francis Joseph Beresford (Gubbins), born , 1865. Frederick William Beresford, born , 1868. Marcus Stamer Beresford, born , 1884. Lucius Burston Beresford, born , 1876. Quintus Evelyn Beresford, born , 1879.

[8] Nina Gertrude, married 31 July, 1871, to Rev. Arthur Gore Ryder, D.D., sub-dean of Christ Church Cathedral, Dublin, and has 5 sons and a daughter.

Harrington Dudley (Ryder), born 26 Sept., 1872. Beresford Burston McMahon, born 27 May, 1877. Ralph St. George Gore, born 15 April, 1879. Lionel Sitric Dudley, born 6 April, 1881. Henry Henry Hugh, born 8 April, 1883. Nina Beryl.

(8e) Elizabeth Honoria (Bateson), died 11 Feb., 1862; married 7 Feb., 1839, to John Neilson Gladstone, Esq., of Bowden Park, Wilts; M.P. Walsall 1841, Ipswich 1842-7, Devizes 1852-63; capt. R.N. (3rd son of Sir John Gladstone, Bart.); born 18 Jan., 1807; died 7 Feb., 1863, having had a son and 7 daughters.

[1] John Evelyn (Gladstone), Royal Wilts yeomanry cavalry; born 23 Nov., 1855.

[2] Catherine, married 2 June, 1881, to Very Rev. William Charles Lake, D.D. (1870), dean of Durham 1869; M.A. Balliol 1841, formerly fellow and tutor; public examiner at Oxford 1853-4; preacher at Chapel Royal, Whitehall; commissioner of army education 1856, of popular education 1858; rector of Huntspill 1858-69, prebendary of (Combe in) Wells 1860-69.

[3] Anne Elizabeth Honoria, married 22 Aug., 1831, to Somerset Richard Lowry - Corry, K.C.M.G., 4th Earl Belmore, and Viscount of co. Fermanagh, and Baron Belmore, of Castle Coole; elected an Irish representative Peer, 1856; P.C. Ireland; under-sec. of state, home department, 1866-7; governor and com.-in-chief of New South Wales, 1868-72; a commissioner of Irish intermediate education; and has 3 sons and 8 daughters,

(1) Armar, Viscount Corry, born 5 May, 1870.

(2) Hon. Cecil, born 20 Mar., 1873.

(3) Hon. Ernest, born 23 Nov., 1874.

(4) Lady Theresa. (5) Lady Florence.

(6) Lady Madeline. (7) Lady Mary.

(8) Lady Winifred. (9) Lady Edith.

(10) Lady Violet, born 15 June, 1881.

(11) Lady Margaret, born 13 July, 1883.

[4] Alice. [5] Clara Frances.

[6] Constance Elizabeth, twin with

[7] Edith Ellen, married 27 Oct., 1870, to William Alexander Dumaresq, M.A. Cantb. barrister-at-law, Inner Temple, J.P. St. Aubins,

Scone, N.S.W. (only surviving son of William Dumaresq); he died 28 May, 1880, having had 3 sons and 2 daughters,

John Saumarez (Dumaresq), born 26 Oct., 1873.
Reginald George Fitzroy, born 2 Oct., 1877.
Herbert William, born 25 April, 1879.
Agnes Susan Elizabeth. Marion Edith.

[8] Lucy Marion (Gladstone), married 29 April, 1876, to Reginald Henry Hardy, J.P., D.L., co. Stafford; lieut. Stafford yeomanry cavalry; barrister-at-law of the Inner Temple 1873 (eldest son of Sir John Hardy, Bart., of Dunstall Hall, co. Stafford), and has had 3 sons,

(1) Bertram (Hardy), born 11 Feb., 1877.
(2) Eustace, born and died, Aug., 1880.
(3) Leonard Henry, born 12 May, 1882.

GAMALIEL LLOYD, of Leeds, Alderman, (Mayor 1790,) afterwards of Bury St. Edmunds, and lastly of London; born 26 May, 1744; died 31 Aug., 1817; married Elizabeth, daughter of James Attwood; she died July, 1818, having had a son and 2 daughters (*f*),

[1*f*] William Horton (Lloyd), of Catton, Yorkshire, &c., F.L.S.; born 10 Feb., 1784; died 18 Feb., 1849; married 13 April, 1826, Mary, 4th and youngest daughter of George Whitelocke, Esq., of London (descended from Sir Bulstrode Whitelocke, ambassador to Sweden, 1663); she died 18 Feb., 1882, aged 84, having had 2 sons,

(1) Gamaliel, born 12 June, 1827; died 6 Nov., 1830.
(2) **George Whitelocke (Lloyd)**, first named, (see p. 654.)

[2*f*] Mary Horton (Lloyd), died ; married , to Stephen John Winthrop, M.D., of Little Bounds, Tunbridge, Kent; he died , having had 4 sons and 2 daughters (*g*),

(1*g*-2*f*) Benjamin (Winthrop), of Hardenhuish, Wilts, J.P.; M.A. Clare Coll., Camb.; in holy orders; born 1800; died 22 Sept., 1885, having married 1834, Anne, daughter of John Harvey Thursby, Esq., of Abington Abbey, Northants, and had 4 sons and 6 daughters.

[1] Benjamin (Winthrop), of Ashley, Box, Wilts; J.P., late lieut. 15th Hussars; born 26 Feb., 1838; married June, 1868, Constance Ellen Susette, daughter of John Christian Boodé, Esq., of Lucknam, Wilts, and has at least 3 sons and 4 daughters.

Walter Thursby, born Dec., 1875; John Gerard, born Nov., 1876; Harvey Stephen, born Nov., 1878; Beatrice Constance; Maude Christine; Cecil Margaret; Monaca Mary.

[2] Stephen, Capt. born ; died on 12 Oct., 1867; married Louisa Dolores Jacoba, eldest daughter of J. Heath, Esq.
[3] Edward (Winthrop), B.A., Worc. Coll., Oxon., 1819; rector of Wolverton since 1873.
[4] William Young (Winthrop).
[5] Marianne Emma.
[6] Eleanor, died ; married , to Rev. Henry Courtney Courtney, M.A., Trin. Coll., Oxon, vicar of Hatton, co. Warwick. since 1875, rector of Wolverton, 1864-73.
[7] Emily.
[8] Florence, married to F. Armstrong, Esq.
[9] Annie (Winthrop).
[10] Constance Ella, married 9 Aug., 1881, as 2nd wife to Francis Nicholas Smith, Esq., of Wingfield Park, Derbyshire (see Foster's *Peerage*, B. CARRINGTON) and has a daughter, born 31 March, 1885.

(2*g*-2*f*) Stephen, died unmarried
(3*g*-2*f*) Edward Gamaliel, died unmarried
(4*g*-2*f*) William, died
(5*g*-2*f*) Mary Ann (Winthrop), died 6 May, 1867; married 10 April, 1826, to Rev. and Hon. Edward Pellew, hon. canon of Norwich, minister of St. Nicholas, Yarmouth (son of Vice-Admiral Viscount Exmouth, G.C.B.; see Foster's *Peerage*); he died 29 Aug., 1869, having had 5 sons and 5 daughters (*h*).

[1*h*-5*g*] Edward Winthrop (Pellew), born 24 Jan., 1830; died unmarried 9 Jan., 1881.
[2*h*-5*g*] George Israel (Pellew), B.A. University Coll. Oxon, 1854; curate of Peterston-Watlington since 1876; chaplain at Avranches, Normandy, 1873-4, &c.; born 10 Jan., 1831.
[3*h*-5*g*] Pownoll William (Pellew), com. R.N.; born 27 Jan., 1837; died 12 March, 1872, having married 20 June, 1867, Mary Elizabeth, daughter of Rev. John Armstrong Bagnell, of Attana, Queen's co., and had a son,

Edward Irving Pownoll, born 3 May, 1868.

[4*h*-5*g*] Fleetwood Hugo (Pellew), commissioner of the Dacca division, B.C.S.; born 13 Dec., 1838; married 3 July, 1869, Dorothy Mary, daughter of late Rev. Philip Anderson, chaplain Colaba, and has a son and 4 daughters,

Fleetwood Hugo Pellew, born 23 Dec., 1871; Dorothy; Margaret Alma; Annie Helen, born 7 Oct., 1880; Caroline, born 29 Aug., 1882.

[5*h*-5*g*] Arthur Samuel (Pellew), born 29 Oct., 1841.
[6*h*-5*g*] Elizabeth Julia (Pellew), married 19 Aug., 1847, to Rev. James Richard Anderson, rector of Barningham, Norfolk, 1866; rector of Matton and Felbrigge; he died 29 May, 1872, having had 3 sons and 4 daughters.

(1) James Winthrop Anderson, born 29 Aug., 1851.
(2) William Donald, born 28 Oct., 1853.
(3) Arthur Robert, born 11 Aug., 1859.
(4) Mary Elizabeth.
(5) Helen Margaret, died
(6) Florence Lydia, married 16 May, 1883, to Hugh Hornby, eldest son of Thomas Hornby Birley, Esq., of Manchester.
(7) Georgina Gertrude.

[7*h*-5*g*] Mary Anne (Pellew), married 11 March, 1852, to Robert Hill Pinhey, puisne judge, High Court, Bombay, since 1873, and has had, with other issue, 7 sons and 2 daughters.

(1) Robert William Spottiswoode (Pinhey), barrister-at-law, Linc. Inn, 1877; advocate Bombay; born 1853.
(2) Edward (Pinhey), engineer P. W. D., Kanara, Bombay; born 1855.
(3) Hugh Theodore, Indian Govt. Telegraph Department; born , 1858.
(4) Alexander Fleetwood, lieut. 2nd batt. the King's (Liverpool) regt.; born , 1861.
(5) Arthur Francis, born , 1863.
(6) Winthrop Molyneux, born , 1870.
(7) Henry Pellew Douglas, born , 1872.
(8) Charles Codrington, born , 1874.
(9) Emily, born 1857; married 1876, to William Bailey Langhorne, Esq.
(10) Mary Georgiana, born , 1868.

[8*h*-5*g*] Emma Susan (Pellew), married 25 July, 1856, to William D'Oyly, Esq., late E.I.C.S., J.P. Notts and Sussex, and has 2 sons and 6 daughters.

Guy Pellew D'Oyly, born 29 June, 1864; Claud Pellew, born 25 April, 1866; Maud Helen; Constance Frances; Eyelyn Bruere; Mabel Emily; Sybil Margaret; Cecily Joane.

[9*h*-5*g*] Frances Helen (Pellew), married 19 Aug., 1858, to Rt. Hon. Sir Louis Mallet, P.C., C.B., under-sec. India since 1874; member Indian Council; 1872-4; assist.-sec. Board of Trade, 1866-72; and has officiated as commissioner in negotiating commercial treaties with France (1860), with Austria (1865, 1866), and has 4 sons.

Bernard Mallet, born 19 Sept., 1859; Stephen Pellew, born 26 Aug., 1860; Louis du Par, born 10 July, 1864; Hugo Eugène, born 9 Dec., 1865.

[10*h*-5*g*] Georgina Caroline (Pellew), married 24 April, 1877, to Frederick Howard, Esq.

(6*g*-2*f*) Elizabeth (Winthrop), married 25 Jan., 1843, to Charles Baring Young, Esq., of Oak Hill, East Barnet, Herts, and of London, merchant (see Foster's *Baronetage*); he died 10 Dec., 1882, having had 2 sons and 2 daughters.

[1] Charles Edward Baring (Young), barrister-at-law, Inner Temple, 1876; born , 1850.

[2] Arthur William Dalton.

[3] Caroline. [4] Margaret.

[3*f*] Anne Susanna Lloyd, died ; married 10 June, 1806, to Leonard Horner, Esq., F.R.S.; he died March, 1864, leaving 6 daughters *(i)*.

(1*i*-3*f*) Mary Elizabeth (Lady Lyell), died April, 1873; married 12 July, 1832, to Sir Charles Lyell, of Kinnordy, Bart., so created 22 Aug., 1864, having been knighted about 1841; D.C.L., F.R.S., F.G.S., president of the Geological Society 1836-7, 1850-1; author of "Principles of Geology," "Antiquity of Man," &c.; died s.p. 22 Feb., 1875.

(2*i*-3*f*) Frances Joanna (Lady Bunbury), married 31 May, 1844, to Sir Charles James Fox Bunbury, 8th Bart., high sheriff Suffolk 1868, s.p.

(3*i*-3*f*) Anne Susanna (Horner).

(4*i*-3*f*) Katharine Murray, married 1848, to Lieut.-col. Henry Lyell, 43rd Bengal native infantry; he died 5 Feb., 1875, having had 3 sons and a daughter.

[1] Leonard Lyell, of Kinnordy and Pitmuis, Forfarshire, born 21 Oct., 1850; married 4 July, 1874, Mary, daughter of Rev. John Mayne Sterling, rector of Mangerville (see Foster's *Baronetage*), and has a son and 2 daughers.

Charles Henry, born 18 May, 1875. Mary Leonora, Eleanor Katharine.

[2] Francis Horner (Lyell), capt. 4th battalion the Gloucestershire regiment; late lieut. 2nd West India regiment; born 11 Feb., 1852; married 12 Aug., 1879, Emily Charlotte, daughter of Francis E. Guise, Esq., and has 2 sons and a daughter.

Henry Guise (Lyell), born 14 Dec., 1881.

Cecil, born 12 April, 1883.

Violet.

[3] Arthur Henry (Lyell), born 26 Nov., 1853.

[4] Rosamond Frances Anne.

(5*i*-3*f*) Leonora (Horner), married 1853, to Chevalier Pertz, librarian of the Imperial Library, Berlin.

(6*i*-3*f*) Joanna Baillie (Horner).

THE DESCENT OF

His Honour Judge de Moleyns, Q.C.

FROM THE

Blood Royal

of England.

EDWARD III., crowned 1 Feb., 1327, b. 13 Nov., 1312, d. 21 June, 1377. = Philippa, 3rd dau. of William, Count of Holland and Hainault, m. 24 Jan. 1328, d. 15 Aug. 1369.

Edmund, Duke of York, K.G., 5th son, d. at Langley, 1 Aug. 1402. = Isabel (1st wife), youngest dau. and co-heir of Peter, King of Castile, m. 1372.

Constance of Langley. = Thomas, 6th Baron le Despencer, cr. Earl of Gloucester, 1397, beheaded at Bristol, 16 Jan. 1400.

Isabel le Despencer, b. 26 July, 1400, m. 27 July 1411, d. 26 Dec. 1440. = Richard Beauchamp, Lord Bergavenny (1st husband), cr. Earl of Worcester 1420, d. 1422.

Elizabeth Beauchamp, Baroness Bergavenny, b. at Hanley Castle, 16 Dec. 1415, d. 18 June, 1447 (1st wife). = Sir Edward Nevill, sum. to parl. as Baron Bergavenny, 1450-72, d. 18 Oct. 1476.

Sir George Nevill, Lord Bergavenny, sum. to parl. 1482-92, d. 20 Sept. 1492. = Margaret (1st wife), dau. and heir of Sir Hugh Fenne, of Sculton, d. 28 Sept. 1485.

Sir Edward Nevill, of Addington Park, Kent, beheaded on Tower Hill, 9 Jan. 1538-9. = Eleanor, widow of Ralph, 8th Lord Scrope, of Masham, dau. of Andrew, Lord Windsor.

——— Royden (1st husband). = Catherine Nevill. = Clement Throckmorton, of Hanley, Warwickshire, d. 19 Oct. 1594.

A, *continued above.*

A, *continued from below.*

Catherine Nevill = Clement Throckmorton.

Martha Throckmorton, bur. at Southwick, 30 Dec. 1600, aged 49. = George Lynne, of South wick Hall, Northants, bur. there 29 Nov. 1617.

George Lynne, of Southwick Hall, d. 5 Nov. 1606. = Isabel, sister of Sir Anthony Forrest, of Morborn, Hunts, Knt.

Martha Lynne = John Blennerhassett, of Ballyseedy, co. Kerry, M.P. Tralee, 1661.

Thomas Blennerhassett, of Littur, co. Kerry. = Ellen, dau. of Anthony Stoughton, of Rattoo, co. Kerry.

Martha Blennerhassett, m. 2nd to Henry Parr. = Frederick Mullins, 1st husband), d. 3 Oct., 1695.

William Mullins, of Burnham, Kerry, d. 3 May, 1761. = Mary, dau. of George Rowan, Esq., of Rathany, Kerry, m. 10 June, 1716.

Sir Thomas Mullins, of Burnham, created a baronet, 1797, and Baron Ventry, 1800, b. 1736, d. 1824. = Elizabeth, only dau. of Townsend Gun, of Rattoo, co. Kerry, m. 5. Oct., 1755, d. 19 Jan., 1823.

Hon. Edward de Moleyns, Major in the army, d. 31 July, 1841, aged 63. = Elizabeth, dau. of Robert Hilliard, Esq., of Listrim, co. Kerry, m. 11 Feb., 1805, d. 10 Feb., 1871.

Thomas de Moleyns, Q.C. County Judge, Ireland, Bencher King's Inn, 1864, b. 24 Jan. 1807. = Jemima, dau. of Cap. Broughton R.N.C.B, m. 17 Jan. 1827, d. 7 April, 1883.

William Bishop de Moleyns, M.A., vicar of Burrington, Somerset, married twice.

Edward Henry Guyon de Moleyns, sol. to the Bank of Ireland.

Elizabeth, m. to John Pennefather, Q.C.

Clara, m. 1st to R. J. Berkeley, Q.C., and 2nd to A. Carden.

Edward Charles, Major R.E. died unm., 1856.

Townsend Aremberg de Moleyns, lieut.-col. R.A., b. 20 June 1838. = Selina Harriet, only dau. of Henry Sneyd French, Esq., of Clonsilla, Dublin, m. 5 June, 1860.

Rose Gertrude, m. 1864, to Lieut.-col. George Eyre Massey, and d. 1 Feb. 1869.

Emmeline Theodora, m. 5 Dec. 1872 to Maj. Loftus Corbet Singleton, who died 1 May 1881.

Richard Philip Aremberg de Moleyns, b. 13 Dec. 1881.

Vera, born 30 May, 1880.

Hugh Hamon George, b. 17 March, 1867.

Henry Townsend Corbet Singleton, b. 27 Jan. 1874.

Violet Theodora.

DAYROLLES BLAKENEY EVELEIGH-DE MOLEYNS, Baron Ventry and a Baronet; elected an Irish representative Peer 10 July, 1871; lieut.-col. commandant Kerry militia since 1854; assumed the additional surname and arms of EVELEIGH by R.L. 1874; 17TH IN DESCENT FROM EDWARD III.; born 22 Jan. 1828; married 12 Sept., 1860, Harriet Elizabeth Frances, elder daughter of Andrew Wauchope, Esq., of Niddrie Marischal, Midlothian, and has 5 sons and 4 daughters.

[1] Hon. Frederic Rossmore Wauchope, lieut. 4th hussars 1882, late 4th batt. Princess Victoria's (R. Irish fusiliers) regiment; born 11 Dec., 1861.
[2] Hon. Arthur William, born 6 April, 1864.
[3] Hon. Edward Dayrolles, born 31 March, 1871.
[4] Hon. Richard Andrew, born 13 June, 1874.
[5] Hon. John Gilbert, born 27 May, 1878.
[6] Hon. Frances Elizabeth, married 21 March, 1881, to Henry Francis, 4th Marquis Conyngham.
[7] Hon. Mildred Rose.
[8] Hon. Hersey Alice.
[9] Hon. Maud Helen.

THE DESCENT OF
RIGHT HON. DAYROLLES, BARON VENTRY,
FROM THE BLOOD ROYAL OF ENGLAND.

EDWARD III., KING OF ENGLAND, Earl of Chester 1320, Duke of Aquitaine, Count of Ponthieu and Montreuil, 1325; crowned at Westminster in his father's lifetime, 1 Feb., 1327; defeated the Scots at Halidon Hill, 1333. In 1339 he assumed the style of "King of France and England, and Lord of Ireland," and quartered the arms of France in the first quarter; gained a great naval victory over the French off Sluys, 1340, and won the celebrated battle of Cressy 26 Aug. 1346; 17 Oct. following the Scots were defeated at Neville Cross, and King David II. taken prisoner to London, where he remained nearly 11 years. Instituted the order of the Garter 1349. His son, the BLACK PRINCE, defeated the French at the battle of Poictiers, 19 Sept., 1356, and brought King John prisoner to London, where he remained nearly five years (for further particulars, see *Royal Lineage*, Foster's *Peerage*). The King died at Sheen, Surrey, 21 June, 1337, having had issue; their descendant,

MARTHA BLENNERHASSETT (eldest daughter of Thomas Blennerhassett, of Littur (see page 639), married 1st, 1685, to Frederick Mullins (son of Colonel Frederick William Mullins, of Burnham, Kerry, M.P. Dingle 1692-5, Tralee 1695-9), he died in the lifetime of his father, 3 Oct., 1695, aged 32. His widow re-married to Henry Parr, of Tralee, and had 2 daughters, Theodora and Anne; by her 1st husband she had 2 sons and a daughter.

[1] **William**, of whom presently.
[2] Frederick, married and had issue.
[3] Jane, married to Peter Ferriter, and had issue.

WILLIAM MULLINS, of Burnham, Kerry, born 1691; died 3 May, 1761; married 10 June, 1716, Mary, daughter of George Rowan, Esq., of Rathany, Kerry (see page 691), and had at least 4 sons and 4 daughters.

[1] George.
[2] Frederick, married Jane, daughter of Rev. Thos. Collis (by his wife Avice Blennerhassett), she re-married as 2nd wife to Rev. Arthur Herbert, of Cahirnane, and Currens, rector of Tralee (see pages 380 and 590).
[3] Richard, 1733.
[4] **Sir Thomas**, created a baronet 1797, and Lord Ventry in 1800, of whom presently.
[5] Mary, married 3 April, 1740, to Captain Thomas

Goddard, of the Earl of Rothes regt.; he made his will 21 Aug., 1756, proved 2 May, 1757; had 3 sons and a daughter,

(1) Thomas (Goddard), buried at Dingle, 18 Dec., 1784.
(2) George. (3) William.
(4) Louisa, married 2 Feb., 1765, to Rev. John Blennerhassett, rector of Tralee (see page 593A).

[6] Frances.
[7] Anne, died 2 Sept., 1824, married to Samuel Crumpe, and had with 2 daughters 2 sons.

(1) Samuel (Crumpe), of the Kerry Militia.
(2) Francis.

[8] Katherine.

SIR THOMAS MULLINS, of Burnham, created a BARONET OF IRELAND 7 Dec., 1797, and BARON VENTRY, of Ventry, co. Kerry, in Ireland, 29 July, 1800; born 25 Oct., 1736; died 11 Jan., 1824, having married 5 Oct., 1755, Elizabeth Margaret, only daughter of Townsend Gun, of Rattoo, co. Kerry (see page 593B); she died 19 Jan. 1823, having had 6 sons and 6 daughters (*a*).

[1*a*] William Townsend, 2nd Baron, M.P. Dingle, co. Kerry, 1800; born 25 Sept., 1761; died 5 Oct., 1827, having married 1st, 12 July, 1784, Sarah Anne, daughter of Sir Riggs Falkiner, Bart.; she died Nov., 1788. He married 2nd, 12 May, 1790, Frances Elizabeth, only daughter of Isaac Sage, Esq. (dissolved by Act of Parliament March, 1796); he married 3rd, 10 Sept, 1797, Clara, daughter of Benjamin Jones, Esq.; she died 17 Jan, 1837, having re-married April, 1832, to Peter Fitz Gibbon Henchy. By his 1st wife he had a son and 2 daughters (*b*).

(1*b*-1*a*) Hon. Thomas (de Moleyns), born 12 Aug., 1798, died 31 May, 1817.

(2*b*-1*a*) Hon. Anne (de Moleyns), died married 9 Feb., 1811, to Richard Orpen-Townsend, of Ardtully, co. Kerry, he died leaving an only daughter.

Anne Sarah (Orpen-Townsend), married to Adrian Taylor, Esq., of Ardtully, co. Kerry.

(3*b*-1*a*) Hon. Elizabeth (de Moleyns), died 20 April, 1820, married 17 Dec., 1810, to Nicholas de la Cherois-Crommelin, of Carrowdore Castle, co. Down, J.P., D.L.; High Sheriff 1821, and High Sheriff co. Antrim 1830; he died 28 March, 1863, having had 3 sons and 4 daughters (*c*).

[1*c*-3*b*] Samuel Arthur de la Cherois-Crommelin, of Carrowdore Castle, co. Down,; High Sheriff, 1852, J.P., D.L.; born 25 Dec., 1817; married 30 Oct., 1845, Anna Maria, only daughter of John Graves Thompson, Esq., and has had 3 sons and 5 daughters.

(1) Louis Nicholas, died Dec., 1869, aged 23.
(2) Arthur Claude, died August, 1869, aged 13.
(3) Frederick Armand, born 7 Nov., 1861.
(4) Lucy Marguerite. (5) Maria Henrietta.
(6) Caroline Anna. (7) Florence Frances.
(8) Evelyn Angélique.

[2*c*-3*b*] Nicholas de la Cherois-Crommelin, of Rockport, Cushenden, Larne; born 7 March, 1819; married 8 Jan., 1851, Annie, 2nd daughter of Andrew Mulholland, Esq., of Bally Walter Park, co. Down, and has 3 sons and 8 daughters.

(1) Thomas William, born 1862.
(2) Nicholas. [3] Andrew.

[3*c*-3*b*] William Thomas de la Cherois-Commelin, B.A. Trin. Coll., Dublin, 1839; vicar of Pawlett, since 1875; incumbent of Comber, co. Down, 1851-68; Vicar of Henlow, Beds, 1868-75; born 14 Feb., 1820; married 23 Oct., 1855, Matilda, daughter William Cairns, Esq. (see Earl Cairns, Foster's *Peerage*), she died 29 Oct, 1856, leaving a daughter,

Matilda Helen, married 23 Nov, 1876, to Pelham Spencer Greenhill, Esq., of Knowle Hall, Somerset, and has 2 sons and 3 daughters.

Pelham Benjamin Knowle (Greenhill), born 21 May, 1881; Hugh Lionel, born 29 Aug., 1883; Helen Mary; Cecil Juliette; Maud Ethel Marie.

[4*c*] Anne Sarah, married 28 May, 1856, to Rev. Frederick Flood, B.A. Trin. Coll., Dublin, 1848, rector of the Rosses, co. Sligo, since 1869. vicar of Kilmood, 1851-69, rural dean, canon of Elphin, member of General Synod, &c., s.p.

[5*c*] Maria Matilda. [6*c*] Clara Suzanne, died young.

[7*c*] Elizabeth Emily, married 12 July, 1840, to John Robert Irwin, Esq, of Carnagh House, co. Armagh, J.P., High Sheriff 1844, served in 25th & 63rd regts., 2 medals for services at Guadaloupe and West Indies; he died 10 March, 1872, having had 5 sons and 2 daughters.

(1) William Arthur Irwin, of Carnagh House, co. Armagh, J.P., late capt. 11th regt.; born 9 June, 1841; married 1870, Eliza, daughter of Major Browne.
(2) Delacherois Thomas (Irwin), Col. Commandant of Artillery, Canada; born ; married Isabella, daughter of Robert Hamilton, of Hamwood, Quebec.
(3) John Frederick, capt. 57th regt, born 17 Sept., 1847; married 18 June, 1884, Annie, daughter of Richard Stanistreet, M.D., of Malahide, Ireland.
(4) Fitz J. Robert, born ; died Dec. 1882; married Sarah, daughter of Andrew Murray Ker, of Newlip, co. Monaghan.
(5) Edmund Herbert, born
(6) Elizabeth Emily. (7) Alice Anna Clara.

[2*a*] Hon. Townsend, born 19 March, 1763; died 1799. having married 1784, Christabella, daughter of Solomon Dayrolles, Esq., of Henley Park, Surrey, gentleman of the privy chamber to GEORGE II. and III.; she died having had an only son,

Thomas Townsend Aremberg, 3rd Baron (see p. 664.)

[3*a*] Hon. Thomas, lieut-col. in the army; d. s.p. February, 1823, having married 18 July, 1810, widow of Major-gen. Archer, and daughter of William Reader, Esq.

[4*a*] Hon. Richard, capt. 31st regiment, served in the West Indies and in the Walcheren expedition; married 2 October, 1798, Jane Guyon Gray, and had 2 sons and 4 daughters. (*d*).

(1*d*-4*a*) Richard Townsend, died 1850; married Sept., 1837 Charity, daughter of William Collis, Esq., of Lismore, Kerry (see MACGILLICUDDY, *Pedigree*, p. 628), she died 5 Nov., 1847, leaving a son.

Guiscarde Henry, died 26 March, 1859, aged 18.

(2*d*-4*a*) Ventry. died 1849.

(3*d*-4*a*) Jane, died 5 Jan. 1866; married 1st, 9 June, 1823, to Richard John Sutcliffe Mellin, Esq., of Wakefield; he died leaving issue; she re-married, 17 March, 1840, to James Henley, 14th dragoon guards.

(4*d*-4*a*) Eliza, died 13 Nov. 1859.

(5*d*-4*a*) Sarah, married Nov. 1829, to Arthur Thomas Blennerhassett, Esq., of Tralee, and had, with other issue (see page 568).

(1) Evelyn Florence, youngest daughter, married 16 July, 1872, to William Townsend de Moleyns,; see next page.

(6*d*-4*a*) Madeline, married 10 April, 1867, to Archibald S. Chartres, C.E.

[5*a*] Hon. Edward, major in the army, J.P., D.L., co.

Kerry; died 31 July, 1841, aged 63, having married 11 February, 1805, Elizabeth, daughter of Robert Hilliard, Esq., of Listrim, co. Kerry (see page 602); she died 10 February, 1871, having had 3 sons and 2 daughters. (*e*)

(1*e*-5*a*) Thomas, Q.C., County Court Judge, Ireland; called to the bar, King's Inns, 1831; bencher, 1864; J.P. cos. Roscommon, Kerry, Tipperary, and Limerick; chairman of quarter sessions, co. Kilkenny; born 24 January, 1807; married 11 January, 1827, Jemima, daughter of William Robert Broughton (see Foster's *Baronetage*), capt. R.N., C.B.; she died 7 April, 1883, having had 2 sons and 2 daughters.

[1] Edward Charles, major R.E., died unmarried 17 Aug., 1856.

[2] Townsend Aremberg, lieut-col. R.A., 1881; major 1872-81; served at the siege and fall of Sebastopol, medal with clasp, and Turkish medal; born 20 June 1838; married 5 June, 1866, Selina Harriet, only daughter of Henry Sneyd French (see B. DE FREYNE in Foster's *Peerage*), of Clonsilla, Dublin, and has a son and daughter.

Richard Philip Aremberg, born 13 Dec., 1881; Vera, born 30 May, 1880.

[3] Rose Gertrude, died 1 Feb., 1869, having married 24 Nov., 1864, as 1st wife to Lieut.-col. George Eyre Massy (see B. MASSY in Foster's *Peerage*), of Riversdale, co. Limerick, and had a son

Hugh Hamon George, born 17 March, 1867.

[4] Emmeline Theodora, married 5 Dec., 1872, to Loftus Corbet Singleton, major 92nd (Gordon) Highlanders, served in Afghan campaign 1880, with General Roberts in his memorable march from Cabul to Candahar, and subsequent engagements; mentioned in despatches; served in Boer campaign, and died 1 May, 1881, of wounds received in the engagement at Majuba Hill. He had 2 sons and a daughter.

(1) Henry Townsend Corbet Singleton, born 27 Jan., 1874.

(2) Loftus Corbet, born 24 Nov., 1879; died 14 Feb. following.

(3) Violet Theodora.

(2*e*-5*a*) William Bishop, M.A., Camb. 1866; Preb. of Wells Cathedral 1876; vicar of Burrington, Somersets. since 1871; hon. chaplain 27th Somerset R.V.; born 4 March, 1821; married 1st, 6 Oct., 1846, Sarah Anne, eldest daughter of Thomas Clark, J.P., of Bellefield, Trowbridge, Wilts.; she died 3 July, 1872. He married 2nd, 5 Aug., 1873, Clara Louisa Elizabeth, eldest daughter of George Thomas Pollard, Esq., of Hundhill, Yorks (see page 634). By his 1st wife he had 2 sons and 4 daughters.

[1] Thomas Edward, B.A. Oxon.; born 20 Oct., 1847; married 16 May, 1877, Kathleen, 4th daughter of James Pike, J.P.

[2] Alured Bayfield, M.A. Queen's Coll., Oxon., 1880; curate of Fleetwood, 1884; born 5 Nov., 1851.

[3] Elizabeth Clara. [4] Emily Madeline.

[5] Alice Vere.

[6] Helen Margaret, died 27 Nov., 1879.

(3*e*-5*a*) Edward Henry Guyon, solicitor to the Bank of Ireland; born 1 Jan., 1823; married 10 Aug., 1858, Maria Louisa, eldest daughter of Edward Day Stokes, Esq., of Tralee (see page 440); she died 15 March, 1862, having had a son and 2 daughters.

[1] Edward Henry, born 17 Sept., 1859; married 3 Sept., 1879, Florence Evelyn, eldest daughter of late Francis Pierson, Esq., of Egerton Lodge, Cheshire (granddaughter of Sir John Baker, Bart.); s. p.

[2] Edith Anne. [3] Maria Louisa.

(4*e*-5*a*) Elizabeth Jemima, died 4 Feb., 1849, having married 8 Aug., 1842, to John Pennefather, Q.C. (son of Right Hon. Richard Pennefather, baron of the exchequer Ireland); he died 8 April, 1855, leaving 2 sons and a daughter.

(1) Alfred Richard PENNEFATHER, Receiver for the Metropolitan Police District, 1883; entered Home Office, 1868; born 10 March, 1845; married 9 May, 1867, Thomasina Cox, youngest daughter of late Thomas Cox Savory, Esq., of London, s.p.

(2) Somerset Edward, M.A., vicar of Jesmond, Newcastle-on-Tyne, since 1882, of Kenilworth, 1875-82, of Christ Church, Wakefield, 1874-5; born 1 March, 1848; married 21 July, 1870, Catherine Emily, daughter of late Thomas Cox Savory, Esq., of London, and has 3 sons and a daughter.

William John Somerset (Pennefather), born 8 June, 1876; Claud Maxwell, born 26 1878; Edward Cyril, born 24 Aug. 1881; Evelyn Maud Pennefather.

(3) Dora Mellicent, married 13 March, 1883, to James Lane, Esq., and has a daughter,

Dora Evelyn (Lane).

(5*e*-5*a*) Clara Maria, married 1st, Oct., 1837, to Robert James Berkeley, Q.C., who died 31 Oct., 1873; she re-married 21 June, 1876, as 2nd wife, to Andrew Carden, of Barnane, co. Tipperary, who died Nov., 1876.

[6*a*] Hon. Frederick Ferriter, in holy orders; died 30 Dec., 1832, aged 54, having married 6 Dec., 1800, Elizabeth, only daughter and heir of William Croker, Esq., of Johnstown, co. Cork; she died having had 3 sons (*f*).

(1*f*-6*a*) Frederick William, of Beaufort House, co. Kerry, M.P., 1831-7; born 29 June, 1804; d. s. p. 17 March, 1854, having married Oct., 1826, Lucia, eldest daughter of Capt. William Robert Broughton, R.N., C.B. (see Foster's *Baronetage*.)

(2*f*-6*a*) William, rector of Killorglin, rural dean; born 15 July, 1806; died 5 March, 1863, having married 30 Aug., 1848, Kate Maria Rochfort, daughter of Capt. John Rae, late 72nd highlanders, and had 2 sons and 3 daughters.

[1] William Townsend, late 50th (Q.O.) regiment; born 16 July, 1850; married 16 July, 1872, his cousin Evelyn Florence, youngest daughter of Arthur Thomas Blennerhassett, Esq., of Tralee, co. Kerry, by his wife, Sarah Mullins (see page 568), and has a son and daughter,

William Frederick, born 1 Dec., 1874.

Evelyn Florence, born 9 Dec., 1877.

[2] Alured Aremberg, born 3 March, 1854.

[3] Rose Blanche, married 2 Jan., 1873, to William Phibbs, capt. 54th regiment, adj. Kerry militia, and has 2 sons and a daughter.

Bertram Owen Frederick PHIBBS, born 2 Jan., 1874; Alured Ventry, born 27 May, 1878; Ethel Rose.

[4] Kate Clara, married 11 April, 1874, to Harry D'Arch Breton, capt. R E., and has had 2 sons and a daughter.

Hubert William BRETON, born 6 April, 1875 Lionel Alured, born 4 June, 1876; died 23 Aug 1879; Adeline May, born 25 Dec., 1880.

[5] Edith Agnes.

(3*f*-6*a*) Alured, died unmarried 3 Aug., 1859.

[7*a*] Hon. Theodora, married 1772, to Edward Brice, Esq., of Scoutbush and Kilroot, co. Antrim, and had 2 sons and 4 daughters (*g*).

(1*g*-7*a*) Edward BRUCE of Scoutbush and Kilroot, co. Antrim, J.P., High Sheriff, 1836, resumed by royal licence the original surname of Bruce; born 27 March, 1783, married 29 Oct., 1807, Maria, eldest daughter of James Coghlan, Esq., of Castlegar, co. Mayo; and had 2 sons and 2 daughters.

[1] Edward (Bruce), in holy orders; born 16 Nov., 1811; married Maria, eldest daughter of late lieut.-col. Head, of Derry Castle, co. Tipperary.

THE DESCENT OF
Alfred Richard Pennefather, Esq.,

FROM THE

of England.

EDWARD III., crowned 1 Feb., 1327, b. 13 Nov., 1312, d. 21 June, 1377. = Philippa, 3rd dau. of William, Count of Holland and Hainault, m. 24 Jan. 1328, d. 15 Aug. 1369.

Edmund, Duke of York, K.G., 5th son, d. at Langley, 1 Aug. 1402. = Isabel (1st wife), youngest dau. and co-heir of Peter, King of Castile, m. 1372.

Constance of Langley. = Thomas, 6th Baron le Despencer, cr. Earl of Gloucester, 1397, beheaded at Bristol, 16 Jan. 1400.

Isabel le Despencer, b. 26 July, 1400, m. 27 July 1411, d. 26 Dec. 1440. = Richard Beauchamp, Lord Bergavenny (1st husband), cr. Earl of Worcester 1420, d. 1422.

Elizabeth Beauchamp, Baroness Bergavenny, b. at Hanley Castle, 16 Dec. 1415, d. 18 June, 1447 (1st wife). = Sir Edward Nevill, sum. to parl. as Baron Bergavenny, 1450-72, d. 18 Oct. 1476.

Sir George Nevill, Lord Bergavenny, sum. to parl. 1482-92, d. 20 Sept. 1492. = Margaret (1st wife), dau. and heir of Sir Hugh Fenne, of Sculton, d. 28 Sept. 1485.

Sir Edward Nevill, of Addington Park, Kent, beheaded on Tower Hill, 9 Jan. 1538-9. = Eleanor, widow of Ralph, 8th Lord Scrope, of Masham, dau. of Andrew, Lord Windsor.

——— Royden (1st husband). = Catherine Nevill. = Clement Throckmorton, of Hanley, Warwickshire, d. 19 Oct. 1594.

A, *continued above.*

A, *continued from below.*

Catherine Nevill = Clement Throckmorton.

Martha Throckmorton, bur. at Southwick, 30 Dec. 1600, aged 49. = George Lynne, of Southwick Hall, Northants, bur. there 29 Nov. 1617.

George Lynne, of Southwick Hall, d. 5 Nov. 1606. = Isabel, sister of Sir Anthony Forrest, of Morborn, Hunts, Knt.

Martha Lynne = John Blennerhassett, of Ballyseedy, co. Kerry, M.P. Tralee, 1661.

Thomas Blennerhasset, of Littur, co. Kerry. = Ellen, dau. of Anthony Stoughton, of Rattoo, co. Kerry.

Martha Blennerhassett, m. 2nd to Henry Parr. = Frederick Mullins, (1st husband), d. 3 Oct., 1695.

William Mullins, of Burnham, Kerry, d. 3 May, 1761. = Mary, dau of George Rowan, Esq., of Rathany, Kerry, m. 10 June, 1716.

Sir Thomas Mullins, of Burnham, created a baronet, 1797, and Baron Ventry, 1800, b. 1736, d. 1824. = Elizabeth, only dau. of Townsend Gun, of Rattoo, co. Kerry, m. 5 Oct., 1755, d. 19 Jan., 1823.

Hon. Edward de Moleyns, Major in the army, d. 31 July, 1841, aged 63. = Elizabeth, dau. of Robert Hilliard, Esq., of Listrim, co. Kerry, m. 11 Feb., 1805, d. 10 Feb., 1871.

Thomas de Moleyns, Q.C. County Judge, Ireland, Bencher King's Inn, 1864, b. 24 Jan. 1807.

William Bishop de Moleyns, M.A., vicar of Burrington, Somerset, married twice.

Edward Henry Guyon de Moleyns, sol. to the Bank of Ireland.

Elizabeth Jemima, m. 8 Aug. 1842, d. 4 Feb. 1849. = John Pennefather, Q.C., d. 8 April, 1855.

Clara, m. 1st to R. J. Berkeley, Q.C., and 2nd to A. Carden.

Alfred Richard Pennefather, receiver for the Metropol. Police District, 1833, b. 10 March, 1845. = Thomasina Cox, youngest daughter of late Thomas Cox Savory, Esq. of London, m. 9 May, 1867.

Somerset Edward Pennefather, M.A., vicar of Jesmond since 1882, b. 1 March, 1843. = Catherine Emily, dau. of late Thomas Cox Savory, Esq., m. 21 July, 1870.

Dora Mellicent, m. 13 March, 1853, = James Lane, Esq.

William, b. 8 June, 1876. Claud 1878. Edward Cyril, b. 24 Aug., 1881. Evelyn Maud.

Dora Evelyn Lane.

[2] James Alexander (Bruce), born 5 Jan., 1826.
[3] Marianne. [4] Rose.
(2g-7a) Thomas Richard (Brice), R.N., born April, 1790; died s.p. married 1817, Jane Suzanne, 2nd daughter of Samuel de la Cherois-Crommelin, Esq., of Carrowdore Castle, co. Down.
(3g-7a) Rose, married 1801, as 2nd wife, to Sir John Blake, of Menlough Castle, co. Galway, 11th Bart., who died 1834, having had a son and 3 daughters.
[1] John Brice (Blake), capt. 47th regt.; married , Elree.
[2] Elizabeth Theodora (Blake), died 25 Oct., 1879; married 18 Aug., 1821, to Thomas, 3rd Lord Ventry, who died 18 Jan., 1868.
[3] Jane Margaret, died 8 May, 1842; married , 1829, as 2nd wife to Rev. Denis Mahony, of Dromore Castle, co. Kerry, who died 21 April, 1851 (see also Day pedigree, page 444), having had 4 sons and 2 daughters.
(1) Denis (Mahony), died unmarried July, 1851.
(2) Edward (Mahony), died unmarried
(3) Henry (Mahony), living unmarried.
(4) John (Mahony), died unmarried
(5) Rose (Mahony), died 20 July, 1870; married 1st, June, 1852, to John, 2nd son of Right Hon. Richard Pennefather, baron of the exchequer Ireland; he died ; she re-married 23 Sept., 1858, to Vice-admiral the Hon. Henry Carr Glyn, C.B., C.S.I., A.D.C. to the Queen 1873-7; capt. of H.M.S. *Serapis*, when H.R.H. the Prince of Wales visited India, 1875-6; capt. successively 1868-75 of H.M.S. *Doris*, *Warrior*, *Agincourt*, and *Duke of Wellington* (see Foster's *Peerage*); he died Feb., 1884, having had 2 sons and 2 daughters.
Henry Richard (Glyn), born 18 July, 1861; Frederick, born 24 Sept., 1864; Rose Riversdale; Alice Coralie.
(6) Margaret (Mahony), married 18 Oct., 1866, as 2nd wife to Comr. the Hon. Reynolds Moreton, late of Lindridge House, co. Leicester, 4th son of Henry, 2nd Earl of Ducie (see Foster's *Peerage*), and has had a son and 3 daughters.
Reginald Ducie (Moreton), born 28 Jan., 1869; Lilly Florence; Mabel Evelyn; Grace Ruth Kathleen, died 9 March, 1880.
[4] Arabella (Blake), born 29 May, 1807; married 1st, 7 Dec., 1827, to Sir Hugh James Moore O'Donnell, Bart., who died 29 July, 1828, and had a posthumous daughter, Arabella; Lady O'Donnell re-married 1830, to John O'Hara, Esq., of Raheen, co. Galway, and had a son and 2 daughters.
(1) Robert (O'Hara), born 17 March, 1836; married October, 1865, Frances, daughter of Colonel Power, and has a daughter, Kathleen.
(2) Frances Anne (O'Hara), married 1 Aug., 1849, to William Wallace Hozier, of Newlands and Barrowfield, co. Lanark, J.P., D.L., convener of the county; formerly lieut. Scots greys, and had a son and 3 daughters.
[1] James Henry Cecil (Hozier), born 4 April, 1851; married 24 May, 1880, Lady Mary Louisa Wellesley Cecil, daughter of William Alleyne, 3rd Marquis of Exeter.
[2] Arabella Rose Evelyn.
[3] Catherine Rose. [4] Mary Houghton.
(3) Rose (O'Hara), died 29 Jan., 1866; married 28 June, 1859, as 1st wife to William Forbes, of Callendar, co. Stirling, N.B., and had issue.
(4g-7a) Eliza (Brice), mrd. R. O'Connell, staff-surgeon.
(5g-7a) Theodora (Brice), Trevor Hill, Esq.
(6g-7a) Charlotte (Brice), married , to Thomas Johnson Smyth, Esq., of Lisburn, and has issue.
[8a] Hon. Elizabeth, died 29 Oct., 1844; married June, 1780, to Richard Blennerhassett, Esq., of Ballymacprior and had issue (see page 567).
[9a] Hon. Arabella, died Dec. 1821; married Feb. 1780, to Richard MacGillycuddy, of the Reeks, who died s.p. 19 Nov., 1826 (see page 627).
[10a] Hon. Charlotte, died s.p. 29 April, 1816, married 2 May, 1792, to Richard Pierse Mahony, Esq., of Dromore, co. Kerry.
[11a] Hon. Catherine, died ; married 28 Dec., 1794, to Capt. James Hozier.
[12a] Hon. Helen Jane, died 24 Dec., 1846; married Sept., 1799, to Arthur Blennerhassett, Esq., of Blennerville (see page 575).

THOMAS TOWNSEND AREMBERG, 3rd Baron, assumed the surname of DE MOLEYNS in lieu of Mullins by royal licence, 16 Feb., 1841; born Jan., 1786; died 18 Jan., 1868, having married 18 August, 1821, Elizabeth Theodora, eldest daughter of Sir John Blake Blake, Bart., aforesaid; she died 25 October, 1879, having had with other issue 4 sons and 4 daughters.

[1] **Sir Dayrolles Blakeney**, 4th and present Baron.
[2] Hon. Frederick William, b. 24 July, 1835; d. 1882.
[3] Hon. Edward Alured, late capt. Kerry militia, born 25 Nov., 1836.
[4] Hon. Denis John, late lieut. 23 R.W. fusiliers; served in Ashantee War, 1874, medal, with clasp; born 12 May, 1844.
[5] Hon. Christabella Rosetta, married 9 June, 1844, to Charles Hawkey, com. R.N. (retired), and has a son.
Charles F Dayrolles HAWKEY, born 12 June, 1846.
[6] Hon. Rose, married 3 March, 1847, as 2nd wife, to Richard Chute, of Chute Hall, and Blennerville, co. Kerry; he died 13 Sept., 1862, having had (by this marriage) 2 sons and 4 daughters.
(1) Thomas Aremberg CHUTE, born 14 Oct., 1853.
(2) Richard Trevor, lieut. 65th foot, b. 17 Sept., 1856.
(3) Marian, married 11 Nov., 1879, to William Shakoor, of Ani Zahalta, Mount Lebanon, Syria.
(4) Theodora Eliza. (5) Rose. (6) Arabella Emily.
[7] Hon. Eliza, married 20 Aug., 1850, to Rev. Henry Joy Tombe, B.D., canon of Christchurch Cathedral, Dublin, and has 2 sons and 3 daughters.
(1) Henry Aremberg (Tombe), born , 1853.
(2) Thomas Aremberg, born , 1856.
(3) Eliza Theodora.
(4) Thomasina Georgina, married 11 May, 1882, to John Fane Vernon, Esq., M.A., barr.-at-law (see Foster's *Peerage*).
(5) Helen Emily.
[8] Hon. Helena Emily, married 22 June, 1865, to Edward James Saunderson, Esq., of Castle Saunderson, co. Cavan M.P.; high sheriff 1859; major Cavan mil., and has 4 sons and a daughter.
(1) Somerset (Saunderson).
(2) Edward.
(3) Armar.
(4) John Vernon.
(5) Rosa.

ARMS—Quarterly, 1st and 4th, Sa., on a chief erm. three fusils gu. DE MOLEYNS. 2nd and 3rd, Per pale or and sa., two chevronnels between three griffins passant counterchanged, EVELEIGH.
CRESTS—1st, The bust of a savage ppr. DE MOLEYNS. 2nd, A goat's head erased per chevron or and sa., holding a branch of laurel ppr. EVELEIGH.
SUPPORTERS—Two lions or, ducally gorged and chained az.
MOTTO—Vivere sat vincere.
SEAT—Burnham House, Dingle, Kerry.